The Art of
Voice Acting

The Art of
Voice
Acting

fifth edition

The Craft and Business of Performing for Voiceover

James R. Alburger

Focal Press
Taylor & Francis Group

First published 1998 by Focal Press

This edition published 2015 by Focal Press
70 Blanchard Road, Suite 402, Burlington, MA 01803
And by Focal Press
2 Park Square, Milton Park, Abingdon, Oxon OX14 4RN

Focal Press is an imprint of the Taylor & Francis Group, an informa business

Notices
Knowledge and best practice in this field are constantly changing. As new research and experience broaden our understanding, changes in research methods, professional practices, or medical treatment may become necessary.

Practitioners and researchers must always rely on their own experience and knowledge in evaluating and using any information, methods, compounds, or experiments described herein. In using such information or methods they should be mindful of their own safety and the safety of others, including parties for whom they have a professional responsibility.

Product or corporate names may be trademarks or registered trademarks, and are used only for identification and explanation without intent to infringe.

Library of Congress Cataloging in Publication Data
[CIP data application submitted]

ISBN: 978-0-415-73697-8 (pbk)
ISBN: 978-1-315-81825-2 (ebk)

Typeset in Arial and Footlight
By James R. Alburger

This edition is dedicated...

To my students, past, present and future ...
To my business partner, Penny Abshire ...
To my many voiceover friends and acquaintances ...
And ...
To the voiceover community as a whole ...
One of the most supportive and helpful groups of
people to be found anywhere!

*Voice acting is the performing craft
of creating believable characters,
in interesting relationships, telling compelling stories,
using only the spoken word.*

*Mastering and applying the skills of voice acting
will take your personal and professional
communication to an entirely new
level of effectiveness.*

James R. Alburger
JamesAlburger.com

Many people stand at the microphone.

But relatively few
take to the mic as if it were a canvas
and are true artists.

Contents

The Craft of Performing for Voiceover

6. Developing Style and Technique

The Business of Voiceover

The Art of Voice Acting

Forward

by Joe Cipriano

Can I just say one thing.

"It ain't about the mic"

Let me clarify. It's so easy to fall into the gear thing when you are just starting out in voiceover.

I hear it all the time. "What microphone did Don LaFontaine use? I really want to get that mic and pair it up with the same pre-amp he used ..." And that's the beginning of the thought process that takes you on the path away from what really matters.

The truth of the matter is, Don could have spoken into two Dixie cups connected by a string and have a career, because as Don used to say to me and to so many others, "Voiceover is not about the voice."

What voiceover IS all about is learning the techniques and skills, gaining confidence in your abilities, creating characters, interpreting copy and studying all of the other pieces of the puzzle and becoming proficient with them. The only way to do that is to take workshops and seminars, and study with qualified coaches and teachers, and above all treat your voiceover career like a career.

When James Alburger asked me to write the forward to the 5th edition of his book, *The Art of Voice Acting*, I was happy to do so because so many times over the past decade I've recommended this very book to people who are interested in pursuing a career in voiceover. Inside the pages of this book is an honest look at what is needed to become relevant and significant in this sometimes very frustrating business.

There is an intelligent way to go about creating a voiceover career and it requires a plan, a commitment on your part and the willingness to never stop learning, never stop growing and most importantly, never give up.

There is no shortage of people who, when you tell them what your dreams are, will say, "You can't do that. There are too many people already doing that. The competition is too steep." Sometimes they are saying these things because they care for you, because they don't want to see you struggle and suffer the disappointments along the way. Yes, there will be struggles and at some point you might even question your decision to take this path, but you can't listen to the naysayers and you should not be deterred by the rejections that may come your way.

Find comfort in something you can believe in, something you can lean on to get you through the tough times. That should involve a belief in your own self, your skills and a commitment to your continuing education.

I've never been booked for a voiceover job and before accepting the gig, ask what kind of microphone I would be talking into. Now, I'm a big fan of finely crafted microphones, but they don't get you a job and having the "right one" won't "make you a voiceover artist."

It's important to remember that a microphone is a tool. What you say into that microphone and how you make your creative decisions in interpreting the copy and creating a character is what is most important and is what WILL always get you the job. Once you become proficient in doing all of that, you can utilize any tool available to deliver the end result of your talents.

So, my advice to you is to focus on what really matters. Learn the techniques, practice them every day, take lessons, read books like this one and soak up all that great information. At the beginning, purchase a microphone that won't break the bank, get the best one you can "afford" without going into debt or having to brown-bag your lunch every day. Put the money in the right place; education, coaches, workshops, seminars and immerse yourself in the important things of building a voiceover career.

Once you do that, you'll be on your way to success and then you can purchase any microphone you want. Then some day, young hopefuls will ask YOU what microphone you use and I hope you'll pass along your own thoughts on what is most important in building a voiceover career.

In reading this book, I hope you enjoy your entrance or continuing education in the world of voiceover. Then go out there and put into practice what you've learned.

Most importantly believe in yourself.

And never give up.

Joe Cipriano

 For more than 25 years, Joe Cipriano has been best known as the voice of the Fox Television Network. He has also served as a signature voice for CBS and NBC, and has been the live booth announcer for the Grammy Awards, The Emmy Awards, and numerous other live television events. Joe's book, *Living on Air*, is a personal account of his early days in radio and how he successfully made the transition from radio to becoming one of the top voiceover talents in the U.S.

Preface
James R. Alburger

The origins of this book go back to the mid-1970's. At that time, my life revolved around my work as a part-time professional magician, my work as audio producer and director at the NBC-TV affiliate in San Diego, and my side jobs of editing music for other performers and working part-time at a local recording studio. I really didn't have much of a social life back then!

Although I was working with voiceover talent on a daily basis, and I had an innate understanding of painting pictures and telling stories through the medium of sound alone, I had no idea that I would one day write a book that has become one of the standard reference works on the craft and business of voiceover.

Each edition of this book has built upon the prior editions by adding more techniques, completely updated information, and more content from many of the top professionals in this industry.

The business of voiceover is one that is in a constant state of flux. Although the fundamental performing techniques may be consistent, there are trends and performing styles that are constantly changing. As voice actors, we must keep up with these trends and maintain our performing skills in order to keep the work coming in. But the reality is, there's actually a lot more to it than that.

What you hold in your hands is a manual for working in the business of voiceover that will take you from the fundamentals of performing to the essentials of marketing ... and everything in-between. Most books on voiceover talk about interpretation—how to deliver phrases and analyze a script, or are more about the author than the craft.

This book is different!

This book was written with the intention of giving you a solid foundation in both the craft *and* business of voiceover. Within these pages you'll find dozens of tools and techniques that are essential for success in this area of show business—some of which you won't find anywhere else. With this book, you will learn exactly how to use these tools, not just in voiceover, but in everything you do. Unlike some other books on voiceover, I don't focus on how I did it, or go into boring stories of my voiceover career. No ... I'll show you how *you* can do it! Every story and every technique you'll read in this book is here for a reason—to teach you exactly how some aspect of this craft and business works, and how you can make it work for you.

The tools and techniques are just that—tools and techniques. Without understanding how to use them, they are little more than words on the page. But once you learn how to use a few of these tools, you'll discover that they can be used to improve relationships, get more customers, resolve problems, close more sales, make you a better actor, improve your public speaking skills, and so on. You won't use every performance tool all the time, and some may not work for you at all. That's fine. Find the tools and techniques that *do* work for you, take them, and make them your own. Create your own unique style. If you can achieve that, you'll be ahead of the game.

This is a book about how you can communicate more effectively than you can imagine. Everything you experience in life holds an emotion that can be used to make you more effective as a voice actor. And even if you never intend to stand in front of a microphone in a recording studio, you can still use what you learn here to become a more effective communicator.

Performing voiceover is much like performing music: There is a limited number of musical notes, yet there is an almost unlimited variety of possibilities for performing those notes. The same is true with a voiceover script. Words and phrases can be delivered with infinite variety, subtlety, and nuance. A voiceover performance is, indeed, very similar to the way a conductor blends and balances the instruments of the orchestra. Your voice is your instrument, and this book will give you the tools to help you create a musical performance. You might think of voiceover as a "Symphony of Words," or "Orchestrating Your Message," both catch phrases I've used to describe the results of what we do as voice actors.

Acknowledgments

This edition of my book would not have been possible without the generous support and help from so many people and companies who work in the world of voiceover every day. As you read through these pages, you will see names, web site links, response codes and other references to the many individuals who have supported my efforts with their contributions. Please join me in thanking them for their willingness to share their knowledge and experience.

A very special thank you goes to my coaching, creative, and business partner, Penny Abshire. As a skilled coach and brilliant copywriter, you're the best! Thank you for your contributions and keen editing eye.

Introduction

"You've got a great voice!"

"You should be doing commercials!"

"You should be doing cartoons!"

I'm going to take a chance here! At some point in the past, someone said something to you similar to the above statements. And you've become inspired! Or perhaps voiceover has been a life-long dream and you finally have time to start learning about what "VO" is all about. Either way, the idea of working in voiceover may have been percolating for a few years, or you may have already dabbled a bit. You picked up this book because you realize that there's a lot you don't know, and you've finally decided to get serious and "take the leap."

Congratulations!

It doesn't matter if you are studying voiceover as part of a higher education curriculum or if you're doing it on your own. Either way, you are about to embark on a journey that will be filled with new concepts, loaded with new knowledge, and certain to be lots of fun. But along your journey, you will face challenging obstacles, frustrating clients, and scripts that seem almost impossible to decipher.

There are no guarantees, but If you are persistent, you will more than likely find success. One thing I can guarantee, though, is that you will learn more about personal communication than you ever imagined.

Maybe working as a professional voice actor is not your primary objective here. Perhaps you simply enjoy making up funny character voices or sounds, or enjoy telling stories and jokes. This book will show you how to do it better and more effectively. Perhaps you need to make presentations as part of your job. If so, this book will definitely give you a new insight into reaching your audience with a stronger message. If you are involved in any line of work for which you need to communicate any sort of message verbally to one or more individuals, this book will help you make your presentation more powerful and more memorable.

This book is about acting and performing, but I won't be talking about performing on stage or working on-camera. In fact, with this kind of acting you rarely, if ever, see your audience or receive any applause. With this kind of acting you create illusions and believable images in the mind of the audience—a listening audience who might never see you, but who, if you do your job well, will remember your performance for many years.

Although the focus here is on developing skills for working in voiceover, the techniques you will learn within these pages can be applied to any situation in which you want to reach and motivate an audience on an emotional level. Radio personalities, professional speakers, video producers, editors, audio engineers, on-camera talent, and even theatrical actors and directors will discover new ways to approach their work simply by gaining an understanding of how voice acting techniques can be applied when telling a story.

And, after all, we are all story tellers in one way or another.

For some, the word "voiceover" is inspirational, describing a job and lifestyle of glitter, big money and stardom. Sorry to say, but that's not an accurate description of this type of work. True, it can happen, but as you will learn in the pages that follow, the business of voiceover is just that—a business. It can be lots of fun and it can be a business that is, at times, very challenging work. And it can be both at the same time!

Voiceover is also an art! It is a highly specialized craft with skills that must be developed. The voiceover performer is an actor who must communicate effectively using nothing more than his or her voice. The business of voiceover should, more accurately, be referred to as the business of *voice acting*. It is most definitely a part of show business.

I'll be perfectly honest with you right from the beginning. Working as a voice actor is not for everyone. It requires an investment of time, energy, persistence, and money to get started. And, perhaps, just a bit of luck. As they say: "Luck is being in the right place, at the right time, with the right knowledge and skills." This book will help with the knowledge and skills ... the rest is up to you.

However ... if you love to play, have the desire to learn some acting skills, can speak clearly, read well, don't mind the occasional odd working hours, don't take things too seriously, have a good attitude, can motivate yourself to be in the right place at the right time, and you are willing to do what is necessary to develop your skills and build your business, this type of work may be just right for you. Even if you have absolutely no acting experience, you may discover a hidden aptitude in communicating through one of the many genres of voiceover—or you may simply find that you are more clearly understood by those you speak to. These skills are not limited to radio and TV commercials.

This book shows you the steps to take to learn the performing skills necessary to be successful as a voice talent. It also has the information you need to build your voiceover business and ultimately get your demo produced and into the hands of those who will hire you. Study these pages and you will gain a solid foundation in both performing and business skills that you can develop to achieve lasting success in the world of voiceover.

You *don't* have to be in Los Angeles, New York, or Chicago to find voiceover work. Work is available everywhere. You *do* need to have the right attitude, the right skills, and a high-quality, professionally produced presentation of your talents, or the casting people won't even give you a second look (or listen). If you master the techniques explained in this book, you will be able to present yourself like a pro—even if you have never done anything like this before.

As comprehensive as this book is, I am only able to scratch the surface of many topics relating to voiceover. So, I've created a web page that includes a lot of information that literally could not fit within the pages of this book. You'll find more information, resources and some unpublished bonus material at **VoiceActing.com.** Click on the **AOVAExtras** menu tab on the website or scan the response code here to take you to the audio files and support materials that are 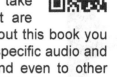 mentioned throughout this book. Sprinkled throughout this book you will find more response codes that will take you to specific audio and video playbacks, PDF support files, image files and even to other websites. Please note that you will need a PDF Reader for your device in order to open some of these links.

As you read the pages that follow, I promise to be straightforward and honest with you. Within these pages are techniques and tricks of the trade that you will not find anywhere else. For those of you considering a move into the business of voiceover, you will learn what it takes to be successful. If you simply want to learn new ways to use your voice to communicate effectively, you will find a wealth of information.

I wish you much success. Please let me know when you land your first national commercial or big contract as a result of using the techniques and information in this book. I can always be reached through **VoiceActing.com**.

In this Chapter

What is Voice Acting?

1

What Is Voice Acting?

"Voiceover" vs. "Voice Acting"

We live in an age of information and communication. We are bombarded with messages of all types 24 hours a day. From 30-second commercials to hour-long infomercials; from feature films, to video games; from corporate presentations to singing greeting cards, and thousands of others. Much of our time is spent assimilating and choosing to act—or not act—on the information we receive.

It is well-known among marketing specialists that there are only two ways to communicate a message: intellectually and emotionally. Of these, the most effective is to connect on an emotional, often unconscious level. This involves drawing the listener (or viewer) into a story or creating a dramatic or emotional scene that the listener can relate to; in short, effective communication is really excellent storytelling. And the best storytellers create vivid imagery through a combination of interpretation, intonation, attitude, and the incorporation of a variety of acting skills. This is exactly what we do as voice actors! The voiceover (VO) performer, in fact, can be more accurately referred to as a voice actor.

Voice actors play a very important role in entertainment, marketing, sales, and delivery of information. As with any other form of acting, it is the voice actor's job to play a role that has been written into the script. To effectively play the role, the performer must, among other things, be able to quickly determine how to best communicate the message using only the spoken word.

If you accept the definition of voiceover as being anything in which you hear the voice but don't see the performer, then, in the strictest sense, anyone who can speak can do voiceover. But that doesn't mean that anyone who can speak has the ability or skill to work professionally as a voice talent. If you've ever recorded an outgoing message on your answering machine, you've done a form of "voiceover." But does that mean you can do voiceover professionally? Probably not. I frequently receive demos from self-proclaimed "voiceover artists" who have just completed a class and produced a demo in an attempt to break into the business. A few of these individuals have some raw talent, but unfortunately, most have not polished their skills or honed their craft to a point where they can effectively compete as voice talent. It is rare that I receive a demo that demonstrates a level of professionalism that shows me the individual has made the transition from "doing voiceover" to performing as a "voice actor."

There is a common misunderstanding that "voice acting" refers only to performing for Japanese films, known as Anime. But the truth about voice acting goes far beyond a single performing genre.

To confuse things even further, the common term used to define all types of work in which the entire performance is delivered only through the sound of the voice is "voiceover."

"So, what's the difference?" I hear you ask.

Let's begin with a simplified definition of voiceover. *Voiceover* can be defined as "any recording or performance of one or more unseen voices for the purpose of communicating a message." The voiceover is the spoken part of a commercial, program, or other announcement that you hear, but do not see the person speaking. It could be anything from a phone message to a television commercial, sales presentation, instructional video, movie trailer, feature film, or documentary narration. It may be nothing more than a single voice heard on the radio or over a public address system. The production may include music, sound effects, video, animation, or multiple voices. In most cases, the message is selling something, providing information, or asking the listener to take some sort of action.

There are several factors that differentiate simple voiceover and professional voice acting. Among them are: competent training, acting ability, interpretive skill, improvisational skills, dedication, business acumen, computer skills, and certain technical recording skills. But the real difference can be summed up in a single word:

Believability

You can listen to the radio or watch TV any hour of any day and hear commercials that literally make you cringe. If you analyze the performance, most of these "bad" commercials have several things in common: they sound flat and lifeless, with every sentence sounding the same; they sound like the script is being read; the performers sound like they are shouting with no clear focus as to who they are speaking to; the performer is talking "at" and not "to" the listener, or they are trying to talk to everyone listening at the same time; there is absolutely nothing compelling about the delivery or the message. In short, the performance lacks "believability."

Here's a simple way to determine if it's "voiceover" or "voice acting." A "voiceover" performance has at least one or more of the following:

- Often "read-y" or "announcer-y" (sounds like reading the script). The focus is on getting the words right.
- Content is information-heavy, primarily intellectual, often with many featured items, and with little or no emotional content.
- The goal of the message is to "sell" the listener on something, and this attitude of "selling" comes through in the performance.
- The overall effect of the message is to create "listener tune-out."
- Delivery of the message may, in some way, actually damage or reduce credibility of the advertiser.

A "voice acting" performance has ALL of the following characteristics:

- The performer creates a believable and real character in conversation with the listener.
- The message is primarily emotional, with a clearly defined focus.
- The focus of the performance is on "telling a story" that the listener can relate to on an emotional level—often coming from a place of helping the listener in some way, rather than "selling."
- The overall effect of the message is one of keeping the listener's attention and creating a memorable moment.

Using this definition, there is certainly a place for voiceover, and if done properly it can be quite effective. But good voiceover is done within the context of a larger performance or is designed for a very specific purpose, and presented from a very specific perspective. The best "voiceover" work is performed from a foundation of "voice acting." For the balance of this book, the terms "voiceover" and "voice acting" will be used interchangeably."

Voice acting is about creating real and believable characters in real and believable situations that listeners can relate to and be motivated by. To do this, a performer must be able to reach the audience on an emotional level. In other words, voice acting is about creating compelling characters in interesting relationships.

We communicate on an emotional level every day in a completely natural manner. But often, when we work from a script, we suddenly flounder: the words are not ours and the life behind those words is not ours. It's not as easy as it may appear to get "off the page" and speak from a script in a manner that sounds natural, real, and conversational. In order to speak as a real and believable character, we must momentarily forget who we are and become that character, or at the very least, understand how to tell a compelling story. That's why it is important to master basic acting techniques.

Types of Voiceover Work

There are only two ways to "do" voiceover: either as a business or as a hobby. Both are completely valid approaches, and this book will help in either case. However, the real focus on this book is in how to work in the voiceover business as a professional voice actor.

You hear voiceover messages many times every day, and you may not even be aware of it. When most people think of voiceover, they think of radio and TV commercials. These are only a small part of the business of voiceover. There is actually much more to it. Scan the code for more information.

Here are just some of the many types of voiceover work that require talented performers, like you:

- Accents and dialects (ethnic)
- ADR—automated dialogue replacement (film)
- Anime—character
- Audio book
- Celebrity spokesperson
- Character—animation, toys
- Character—announcer, tags
- Character—celebrity sound-alike
- Character—real people
- Character—sound effects
- Character—video game
- Commercial—radio
- Commercial—television
- Commercial—web
- Dialogue—multiple voices
- DJ—radio personality
- E-Learning (online training)
- Foreign language
- Imaging (radio)
- Industrial—training
- Industrial—video kiosk
- Industrial—web learning
- In-store messaging
- Jingles (singing)
- Live event announcer
- Looping—film backgrounds
- Narration—corporate marketing
- Narration—documentary
- Narration—medical/technical
- Narration—multi-media
- New Media—web
- Political
- Specialty
- Spokesperson
- Talking toys & games
- Telephony—IVR (Interactive Voice Response)
- Telephony—message-on-hold
- Telephony—phone prompts
- Television—news
- Television—programming
- Television—promo
- Theatrical—various
- Trailer (film)
- Video game
- Youth (real or child sound-alike)

The Essentials

Regardless of the type of voiceover work you do, there are several basic requirements:

- **A decent speaking voice:** The days of the "Golden Pipes" are history! Voice acting is *not* about your voice—it's about what you can *do* with your voice. And that means acting ability.
- **Excellent reading skills:** All voiceover work requires excellent reading skills. There is no memorization in voiceover work.
- **Directable talent:** You must be able to act and change your delivery or interpretation at the whim of the director.
- **Passion:** You must be willing to spend the time, energy, and money necessary to develop your acting and business skills, install a home studio, and market and promote your talent.

All four of these minimum requirements are necessary to achieve even the slightest degree of success as a voiceover performer. If one or more of these is missing, the journey to becoming a professional voice actor will be long and arduous.

Breaking into the Business of Voiceover

Learning basic voice acting techniques for reading and interpreting a script is a good start. But don't stop there. If performing with your voice is something you love to do, keep studying: take acting and improvisation classes; study commercials and analyze what the professionals are doing to create character and make their scripted words sound real; learn how to take direction; read every book on this craft you can get your hands on; visit talent websites and listen to the demos to learn what works and what doesn't; watch television programs about acting and theater, and finally ... never stop learning.

Even if you are an experienced actor, you need to know that the disciplines of "voice acting" are different from stage, film, or TV. In all other forms of acting, your lines are committed to memory and you have time to internalize, understand, and develop your character. In voice acting, you may have only a few minutes to create a believable character, find the voice, and deliver a compelling performance as you read from a script.

5

Voice acting is creative, fun and potentially lucrative—if you know what you are doing and have the patience to master the necessary skills! To be a successful voice actor, learn how to be natural, confident, real, and most of all … believable.

Most people think voiceover work is easy. You have probably even said to yourself after listening to a commercial, "I can do that!" For some people, it is easy. For most, though, voiceover—just like theatrical acting—is an ongoing learning process. In our VoiceActing Academy Performance Workshops, it is not uncommon for someone, after only a short time, to say "Oh, my! I had no idea there was this much to voiceover! This really isn't about just reading a script!"

Even experienced professionals will tell you that voiceover work is far more difficult than on-camera or on-stage acting. There is no memorization and the advantages of props, scenery, wardrobe, makeup, and lighting are not available to the voice actor. Voiceover is truly theater of the mind. The drama, comedy, emotions, and subtext of a message must be communicated solely through the spoken word to elicit the desired response in the listener's imagination. This requires a tremendous amount of focus and concentration, plus an ability to make quick changes in midstream. Prior acting experience is an advantage, but the essential performing skills can be picked up as you go, so don't let a lack of experience stop you. If you can use your imagination, tell a story with vivid imagery, and take direction, you can do voiceover.

One of the greatest misconceptions is that you need a certain type of voice to do voiceover. You do not need a "good" voice, or "announcer" voice. You do need a voice that is easily understood. If your voice has a unique quality or sound, you can use that to your advantage, especially for animation and character work. But a unique voice quality can also become a limitation if that is the only thing you do. You may find you are better suited to one particular type of voiceover work—corporate/industrial, for example. If that's the case, you can focus on marketing yourself for that type of work. Still, you should consider other types of voice work when the call comes.

Variety is an important aspect of voiceover performing. By variety I mean being able to use your voice to convey a wide range of attitudes, delivery styles, personality, interpretation, energy, and emotions. These are the characteristics of your voice presentation that will allow you to effectively tell a story that contains a message. And communicating a message is what working as a voice actor is all about.

Many people think that because they can do lots of impersonations or make up crazy character voices, they can do voiceover work. Vocal versatility is certainly valuable; however, success in the world of voiceover also takes focus, discipline, and an ability to act. Remember, it's not about your voice, it's about what you can do with your voice.

So, just how do you learn voiceover performing skills, break in, and get yourself known as a voice actor? There is no simple answer to this question. To be successful, you should learn everything you can about acting, communication, and marketing. In this business, an old adage, "It's not what you know, but who you know," is also very true. Getting voiceover work is largely a numbers game—a game of networking and making yourself known in the right circles.

There's another adage that holds a lot of truth: "Luck is being in the right place at the right time with the right skills." This book will be a great start toward acquiring the right skills. The other parts you'll need to do on your own.

To be successful you cannot be shy. Let every person you meet know what you do! But you must also possess both the performing and business skills that qualify you as a professional, and that is what this book is really about!

Or, you can do voiceover as a hobby!

In this Chapter

The Best Kept Secret

2

The Best Kept Secret

The Realities of Voice Acting

Let's face it—if everyone were equally good at every job, there would be no need for résumés or auditions. Fortunately, every person has uniquely different talents, abilities, and levels of skill. It is this variety that makes the voiceover business a potentially profitable career for anyone willing to invest the time and effort.

For years, voiceover was one of the best-kept secrets around. The job can be loads of fun and very profitable, but it is not an easy business to break into. Today, there are roughly five times as many people who claim to be voiceover talent as there are actors trying to break into TV and movies. Add to that the major film stars who have discovered that voiceover work is more fun than spending many hours in makeup each day. The simple truth is that competition is tough, and it is easy to become frustrated when just beginning.

Voiceover work is part of "show business." As such it has all the potential excitement, celebrity status, and opportunities as other areas of show business, as well as the long periods of waiting, frustrations in getting "booked," and problems dealing with agents, producers and clients.

Because voiceover is part of "show business," it can take many years of study and constantly being in the right place, to achieve a level of success. One voiceover coach I know suggests that it takes 15 years to become successful in voiceover. I disagree with that! Everyone defines "success" differently. Sure, if you define success as being in high demand and making the "big bucks," it might take 15 years or longer to get there. But if you are doing voiceover because you really love it, and you wonder why you're not paying them to let you get in front of the mic, then success can be as soon as next week.

Like most of the performing arts, voice acting is a hurry-up-and-wait kind of business. By that I mean you will spend a lot of time waiting: waiting for auditions, waiting for a callback, waiting in the lobby of a recording studio, waiting for the email with your script, and waiting to get paid. Once a voiceover recording session begins, things tend to happen very fast. But you may still find yourself waiting as the producer works on copy changes, or while the studio engineer deals with a technical problem.

If you are recording in your home studio, which has become a standard practice for voiceover work at all levels, you will be expected to deliver studio-quality recordings. You'll also be expected to know how to do some limited production and editing—even though you are not a recording engineer. That means you need to be computer-literate and you'll need to invest in the training, equipment, software, and acoustic improvements necessary to build a functional recording facility in your home.

From a performance standpoint, producers assume that you know what you are doing and expect you to deliver your lines professionally. You are expected to be able to deliver a masterful interpretation of a script after only a short read-through—usually within the first two or three takes. Direction or coaching from the producer or director often comes very fast, so you must listen closely and pay attention. Sometimes, the producer or director completely changes the concept or makes major copy changes in the middle of an audition or session—and you need to be able to adapt quickly. More often than not, you won't get any direction at all. If you're recording in your home studio, the session may be director-less and producer-less, meaning you are on your own! You need to develop excellent interpretive skills and be a versatile performer with the ability to self-direct and provide what your client is asking for, even when you're not certain exactly what that is.

Your job as a voice actor is to perform to the best of your abilities. When you are hired, either from your demo or after an audition, your voice has been chosen over many others as the one most desirable for the job. Unless there is a serious technical problem that requires your being called back, or if there are revisions that are made after the session has ended, you will not get a second chance after leaving the studio or sending your files.

Full~Time or Part~Time

If you think voiceover work is for you, you have some decisions to make. Not right this minute, but soon. Do you want to do voiceover work as a full-time career, or as a part-time avocation? What niche area of voiceover do you want to focus on? Should you move to a different city in search of work in your niche area? The choices may be many and may not be easy!

Doing voiceover work on a full-time basis is unlike just about any other job you can imagine. You must be available on a moment's notice when you are called for an audition. In addition, you must constantly market yourself, even if you have an agent.

Full-time voiceover work may also mean joining a union, and possibly even moving to a larger city—if that's where your destiny leads you. Los Angeles, Chicago, New York, and other major cities are strong union towns for voiceover work, and you must be in the union to get well-paying jobs in these cities. Although the possibility for non-union work does exist in larger cities, it may require some additional effort to find it.

The union for voiceover in the United Stages is SAG-AFTRA, a merger of the Screen Actor's Guild and the American Federation of Television and Radio Artists. If you are just getting started in voiceover, union membership will best be reserved for some time in the future. You'll find more about unions in Chapter 19.

Since voiceover is a part of show business, it is very important to know exactly what you are doing before "taking the leap." In other words ... don't quit your day job! But that can create a challenge of how you will study your craft, promote your business, and submit auditions all while earning an income with a completely unrelated job. So, the question now is, "Can I break into voiceover on a part-time basis?" Good question!

Although working as a voice actor on a part-time basis is possible, you won't be doing the same kind of work as you would if you devoted more time to it—and it will likely take you considerably longer to reach your goals. You will most likely do some corporate or industrial work, telephone messages, and smaller projects for clients who have a minimal or nonexistent budget. Some of your work may be voluntary, barter, or you will do it just because you want the experience. The pay for nonunion freelance work is usually not terrific—but freelance work is a very good way of getting voiceover experience. You can gradually build up a client list and get copies of your work that you can use to market yourself later on when, or if, you decide to go full-time.

The biggest challenge with doing voiceover work part-time is that you may find it difficult to deal with last-minute auditions or session calls. If you have a regular full-time job, you will usually need to arrange your voiceover work around it, unless you have a very understanding employer. Part-time voiceover work can, however, be an ideal opportunity for the homemaker or self-employed individual with a flexible schedule.

With the advent of Internet audition services and advanced computer technology, it has become very convenient to record auditions and paid projects in a home studio and submit them as MP3 files via the Internet.

Doing voiceover work can be very satisfying, even if you only do an occasional session. Yet, the day may come when your skills are at a level where you decide to go for the big money in L.A., Chicago, or New York. In the meantime, don't be in a hurry. Make the best of every opportunity that comes along and create your own opportunities whenever possible. Networking is extremely important! You never know when you might be in just the right place to land that important national spot that changes your entire life!

Seven Things You Must Know about Voiceover Work

On the surface, voiceover appears "easy," but in reality there is a LOT to learn! Here's a list, inspired by VO pro Michael Minetree, of some essential things you need to know about voiceover before you take the leap:

1. You can't learn how to perform for voiceover on your own. You need the guidance of a qualified coach who knows the business.

2. You can't learn how to perform for voiceover by reading a book. Any VO book (yes, even this one!) is only as good as the information it contains. The purpose of a book is to provide you with the information you need so you can more effectively learn the skills. You need talent, dedication, passion, and training that goes beyond the information contained in a book.

3. You can't learn how to perform for voiceover from a tele-course. A tele-course will give you lots of information, but by its very nature, will be limited in the effectiveness of any performance coaching. You may get the general idea of how to use a technique, but it won't qualify you to compete in this business. Personal coaching and experience are your best training.

4. You can't learn this craft from a single workshop. Some workshops are excellent—and some are, well … not. Any workshop (yes, even ours!) will only be good enough to get you started on the path. You need to take the next steps with additional training. Professional film, stage, and television actors are constantly taking classes between projects. Continued training is essential in the voiceover business. Throughout this book, I'll encourage you to do the same.

5. If you produce your demo immediately following a workshop, you will be wasting your money. Your money will be better spent on additional training and personalized coaching. Do not even think about spending money on producing your demo until **you** *know* you are ready. See Chapter 21, "Your Voiceover Demo," to learn more about how to prepare for your demo.

6. If a demo is included as part of a course … find a different course! No one is ready for a demo after a single workshop. Your demo must be great—it cannot be merely "good." Even more than that, your performance must be comparable to the best voice talent out there. That level of skill only comes with time and proper training.

7. Be wary of workshops and coaches who promise success and a substantial income from taking their course. No one can promise you success, and no one can promise your demo will even be heard. Your degree of success in voiceover will be directly related to your dedication to running your business in a professional manner.

In this Chapter

Voiceover Basics

3

Voiceover Basics:
Where to Start

Are You an Actor or a Salesperson?

When you stand in front of a microphone as voice talent, your job is to effectively communicate the message contained within the words written on the paper in front of you. You are a storyteller. Although the ultimate objective of your performance might be for the listener to make a purchase, rarely will your job be to actually "sell" something. There's a difference between telling a story in a way that motivates a purchase and speaking in a way that sounds like you are selling something. People love to buy, but people do not like being "sold." Part of your job is to figure out how to speak the words in such a way that your listener understands the message and is motivated to act on what they hear.

YOUR ROLE AS A VOICE ACTOR

You are an actor! The words, by themselves, are nothing but ink on a page. As a voice actor, you must interpret the words in such a way as to effectively tell the story, bring the character to life, and meet the perceived needs of the producer or director in terms of communicating the message. I say "perceived needs" because many producers and writers only have an idea in their heads. The producer may think he knows what he wants, when, in reality, he hasn't got a clue as to the best way to deliver the message. This is where your acting skills and performance choices come in. You may find yourself in the enviable position of solving many of your producer's problems simply by performing the copy in a way that you feel effectively communicates the message.

Your acting abilities are the vital link between the writer and the audience. You are the actor playing the role of the character written in the script. On the surface, that may sound like a fairly simple task. However, mastering the skills to create interesting and compelling characters on a consistent basis can be very challenging. Unlike stage performers, who may have several days, weeks, or months to define, internalize, and develop their characters, you may have only a few minutes. You must use your best acting skills to deliver your best interpretation of the copy—and you must do it quickly. Your job is to breathe life into the script, making the thoughts of the writer become real through the character you create. You need to be able to quickly grasp the important elements of the script, figure out who you are talking to, understand your character in great detail, find the key elements of the copy, and choose what you believe to be the most effective delivery for your lines. Every script is written for a purpose and you must be able to find and give meaning to that purpose, regardless of how or where the voice track will be recorded. In many cases, especially in studio sessions, the producer or director will be coaching you into the read that gets you as close as possible to his or her vision. However, with the increasing prevalence of high quality home studios, more and more voice talent are being asked to provide self-directed, unsupervised, sessions.

A COMMON MISTAKE

One mistake made by many beginning voiceover performers is that they get nervous when they approach the microphone. They are focused on their voice or the words in the script, not their performance. They fidget, stand stiff as a board, cross their arms, or put their hands behind their backs or in their pockets. It is impossible to perform effectively under those conditions.

What is needed is to get into the flow of the copy, breathe naturally, relax, have fun, and let the performance take you where it needs to go. Discover your character and let that character come into you so that you can create a sense of truth and reality for the character. If you think too much about what you are doing, your performance will usually be forced and sound like you are acting or selling. When you allow yourself to "become the character" you will be able to "live the voice."

UNDERSTAND YOUR AUDIENCE

Every message (script) has an intended (or target) audience. Once you understand who the audience is and your role as the actor, you will be well on your way to knowing how to perform the copy for the most effective delivery. In order to know your audience, you must begin by understanding the story. Only then you can figure out who you are talking to. Narrow it down to a single individual and relate to that person on an emotional level. This is the first critical step to creating an effective performance and a believable character.

THE VOICE ACTOR AS A SALESPERSON

It can be argued that virtually all voiceover is "selling" something. Commercials sell products or services, or try to get an emotional response to motivate action; instructional products sell procedures; audio books sell entertainment; and so on. The argument goes that acting is the means by which any of these messages can be effectively communicated, the story told, and the listener motivated to take action. So, technically, you are not only a performer, but, in a sense, you are also a salesperson. For the time you are in the recording studio, you are an employee of your client's business. In fact, you, as an actor, are the advertiser's top salesperson and must present yourself as a qualified expert. And you, as the actor playing that character, must be perceived as real and honest.

Your acting job may only last a few minutes in the studio, but that performance may be repeated thousands of times on radio or TV. Your voice may be heard by more people in a single minute than might walk through the front door of a business in an entire year. But even though you may be playing the role of a salesperson, you must never sound like you are selling. The credibility of the product or advertiser—and the success of an advertising campaign—may be directly related to the authenticity, effectiveness, and believability of your performance. Tell the story ... Never sell it!

Are you beginning to see there's more to this thing called voiceover than merely reading words on a page? And we're just getting started!

Getting the Skills You Need

The bottom line here is to get experience—as much as you can, wherever you can, any way you can! Take classes in acting, voiceover, improvisation, business, and marketing. Get as much experience as you can reading stories out loud. Read to your children. Read to your spouse. Volunteer. Practice telling stories with lots of variety in your voice.

Analyze the characters in the stories you read. Take more classes. Read the same copy in different ways, at different speeds, and with different feelings or emotional attitudes—loud, soft, slow, fast, happy, sad, compassionate, angry. If possible, record yourself and listen to what you did to see where you might improve. Take some more classes. Become a master of performing on a microphone. You can't take too many classes!

One of the best ways to acquire voice acting skills is to listen to other voice actors. Mimicking other performers can be a good start to learning some basic performing techniques, but your ultimate goal should be to develop your own, unique interpretive skills and your own, unique delivery style. To really get an understanding of communicating on an emotional level, listen to how other professional voice actors deliver their lines and tell their stories:

- How do they interpret the message?
- How do they reach you emotionally?
- How do they use inflection, intonation, pacing, musicality, and express feelings?
- Is their delivery conversational and natural or not?
- How do you respond to their interpretation?

In short, do they sound as if they are reading or do they sound natural and believable? Use what you learn from studying others and adapt that information to your own voice and style. Learn how to "make the copy your own." This simply means that you bring to the performance something of yourself to give the character and copy truth and believability. That's good acting! Chapters 5 through 10 will show you how to do it!

A TWIST OF A WORD

The best voice actors do not sound like someone "doing" voiceover. They sound like your best friend talking to you—comfortable, casual, friendly, and most of all, not "announcery." A good performer can make even bad copy sound reasonably good—and what they can do with good copy is truly amazing.

Create an emotional, visual image in the mind of the audience with a twist of a word. A slight change in the delivery of a word—a shift of the nuance—can change the entire meaning of a sentence. Speaking a word softly or with more intensity, or perhaps sustaining a vowel, making the delivery crisp, or taking the inflection up or down can all affect the meaning of a sentence and its emotional impact in the mind of the listener. These are skills that are acquired over time and require an in-depth understanding of basic acting techniques that help to create an emotional connection with the audience.

To be an effective voiceover performer you need to discover the qualities and characteristics of your voice that will make you different from all those other voices out there. Keep developing new techniques. Keep practicing and studying the work of others in the business. Find your unique qualities and perfect them. Learn how to make any piece of copy your own, and you will be in demand. Remember, it's not about your voice, but what you can do with it.

VOICEOVER "READS"

There are more than two dozen different genres in voiceover, ranging from commercials to talking toys, and each of them has its own unique delivery style, or "read." Some of the more common styles are: conversational, story teller, announcer, objective narrator, authoritative narrator, attitude personality, real person, whimsical, contemplative, and extreme character, among others.

Although the term "read" is commonly used in this industry, it is really a misnomer, because literally all of these delivery styles require at least some acting ability and a mastery of performing techniques. The term "read" implies that it's the words that are important, but the reality is that voiceover is all about acting.

CLASSES

One observation that has appeared in discussions of this book over the past several editions is my repeated recommendation for continued training. The simple truth is that the only way you will learn the diverse range of performing and business skills needed to be a successful voice actor is to take classes. The necessity to keep up with business trends and constantly hone performance techniques cannot be over-emphasized! It is impossible to take too many classes! There is always something new to be learned. Even if you leave a class with only one small piece of useful information, that small gem may someday pay big dividends. The same is true of books and articles. You will be amazed at where you can find a tip or trick that will help you create a believable performance.

There are four types of classes that are most valuable for the voiceover performer: acting, voiceover, improvisation, and business. Acting classes will give you opportunities to learn about directing, dramatic structure, comedic timing, stage presence, emotional delivery, and innumerable other fine points of performing. Voiceover classes will give you opportunities to learn about other niches of this business, practice your skills on-mic and study new techniques with personalized coaching. Improvisation in voice work is common with dialogue or multiple voice copy and is an essential skill for commercials, animation, video game and other niche areas of the business. This type of training helps improve your spontaneity and ability to adapt quickly. You will also learn skills that can be applied to character development and copy interpretation. And because the nature of voiceover work today is largely entrepreneurial, it is imperative that you have at least a basic understanding of fundamental business skills. I truly encourage you to take some classes, attend a workshop, or even spend a few days learning from the pros at a voiceover convention. Continued training is an incredibly worthwhile investment in your performing career. I promise you will learn a lot, and you might actually have lots of fun. Here are some of the places you can find classes:

- Community theater groups are constantly in need of volunteers. Even if you are working on a crew, you will be able to study what goes on in the theater. Watch what the director does, and learn how the actors become their characters. Don't forget that voice acting is theater of the mind—without props, scenery, or lighting.

- Most community colleges offer continuing education classes, often in the evenings or on weekends. Tuition is usually reasonable and the skills you can learn will pay off later on. Suitable courses can also be found in most college theater arts and business curriculums.

- Many cities have adult education classes in voiceover, acting, comedy, improvisation, and other subjects that can give you opportunities to acquire the skills you need. Check your local adult or continuing education office, or local colleges and universities for classes offered in your area.

- Many cities have private acting and voiceover courses. They are usually not advertised in the phone book, so they may be somewhat difficult to locate. An Internet search for "voiceover (or voice acting) Your City" may bring up some interesting results. Talent agents in most cities may be aware of local training and may be able to refer you to a class or coach. Check the classifieds of the local subscription and free newspapers in your area. You can also call the drama department at high schools and colleges for any referrals they might be able to make. Your local professional and community theater groups may also be able to give you some guidance. You'll find a comprehensive listing of voiceover coaches in the Resources area at **VoiceActing.com**.

- For voiceover classes, try calling some of the recording studios or talent agents in your area. Many recording studios work with voiceover performers every day and can offer some valuable insights or give you some good leads. Some studios offer classes or do the production work for a class offered by someone else. Or they might be able to simply point you in the right direction by suggesting local workshops or refer you to a local talent agent who might be able to give you some direction.

A WORD OF CAUTION

Larger cities, such as Los Angeles and New York, have many voiceover workshops and classes available. Most are reputable and valuable resources. Be careful, though, because some classes are little more than scams designed to take your money. Usually the scam classes will begin with a short "teaser" class or workshop where they provide you with information that you can often find elsewhere for free or from a book. They tell you just enough to get you excited—usually conveniently underplaying the true realities of the business. Then they tell you they will produce and market your demo for a fee—anything from $500 to $5,000. You may even be required to take their class if you want them to produce your demo. Demo fees are usually in addition to the fees you pay for the class, although some will include a demo as part of their overpriced tuition. You may get a demo from these classes, but the quality will likely be poor, and their promises of marketing your demo or sending it out to agents are usually worthless.

Many legitimate classes will also offer their services to assist with your demo. The difference is that you will not be pressured into buying their services and the demo will not be a condition of taking the class. An honest and reputable voiceover instructor will not encourage you to do a demo until you are ready. When they do assist with your demo, the production quality is generally very high. Regardless of who you hire to produce your demo, be sure to check them out. Get copies of some demos they have done and get a list of former clients who you can call to ask about their experience with the producer. If they are legitimate, the demo producer will be happy to help you. Some will even give you a free consultation.

Be aware that no workshop coach or demo producer can guarantee your demo will be heard by an agent or talent buyer, or even that you will be accepted for voiceover representation or work. No matter what they tell you, you are the only person who will determine your success in this business. Do not rely on someone else to do it for you.

In this Chapter

Using Your Instrument

4

Using Your Instrument

Where do You Sit in the Voiceover Orchestra?

As a voice actor, the tool of your trade—the instrument for your performance—is your voice. Just as any other craftsperson must know how to care for the tools of his or her trade, before you can begin to learn the craft of performing for voiceover, it is vital that you first learn how to properly use, and care for, the most important tool you have ... your voice! So, with that in mind, this chapter includes some essential information about how your voice works, how to deal with common vocal problems, simple warm-up exercises, and tips for keeping your voice healthy. You'll also find some resources for further research if you feel that necessary. If you've never thought much about your voice, you'll probably find most of the exercises and tips helpful, some merely interesting, and a few perhaps totally weird.

All voice actors are not created equal! Sorry, but that's just the way it is. The world of voiceover is one of diverse talent, abilities, and sounds. Some people seem to master voiceover quickly and easily while others struggle for years to "break in." You must begin with some basic talent. You simply have to have it—talent cannot be taught. If you didn't have at least some level of talent, chances are you wouldn't be reading this book, so I'll assume that isn't an issue. Once you've discovered your basic talent, the next step is to build upon it and nurture it as you develop performing and business skills.

Learning the craft and business of voiceover is much like learning how to play a musical instrument. Some people are more adept at learning piano, while others choose to study flute, some will play string instruments, and still others have the ability to play a variety of instruments. Some dedicated musicians become virtuosos while others never advance their level of skill beyond the beginner stage. The simple truth is that some people simply have more talent for learning what it takes to play their chosen instrument. If you've ever taken lessons to learn how to play guitar, piano, violin, oboe, or some other musical instrument, you have a good idea of what to expect as you begin your study of voiceover. If you have the basic talent, and you're willing to dedicate yourself to mastering the necessary skills, there's a very good chance that you'll find your place in the voiceover orchestra.

In the context of an orchestra, each voice actor has a seat—and not everyone can be section leader. Each section of an orchestra consists of several musicians seated according to their skill level and expertise. A musical composition is broken down into several parts for each section. For example the first violin part may be played by several musicians and will usually carry the melody and be technically demanding. The second violin part, also played by several musicians, will be less demanding, but still critical to the overall composition. The third and successive parts are progressively less demanding, but all are essential parts of the whole. The violinist seated to the conductor's left is also known as the Concertmaster and is second in command after the orchestra conductor. This individual has earned their position through constant study and a demonstration of a high level of expertise with their instrument.

Do you know where you sit in the voiceover orchestra? Do you know which part you play? Do you know your level of expertise at playing your instrument? Do you even know what instrument you play?

If you're reading this book to learn what voiceover is all about and how to get started, your answers to the above questions are most likely all "no." And that's OK. By the time you finish this book you should be in a much better position to answer these questions with a resounding "yes."

At this point you should be aware that your instrument is your voice. But there's more to it! Just as every musician in an orchestra plays an instrument, every voice actor uses their voice. In an orchestra some instruments have a deep, resonant, low tone (string bass, cello, bassoon, and tuba), while other instruments have a high, clear tone (piccolo, flute, trumpet, and percussion bells). Other instruments have a raspy, edgy tone (violin, clarinet, oboe and saxophone), or a percussive, harsh attack (piano, harpsichord, percussion). Even within sections of the orchestra there are a variety of instruments that are of the same basic design, yet exhibit a uniquely different tone:

- Brass: trombone, trumpet, French horn, tuba
- String: violin, viola, cello, upright bass, guitar, piano
- Wind: flute, piccolo, clarinet, oboe, bassoon, saxophone
- Percussion: xylophone, tympani, drums, cymbals, bells

Voice actors are no different than the instruments in an orchestra. As you study this craft you'll begin to discover things about your instrument. Do you have a smooth, mellow, clear tone like a trumpet? Do you have a voice that is high pitched, or as a friend of ours says: "baritone challenged," like a piccolo? Or perhaps you will discover that your voice is deep and resonant with limited range, like a bassoon.

Your determination of the tonality and texture of your voice is a very important discovery because it will ultimately guide you through your study of this craft. If you have a voice with deep "golden tones" you'll find it a challenge to perform a script written for a high pitched, fast-talking character voice. By the same token, if your vocal tone resides in the mid-range, you may find it difficult to work at either extreme without sounding artificial and unreal. All music uses the same written notes, just like all voiceover copy uses the same words. Although you might hear a tuba solo, you'll never hear a tuba trying to sound like a flute.

There is still one instrument I haven't mentioned yet, and you may discover that this is where you fit in the voiceover orchestra. That instrument is the digital MIDI keyboard. Press a button on this keyboard and you have a string section. Press a different button and you're playing a piano. Press yet another button and it's now a trumpet. The possibilities are endless.

Many voice actors specialize in mastering the skills for performing within the primary range and tone of their voice. They become the best violin, trumpet, or bassoon they can be, with an ability to convey the subtlest nuance through their performance.

Most voice actors who work in animation or video games fall in the digital keyboard category. Through their years of study, they have mastered the ability to create a wide range of very real and believable voices on demand.

What instrument do you play? Are you a highly proficient first violinist capable of playing complex melodies at ease? Or are you a third trombone, able to get all the notes right, but still learning how to master the nuance of your instrument? Maybe, just maybe, you're a digital keyboard with the ability to create radically diverse voices with different tonalities and textures, all of which sound completely authentic. The only way you'll know is to discover your unique talent by studying performing techniques and experimenting to learn what works best for you.

The beauty of both music and voiceover is that the performance is not dependent on what's on the paper. The performance is the end result of how the performer plays their instrument.

All About Breathing

Your voice is a wind instrument and as with any other wind instrument, it is essential that you know how to play your instrument properly. In other words, you need to know how to breathe. Proper breathing provides support for your voice and allows for emotional expression. It allows you to speak softly or with power, and to switch between the two styles instantly. Proper breathing is what makes possible the subtleties of communicating a broad range of information and emotion through the spoken word.

Breathing comes naturally, and it is something you should not be thinking about while performing. From the moment we are born, we are breathing. However, during our formative years, many of us were either taught to breathe incorrectly, or experienced something in our environment that left us with an improper breathing pattern. It may be that we learned to breathe from our chest, using only our lungs. Or perhaps, we adapted to our insecurities and created a mental block that inhibits our ability to breathe properly.

YOUR VOCAL PRESENTATION

Arthur Joseph, a voice specialist and creator of Vocal Awareness (**vocalawareness.com**), describes vocal presentation as the way in which others hear and respond to you. The way you are perceived by others is directly related to your perception of yourself. If you perceive yourself to be outgoing, strong, forceful, and intelligent, your voice reflects these attitudes and perceptions with a certain loudness and assertiveness. By the same token, if you perceive yourself to be weak, helpless, and always making mistakes, your voice reflects your internal beliefs with qualities of softness and insecurity. How you breathe is an important factor in your individual vocal presentation because breath control is directly related to the loudness, tonality, and power behind your voice.

Your perception is your reality. So, if you want to change how you are perceived by others, you must first change how you perceive yourself—and that requires awareness. In most cases, a problem with vocal presentation is a habit directly related to a lack of vocal awareness—and habits can be changed. Changing a habit requires an extreme technique, discipline, conscious diligence, and constant awareness. A number of vocal presentation problems, and exercises for correcting them, are discussed later in this chapter.

Many of the exercises in this book will help you discover things about yourself and your voice, of which you might not have been aware. They will also help you improve or change your breathing technique and vocal presentation, and maintain the new qualities you acquire. The lessons you learn about your voice from this and other books will help give you awareness of your voice and will be of tremendous value as you proceed on your voice-acting journey. From this new awareness, you will be able to adapt and modify your vocal presentation to create believable, compelling characters.

Joni Wilson has written an excellent series of books for improving and maintaining the sound of your voice. The first book of the series, *The 3-Dimensional Voice* is the much-needed owner's manual for the human voice and introduces her ideas and techniques. You can learn more about Joni and her books by visiting **joniwilsonvoice.com**. Scan this response code to listen to Joni describe 20 facts you need to know about your voice.

BREATH CONTROL FOR THE VOICE ACTOR

The first lesson you must learn before you can begin mastering the skills of voice acting is how to breathe properly. Take a moment to observe yourself breathing. Is your breathing rapid and shallow? Or do you inhale with long, slow, deep breaths? Observe how you breathe when you are under stress or in a hurry, and listen to your voice under these conditions. Does the pitch of your voice rise? When you are comfortable and relaxed, is the pitch of your voice lower and softer? Feel what your body is doing as you breathe. Do your shoulders rise when you take a deep breath? Does your chest expand? Do you feel tension in your shoulders, body, or face? Your observations will give you an idea of how you handle the physical process of breathing that we all take for granted.

Of course, the lungs are the organ we use for breathing, but in and of themselves, they cannot provide adequate support for the column of air that passes across your vocal cords. Your lungs are really nothing more than a container for air. It is the diaphragm, a muscle situated below the rib cage and lungs, that is the real source of support for proper breathing.

Allowing your diaphragm to expand when inhaling allows your lungs to expand more completely and fill with a larger quantity of air than if a breath is taken by simply expanding your chest. When you relax your mind and body, and allow a slow, deep, cleansing breath, your diaphragm expands automatically. Contracting your diaphragm, by pulling your lower abdominal muscles up and through your voice as you speak, gives a constant means of support for a column of air across your vocal cords. For a performer, correct breathing is from the diaphragm, not from the chest.

Good breath control begins with a relaxed body. Tense muscles in the neck, tongue, jaw and throat, usually caused by stress, constrict your vocal cords and cause the pitch of your voice to rise. Tension in other parts of your body also has an effect on the quality of your voice and your ability to perform. Relaxation exercises reduce tension throughout your body and have the additional benefit of improving your mental focus and acuity by providing increased oxygen to your brain. Later in this chapter, you'll find several exercises for relaxing your body and improving your breathing.

Good breath control and support can make the difference between a voice actor successfully transcending an especially unruly piece of copy or ending up exhausted on the studio floor. A voice actor must be able to deal with complex copy and sentences that seem to never end, and to make it all sound natural and comfortable. The only way to do it is with good breath control and support.

The following piece of copy must be read in a single breath in order to come in at :10, or "on-time." Even though the words will go by quickly, it should not sound rushed. It should sound effortless and comfortable, not strained or forced. It should be delivered in a conversational manner, as though you are speaking to a good friend. Allow a good supporting breath and read the following copy out loud.

 Come in today for special savings on all patio furniture, lighting fixtures, door bells, and buzzers, including big discounts on hammers, saws, shovels, rakes, and power tools, plus super savings on everything you need to keep your garden green and beautiful.

How did you do? If you made it all the way through without running out of air, congratulations! If you had to take a breath, or ran out of air near the end, you may need to increase your lung capacity and breath support. Long lists and wordy copy are commonplace and performing them requires a relaxed body, focus, concentration, and breath support. You need to start with a good breath that fills the lungs with fresh air.

Check your breathing technique by standing in front of a mirror. Place your fingers just below your rib cage, with thumbs toward the back and watch as you take a slow, deep breath. You should see and feel your stomach expand and your shoulders should not move. If your hands don't move and your shoulders rise, you are breathing from your chest.

As the diaphragm expands, it opens the body cavity, allowing the rib cage to open and the lungs to expand downward as they fill with air. If you breathe with your chest, you will only partially fill your lungs. It is not necessary for the shoulders to rise in order to obtain a good breath. In fact, rising shoulders is a sign of shallow breathing, indicating that the breath is getting caught in the chest or throat. Tension, fear, stress, and anxiety can all result in shallow breathing, causing the voice to appear weak and shaky and words to sound unnatural.

Breathing from your diaphragm gives you greater power behind your voice and can allow you to speak longer before taking another breath. This is important when you have to read a lot of copy in a short period of time, or when the copy is written in long, complicated sentences.

Do the following exercise, then go back and read the copy again. You should find it easier to read the entire piece in one breath.

- Begin by inhaling a very slow, deep, cleansing breath. Allow your diaphragm to expand and your lungs to completely fill with air. Now exhale completely, making sure not to let your breath get caught in your chest or throat. Rid your body of any remaining stale air by tightening your abdominal muscles after you have exhaled. You may be surprised at how much air is left in your lungs.
- Place your hands below your rib cage, lower your jaw, and allow two very slow preparatory breaths, exhaling completely after each one. Feel your diaphragm and rib cage expand as you breathe in and contract as you exhale. Your shoulders should not move. If they do, you are breathing from your chest for only a "shallow" breath.
- Allow a third deep breath and hold it for just a second or two before beginning to read. Holding your breath before starting gives stability to your performance by allowing you to lock your diaphragm so you can get a solid start with the first word of your copy.

A slow, deep, cleansing breath is a terrific way to relax and prepare for a voice-acting performance (see Exercise 1 on page 41). It will help center you and give you focus and balance. However, working from a script requires a somewhat different sort of breathing. You will need to find places in the copy where you can take a breath.

For some scripts you may need to take a silent catch breath. At other times you might choose to vocalize a breath for dramatic impact, or take a completely silent breath so as to not to not create an audible distraction.

If you breathe primarily from your chest, you will find that breathing from your diaphragm makes a difference in the sound of your voice. Your diaphragm is a muscle and, just as you tone other muscles in your body, you may need to tone your diaphragm.

Here's a quick exercise from Joni Wilson that will help you develop strong diaphragmatic breathing. You'll find other exercises in her book *The 3-Dimensional Voice*[1]:

- Put the fingers of both hands on the abdominal diaphragm and open the mouth in a yawn position. Inhale the air, then say as you exhale the air, "haaaaaaaaaaaaaa," manually pushing the diaphragm with your fingers in toward the spine for as long as air comes out of the mouth.
- When there is no more air, and what comes out begins to resemble a "death rattle," slowly relax the pushing and allow the diaphragm to drop back down and suck the air back into the lungs. You may experience some dizziness. Stop for a moment, and let it pass before you do the exercise again. You can do this throughout the day to strengthen the diaphragm.

BREATHE CONVERSATIONALLY

One of the secrets for proper breathing with a voiceover performance is to only take in enough air for what you need to say. We do this instinctively in normal conversation. If you only need to say a few words, there's no point in taking a deep breath. Inhaling too much air may result in a very audible breath or a sudden and unnatural exhale at the end of your line.

Listen to how you and others speak in conversation. You'll notice that no one takes a deep breath before they speak, and no one waits until someone else finishes talking before they take a breath. In conversation, we breathe in a natural and comfortable manner— even when others are speaking. When we speak, we only take in enough air for the words we say, and we breathe at natural breaks in our delivery without thinking about what we are doing. When you understand how to properly use your diaphragm to provide breath support you will eliminate the need for frequent deep breaths and rapid catch breaths.

You do need to breathe, and you will sometimes be working a script with extremely long, complicated sentences. Breath points in most copy usually occur after a portion of a thought has been stated or a question has been asked. Listings provide natural break points between each item. You normally won't want to breathe between each item of a list, but the punctuation of a list will usually provide an opportunity if you need it.

Of course, when we are performing from a script, the words aren't ours, but as voice actors we must make the words sound conversational and believable as if they are ours. A common problem for many people just starting in voiceover is that they become too focused on the words or feel like they may not be able to "get through" the script, especially if the sentences are long. The result is that they tend to take a deep breath and read as much as they can until they begin to run out of air, somehow thinking that by reading the copy without breathing will help. Although some may be able to deliver the words with a reasonable interpretation for short bursts, most will sound rushed and detached from the meaning of the words. In this case, there is no acting or performance taking place and no connection with the intended audience. The voice talent is merely being themselves while struggling through a highly stressful situation.

The remedy for this common ailment is to realize that the words are just words on a piece of paper, and that our job is to simply speak those words in an appropriate manner. The stress of the moment is completely self-imposed and need not exist. Nowhere is it written that a voice actor must read, or "get through," a script without breathing. The truth is that breathing is an essential part of communicating the meaning of those words. It's part of the natural flow of conversational phrasing.

The challenge is in learning how to breath naturally while reading from a script, allowing the breath to happen at appropriate places. In order to find the natural breath points in a script, you need to understand the story, your character, and myriad other details in the script. When you play the role of a character you create, the stress of working with a script can be completely eliminated because the character already knows how—and where—to breathe.

Be Easy on Yourself

My first recommendation as you begin studying the craft of voiceover is for you to record yourself reading copy every chance you get. I guarantee that you will likely not care for the way you sound, and what you hear as you listen to your recorded voice may surprise you—and for good reason. When you speak, you are not actually hearing your own voice in the same way others do. Much of what you hear is actually resonance of vibrations from your vocal cords traveling through your body and bones to your inner ear. When other people hear you, they don't get the advantage of that nice resonance. The way your voice sounds to other people is what you hear when your voice is played back from a recording.

I suggest you find a way to record your voice. In this age of digital audio, there are new devices coming out every day for recording audio. Some offer extremely high-quality recordings, while others are marginal. What you need, at least to start, is a way to record a reasonably high quality voice recording so you can play it back to study what you are doing. For the purpose of rehearsal and mastering your technique, you don't need to spend a lot of money on building a home studio. The time for that will come when you start marketing yourself as a professional voice talent. For now, an old tape recorder, handheld digital recorder, or some simple recording software and a microphone for your computer will do the job.

Practice reading out loud—the newspaper, magazine ads, pages from a novel—anything that tells a story. Record yourself reading a few short paragraphs. Begin by reading as if you were simply reading out loud to someone else. Observe how you breathe as you read. Listen to yourself to hear if you read with a monotone or if you tell the story with vocal variety.

Now change your interpretation of the story. Pretend you are a different person with a different attitude. If your first read-through was up-beat and friendly, this time go for the opposite—serious and dramatic. If your first read-through was fast, this time slow down.

Again, observe how you breathe and listen for changes in the vocal variety of your delivery. When you change the component parts of your delivery, you should hear noticeable differences with each read-through.

Each time you read the story, make some adjustments to the pitch of your voice, make your voice louder or softer, and vary the dynamics of pacing, rhythm, and emotion. Practice looking for the most important elements of the story and explore different ways of making those parts of the story interesting. As you work on this, you will begin to discover many things about yourself as a performer and you will be scratching the surface of what it takes to create interesting and compelling characters.

One of the best ways to learn this craft is to listen to voiceover work at every opportunity. How do you compare? Adapt your style to imitate the delivery of someone you have heard on a national radio or TV commercial. Don't try to be that other performer, but rather imitate their tone of voice, attitude, vocal placement, pacing and phrasing. Notice what feels right and what doesn't seem to work for you. This process will help you to discover how various performing techniques work and will ultimately help you to develop your personal style. The exercises in this chapter will help you explore your performing capabilities .

Listen to your recordings to evaluate what you are doing, but don't be too hard on yourself. Don't be concerned about what your voice sounds like or getting all the words spoken correctly. At this stage of developing your performing skills, it's more important to focus on what it feels like as you work on your reading. The rest will come in time.

Be as objective as you can and make notes about the things you hear that you would like to correct. Practice the exercises and techniques in this book that apply. Recording and listening to yourself can be an enjoyable process and a great learning experience that helps give you an awareness of what you are doing with your voice. Remember, it's not about your voice, it's about what you can do with your voice—and it might take some time before you really discover what you can do, especially if you're doing it on your own.

One other tip: If you have a webcam or video camera, you might want to record yourself on video as you work on your vocal delivery. As you will discover later, studying your physical movement will make a big difference in the way you sound.

Exercising Your Voice

Two things are essential when exercising your voice: (1) a deep breath with good breath control and (2) making a sound. Your vocal cords are muscles, and as with all other muscles in your body, proper exercise and maintenance will provide greater endurance and stronger performance. The vocal cord muscles are little more than flaps that vibrate as air passes over them. Sound is created by a conscious thought that tightens the vocal folds, enabling them to resonate as air passes by. Overexertion and stress can cause the vocal cords to tighten too much, resulting in hoarseness and an impaired speaking ability. A sore throat, cold, flu, or other illness can also injure these muscles. If injured, your vocal cords will heal more rapidly if they are allowed to stay relaxed. However, if you don't correct the source of the vocal injury, the problem will reoccur.

The manner in which we speak, breathe, and use our vocal and facial muscles, can often be traced to our childhood. Cultural and regional speech patterns influence the way we speak, as do family attitudes and speaking habits. From the time we first began to talk, we developed speaking habits and attitudes that remain with us today. We became comfortable with these habits because they worked for us as we learned to communicate with others. Some of these habits might include a regional accent, rapid speech, slurred speech, not thinking thoughts through before speaking, a lack of confidence in our ability to communicate, and shallow or poor breathing.

Changing a habit will take approximately 21 days and at least 200 or more repetitions. For most people, it takes about seven days of consistent repetition of a new behavior pattern before the subconscious mind begins to accept the change. It takes another 14 days, more or less, for a new habit pattern to become established in the mind. This time frame is true for changing just about any habit and will vary from person to person. As much as we might wish otherwise, achieving the desired results of a changed habit will take a concentrated effort and constant awareness.

Later in this chapter are numerous exercises designed to help you modify old habits or strengthen new habits. Discover which of the exercises in this chapter are most helpful and do them on a regular basis, setting aside a specific time each day for your voice exercises. A daily workout is especially important if you are correcting breath control or a specific speaking habit.

Correcting Speech Problems and Habits

As you exercise your voice, awareness of what is happening physically is vital to improving your ability to experience yourself as you work on changing a habit. Observe what is happening with your voice, diaphragm, body, and facial muscles. Self-awareness helps you discover and correct problems with your speech. Without it, you will not be able to recognize the characteristics you need to work on. Your recordings will be a good start to developing self-awareness skills, but you will eventually need to be aware of how you speak in real-time. As you develop self-awareness skills, you will also be developing instincts for delivery and interpretation that will be of tremendous benefit during a performance.

It is often helpful to have another set of ears listening to you as you work on correcting a problem or speaking habit. A speech therapist, voice coach, or a local voiceover professional can be invaluable to improving your speaking voice. You can also get constructive criticism designed to improve your communication skills from acting classes and workshops.

There are many common speech problems and habits that can be corrected by simple exercise and technique. However, all these problems have an underlying cause that requires self-awareness to correct them. In her book *Voice and the Actor* (1973),[2] Cicely Berry discusses the human voice and methods to improve a vocal performance in great detail. She also explains some of the following common speech problems and how to correct them.

UNCLEAR DICTION OR LACK OF SPEECH CLARITY

Usually, unclear diction or lack of speech clarity is the result of not carrying a thought through into words. A lack of focus on the part of the performer or an incomplete character development can affect diction. This problem can be heard in the voice as a lack of clarity or understanding, often communicated through inappropriate inflection or attitude. An indicator of this problem in conversational speech is starting a new thought without first completing the original thought.

To correct this, you'll need a clear understanding of each thought before you speak. Then, speak more slowly than what might feel comfortable to you. Speaking slowly forces you to focus on what you are saying and improves intelligibility. In some cases, a speech therapist is recommended to help overcome the problem.

Stuttering can be classified in this problem area. Although the actual cause of stuttering is still not known, research has shown that it may have different causes in different people and is generally a developmental disorder. Stuttering can also be a side effect of stroke, traumatic brain injury or other neurologic episodes. Even though research has found three genes that appear to cause stuttering, there is no evidence that all stutterers have these genes or that stuttering is an inherited trait.

There are two traditional therapies to correct stuttering. The first is *stuttering modification therapy,* focusing on reducing fears and anxieties about talking. It can be done with a self-therapy book or with a speech pathologist. The second is *fluency shaping,* normally done at a speech clinic.[3] This therapy teaches the stutterer to talk all over again by beginning with extremely slow, fluent speech and gradually increasing the speaking rate until speech sounds normal.

OVER-EMPHASIS, EXPLOSIVE CONSONANTS, AND OVER-ENUNCIATION

The source of over-emphasis or over-enunciation usually derives from the actor's insecurity or lack of trust in his or her ability to communicate. As a result, the tendency is to push too hard to make sense and start to explain. Typical over-emphasis is vocalized as excessive weight placed on certain words. Over-enunciation, or over-articulation, appears as the precise pronunciation of words. The result of both of these problems is that sentences tend to lose their natural flow. Both are often the result of trying too hard or over-thinking the thought. The moment you begin to over-emphasize, you lose the sense.

The simplest, although often challenging, solution is to stop worrying about the listener understanding what you are saying. Stay focused on your thought and just tell the story. Don't explain it, just tell it. It may help to soften the tone of your voice, lower your volume, slow down, or simply focus on talking to a single person. If you find yourself over-emphasizing, you may be trying too hard to achieve good articulation.

Sibilance, the over-emphasis of the "s" sound, is often caused by not differentiating between the "s," "sh," and "z" sounds. It can also be the result of a clenched or tight jaw, dental problems, loose dentures, or missing teeth. Minor sibilance problems can be corrected in the studio with a "de-esser," but serious problems can only be corrected with the help of a speech therapist or perhaps a good dentist.

Some individuals may tend to speak consonants with excessive clarity. This is an aspect of over-articulation and frequently appears as an overly crisp sound of consonants in mid-word or at the end of the word. This form of articulation may be useful for some voiceover styles or characters, but used incorrectly, crunchy or explosive consonants can be a problem worthy of being addressed.

LOSING, OR DROPPING, THE ENDS OF WORDS

This is the direct opposite of explosive consonants or over-enunciation. In some circles, this is simply referred to as "lazy mouth," which is simply another way of saying poor articulation. A habit common to many people who are just starting in voiceover and acting is to simply not pronounce the ends of words. Words ending in "b," "d," "g," "p," "t," and "ing" are especially vulnerable.

One source of this problem can be learning to speak with a cultural or regional dialect. Or the source of this may be simply not thinking through to the end of a thought. The brain is rushing from one thought to another without giving any thought an opportunity to be completed. This is usually due to a lack of trust in one's abilities, but can also be the result of a lack of focus or concentration.

Awareness of this problem is critical to being able to correct it. This problem can be corrected by forcing yourself to slow down—speaking each word clearly and concisely as you talk. Think each thought through completely before speaking, then speak slowly and clearly, making sure that the end of each word is spoken clearly. You may find this difficult at first, but stick with it and results will come. Correcting a cultural or regional dialect may be considerably more challenging and the assistance of a speech therapist or accent reduction coach may be in order. Exercise #9, *The Cork*, on page 44 addresses this problem.

LACK OF MOBILITY IN THE FACE, JAW, AND LIPS

A person speaking with lack of mobility is one who speaks with only minimal movement of the mouth and face. This can be useful for certain types of characterizations, but is generally viewed as a performance problem. Lack of mobility can be due in part to insecurity or a reluctance to communicate; however, it can also be a habit.

To correct this problem, work on the facial stretching exercises described later. Practice reading out loud in front of a mirror. Watch your face as you speak and notice how much movement there is in your jaw, lips, forehead, and face. It may help to incorporate other body movement into your exercises. Body movement and gestures can help you discover the emotions associated with facial expressions, which will in turn, help you to be more expressive. Work on exaggerating facial expressions as you speak. Raise your eyebrows, furrow your brow, put a smile on your face, or frown. Stretch your facial muscles. Go beyond what feels comfortable.

CLIPPED VOWELS

This is yet another common speaking problem with a solution similar to other articulation issues. Many people think in a very logical sequence. Logical thinking can result in a speech pattern in which all parts of a word are treated equally. This often results in a monotone delivery with vowels being dropped or a rapid delivery in which vowels are truncated or clipped. In either case, there is little emotion attached to the words being spoken even though an emotional concept may be the subject.

Vowels add character, emotion, and life to words. To correct the problem of monotony, search for the emotion in the words being spoken and commit to the feeling you get. Find the place in your body where you feel that emotion and speak from that center. Listen to your voice as you speak and strive to include emotional content and a variety of inflections in every sentence. Working with someone who can bring continued awareness to the problem may be helpful. For someone who is in the habit of speaking rapidly or in a monotone, this problem can be a challenge to overcome, but the rewards are well worth the effort. Once again, slowing down as you speak can help you overcome this problem.

BREATHINESS AND DEVOICING CONSONANTS

Breathiness is the result of exhaling too quickly while speaking, or exhaling before starting to speak. Improper breath control, resulting from nervousness or an anxiety to please, is the ultimate cause. This is similar to other articulation problems, but is directly related to breath support and personal confidence. Consonants and ends of words are often dropped, or unspoken, and breaths are taken at awkward or inappropriate places within a sentence.

To correct this problem, work on breathing from your diaphragm. Take a good breath before speaking and maintain a supporting column of air as you speak. Also, be careful not to rush, and think each thought through completely. As your breath support and delivery improve, you will become a more confident performer.

EXCESSIVE RESONANCE OR AN OVEREMOTIONAL QUALITY

This problem arises from an internal involvement with an emotion. It is usually the result of becoming more wrapped up in the emotion than understanding the reason for the emotion. Actors trained in Shakespearian theater or whose performing background is primarily theatrical will sometimes fall into an overly dramatic delivery in an attempt to reveal the emotion of the scene.

To correct this, you may need to learn how to look at things a bit more objectively. People who exhibit this problem are generally reactive and live life from an emotional center. For them life is drama. Work on looking at situations from a different angle. Try to be more objective and less reactive. When you feel yourself beginning to react, acknowledge the feeling and remind yourself to step back a bit from your emotional response.

ACCENT REDUCTION OR MINIMIZATION

Many people feel their natural accent or dialect is a problem when doing voiceover. This can certainly be true if you are unable to adapt your style of vocal delivery. In some cases, an accent or dialect can be used to your advantage to create a distinctive style for your performance, when you create a character, or when you are working in only a certain region. However, if you want to be well-received on a broad geographic level, you will need to develop the skill to modify your delivery style to one that is expected, and accepted, by the general population of your region. In But even though there may be a generally accepted "standard," different regions of a country may respond better when hearing a message in their regional accent.

Many famous actors have learned how to either use their accent to enhance their performance image, or have learned how to adapt their voice to create uniquely believable characters: Sean Connery, Mel Gibson, Patrick Stewart, Nicole Kidman, Meryl Streep, and Tracy

Ullman to mention only a few. Mel Gibson has a thick native Australian accent, yet he can play a very believable American. Tracy Ullman has a native British accent, yet she creates dozens of characters from around the world. And Meryl Streep has developed a reputation for creating incredibly authentic and believable foreign accents, even though she is American.

When we first learn to speak, we imitate and mimic those around us as we develop our speaking skills. By the time we are two or three years old, the mannerisms and vocal styling that we adopt become the habit pattern for our speaking. Over the years, we become very comfortable with our speaking patterns to the point where it can be difficult to modify them.

In the United States, most voiceover talent perform with the standard non-accented American English. Regional inflections, dialects, and other tonalities are, for the most part, absent unless required for a character in the script, or unless the production is intended for a regional audience. Although this has become the generally accepted sound for American voiceover, it does not mean that someone who speaks with an accent or dialect cannot be successful. The most successful voice actors are those who are versatile with their speaking voice and who possess the ability to create a variety of believable characters. If you have an accent (foreign or domestic) there are several things you can do to make yourself more marketable as a voice actor:

1. Refine your accent and learn how to use it to your advantage. Although you may be able to create a unique performing style, you may find that you are limited in the types of projects you can do if you focus only on improving your native accent.
2. Learn how to adapt your speaking voice to mimic other accents for the purpose of creating believable characters. Learn to do this well and you can develop the ability to create any character on demand.
3. Work with a diction coach or study methods of modifying your speech patterns. All of these will require some time and effort on your part, but the results will be well worth it.

Accent reduction, modification, or minimization is, in essence, a process of learning or acquiring new habit patterns for speaking. The process of retraining your speaking habits can be lengthy and, for most adults, it is impossible to completely eliminate their native or regional accent. However, reducing the accent or modifying the way words are formed is certainly possible. There are many good books and audio programs designed to help people speak with a more "natural" American, regional, or foreign accent. An Internet search for "accent reduction" will result in a wealth of resources. Contact your local University's speech department for recommendations of a licensed speech pathologist, or look into an English as a Second Language (ESL) program in your area. You can even acquire a basic level of accent reduction or modification simply by listening to someone with the desired accent. Study the sound of their speech, mimic the sound of their words, and practice the speaking pattern until it feels comfortable. This is essentially how actors do it.

Voice and Body Exercises

WARM UP TO SAVE YOUR VOICE

Would you begin running a marathon or heavy exercise without warming up? Of course not! If you strain your muscles, you'll feel it for days. Warming up prepares your muscles for the stress to come. You should be careful to take the same care by warming up your voice before performing.

Your vocal cords are muscles that can be strained just like any other muscles in your body. If you don't warm up your voice, an extreme performance can literally blow out your vocal cords resulting in laryngitis that can put you out of work for several days.

But warming up has other benefits in addition to preparing your vocal muscles for work. As you will soon discover, warming up your voice can also prepare your body and mind for your performance. It can help you to discover aspects of a performance that might otherwise be overlooked. It can help you establish believability from the very first word of the script.

You will find it much easier to get into the flow of a script and concentrate on your performance if you are warmed-up and in a relaxed and alert state of mind. A variety of methods to help care for your voice are covered later in this chapter. But first, let's begin with some ways to create a relaxed body and mind. That will be followed by a variety of exercises designed to tune your voice and exercise the muscles that comprise your vocal instrument.

When doing breathing or relaxation exercises, it is important for you to breathe correctly. Most of us were never taught how to breathe as children—we just did it. As a result, many of us have developed poor breathing habits. See the *All about Breathing* section starting on page 26 for breathing techniques and exercises to help you become comfortable breathing from your diaphragm.

The exercises that follow will help you relax and serve to redirect your nervous energy to productive energy that you can use effectively as you perform. Breathe slowly and deeply, and take your time as you allow yourself to feel and experience the changes that take place within your body. Try to spend at least a few minutes a day with each of these exercises. It's best if you can do these in a quite place where you won't be disturbed.

EXERCISE 1: RELAX YOUR MIND

This exercise is a basic meditation technique best done while sitting in a quiet place. Begin by allowing a very slow, deep breath through your nose. Expand your diaphragm to bring in as much air as you can, then expand your chest to completely fill your lungs. Hold your breath for a few seconds, then slowly exhale through your mouth—breathe out all the air. As you do this, think calm thoughts, or simply repeat the word "relax" silently to yourself. Take your time. Do this about 10 times and you will find that your body becomes quite relaxed, and your mind will be much sharper and focused. You may even find yourself becoming slightly dizzy. This is normal and is a result of the increased oxygen going to your brain.

This exercise is an excellent way to convert nervous energy into productive energy. Do this in your car before an audition or session—but not while driving.

EXERCISE 2: RELAX YOUR BODY

Deep breathing to relax your mind will also help to relax your body. Even after some basic relaxation, you may still experience some tension in certain parts of your body. An excellent way to release tension is to combine breathing with stretching. There are several steps to this stretching exercise, so take it slow and if you feel any pain, stop immediately.

Stand with your feet about shoulder width. Close your eyes and breathe deeply from your diaphragm, inhaling and exhaling through your nose. Extend your arms over your head, stretching to reach the ceiling. Stretch all the way through the fingers. Now, slowly bend forward at the waist, lowering your arms as you stretch your back. Try to touch the floor if you can. If you need to bend you knees, go ahead. The idea here is to stretch the muscles in your arms, shoulders, back, and legs. When you feel a good stretch, begin to slowly straighten your body, allowing each vertebra to straighten one at a time as you go. Don't forget to keep breathing.

Now that you are once again standing, with your arms still over your head, slowly bend at the waist, leaning to the left, reaching for a distant object with both arms. You should feel a stretch along the right side of your body. Slowly straighten and repeat with a lean to the right, then straighten.

Next, lower your arms so they are directly in front of you. Rotate your body to the left, turning at the waist and keeping your feet pointing forward. Allow your hips to follow. Slowly bend at the waist as you stretch your arms out in front of you. Keep your head up and your back as straight as you can. Now, rotate forward and repeat the stretch as you reach in front of you. Finally, repeat to the other side before returning to an upright position.

EXERCISE 3: RELAX YOUR NECK

A relaxed neck helps keep the vocal cords and throat relaxed. Begin by relaxing your mind and body with the techniques described in Exercises 1 and 2. If you want to close your eyes for this one, feel free.

This exercise should be done very slowly and it can be done sitting or standing. If you begin to feel any pain in your neck, stop immediately. There may be a neck injury present that your doctor should know about. Begin by sitting or standing up straight. Slowly tilt your head forward until your chin is almost resting on your chest. Allow your head to fall forward, slightly stretching your neck muscles. Slowly rotate your head to the left until your left ear is over your left shoulder; then move your head back and to the right. Continue to breathe slowly as you move your head around until your chin returns to its starting point. Now rotate your head in the opposite direction. This exercise will help release tension in your neck and throat.

EXERCISE 4: RELAX YOUR ARMS

This exercise helps remind you to keep your body moving and converts locked-up nervous energy into productive energy you can use. When you are in a session, it often can be helpful to simply loosen up your body, especially if you have been standing in front of the mic for a long time. Remember that moving your body is a very important part of getting into the flow of the script. Loosen your arms and upper body by letting your arms hang loosely at your side and gently shake them out. This relaxation technique works quickly and can be done inconspicuously. You can also expand your shake out to include your entire upper body.

EXERCISE 5: RELAX YOUR FACE

A relaxed face allows you to be more flexible in creating a character and can help improve articulation. You can use your facial muscles to add sparkle and depth to your delivery. Your face is one of the best tools you have as a voice actor.

Begin by relaxing your body. Then, scrunch up your face as tight as you can and hold it that way for a count of 10. Relax and stretch your face by opening your eyes as wide as you can. Open your mouth wide and stretch your cheeks and lips by moving them while opening and closing your jaw. The process of stretching increases blood flow to your face and gives a feeling of invigoration.

EXERCISE 6: HORSE LIPS

Take a long deep breath and slowly release air through your lips to relax them. Let your lips "flutter" as your breath passes over them. This is a good exercise to do alone in your car on your way to a session. By forcing the air out of one side of your mouth or the other, you can also include your cheeks as part of this exercise. As with the face stretch, this exercise will help you in creating character voices and aid in improving articulation.

EXERCISE 7: RELAX YOUR TONGUE

This may sound odd, but your tongue can get tense too. A simple stretching exercise can relax your tongue, and also helps relax the muscles at the back of your mouth. You may want to do this exercise in private.

Begin by sticking out your tongue as far as you can, stretching it toward your chin. Hold for a count of five, then stretch toward your right cheek. Do the same toward your left cheek and finally up toward your nose.

Another tongue stretch that also helps open up the throat is to gently grasp your extended tongue with your fingers. You might want to use a tissue or towel to keep your fingers dry. Begin with a deep breath and gently stretch your tongue forward as you slowly exhale and vocalize a "HAAA" sound, much like the sigh you make when yawning. In fact, this exercise may very well make you feel like yawning. If so, good. Yawning helps open your throat.

EXERCISE 8: YAWNING

As you do these exercises, you may feel like yawning. If that happens, enjoy it. Yawning is a good thing. It stretches your throat, relaxing it and opening it up. More important, yawning helps you take in more air, increasing the flow of oxygen to your brain, improving your mental acuity. It also helps lower the pitch of your voice and improves resonance.

To increase the feeling of relaxation, vocalize your yawn with a low pitch "HAAA" sound, concentrating on opening the back of your throat. It is also important that you allow yourself to experience what happens to your body as you yawn.

EXERCISE 9: THE CORK EXERCISE

You may find this exercise a little odd at first, but the results will most likely amaze you. Although a pencil is a suitable substitute, using a cork will give you quicker results simply because it forces you to work your muscles harder.

Get a wine bottle cork—save the wine for later, or have it first  (your choice). Now, find a few good paragraphs in a book or newspaper. Before doing anything with the cork, begin by recording yourself reading the copy out loud. Stop the recorder. Now place the cork in your mouth horizontally so that it is about one-quarter inch behind your front teeth—as though biting on a stubby cigar. If you use a  pencil, place it lengthwise between your teeth so you are gently biting it in two places. Don't bite hard enough to break the pencil, and don't place the pencil too far back—it should be positioned near the front of your mouth. Now read the same paragraphs out loud several times. Speak very slowly and distinctly, emphasizing every vowel, consonant, and syllable of each word. Don't cheat and be careful not to drop the ends of words. In a very short time your jaw and tongue will begin to get tired.

After you have spent a few minutes exercising your mouth, remove the cork, turn the recorder back on, and read the copy one more time. Now, play back both recordings. You will notice a remarkable difference in the sound of your voice. The *after* version will be much clearer and easier to listen to.

The cork is an excellent warm-up exercise for any time you feel the need to work on your articulation or enunciation. You can even do this in your car, singing to the radio, or reading street signs aloud as you drive to an audition or session.

EXERCISE 10: THE SWEEP

Vocal range is important for achieving emotional attitudes and dynamics in your performance. By vocal range, I am referring to the range from your lowest note to your highest note. Start this exercise by taking a deep breath, holding it in, and releasing slowly with a vocalized yawn. This will help to relax you. Now fill your lungs with another deep breath and release it slowly, this time making the lowest note you can with a "HAAAA" sound. Gradually increase the pitch of your voice, sweeping from low to high. It may help to start by holding your hands near your stomach and gradually raise your hands as you raise the pitch of your voice.

You will quite likely find one or two spots where your voice breaks or "cracks." This is normal and simply reveals those parts of your voice range that are not often used. Over time, as you practice this exercise, your vocal range will improve and as your vocal cords strengthen, the "voice cracking" will become less or may even go away entirely. This is also a good breathing exercise to help you with breath control. If your recordings reveal that you take breaths in midsentence or that the volume (overall loudness) of your voice fluctuates, this exercise will help. Practicing regularly will improve your lung capacity and speaking power, as well as vocal range.

EXERCISE 11: ENUNCIATION EXERCISES

The following phrases are from a small but excellent book titled *Broadcast Voice Exercises* by Jon Beaupré (1994).[4]

To improve diction and enunciation, repeat the phrases that follow. Do this exercise slowly and deliberately making sure that each consonant and vowel is spoken clearly and distinctly, stretching your lips and cheeks as you read. Don't cheat on the ends of words. Watch yourself in a mirror, listen to yourself carefully, and be aware of what you are feeling physically and emotionally. Remember that consistent repetition is necessary to achieve any lasting change. For an extra challenge, try these with the cork.

Specific Letter Sounds—do each four times, then reverse for four more. Make a clear distinction between the sounds of each letter.

Gudda-Budda (Budda-Gudda)
   [Emphasize the "B" and "G" sounds.]
Peachy-Weachy (Weachy-Peachy)
   [Emphasize the "P" and "W" sounds.]
Peachy-Neachy (Neachy-Peachy)
   [Emphasize the "P" and "N" sounds.]
Peachy-Leachy (Leachy-Peachy)
   [Emphasize the "P" and "L" sounds.]
Fea-Sma (Sma-Fea) [pronounce as FEH-SMA]
   [Emphasize the difference between the "EH" and "AH" sounds.]
Lip-Sips (Sip-Lips)
   [Make the "P" sound clear and don't drop the "S" after lips or sips.]

TTT-DDD (Tee Tee Tee, Dee Dee Dee)
[Emphasize the difference between the "T" sound and the "D" sound.]

PPP-BBB (Puh Puh Puh, Buh Buh Buh)
[The "PUH" sound should be more breathy and have less vocalizing than the "BUH" sound.]

KKK-GGG (Kuh Kuh Kuh, Guh Guh Guh)
[Emphasize the difference between the "K" and "G." Notice
where the sounds originate in your mouth and throat.]

Short Phrases—make sure every syllable is spoken clearly and that the ends of words are crisp and clear.

Flippantly simpering statistics, the specifically Spartan
strategic spatial statistics of incalculable value

[This one works on "SP" and "ST" combinations. Make
sure each letter is clear.]

She stood on the steps
Of Burgess's Fish Sauce Shop
Inexplicably mimicking him hiccuping
And amicably welcoming him in.

[Make each word clear—"Fish Sauce Shop" should be
three distinctly different words and should not be run
together. Once you've mastered this, try speeding up your
pace.]

TONGUE TWISTERS

Tongue twisters are a great way to loosen up the muscles in your face and mouth. Go for proper enunciation first, making sure all letters are heard and each word is clear. Begin slowly at first, then pick up speed. Don't cheat on the end of words. For an extra challenge, practice these using your cork. With repeated practice, they will be a bit easier to do.

I slit a sheet; a sheet I slit, upon the slitted sheet I sit.

A proper cup of coffee in a copper coffee pot.

A big black bug bit a big black bear, and the big black bear bled blood.

The sixth sick sheik's sixth sheep's sick.

Better buy the bigger rubber baby buggy bumpers.

Licorice Swiss wrist watch.

Tom told Ted today to take two tablets tomorrow.

The bloke's back brake block broke.

Most Dr. Seuss books can provide additional tongue twisters, and can be lots of fun to read out loud in a variety of styles. Some excellent tongue twisters can be found in *Fox in Sox* and *Oh, Say Can You Say* (1979). Another good book of tongue twisters is *You Said a Mouthful* by Roger Karshner (1993). Most retail and online booksellers can help you find a variety of other tongue twister books.

In 1984, while at a dinner party with people from 12 countries representing more than 15 languages, Michael Reck, of Germany, began collecting tongue twisters. Since then, he has compiled the largest collection of tongue twisters to be found anywhere—"The 1st International Collection of Tongue Twisters." There are more than 3560 entries in 118 languages at **uebersetzung.at**. Select your language and click on the Tongue Twisters link on his home page for the list of languages. If you think the English tongue twisters are challenging, try some of the other languages (assuming, of course, you can read them!). Click on this response code to go directly to the page of English tongue twisters.

24 Tips for Maintaining Your Voice and Improving Your Performance

Keeping your voice in good condition is vital to maintaining peak performing abilities. Some of the tips here were taken from the private files of top voiceover professionals. None of them is intended to be a recommendation or endorsement of any product, and as with any remedy, if you are unsure please consult your doctor.

TIP 1: SEEK GOOD TRAINING

A good performer never stops learning. Continued training in acting, improvisation, voiceover, singing, and even classes in marketing and business management can be helpful. Learn the skills you need to become the best performer and business person you can be. Study other voiceover artists. Watch, listen, and learn from television and radio commercials. Observe the trends. Practice what you learn to become an expert on the techniques. Rehearse regularly to polish your performing skills. Take more classes. Learn everything you can about your home studio equipment so you can provide the best possible recordings of your work. Master marketing techniques, develop strong negotiating skills, and learn how to run your business. You can get a lot of this information from books, but the best way to learn will be to study one-on-one with professionals who can teach you the skills you need to know.

TIP 2: NO COFFEE, SOFT DRINKS, SMOKING, ALCOHOL, OR DRUGS

Coffee may be a great "pick-me-up," but it contains ingredients that tend to impair voice performance. Although the heat from the coffee might feel good, and you might get that "needed" energy boost, the caffeine can cause constriction of your sinuses or throat. Coffee is also a diuretic. The same is true for most soft drinks. Soft drinks also contain sugar that can cause your mouth to dry out.

Smoking is a sure-fire way to dry out your mouth quickly. Smoking over a long period of time will have the effect of lowering your voice by damaging your vocal cords, and presents potentially serious health risks.

Alcohol and drugs both can have a serious effect on your performance. You cannot present yourself as a professional if you are under their influence. Using alcohol and drugs can have a serious negative influence on your career as a voice actor. Word can spread quickly among talent agents, studios, and producers affecting your future bookings. I have seen sessions cancelled because the talent arrived at the studio "under the influence."

TIP 3: KEEP WATER NEARBY

Water is great for keeping the mouth moist and keeping you hydrated. But cold liquids can constrict your throat, so it's a good idea to keep your water at room temperature when doing voice work.

As your mouth dries out, tiny saliva bubbles begin to form, and pop as you speak, creating audible clicks. Well-known voice coach Bettye Pierce Zoller recommends keeping a squirt top bottle of water handy. When *dry mouth* is noticed, squirt all areas of the mouth wetting the cheeks, teeth, and tongue—even underneath it. Then, do not swallow right away, but instead swish for about five seconds or more to get all mouth tissues wet. This will help reduce dry mouth temporarily, but only hydration will correct the cause.

Here are some interesting statistics about water, hydration, and the human body:

- It is estimated that up to 50% of the world population is chronically dehydrated.
- It is estimated that in 37% of Americans, the thirst mechanism is so weak that it is often mistaken for hunger.
- Mild dehydration can slow the human metabolism up to 3%.
- One glass of water shuts down midnight hunger pangs for almost 100% of dieters studied in a University of Washington study.

- Lack of water is the #1 trigger of daytime fatigue.
- Research indicates that drinking 10 glasses of water a day may significantly ease back and joint pain for up to 80% of sufferers.
- A drop of 2% in body water can trigger fuzzy short-term memory, trouble with basic math, and difficulty focusing on a computer screen or a printed page.
- Drinking five or more glasses of water daily may decrease the risk of colon cancer by 45%, slash the risk of breast cancer by 79% and reduce the likelihood of bladder cancer by up to 50%.
- It takes about 45 minutes for a drink of water to achieve proper hydration. You may want to start drinking water well before you leave for a session.

TIP 4: DEALING WITH MOUTH NOISE (a.k.a. DRY MOUTH)

Every voice actor dreads the inevitable *dry mouth*. There are many causes of mouth noise including stress, illness, smoking, dairy products, foods containing sugar, antihistamines, decongestants, pain relievers, and other medications. But mouth noise is most often simply the result of saliva bubbles popping from lack of hydration.

Sooner or later you will experience dry mouth. Some of the hundreds of solutions voice actors have come up with to deal with this common problem include: distilled water with Emergen-C (**emergenc.com**) (one packet per quart); no dairy for two days prior to a VO session; or a swish of carbonated water.

Allowing a throat lozenge or cough drop to dissolve slowly in your mouth can help keep your throat and mouth moist. However, most lozenges are like hard candy and contain sugar that can actually dry your mouth. A few exceptions are Fisherman's Friend lozenges (**fishermansfriend.com),** Grether's Redcurrant or Blackcurrant Pastilles (**grethers-pastiles.ch**), and Ricola Pearls natural mountain herbal sugar-free throat lozenges and breath mints (**ricola.com**). The best time to use a lozenge is about 30 minutes before a session. Be aware that holding a lozenge in your mouth as you speak can cause unwanted clicks or adversely affect your articulation. Dissolving a lozenge or two in a bottle of water is another option. The lozenge-treated water will not only give you the benefits of the lozenge, but will also help keep you hydrated.

Some throat sprays and over-the-counter remedies will work nicely to control dry mouth, such as Thayer's Dry Mouth Spray (**thayers.com**), Entertainer's Secret (**entertainers-secret.com**), Singer's Saving Grace (**herbsetc.com**), Oasis Moisturizing Mouthwash (**oasisdrymouth.com**) and Biotene (**biotene.com**). Lubricating sprays can be used at any time.

TIP 5: SWISH VIRGIN OLIVE OIL

Swish a small amount of virgin olive oil to reduce or kill mouth noise and clicks. About a capful will do nicely. Work the olive oil into every corner of your mouth. The olive oil has a mild taste and leaves a coating on the inside of the mouth that holds moisture in. This clever trick came from one of our students who is also an opera singer—and it really does work!

TIP 6: EAT GREASY POTATO CHIPS

Here's another insider secret that might sound a bit weird. During a session an singer asked if I had any potato chips handy. This, of course, raised my curiosity. She then explained that a trick opera singers will use is to eat greasy food, like potato chips, before a session or performance to lubricate their mouth and throat. Odd as it may sound, it does seem to work.

TIP 7: HAVE SOME JUICE

Some juices can help keep your mouth moist and your throat clear. Any of the Ocean Spray brand juices do a good job of cleansing your mouth. A slice of lemon in a glass of water can also help. Grapefruit juice, lemonade, or any other acidic fruit juice without pulp or added sugar, can help strip away mucus and cleanse the mouth. Be careful of fruit juices that leave your throat "cloudy" or that leave a residue in your mouth. Orange juice, grape juice, carrot juice, and a few others others can be a problem for many people.

TIP 8: THE GREEN APPLE THEORY

This is a good trick for helping reduce "dry mouth." Taking a bite of a Granny Smith or Pippin green apple tends to help cut through mucous buildup in the mouth and clear the throat. It appears that it is the pectin in green apples that makes this work. Red apples may taste good, but they don't produce the same effect.

TIP 9: AVOID DAIRY PRODUCTS

Dairy products, such as milk and cheese, can cause the sinuses to congest. Milk will also coat the inside of the mouth, affecting your ability to speak clearly. Stay away from milk and cheese products when you know you are going to be doing voiceover work.

TIP 10: CLEARING YOUR THROAT

One of the worst things you can do to your vocal cords is to clear your throat. When you need to clear your throat, do it gently with a mild cough. A hard, raspy throat clearing, can actually hurt your vocal cords. Try humming from your throat, gradually progressing into a cough. The vibration from humming often helps break up phlegm in your throat. Always be sure to vocalize and put air across your vocal cords whenever you cough. Building up saliva in your mouth and swallowing before a mild cough is also beneficial. Be careful of loud yelling or screaming and even speaking in a harsh, throaty whisper. These can also hurt your vocal cords.

TIP 11: DON'T COVER UP THROAT PAIN

Covering up throat pain will not improve your performance and may result in serious damage to your vocal cords. If you feel you cannot perform effectively, the proper thing to do would be to advise your agent or client as soon as possible so that alternative plans can be made. The worst thing you can do is to go to a session when you are ill. If you must attend a session when your voice is not in top form, be careful not to overexert or do anything that might injure your vocal cords.

TIP 12: BE AWARE OF YOURSELF AND YOUR ENVIRONMENT

Get plenty of rest and stay in good physical condition. If you are on medication (especially antihistamines), be sure to increase your intake of fluids. If you suspect any problems with your voice, see your doctor immediately. Be aware of dust, smoke, fumes, pollen, and anything environmental that may affect your voice. Be aware of any allergies or reactions to food, how they might affect your voice, and what you can do about them. An Internet search for "allergies" will reveal resources with lots of information you can use.

TIP 13: AVOID ANYTHING THAT CAN DRY OUT YOUR THROAT

Air conditioning can be very drying for your throat. Be careful not to let cold, dry air be drawn directly over your vocal cords. Smoke and dust can also dry out your throat.

TIP 14: AVOID EATING BEFORE A SESSION

Eating a full meal before a session can leave you feeling sluggish and may leave your mouth in a less-than-ideal condition for performing. If you do need to eat, have something light and rinse your mouth with water before performing. Avoid foods that you know will cause digestive problems or produce excessive saliva.

TIP 15: KEEP YOUR SINUSES CLEAR

Clogged or stuffy sinuses can seriously affect your performance. The resulting de-nasal sound (no, or limited, air moving through your nose) may be appropriate if it is consistent with a character, or if it is part of a style that becomes something identified with you. Usually, however, stuffy sinuses are a problem.

Clearing the sinuses with a nasal spray tends to work more quickly than tablets or capsules. Be careful when using medications to clear your sinuses. Although they will do the job, they can also dry your mouth and can have other side effects. Even over-the-counter decongestants are drugs and should be used in moderation.

When used over a period of time, the body can build up an immunity to the active ingredient in decongestants, making it necessary to use more to achieve the desired results. Once the medication is stopped, sinus congestion can return and may actually be worse than before. Some decongestants can make you drowsy, which can create other problems.

An alternative to decongestants is a saline nasal rinse, technically known as Buffered Hypertonic Saline Nasal Irrigation. That's a technical phrase that simply refers to rinsing the nasal passage with a mixture of warm saline solution. This is a proven method for treating sinus problems, colds, allergies, post-nasal drip, and for counteracting the effects of environmental pollution.

There are a variety of ways to administer the nasal wash, including a syringe, bulb, water pik, and the Neti™ Pot, a small pot with a spout on one end. You'll find an assortment of Neti Pots at **netipot.com**. Other nasal rinse systems include pre-measured saline packets and specially designed bottles for applying the rinse.

Although the nasal wash can be done using only a saline solution, some studies have shown that the addition of baking soda (bicarbonate) helps move mucus out of the nose faster and helps the nose membrane work better. An Internet search for *nasal rinse* will bring up numerous resources and recipes.

TIP 16: IF YOU HAVE A COLD

You know what a cold can do to your voice! If you feel a cold coming on, you should do whatever you can to minimize its effects. Different precautions work for different people. For some, Alka Seltzer changes the blood chemistry and helps to minimize the effects of a cold. For others, decongestants and nasal sprays at the first signs of a cold help ease its onset. Lozenges and cough drops can ease cold symptoms or a sore throat, but be aware that covering up the soreness may give you a false sense of security and your vocal cords may actually be more easily injured in this condition.

The common cold is a viral infection characterized by inflammation of the mucous membranes lining the upper respiratory passages. Coughing, sneezing, headache, and a general feeling of "being drained" are often symptoms of the common cold. In theory, there are more than 200 strains of rhinovirus that can enter the nasal cavity through the nose, mouth, or eyes. Once in the nasal cavity, the virus replicates and attacks the body. Most cold remedies rely on treating the symptoms of a cold to help you "feel better" while your body's immune system attempts to repair the damage.

Zicam® is a homeopathic cold remedy that has been shown in clinical studies to reduce the duration and severity of the common cold. According to Gel Tech, LLC (**zicam.com**), Zicam's active ingredients are Zincum Aceticum and Zincum Gluconicum. I'm not quite sure what they are, but I do know it works for me, and many people to whom I've recommended Zicam®.

Other OTC remedies that claim to reduce a cold's severity and duration include Airborne®, developed by second-grade teacher Victoria Knight-McDowell (**airbornehealth.com**); Emergen-C®, a vitamin drink mix manufactured by Alacer Corp. (**emergenc.com**) and Cold-Eeze® lozenges, oral spray and quick-melts manufactured by Quigley Pharma, Inc. (**coldeeze.com**).

Health food and online specialty stores are a good source for herbal remedies. Many voice actors recommend special teas from online stores like **traditionalmedicinals.com** (Throat Coat products and Breathe Easy Tea), **yogiproducts.com** (Breathe Deep Tea), and Chinese cold remedies from **yinchiao.com**, and others. As with OTC remedies, some herbal remedies may work better for some people than others.

Many people swear by Grapefruit Seed Extract (GSE) as a means of boosting the immune system to either head-off or minimize the effects of a cold and other ailments. GSE is available at health food stores.

TIP 17: SOME COLD REMEDY RECIPIES

There are literally dozens of herbal remedies that reportedly reduce the symptoms of a cold.

One cold and sore throat remedy that seems to do the job for many people is this rather tasty recipe: 1 can of regular Dr. Pepper (not diet), 1 fresh lemon, 1 cinnamon stick. Pour Dr. Pepper into a mug, add 1 slice (circle) of lemon and heat in the microwave. Remove and add one cinnamon stick. Relax and sip slowly.

For the more adventurous, here's a recipe for Cold Killer Tea given to us by one of our workshop students. To one cup of tea (Green Tea is an excellent choice) add 1 tsp. lemon juice, 1 tsp. honey, 1 tsp. apple cider vinegar, and a dash of cayenne pepper. The key ingredients are the vinegar and the cayenne pepper. Ingredients can be adjusted for taste.

For many, the effects of a cold can be temporarily offset by drinking hot tea with honey and lemon. The heat soothes the throat and helps loosen things up. Honey is a natural sweetener and does not tend to dry the mouth as sugar does. Lemon juice cuts through the mucus, thus helping clear the throat. The only problem is that some tea contains caffeine, which may constrict or dry the throat.

Bill Smith of The Acting Studio in Denver, CO recommends this mixture of Tabasco sauce and water: Mix 8 drops of Tabasco sauce into an 8 ounce glass of luke-warm water. Stir. Gargle and spit. Repeat. Then drink and swallow regular water. According to Bill, at this solution level, you may taste the Tabasco sauce but you won't "experience" its hotness. You'll notice that most of the phlegm has been cleared from the back of the soft palate and all the way down past the vocal cords to the esophagus. One of the key benefits of this mixture is that the key ingredient in Tabasco sauce is Capsaicin. Although this ingredient is what gives Tabasco sauce its hotness, Capsaicin is also used in pain neuropathy to reduce inflammation of damaged tissues and nerve endings. As a result of gargling this mixture, the tendency to cough or clear the throat is reduced.

Carolynn Mincin (**carolynnmincin.com**), a professional actress and voice actor suggests the following remedies, depending on the severity of the cold and if it includes coughing: 1) Gargle with warm water and Himalayan salt and use the mixture to irrigate the sinuses. 2) A teaspoon of Wasabi on your tongue clears the sinuses for about five minutes, 3) Put 4 chopped garlic cloves in a cup of honey (let it stay over night before using for better results) and then take two teaspoons twice a day. 4) Add a tablespoon of cinnamon to the mixture for even better results. 5) Vicks on your chest and vicks on the soles of your feet covered with socks will also help.

Here's another remedy for a severe cold with cough that is simply known as "Maggie's Cough Remedy." This one burns like crazy for a few seconds, but it will stop a throat tickle dead in its tracks! Intended for adults only, this concoction will take about 10 minutes to prepare. Warning: This remedy is extremely potent! Ingredients: 1/4 - tsp cayenne pepper, 1/4 - tsp ginger, 1 Tbsp cider vinegar (organic preferred), 2 Tbsp water, 1 Tbsp honey (locally produced raw - if possible). Directions: 1. Dissolve cayenne and ginger in cider vinegar and water. Add honey and shake well. Take 1 Tablespoon as needed for cough.

It should be noted that this is a potent albeit watery syrup. It doesn't dissolve perfectly. Always shake well before using. If you make this in small batches as the recipe is written, there is no need to refrigerate. If you prefer, you may refrigerate this. It keeps as long as you need it.

Another interesting way to control coughs and colds is through acupressure. One pressure point is the high spot on the muscle on the hand at the point where the thumb and index finger meet. For more cough and cold acupressure points, scan this response code.

You may not be able to prevent a cold, but if you can find a way to minimize its affects, you will be able to perform better when you do have a cold. If you have a cold and need to perform, it will be up to you to decide if you are fit for the job.

TIP 18: SORE THROAT

Make Jello®, but instead of chilling it, heat it in the microwave for 30 seconds, then add a table spoon of honey. According to experts, the warm Jello will coat and soothe your throat, and the honey's antimicrobial properties will kill bacteria. For more than a dozen additional homeopathic sore throat remedies, scan this response code.

TIP 19: LARYNGITIS

There can be many causes of laryngitis, but the end result is that you temporarily lose your voice. This may be the result of a cold or flu infection that has moved into the throat and settled in your larynx, or you might strain your vocal cords by screaming or overexertion.

When this happens to a voice actor, it usually means a few days out of work. The best thing to do when you have laryngitis is nothing. Your vocal cords have become inflamed and need to heal. They will heal faster if they are not used. Don't talk ... don't even whisper ... just get lots of sleep and let your vocal cords heal. Although not a cure for laryngitis, hot tea with honey and lemon juice will often make you feel better.

A classic remedy is a mix of hot water, Collins mix, and fine bar sugar. This is similar to hot tea, lemon juice, and honey with the benefit of no caffeine. It's sort of a hot lemonade that can be sipped slowly. Many performers claim this mixture helps restore their voice.

Another remedy that is said to be effective is to create a mixture of honey, ground garlic cloves, and fresh lemon juice. This doesn't taste very good, but many have reported a quicker recovery after taking this remedy. Garlic and honey are both known to strengthen the immune system, which may be a factor in its effectiveness.

Similar to hot tea with honey and lemon is a remedy popular in the eastern United States. This was given to me by one of my voice students and seems to work quite well. Boil some water and pour the boiling water into a coffee cup. Add 1 teaspoon of honey and 1 teaspoon of apple cider vinegar. The mixture tastes like lemon tea, but with the benefit of having no caffeine. Slowly sip the drink allowing it to warm and soothe your throat.

TIP 20: ILLNESS

The best thing you can do if you have a cold, laryngitis, or just feel ill is to rest and take care of yourself. If you become ill, you should let your agent, or whoever cast you, know immediately and try to reschedule. Talent agents and producers are generally very understanding in cases of illness.

However, there are times when you must perform to the best of your abilities, even when ill. These can be difficult sessions, and the sound of your voice may not be up to your usual standards. In situations such as this, be careful not to force yourself to the point of causing pain or undue stress on your voice. Use your good judgment to decide if you are capable of performing. You may cause permanent damage to your vocal cords.

TIP 21: DEALING WITH GERD

Most people will experience Gastroesophageal Reflux Disease (technically known as laryngopharyngeal Reflux) at one time or another. For some it is an ongoing condition that must be dealt with on a daily basis. It is a condition in which stomach acid backs up from the stomach into the swallowing tube or esophagus. For a voiceover talent, this condition can present a serious problem. It's not that GERD will directly affect the sound of the voice, but the physical discomfort of the condition, and some of its symptoms, can get in the way of an effective performance.

Many of the tips in this section will have a direct effect on GERD, and there are several over-the-counter and prescription remedies that address the problem. Basically, all digestive processes will produce stomach acid which can result in GERD. Some recommendations for dealing with the condition are: 1) avoid acidic foods, 2) avoid eating *anything* within two hours of bed, and 3) avoid alcohol for at least two hours before bed. Any digestive disorder lasting more than a few days should be checked by consulting a physician. For more "dos and don'ts," see Elley-Ray Hennessey's "Healthy Eating" in Chapter 29, Tips, Tricks & Studio Stories.

TIP 22: BE PREPARED

Sooner or later you may find yourself at a session recording in a very strange environment, or the studio may be out of pencils or not have a pencil sharpener, the water may be turned off, or any number of other situations might occur. It's a good plan to arrive prepared.

Enter the Voiceover Survival Kit! You can purchase a small bag or pouch to hold the essential items and keep it with you whenever you go to an audition or session.

TIP 23: PRACTICE CREATING VISUAL MENTAL PICTURES

Visual images will help you express different emotional attitudes through your voice. Close your eyes and visualize the scene taking place in the copy or visualize what your character might look like. Lock the image in your imagination and use it as a tool to help feel and experience whatever it is that you need to express in the copy. Visualization will also help create a sense of believability as you read your lines. Don't worry if you can't visualize in "pictures." However you use your imagination is how you visualize: colors, sounds, or images. Use whatever works for you.

TIP 24: HAVE FUN

Voiceover work is like getting paid to play. Whether you're working from your home studio or at a recording studio, your auditions and sessions will go more smoothly when you are relaxed, prepared, and ready to perform. Choose to not worry about mistakes you might make. Use these as opportunities to learn more about your craft and to hone your skills.

[1] Wilson, J. (2000). *The 3-Dimensional Voice*. San Diego: Blue Loon Press.

[2] Berry, C. (1973). *Voice and the Actor*. New York: Macmillan.

[3] Kehoe, TD. (1997). *Stuttering: Science, Therapy and Practice*. Boulder: Casa Futura Technologies.

[4] Beaupré, J. (1994). *Broadcast Voice Exercises*. Los Angeles: Broadcast Voice Books.

In this Chapter

5

Voice Acting 101

It's Not About Your Voice ...
It's About What You Can DO With Your Voice!

As you have no doubt figured out by now, voiceover has very little to do with the sound of your voice and everything to do with your acting ability or, in other words, how you play your instrument.

Acting, at its essence, is defined as "playing the role of another character," but the reality is that there is much more to it than that. A good actor doesn't merely "play" the role of another character. A good actor "becomes" the other character, resulting in a sense of believability and authenticity in the mind of the audience.

Creating a believable and authentic character requires certain performing skills and a working knowledge of techniques and processes that are designed to help the actor step outside their own reality and into that of the character they are playing. As you begin to master these techniques, you will find your voiceover delivery becoming increasingly effective. You will also discover that you will become better able to handle a wider range of delivery styles, emotions, and attitudes.

It is important to understand that the techniques you use are *not* your performance. The techniques you will learn in this and the next few chapters are there to support and assist you in achieving the objectives of your performance. It's much like building a house: the hammer, saw, nails, and boards are only tools and components that are used to build the house. Acting techniques and processes are the tools and component parts of your performance. They are the tools you use as you play your instrument.

Understanding how to use a technique in and of itself is of only limited value. You also need to know how to apply the techniques you use in the broader scope of your performance. This chapter covers concepts and performing principles that are basic to theatrical acting, and any or all will be of tremendous value to you as a voiceover performer.

Commit to Your Choices ... and Adjust

All acting is based on initial choices and adjustments made to those choices as a performance develops. As you work with a piece of copy, you will be making lots of decisions and choices about dozens of aspects of the story that can affect your performance. It is important to commit to these choices in order to be consistent throughout the recording session.

Of course, as new choices are made to enhance your character or performance, you must commit to these also. In some cases, you may find that the choices you have committed to no longer work as well as you or the director might like. You may find it necessary to completely change or revise some of your choices. That's OK! Your choices are not engraved in stone. Learn how to explore a variety of choices and be flexible as a performer so you can make adjustments quickly, without thinking. As new choices are made, commit to them to maintain a consistent performance. As you discover and commit to the best choices that develop the character and strengthen the delivery or emotional impact of the message, you will be creating realism and believability in your performance.

The process of working through your performance to make valid choices is called *wood shedding*. This will be covered in detail in Chapter 10, "Wood shedding and Script Analysis."

BE IN THE MOMENT

This is one of the basic precepts of acting. You must be focused on your performance. You cannot be thinking about what you are doing later that afternoon and expect to give a good performance. You also cannot be in the moment if you are struggling to get the words right or dealing with interpretation or worrying that your client might not like what you are doing. If you are even, in the slightest way, *not* focused on the copy and your performance, you will sound as though you are reading. To be in the moment, you must become comfortable with the words to the point where they become yours, and you are not thinking about what you are doing.

Being in the moment means that you understand on an instinctive level, your character, who your character is speaking to, the message in the script, your character's intentions, and innumerable other details. It also means that you speak the words in the script with a truth and honesty that comes from the heart of the character. A good way to be and stay in the moment is to practice the techniques in this chapter. Mastering this skill can take some time, so don't be discouraged if you find yourself drifting out of character or starting to think about what you are doing. Keep working at it and it will come. Some actors will spend many years developing this skill.

Your best and most real performance will be achieved when you are truly *in the moment* of the scene taking place—aware of what you are doing, but not consciously thinking about it.

BE YOUR OWN DIRECTOR—MASTERING SELF-DIRECTION

You need to learn how to look at your performance objectively, as if observing from a distance. This director in your mind will give you the cues to keep your performance on track. *Self-direction* is not only a valuable skill that you can use constantly—even when there is a director on the other side of the glass—but it is a skill that becomes absolutely essential when you record voice tracks from the comfort of your personal home studio.

When you are wearing your "director" hat, you need to be listening for all the little things in your delivery that are, and are *not* working. Look for the important words in the copy that need to receive importance or value. Look for the parts that need to be softened. Look for places to pause—a half-second of silence can make all the difference. Listen for the rhythm, the pace, and the flow of the copy. As the director, you are your own critic. Your goal is to constructively critique your performance to increase your effectiveness in communicating the message.

Self-direction can be a difficult skill to master if you are working alone. The difficulty lies in the fact that if you think about what you are doing as you perform, you will break character. Your "director's" listening process needs to be developed to the point where it happens at an unconscious level, yet you still have a conscious awareness of what you are doing as your character. The best way to learn this is to work with a voice coach or take some classes to learn what directors look (or listen) for and how they work with performers to get the delivery they want. Watch and learn as others are directed. Observe how the director focuses the performer on the particular part of the copy that needs improvement. More importantly, study the process by which the director adjusts the actor's performance.

Another way to learn self-direction is to record your practice sessions and have a skilled director listen to your recordings to give you suggestions on what you can do on your own. As you gain experience and confidence in your performing abilities, your performance and self-direction become as one, and you will soon instinctively know how to deliver a piece of copy. At an advanced level, you will be able to hear very subtle flaws in your performance and be able to make instantaneous adjustments.

MAKE IT THE FIRST TIME EVERY TIME

Be spontaneous, every time! Use your acting and imagination skills to keep the copy, and your performance, fresh. Each performance (or take) should be as though the character is experiencing the moment in the script for the first time. You may be on take 24, but your character in the copy needs to be on take 1—for every take. Use your imagination to create a clear visualization of a scene, character, or situation to help make your performance real and believable take after take.

In the preface to the book *Scenes for Actors and Voices*, Daws Butler is quoted from one of his workshops[1]:

> *I want you to understand the words. I want you to taste the words. I want you to love the words. Because the words are important. But they're only words. You leave them on the paper and you take the thoughts and put them into your mind and then you as an actor recreate them, as if the thoughts had suddenly occurred to you.*

Learn how to be consistently spontaneous! This doesn't necessarily mean that every time you deliver a line of copy it must sound exactly the same—that will depend on your choices, any adjustments you make, and the direction you receive. What this means is that you need to be able to deliver each line of your performance as though it was the first time your character ever thought of those words.

TELL THE STORY EFFECTIVELY

Don't just read the words on the page. You are a storyteller—no matter what the copy is. Search for an emotional hook in the copy—it's in there someplace—even in a complex technical script. Find a way to close the gap between the performer and the audience. Find a way to connect on an emotional level with that one person who needs to hear what you are saying.

Your emotional connection may be in the softness of your voice. Or it may be in the way you say certain words. It may be in the way you carry your body as you speak your lines. Or it may be in the smile on your face. Make that connection, and you will be in demand.

The late Don LaFontaine (1940–2008) was once asked what he did as he performed. His answer was, "I create visual images with a twist of a word." It is the little shift of inflection or subtlety in the delivery of a word or phrase that makes the difference between an adequate voiceover performance and an exceptional voice acting performance. Effective storytelling is using the subtleties of performance to reach the audience emotionally and create strong, memorable visual images.

FIND THE RHYTHM IN THE COPY

Consider voiceover copy in terms of a musical composition. Music has a range of notes from high to low, being played by a variety of instruments (the voices). The tempo of the music may be generally fast or slow (the pace), and the tempo may fluctuate throughout the composition. The music also has a range of loud-to-soft (dynamics). These elements combine to create interest and attract and hold the listener's attention. Voiceover copy works the same way.

All copy has a *rhythm*, a *tempo*, and a *flow*. Rhythm in voiceover copy is much the same as rhythm in music. There are many pieces of music that run the same length of time, but each has a unique rhythm. Many times, the rhythm will change within the composition. Rhythm in voiceover copy is as varied as it is in music. Some copy has a rhythm that is smooth, classy, and mellow. Other copy has a choppiness that is awkward and uncomfortable.

Some of the factors that affect rhythm in voiceover copy are pacing, pauses, breaths, the subtle emphasis of key words, and even diction and intonation. In dialogue, rhythm also includes the timing of the interaction between characters. Find the rhythm in the copy and you will win auditions.

Rhythm is something that can only be found by making the copy your own. You cannot get into a rhythm if you are just reading words off a page. Make the words your own by knowing your character, and you will be on your way to finding the rhythm. You might find it interesting to record yourself in a conversation. You may discover that you have a unique rhythm in the way you speak, which is quite different from the rhythm of others in the conversation.

A conversation has several things going on at once: There is a rhythm to the words, a tempo or pacing, and the interaction between the people having the conversation. Listen for pauses, people talking at the same time, the energy of the conversation, and the way in which certain words are emphasized. Observe how they move their bodies, especially when expressing an emotion or feeling. All these elements, and more, go into creating the rhythm of a conversation.

An excellent way to study vocal rhythm is to watch classic black and white movies from the 1940s. Many of these films feature some incredible character actors with interesting voices who use rhythm, tempo, phrasing, and vocal texture in powerful ways.

Getting Away from the Read

One of the most challenging things to do when reading a script is to read it without sounding like you are reading. When you learned to read, you most likely learned to pronounce individual words and combine those words into meaningful sentences. When reading "silently," most of us read a linear series of individual words and develop our interpretation of those words as our brain processes the information. When reading "out loud," the result often sounds like a monotonous series of words spoken with little meaning. This is simply not acceptable in voiceover.

As a voice actor, you will need to learn how to read out loud in a way that sounds like you are just talking to another person, as if you were having a casual conversation. If you have children, you may have read lots of stories to them out loud, which can put you a bit ahead of the curve. But if you're like most people just starting in voiceover, learning how to read in a conversational delivery is something that will require learning some new skills and a bit of practice.

UNDERSTAND THE BIG PICTURE WITH SIX "WS" AND AN "H"

One of the best places to start for getting out of the "read" is to have a full and complete understanding of the story you are telling. The more you understand the story, the more internalized it will be, and the less you will need to rely on the words in the script in order to tell the story effectively.

Begin by simply reading the script. This will give you a very superficial understanding of the story. To gain a more in-depth understanding, start from the beginning again and look for the basic dramatic elements of a story as you study a script. These are the basic journalism five Ws—who, what, when, where, and why; and, of course, the ever popular "how." As an actor, it's very helpful to add a sixth W to define the environment in which the story is taking place—

the "weather." The more details you can discover, the more accurately you will be able to portray a believable character.

Here are some examples of what you can ask as you work your way through the six Ws and an H:

- Who is your character?
- Who are the other characters in the story?
- Who is your character speaking to?
- What does your character want or need at this moment in time?
- What is your character responding to?
- What is the plot of the story?
- What is the emotional relationship between the characters?
- What is the conflict?
- What complications arise?
- What events brought your character to this situation?
- When does the story take place?
- When does the peak moment happen?
- Where is the story taking place?
- Where, geographically, are other characters or objects in relation to your character?
- Why is your character in the situation he or she is in?
- Why does your character behave the way he or she does?
- Weather:Is the environment cold, hot, steamy, dry, wet, dusty, or cozy? Allow yourself to feel the temperature and other conditions of the environment so you can fully express the feelings and emotions of the story.
- How is the conflict resolved, or not resolved?
- How is the message expressed through the resolution or nonresolution of the conflict?

Ask yourself a lot of questions! By understanding what is taking place, you will discover your role in the story. A dramatic story structure with a definite plot is most often found in dialogue scripts. However, many single voice scripts have a plot structure that evolves through the course of the story.

Unfortunately, many small-market and lower-end scripts are written solely to provide intellectual (or logical) information. Information-based copy, also known as spokesperson copy, rarely has much of a story or plot, and thus there is little or no conflict. With no conflict to be resolved, it can be very challenging to find an emotional hook. Industrial copy often falls into this category. Even with no plot, you still need to determine who you are talking to, your role in the story and all the other things you would look for in any other script. You also need to find a way to bridge the gap between you as the performer and audience you are talking to. Building that bridge can be a much greater challenge with dry, narrative copy than it is with a plot-based story script. However, an emotional connection can be created with any script through a thorough understanding of the 6 Ws and an H.

ASK "WHAT IF ... "

While working with a script, you will often find that you deliver the copy in a style that is very comfortable for you, but which may not be the most effective for your client. As you develop your performance, you'll begin to make choices that will affect the many aspects of your delivery and how the words will be perceived. As your interpretation of the script develops, you settle on your choices, and that's how you will perform the script.

But "what if" you slowed down on part of a line that you hadn't considered before? Or sped up on a different line? Or maybe changed your tempo or rhythm? "What if" you lowered your volume to a point just above a whisper? "What if" you gave one word in each sentence a great deal of value and importance? "What if" you chose a different person to talk to? "What if" your character had a different physical posture or facial expression? "What if" your character wanted a different outcome? "What if ..."

Just because you think you've got a "killer" delivery for a script doesn't mean that what you've come up with is what the director is looking for—or that it's the only way to deliver the script. If you get yourself stuck with one delivery, you may be in trouble when the director asks you for something different. By asking "what if ..." throughout your wood shedding process, you'll come up with lots of options which will prepare you for anything the director might throw at you. Ask "what if ..."

CHARACTER DEPARTURE

One of the best examples of "what if" is a called a *character departure*. As you work with each line of a script, deliver the line in completely different ways. There should be absolutely no similarity between your various departures. If your initial choice is to speak a line slowly, run it again very fast and with a different attitude. Then run the line again with a varying tempo with another attitude or emotional subtext. If, through your wood shedding process, you choose a vocal characteristic or character voice for the line, run it again with a completely different voice.

It is only through exploring these departures from your initial choices and the other "what ifs" that you will be able to make the strongest choices for delivering your copy.

LISTEN AND ANSWER

An actor's job is to respond. And the best way to have a believable response is to listen. Be aware of what is going on in the copy so you have an understanding of the story and can respond appropriately. Don't just read words on the page.

- Listen to your *audience* so that your response is appropriate.
- Listen to your *character*, and to the other performers if you are doing dialogue copy. Interact with what is being said. Be real! Respond to the message emotionally and physically. Remember that acting is reacting.
- Listen to yourself as you deliver the lines, and observe your internal response to the words you are saying. Then react or respond accordingly. This technique can give life to an otherwise dull script.
- Listen to the director in your mind to stay on track. Learn to think critically to constantly improve your performance.
- Listen to the producer or director to take your performance where it needs to go. Your performance needs to reach the producer's vision.
- Listen to your body to find the physical tension and emotional energy needed for a believable delivery. Without physical energy, there is little more than just words.

It is only by careful listening that you will be able to respond appropriately and ultimately get out of your own way to create a believable performance.

MAKE UP A LEAD-IN LINE (PRE-LIFE)

Here's a trick to fool your brain when searching for the proper inflection of a line of copy. A *lead-in line* is simply a short statement of a possible *back story* that will give your character *pre-life* before the first line of copy. Before delivering your first line, you say something that would be a logical introductory statement, or lead-in. You can say it silently, or out loud. If you say the pre-life line out loud, leave a beat of silence before your first line of copy so that the editor can remove the unwanted lead-in line.

For example, if you are reading copy for a spokesperson commercial, you might want to have a lead-in line that sets up who you are talking to. Let's say you have determined that your audience is a man or woman in their thirties or forties, self-employed, and financially well-off. You have set your character as someone who is equal to the audience, so you won't be patronizing; however, you will be conveying some important information. Here's the copy:

> Traffic! Seems like it's getting worse every day. If your daily commute feels like being trapped in a parking lot, the answer to your problem is just around the corner. Take the New Bus. It's not the ride you think it is.

For a *lead-in line*, you might set up the copy by putting yourself in the position of talking to your best friend, John. Rather than starting cold, set a visual image in your mind of a conversation between you and John. Deliver your lines starting with:

> *(Silently: I learned something really interesting today, and you know, John ...)*
> Traffic! Seems like it's getting worse every day ...

Your lead-in line (*pre-life*) sets up a conversational delivery that helps you to close the gap and communicate your message on an emotional level, like a warm-up for the conversation. This approach works for all types of copy in any situation. The *lead-in line* can be anything from a few short words to an elaborate story leading into the written copy. Generally, the shorter and more specific, the better.

MAKE UP A LEAD-OUT LINE (AFTER LIFE)

Your character lives before the first word of the script and continues to live after the last word of the script. Just as a *lead-in line* will give your character *pre-life* to help you to find the energy, attitude, and proper manner for responding, a *lead-out line* will help you to maintain your character beyond the last word spoken. And, occasionally, a *lead-out line* can help you determine the appropriate mood, attitude, or emotion for a line.

A common problem many beginning voice talent experience is that as they near the end of a script, their delivery begins to fall off, and any character they've created loses believability. There can be several reasons for this, but the most common is simply the way our brains work. Most voice talent will be reading about six to eight words ahead of the words being spoken. As the eye reaches the end of the script (or in some cases a line of copy), the brain sees its job as being done, so it relaxes and waits for the mouth to catch up. The result is a fade out in energy and delivery.

When you create a *lead-out line*, you are giving extra life to your character. The lead-out line needs to be something that is appropriate for the context of the story. It can be used to set the tone and emotional attitude for a line of copy or the end of a script.

Find an interpretation and deliver the following line of copy, first only by itself ...

Please don't park the car over there.

Now, using each of the following lead-out lines, deliver the same line of copy again. Just hold the after-sentence in your head—don't verbalize it. Notice how the intention of each lead-out line can completely change your delivery of the copy just by the thought you hold in your mind:

Sweetheart!
You idiot!
I don't want it to get wet!
You'll wake the family!

Use *lead-in* and *lead-out* lines to help maintain your character and lock in the attitude and emotional subtext of your delivery.

BILLBOARDING KEY WORDS AND PHRASES

If a client or product name appears in a script, you may want to do something in your delivery that will help give it some special impact. This may also apply to a phrase or clause that needs some special treatment. Giving a word or phrase that extra punch is often referred to as *billboarding*. Typical methods for billboarding a word or phrase include: leaving a slight pause before or after you speak the words, slowing down slightly, changing your body language or facial expression, changing the inflection on the word or phrase, or even reducing the volume of your voice. All of these have the effect of giving more value and importance to the word or phrase—but only if you have the appropriate thoughts behind the words.

Emphasis is usually what directors will ask for when requesting extra punch on a word. Most people incorrectly interpret the word as meaning "to get louder," "accent," or "punctuate" in some way. By definition, the word *emphasis* means to change the intensity to add importance or value, specifically in terms of adding vocal weight to specific syllables. If you deliver a word by only making it louder, or "punching" the word, it will sound artificial and unnatural. There must be a thought in your mind in order for an *emphasized* word or phrase to have any meaning. Without the thought, it's just a louder word.

I'd recommend removing the word "emphasis" from your vocabulary. When a director asks you to emphasize a word, change the way you think to interpret the request as asking for you to give greater importance and value to the word or phrase.

If you billboard, or place extra emphasis, on too many words or phrases, your delivery will sound artificial and forced, losing believability and credibility. Experiment with different ways to give value and importance to names, places, and phrases in a script. You will soon find one that sounds right. As a guide to help with your delivery, underline words you feel are important. As you work on your delivery, you may discover that underlining only the syllable that should receive value, rather than the entire word, can completely change the meaning or create a regional delivery. For example: defense could be spoken as <u>de</u>fense or de<u>fense</u>.

PERSONAL PRONOUNS—THE CONNECTING WORDS

First person personal pronouns—I, me, we, us, our, you, and your—are all words that listeners tune in to. These are *connecting words* that help the voice actor reach the audience on an emotional level. Use these words to your advantage. Take your time with these words and don't rush past them.

In some copy, you will want to give these words a special importance for greater impact. Most of the time, you will want to underplay the personal pronouns and give extra value to words that are the subject of a sentence. For example, the sentence—"It's what you're looking for!"—could have value placed on any of the five words, or a combination of two or more. The contractions—"it's" and "you're"—could even be separated into "it is" and "you are." Each variation gives the sentence a unique meaning. Read the line out loud several different ways to see how the meaning changes. Placing the greatest value on the word "you're" may not be appropriate if the context of the script is all about searching for exactly the right product. In that case, "looking" would probably be the best word to receive the greatest importance. Experiment by changing the context to find a delivery that sounds best for you.

It's what you're looking for.

A general rule-of-thumb is that when you emphasize or "punch" personal pronouns, the meaning shifts from the subject of the sentence to the individual being addressed. In the example above, the most important part of the line in the context of the story might be the aspect of finding that special thing everyone is "looking" for. By placing importance on the word "you're," the focus of the intent is shifted to the person and moved away from the action of looking. The result for the listener is that the meaning can be unclear, confused, or in some cases just doesn't make any sense.

There are certainly many situations in which the pronoun is exactly the proper word that needs to receive importance and value. However, this is usually only a valid choice when the individual being addressed is the subject of the intention for that line of copy.

WORK THE CONSONANTS

Bringing life to a script will often mean giving value and importance to certain words and phrases. But you can achieve similar results on a smaller scale when you *work the consonants*. Rather than emphasize an entire word, limit the emphasis or value to only the primary consonant in the word. This approach will help a word "pop" giving it a crisper edge in the context of a sentence. To do this, simply give the consonants a bit crisper articulation. The trick with using this technique is to find the correct amount of emphasis or articulation. If you hit the consonant too soft, the word can get lost in the mix. If you hit the consonant too hard, it can sound artificial.

This technique works well with copy that is descriptive, or which must be delivered quickly. There may not be enough time to spend with specific words and working the consonants will often achieve the same result. Also, working the consonants may be helpful for discovering a strong delivery for a line of copy. For example, in the following line of copy, the strongest delivery will be one which enables the listener to taste the food.

Crispy duck lumpia, basil scented prawns

Working the consonants in a way that lets you taste the food, will help the listener taste the food. For fast copy, working the consonants can help your delivery "cut through" the mix when music and sound effects are added. Deliver the following line first in a conversational style, then by giving the consonants just a bit more articulation or emphasis at a faster pace, and observe the difference.

The greatest deals of the decade at our grand opening sale.

Notice how *working the consonants* almost forces you into a certain delivery style. If your delivery needs to be conversational, this technique may not be appropriate as it can produce a choppiness or insincere delivery style. Use care when applying this technique. It may not work for every script, but this is definitely a technique worth keeping in your back pocket.

BUILDING TRANSITION BRIDGES

A copy *transition* is a *bridge* between concepts within a line, between subjects within a script, or between characters, and it can take many forms. It may be a transition of a character's mood or attitude. Or it may be a transition in the rhythm or pace of delivery. It might be a transition from a question asked to an answer given. It could even be a transition between concepts or products within a list.

In a script these transitions may be indicated by an ellipsis, a comma, a hyphen, a colon, a semicolon, or even no punctuation at all. As an actor, you are at liberty to include transitions wherever they feel appropriate as you perform a script.

Transitions help "hook" the audience and keep their attention. Look for transitional phrases in the script and decide how you can make them interesting. Change your physical attitude, movement, mental picture, or use some other device to let your audience know that something special has happened, or that you have moved on to a new idea.

> In a perfect world, there'd be no grime, no soot, no
> stains and no yellowing. In a perfect world, your
> clothes would stay clean. But it's not a perfect world!
> That's why you've got Presto! Presto keeps your
> clothes looking like new ... just like magic!

Sometimes all that is needed is a slight change in your facial expression or body posture. Sometimes a shift in volume, importance, back story, or who you are talking to will create the *transition bridge*. And sometimes, a simple pause in your delivery will do the trick. Experiment with different techniques to find out what will work best for the copy you are performing. In time you will develop a style that sets you apart from other voice talent.

USING CONJUNCTIONS

How do you handle the *conjunctions* "and," "but," and "or" when they appear in a script? These three words are loaded with opportunity for creating transitions and building interest through your performance. "And" is an additive word used to connect two or more things: "We have small and medium and large sizes." "But" indicates opposites: "Oranges are sweet but lemons are sour." And "or" connotes a comparison between two things: "Do you prefer red or blue?" These little words can be stretched, emphasized, sped up, slowed down, charged with emotion, or thrown away.

How you handle these words when they come up will largely depend on your interpretation of the copy, the character you choose, and countless other choices. The challenge with conjunctions is that many voice talent will emphasize the conjunction in a misguided attempt to make whatever follows appear more important. What often happens is that the listener only hears the emphasized conjunction and what follows actually loses value.

There are many occasions when giving value, or emphasis, to the conjunction will enhance the meaning of the phrase. On the other hand, there are just as many, if not more, occasions when it will be more effective to deemphasize the conjunction. Be cautious when emphasizing conjunctions. The only way you'll truly know what works best in the context of a script is to test the phrase in different ways.

DEALING WITH LISTS

Lists are common in all types of voiceover work, but the way a list is handled may differ depending the context of the script, the character speaking, or the genre of the voiceover work.

Some aspects of working with lists have been covered earlier. For example, in commercials, a list will most often be delivered with varying inflections that allow each item to stand alone, yet still be tied to the list as a whole. However, a list in a promo will often be delivered with each item given a downward inflection to create a sense of intensity and dramatic impact.

The ideas of substitution and adding or subtracting a word or two, discussed on pages 123 and 124, are extremely useful when working with lists. If time permits, adding conjunctions between items of a list can add impact and eliminating conjunctions from a scripted list can create a sense of authority and drama.

CONTRAST AND COMPARISON

A common writing technique is to present a comparison between two or more items, or to contrast the positive versus negative or other aspects of a topic. In almost all cases, a contrast and comparison will be followed by a benefit as to why one or the other is better. When you see a contrast or comparison in a script, your job is to make the difference very clear to the listener. Here's an example:

> Most digital cameras require expensive, hard-to-find
> batteries. The new Sigma Solar camera doesn't use
> batteries—it uses the power of light. So you'll never have
> to worry about a dead battery again.

This script contains both a contrast and comparison. The comparison is between regular digital cameras that require batteries and the new solar camera. The contrast is between expensive, hard-to-find batteries and solar (light) power. The benefit is stated in the last line.

A contrast and comparison is best delivered by understanding the meaning of all aspects of the comparison and the ultimate benefit being discussed. When you understand the benefit you can create an emotional connection to that benefit and an appropriate thought that corresponds to that feeling. Use the feeling and thought as you speak the words for both parts of the contrast and comparison to create a believable delivery. If you don't truly understand the comparison or why the contrast is important, your delivery of the copy will be flat and emotionless.

A good technique for getting to the heart of the contrast or comparison quickly is to remove the unessential parts of the script.

> Most digital cameras require ... batteries.
> The new Sigma ... uses the power of light.

Once you've got the essence of the contrast or comparison, it's a simple matter to experiment with a variety of delivery options.

AD-LIB TO CREATE REALISM

One of the cardinal rules in voiceover is to never alter the copy when you are performing. This is true and absolutely must be adhered to when delivering audio books, most e-learning scripts, certain animation characters, legal disclaimers, and any commercial or narration copy that has been run through a company's legal department for approval. Lawyers are paid a lot of money to make sure the words in an advertisement are exactly correct—whether they actually make sense or not.

But rules are often made to be broken, so there may be some opportunities for ad-libbing even with copy that is "locked-in." When you come across a script that is obviously written for the eye and not the ear, it might be worth asking your producer or client if they are open to you making some minor adjustments to help make your delivery more conversational. But, unless your client has specifically given you permission to adjust the copy, it must be read "as written."

Advertising, however, is a different story. Most radio and television commercials are intended for a audience of real people and their scripts need to be delivered in a conversational and approachable manner. If the words sound like they are being read out loud, the advertising message will be completely lost.

Unfortunately, most voice talent are concerned that if they, even slightly, alter the copy, the script police will come knocking on their door or the client will be upset because the copy was changed. The reality is that most clients will welcome the help to bring the words of their script to life.

An excellent way to add a layer of realism to your performance is to slightly embellish the script by adding natural, and appropriate, "humanisms" as you speak. At appropriate places within the copy, you can add human sounds or "crutch words" like "um," "uh," or "uh-huh." Sometimes a vocalized sigh or breath can add a sense of realism. Or, you might add natural, personal responses like "ya know," "like," "okay," and "so," among others. For some scripts, you might want to add or remove a word or two to help the copy make more sense or to be more conversational. Obviously, you can't change the context of the copy. But you can take some liberties of embellishment to breathe some life into the script. For example, the following script makes sense as written, but it can be made more conversational with a few simple adjustments:

> When my ship comes in, I'll probably be at the airport.
> That's just the kind of person I am. But this time, I did
> it right. I just bought the new PowerPlay media player
> from Best Price. It has everything I want in a media
> player, with tons of features. It plays everything! It's just
> what I've been looking for! If you're looking for the
> perfect media player, you can pick up your own
> PowerPlay at your neighborhood Best Price.

To make this script more conversational, a few carefully chosen adjustments can be made that will bring the script to life. Adding "Ya know," and "I mean" on the first two sentences helps to bring the character to life and takes the performance out of a potentially sterile delivery. On the line "But this time, I did it right," the word "But" is OK, but the line can be made more personal by changing the word to "Well." And if the word "well" is spoken with a smile on the face, the true meaning of the message is more likely to come through. Also notice that later in the script the two sentences "It plays everything! It's just what I've been looking for" have been made into a single sentence with the conjunction "and" inserted in between. Adding "See" in front of the new sentence helps to drive home the personal impact the purchase has had on this character. And finally, the word "So" is added to make the closing more personal.

Ya know, when my ship comes in, I'll probably be at the airport. **I mean,** that's just the kind of person I am. **Well ...** this time, I did it right. **Yeah!** I just bought the new PowerPlay media player from Best Price. **See,** it has everything I want in a media player, with tons of features. It plays everything, **and** it's just what I've been looking for! **So,** if you're looking for the perfect media player, you can pick up your own PowerPlay at your neighborhood Best Price.

The idea with ad-libbing is to help bring the words to life by making the delivery more real and authentic. This can work brilliantly when the embellishments are consistent with the character and attitude of your performance. But it can also backfire, sounding phony and artificial, if overdone or not done correctly.

Don't worry about modifying the copy with minor ad-libs. You're not changing the context of the message. You are not re-writing the script. You are simply making the words more real by making them more conversational.

Marc Cashman, a voice actor, producer, audio book narrator, and performance coach, describes ad-libbing in voiceover to be like adding seasoning to a meal to bring out the taste. All it might take is a little salt or pepper to bring out the flavor. You aren't changing the food, you're just enhancing it a bit to make it more interesting.

Ad-libs and embellishments are discussed further in Chapter 11, "Character in the Copy," as a concept I refer to as *Character has Precedence Over Copy.*

THE TELL

The biggest challenge with voiceover copy is to create a sense of authenticity, truth, reality, and knowledge through the performance. Without this, you stand a good chance of losing credibility with the listener and all your well-intended efforts will be for naught.

If you've ever played a game of poker, you know that a player can reveal their position through a simple unconscious gesture or facial expression. Another player who can read this *tell*, and knows what it means, may be able to maneuver the game to his advantage.

Voiceover has its tells as well, and many of them are discussed in this book. Voiceover tells are those performance characteristics that affect the believability of the character and credibility of the message. The critical tell in fast-paced commercials is a catch-breath, or short, audible breath between phrases. The catch-breath, along with a pause are both also common in long-form narration. These breaks in the continuity of the delivery are a clear indication to the listener of a lack of confidence, expertise, or knowledge in the presenter. It doesn't take much for a listener to know what this tell means. In fact, it is understood on a subconscious level and can result in an instantaneous loss of credibility. The result is often a performance that shifts from a believable communication to one that sounds like the performer is reading the script or simply doesn't care.

The best way to avoid this tell is, first, to be aware that you are doing it, and second, to master breath control and the ability to create a character and performance style that does not allow for this tell to take place. Training, practice, and study with a competent voiceover coach or director are the best ways to eliminate all tells from your performance.

MAINTAIN YOUR CHARACTER'S VOCAL RANGE

Every character has a vocal range in which their voice will sound genuine and authentic. This vocal, or tonal, range traverses from a comfortable low note, often heard in a relaxed tone of voice, to a pleasant, higher note usually heard when the character expresses joy or excitement, often accompanied by a big smile or open facial expressions. The musical range of the voice between these two comfortable spots is the character's primary vocal range.

The strength of your voiceover delivery will always lie in your primary vocal range. When the voice goes outside of this primary range—either too low or too high pitched, the effectiveness and believability of the delivery will often suffer.

One common occurrence of breaking out of the primary vocal range happens at the end of a sentence. Instead of concluding a thought at the end of the sentence, the voice actor will sometimes take the delivery to a higher pitch, sometimes with an upward inflection. The result is that the thought behind the line of copy is "thrown away," or discarded. At an unconscious level, this can leave the listener unsatisfied or desiring closure on the thought. The overall effect is that the message is diluted, or worse, lost entirely.

In order to maintain your primary vocal range, you first need to know what it is for a given character, and to have the awareness to hear when you step outside of that range. Working with a qualified voiceover coach is usually the best way to learn how to maintain your character's vocal range.

FASTER AND FLATTER

If there is one concept that will do more to take you out of the read and get you into a conversational delivery, this is it: speak faster and flatten your delivery. It's really that simple!

This is a trick used by many film directors for their on-camera talent, and it works like a champ for voiceover. When you speak faster and flatter, you don't have time to think about the words or what you are doing as you speak. Your pacing and inflections will be more natural and your overall phrasing will be more conversational.

People in real conversations speak quickly and don't focus on the words as they speak. Conversational delivery is often more like a verbalized stream of thought.

Speaking faster is not complicated. Simply speed up your tempo to create a more believable sense of reality. Flattening your delivery, however, may be a bit trickier, but it's not difficult. When, reading out loud, most people tend to "work the words," often slightly over-articulating, over-dramatizing or adding too much musicality as they speak. Flattening the delivery simply means to just speak the words. Don't focus on how you think they are supposed to sound. Just speak the words.

As long as you understand what you are saying, speaking faster and flatter can give your conversation a more natural musicality and phrasing.

Physical Attitudes to Help Delivery

M.O.V.E.

The degree of physical energy you use when performing will have a direct relation to the effectiveness and believability of your performance. Most beginning voice actors assume, falsely, that all they need to do is stand in front of the microphone and talk. They seem to believe that if they "think" the attitude or emotion in their head, it will come out of their mouth. The truth is that it takes much more than just thinking about it to convey a feeling, emotion, or attitude through only the sound of the voice.

Don't be afraid to be physical when you are in front of the microphone. Allow more than just your lips to move. You do need to keep your head at a consistent distance from the mic without moving it too much. But from the neck down, it's anything goes—as long as there is no clothing noise and you don't make any unwanted sounds.

Body movement is an expression of emotion, and your expression of emotions or feelings is the result of the thoughts you hold in your mind. When you verbalize those thoughts the meaning of the words will communicate through the tone of your voice. Move your body in whatever manner works for you to effectively get to the core emotion of the message. Your **M**ovement **O**rchestrates your **V**ocal **E**xpression! M.O.V.E.

Try the following using this phrase: "You want me to do what?" Begin by standing straight and stiff, feet together, arms at your sides, head up, looking straight ahead with an expressionless face. Now, say the phrase out loud—without moving your body, arms, or face—and listen to the sound of your voice. Listen to the lack of expression in your voice. Listen to how totally boring you sound.

While keeping the same physical attitude—and still without moving, say the same phrase again and try to put some emotion into your reading. You will find it extremely difficult to put any emotion or drama into those words without moving. When you begin to communicate emotions, your body instinctively wants to move.

Now, relax your body, separate your feet slightly, bring your arms away from your sides, and loosen up. Think of something in your past that you can relate to the phrase and recall the physical tension or feeling you originally felt. Say the phrase again—this time moving your arms and body appropriately for that original feeling. Observe how your physical attitude and facial expression change the sound of your voice. Try this with different physical positions and expressions and you may be amazed at the range of voices you will find. A smile will add brightness and happiness to the sound of your voice. A furrowed brow will give your voice a more serious tone. Tension in your face and body will communicate stress through your voice.

It's a mistake to stand in front of the microphone with your hands hanging limp at your sides or stuffed in your pockets—unless that physical attitude is consistent with your character in the copy. Start your hands at about chest level and your elbows bent. This allows you the freedom to move your hands as you speak.

The way you stand can also affect your voice performance. Although body stance primarily communicates information visually, it can also be very important when creating a character. Body language, just as facial expression, translates through the voice. For example, to make a character of a self-conscious person more believable, you might roll your shoulders forward and bring your arms in close to the body, perhaps crossing the arms at certain points in the copy. To create a sense of pride and accomplishment in the voice, simply stand straighter, puff your chest, lift your chin and speak in an assertive, positive tone of voice.

Your body posture and physical movement assist in framing the attitude and personality of the character. The following are some typical body postures that will help you understand how body stance can affect your performance. If used unconsciously, these postures can have an adverse affect on your performance because they will have a direct impact on your speaking voice. However, when consciously applied to a character or attitude, these and other body postures can be used to enhance any voice performance:

- **Arms behind back ("at-ease" stance)**—This body posture reflects nervousness and implies that the speaker doesn't know what to do with his or her hands or is uncomfortable in the current situation. Clasping the hands behind or in front of the body tends to minimize other body movement and can block the flow of energy through your body. This in turn may result in a "stiffer" sound with a restricted range of inflection and character.

- **Straight, stiff body with hands at the side ("attention" stance)**— Standing straight and tall, with chest out, head held high and shoulders back implies authority, control, and command of a situation. This projection of power and authority can be real or feigned. This stance is sometimes used as a bluff to create an outward image of authority to cover for an inward feeling of insecurity. This body stance can be useful for a character who must project power, authority, or dominance over a situation.

- **Arms crossed in front of the body ("show me" stance)**— Crossed arms often represent an unconscious feeling of self-consciousness and insecurity, creating an attitude of defiance or being defensive. Crossed arms can also imply a certain level of dishonesty.

- **Hands crossed in front of the body ("Adam and Eve" stance)**— As with the at-ease stance, this posture implies that the speaker doesn't know what to do with his or her hands. This stance, with the hands crossed like a fig leaf, is commonly perceived as an indication that the speaker has something to hide. This stance can be useful in helping create a character who projects suspicion.

- **Hands on the hips ("mannequin" stance)**—This posture makes the speaker appear inexperienced or unqualified. Hands on the hips also blocks the flow of energy through the body and limits the performer's ability to inject emotion and drama into a performance. This stance can be used to create an attitude of arrogance.

A simple adjustment of your *physical energy* can make a huge change in your performance. I have seen voiceover performers do some of the strangest things to get into character. The basic rule is "whatever works—do it." I once worked with a voice actor who arrived at the studio wearing a tennis outfit and carrying a tennis racket. Throughout the session, he used that tennis racket as a prop to help with his character and delivery. I've seen other voice actors go through a series of contortions and exercises to set the physical attitude for the character they are playing. A friend of mine was working a dialogue script that required a very intimate delivery and her male dialogue partner was having trouble getting into the right tone of voice. To get into the proper attitude, the booth lights were dimmed, the mics were adjusted, and the two of them actually laid down on the studio floor as they delivered their lines.

Your analysis of the copy can give you a starting point for your physical attitude. When you've decided on your physical attitude, commit to it and use your body to express yourself.

TO CARE OR NOT TO CARE

Many people are self-conscious when just starting in this business, and that's normal. However, when you are in the "booth," you really need to leave any judgments you may have about your performance outside. If you are concerned about what the people in the control room think about you as you are performing (rather than what they think about your performance), you will not be able to do your best work. It comes down to taking on an attitude of "I don't care" when walking into the booth or studio. It's not that you don't care about doing your best, or making the character in the copy real and believable. You must care about these things. But you cannot afford to care about what others think of you and what you are doing as you perform to the best of your abilities. And besides, as you may be starting to realize, it's not you delivering those words anyway—it's really your character who's speaking!

If getting to your best performance means moving your entire body and waving your arms wildly are appropriate for your character, that's what you need to do. You can't afford to worry that the people in the control room might think you are crazy. The engineer and producer certainly don't care! They are only interested in recording your best performance as quickly as possible, and I guarantee they've seen some pretty strange things.

Usually you can perform better if you are standing, but in some cases, sitting may help. If you sit, remember that a straight back will help your breathing and delivery. If possible, use a stool rather than a chair. Sitting in a chair tends to compress the diaphragm, while a stool allows you to sit straight and breathe properly. If a chair is all that's available, sit forward on the seat rather than all the way back. This helps you keep a straight back so you can better control your breath. Most studios are set up for the performers to stand in front of the microphone. Standing allows for more body movement and allows for a wider range of motion without being restricted.

FEEL THE TENSION

Your physical attitude is expressed through the relaxation and tension of your face and other muscles. All human emotions and feelings can be communicated vocally by simply changing physical attitudes. Often, the words in a script will describe a specific emotion or attitude. When you see that, find a place in your body where you can feel the tension of that emotion or attitude—and hold it there. Holding tension in your body contributes to the realism and believability of your character. Focus on centering your voice at the location of the tension in your body and speak from that center. This helps give your voice a sense of realism and believability.

A tense face and body will communicate as anger, frustration, or hostility. A relaxed face and body result in a softer delivery. Try reading some light copy with a tense body or clenched fists; you will find it very difficult to make the copy believable. You can make your delivery friendlier and more personable simply by delivering your lines with a smile on your face. Tilting your head to the side and wrinkling your forehead will help convey an attitude of puzzlement. Wide-open eyes will help create an attitude of surprise. Practice reading with different physical attitudes and you will be amazed at the changes you hear.

Another physical gesture that can make a big difference in your delivery is something commonly referred to as *air quotes*. When a word or phrase needs special emphasis or needs to be set apart from the rest of the copy, simply raise both hands and use your index and middle fingers to simulate making quotation marks in the air surrounding the words as you speak. The mere gesture almost forces you to say the words differently by separating them from the rest of the sentence with a distinctive shift of attitude. Air quotes are best used in moderation and must be part of the fluid physicality of your performance. The challenge with using air quotes is to maintain the authenticity of your character and the context of the phrasing. This gesture may not be appropriate for all copy, and excessive use of air quotes can result in a delivery that sounds choppy and artificial. If you do nothing more than this single gesture, you will hear a difference, but when you use air quotes in combination with other physical movement, the effect can be profound.

Your Clothes Make a Difference

Wear comfortable clothes when recording. Tight or uncomfortable clothing can be restricting or distracting. You do not want to be concerned with shoes that are too tight when you are working in a high-priced recording studio. Stay comfortable. The voiceover business is a casual affair. With the increase in home studios for voiceover work, you can now even record in your jammies and no one will know the difference. I even know of one voice actor who will occasionally record—how shall I say this—in the all-together. He says it's a very freeing way to work.

Another note about clothing: A studio microphone is very sensitive and will pick up every little noise you make. Be careful not to wear clothing that rustles or "squeaks." Nylon jackets, leather coats, and many other fabrics can be noisy when worn in a recording studio. Other things to be aware of are: noisy jewelry, loose change, cell phones, and pagers. If you do wear noisy clothing, it may be necessary for you to restrict your movement while in the studio, which can seriously affect your performance. Maybe my friend who records in the all-together has something!

If you are recording in your home studio, you'll need to not only be aware of clothing noise, but also the many other potential noise sources around your home, both inside and out. Dealing with environmental noise will be covered later in the section on home studios.

The Magic of Your Mind:
If You Believe It, They Will!

One of the objectives of voice acting is to lead the listener to action. The most effective way to do that is to create believability through a *suspension of disbelief.* You suspend disbelief whenever you allow yourself to be drawn into a story while watching a movie or play or when you read a book. You are fully aware that what is taking place in the story really isn't real. However, as you experience it, you suspend your disbelief and momentarily accept the appearance of the reality of what is happening in the story.

Suspension of disbelief in voiceover is essential for creating a sense of believability. The audience must believe you, and for that to happen, *you* must, at least momentarily, believe in what you are saying.

Use your imagination to create a believable visual image in your mind for the message you are delivering. The more visual you can make it, the more believable it will be for you and for your audience. On a subconscious level, your mind does not know the difference between illusion and reality. Just as your physical attitude affects the sound of your voice, if you create a strong enough visual illusion in your mind, your words will be believable.

Creating a visual illusion is a technique used by most great actors and virtually all magicians. For a magician to make the audience believe that a person is really floating in the air, he must momentarily believe it himself. The performer's belief in what is taking place contributes to establishing the suspension of disbelief in the audience. If the magician is focused on the mechanics of his illusion, he will not give a convincing performance.

If you are focused on the technical aspects of your performance you cannot possibly be believable. The technical aspects and techniques of your voiceover work must become completely automatic to the point where you are not even aware of them. The words on that script in front of you must come from within you—from the character you create. Only then will you be able to successfully suspend disbelief. This is what's meant by the phrases "making the words your own" and "getting off the page."

Visual imagery is a powerful technique for creating believability when delivering any type of copy. Read your script a few times to get an understanding of what you are saying. Then, set your visual image and let your character come in and be the storyteller, the expert, the spokesperson, the salesperson, the inquisitive customer, the kooky boss, the eccentric neighbor, and so on. By allowing your character to take over, you automatically shift your focus from the technical aspects of reading the copy to the creative aspects of performing and telling the story. This concept will be re-visited several times throughout this book.

A visual image helps give life to your character, reason for its existence, an environment for it to live in, and motivation for its words. Visualization helps make your character believable to you. If the character is believable to you, its words become true, and the message becomes believable to the audience. To put it another way: If you believe it, your audience will.

Trends

A considerable amount of voiceover work is in the form of advertising as radio and television commercials. The advertising industry is generally in a constant state of flux simply because its job is to reach today's customers in a way that will motivate them to buy the current "hot item." In order to do that, advertisers must connect on an emotional level with their audience. And, in order to do that, the delivery of a commercial must be in alignment with the attitude and behavior of the current target audience. Each generation seems to have a unique lifestyle, physical attitude, slang, and style of dress. These constantly shifting *trends* are reflected in the advertising on radio and TV. In other words, what is "in style" today may be "out of style" tomorrow.

As a voice actor, it is important that you keep up with the current trends and develop flexibility and versatility in your performing style.

You may develop a performing style that is perfect for a certain attitude or market niche, but if you don't adapt to changing trends you may discover that your style is no longer in demand. During the mid 1990s, the Carl's Jr. restaurant chain ran an advertising campaign that featured a very droll, flat, almost monotone voiceover with a very definite lackadaisical, yet sardonic attitude. The key phrase of the campaign was "If it doesn't get all over the place, it doesn't belong in your face." The delivery style became a trend. Suddenly there were commercials everywhere that had a similar delivery style. The trend lasted for a few years, during which a handful of voice talent who could effectively perform in that style did quite well, financially. But when the trend had run its course, that flat, monotone delivery style vanished from the advertising scene almost overnight. Those voice actors who were at the top of their game during those few short years found it necessary to adapt and follow the current trends if they were to continue to be successful in their voiceover careers.

Probably the best way to keep pace with current trends is to simply study radio and television advertising that is on the air today. Listen to what the major national advertising producers are doing in terms of delivery attitude, pace, and rhythm. Observe the energy of the music and how the visuals are edited in television commercials and notice how the voiceover works with or against that energy. Look for commonalities among the commercials you study, and you will begin to notice the current trends.

One thing you will notice is that most locally produced advertising does not follow national advertising trends, or at best, is several months behind.

You don't really need to do anything about these trends, other than to be aware of what they are and how they might affect your performance. That awareness will prove to be another valuable tool for you to use when you audition or are booked for a session. Use it to your advantage.

---

[1] Butler, D. (2003). *Scenes for Actors and Voices*. BearManor Media.

In this Chapter

Developing Style

6

Developing Style and Technique

What's in Your Tool Kit?

Think of *style* as your unique approach to interpretation and delivery, and think of *technique* as the tools of your trade. Your individual style is something that will develop as you begin to understand and master the myriad performing techniques, or tools, for working as a voice actor. There are some tools that you will use on a daily basis, and there are some tools that will stay at the bottom of your tool kit for a long time, and there are always new and improved tools coming along that can make your life and work easier, and further define your style.

A voiceover technique is really nothing more than a skill you develop or a process that you use that allows you to become a better performer. Sure, you can do voiceover without mastering any skills, or you may already have an innate ability with many of them. However, having an understanding of basic acting and voiceover techniques gives you the knowledge necessary to work efficiently under the pressure of a recording session—and to make your performance more real and believable.

As a voice actor, your job is to give life to the words in a script. The writer had a sound in mind when writing the script and you must find that sound by making the words compelling, interesting, real and believable. This is achieved through your performing technique. It is the foundation for your performance. It is the structure on which your character, attitude, and delivery are built. Technique must be completely unconscious. The moment you begin thinking about it, the illusion is broken and the moment is lost.

As you study and learn the techniques in this book, you will find yourself at first thinking a lot about what you are doing. Be careful not to get too analytical as you work with these concepts. Avoid the tendency to over-think the process. Just know that these techniques work. They are much like a frog … you can dissect the thing, but it will die in the process. As you gain experience and become more comfortable, your technique will become automatic, and you will be able to adapt quickly to changes without having to think. Acting techniques are much like riding a bicycle. Once you've mastered the process, it becomes automatic.

Style

It is interesting to note that using the voice is the only art form in which an individual style may be developed out of an inability to do something. It may be an inability to form certain sounds, or it may be a cultural affectation (an accent or dialect) that results in a quality uniquely your own.

One person's vocal style might emphasize lower frequencies, creating an image of strength and power. Someone else may not be able to reach those low tones, and his or her style might be based on a somewhat warped sense of humor expressed through attitude as he or she speaks. Each of us has developed a unique vocal style for speaking in our everyday lives, and for most, it is possible to build upon this natural style to create a "sound" or performing style that can be a marketable commodity.

Your natural speaking style is a reflection of how you perceive yourself, and it may change from moment to moment as you move from one situation to another. When you are confident of what you are doing, you might speak with determination and solidarity. But when your insecurities take over, your voice might become weak, breathy, and filled with emotion.

Your style as a voice actor comes first from knowing who you are, and then expands on that by adding what you know about human nature, personality, character development, and acting. Developing your vocal style is an ongoing process. You start with your voice as it is now, and as you master new acting and performing skills your style will begin to develop. Your vocal range will expand, as will your ability to express attitude, emotion, subtlety, and nuance in your delivery.

You may believe that you have certain limitations with your vocal range, perhaps due to the way your vocal instrument is constructed, and that these limitations may prevent you from developing a marketable style. The truth is that there are many very successful voice artists who have taken what might be viewed as a vocal limitation, and developed it into a highly successful performance style. With proper training, your perceived "limitations" can often be polished and honed into a style that is uniquely yours. The challenge is to first discover your potential, and second, have the dedication and persistence to discover where that potential may lead. The style you ultimately discover may be that of a single "signature voice" or a style that covers a broad range of characterizations and attitudes.

Your Signature Voice

As you master voiceover performing techniques you will begin to discover that you fit into one of two basic categories as a voice talent: 1) you may find that you can easily create a wide variety of vocal placements and character voices, or 2) your vocal instrument is limited in range and you are learning how to create a variety of delivery styles that fall within the predominant sound of your voice. In either case, you will ultimately discover a fundamental sound or style that you are most comfortable with when performing different types of copy. This style is often referred to as your *signature voice*. It's the "voice" that gets you booked and it may be different for different genres of voiceover work. If you have the ability to create many unique character voices, you may or may not have a specific signature voice for your character work, but you still may have one signature voice for other types of voiceover work.

Your signature voice is your marketing base. When a talent buyer books you based on your demo or an audition, they believe you will be able to deliver what they need to make their project work. What the talent buyer hears may or may not be what you consider to be your signature voice—or even what you think you do best. You may be booked based on your signature voice or from a variation presented in an audition, but during a session you may be asked to take your performance in an entirely different direction. That new direction may be radically different from what got you the job, and it may even take you into unfamiliar territory.

It is unwise and unprofessional to think that you are being hired only for the one "style" you think you do best. As a professional voice actor, it is expected that you have the talent and ability to make adjustments with your performance and delivery style. What you think you do best—no matter what that may be—means very little to a producer. Learn how to get past your ego! You must be able to adapt your delivery style, interpretation, attitude, emotional subtext, vocal placement, dynamics, and characterization to what your client needs. This does not mean that you need to be able to do wacky character voices, or take your performance to something that is beyond your abilities. But it does mean that you need to develop the skills to perform with a variety of attitudes and dynamics. And you need to do this without your ego getting in the way.

The techniques in this chapter are intended to help you develop range and variety, which will ultimately help you to develop your unique style. As useful as these techniques may be, they will only be effective when combined with some basic acting skills.

The Road to Proficiency

Acquiring a skill, and becoming good at that skill, is called *competency*. Becoming an expert with the skill is called *proficiency*. You must first be competent before you can become proficient. Sorry, but it just doesn't work the other way around.

BECOMING COMPETENT

Your degree of competency with any skill actually falls into the following four distinct levels. Each person works through these levels at his or her own pace and with varying degrees of success.

LEVEL #1: *Unconscious incompetence.* At this level you are not even aware that you don't know how to do something. You have absolutely no skill for the task at hand.

LEVEL #2: *Conscious incompetence.* You become aware that there is something you don't know or understand, and you begin to take steps to learn what you need to know.

LEVEL #3: *Conscious competence.* You have the basic skills necessary to accomplish a task. However, you must consciously think about what you are doing at each step of the process.

LEVEL #4: *Unconscious competence.* When you reach this level, you have mastered the skills necessary to accomplish a task without thinking about what you are doing. At this stage, you may or may not yet be proficient.

THREE STAGES TO ACHIEVING PROFICIENCY

There are three stages to acquiring a proficient level of skill to become an expert. These must be worked through regardless of the skill that is being learned. Playing the piano, building a table, or performing in a recording studio all require the same three stages of learning and perfecting the skills needed to achieve the end result.

STAGE #1: *Understand the underlying mechanics.* Every skill requires an understanding of certain basic mechanical techniques that must be learned before any level of expertise is possible. In the craft of voice acting, some of these mechanics include: breath control, pacing, timing, rhythm, inflection, acting, and effective use of the microphone, computer and recording software. To be proficient as a voice actor, you must have an innate understanding of performing technique to the point where you can almost instantly identify the appropriate technique for a given line of copy.

STAGE #2: *Understand the theory and principles that are the foundation for using the skill effectively.* In voice acting, these principles include script analysis, interpretation, character development, audience psychology, and marketing. To be proficient, these fundamental skill sets must be honed and polished to the point of becoming second nature.

STAGE #3: *Apply the knowledge learned in the first two stages and continually improve on the level of skill being achieved (practice and rehearsal).* For the voice actor, this means constantly studying acting techniques, taking classes and workshops, studying performances by other voice actors (listening to commercials, etc.), following the trends of the business, and working with what you learn to find the techniques that work best for you.

The question often asked is "Do I really need to be at a high level of proficiency to work as a voice actor?" The short answer is "no." You can audition and even get work with only a basic understanding of the craft, working at the level of unconscious competence. However, it is only when you reach a high level of proficiency in both the craft and business of voiceover that you will begin to consistently book the higher paying sessions and national jobs.

Three Steps to Creating an Effective Performance

In all areas of performing, there are three steps to creating an effective performance; the end result of any task can be considered a performance. For example, when building a table, you are performing a series of tasks required to result in a finished table. Your degree of proficiency (expertise) at performing the various tasks will determine how sturdy your table is and what it looks like when you are finished.

The following three basic steps to performing any task are necessary in the business of voice acting as well:

1. Practice—learning the skills and techniques
2. Rehearsal—perfecting and improving techniques and skills
3. Performance—the end result of learning and perfecting

The steps must be done in that order. You, no doubt, have heard the phrase "practice makes perfect." Well, guess what! It's a misnomer. Even *perfect* practice may not make perfect, because it is possible to practice mistakes without realizing it—only to discover too late that the end result is ineffective—and you may not understand why.

A voiceover performance will rarely be "perfect." So what we need to do as a voice actor is to practice with a mind-set of knowing that there may be dozens of ways to apply a certain technique or deliver a line of copy. Our mastery of a technique will be achieved through testing and experimentation as we discover how it works when combined with other techniques. This is one of the reasons why continued training from qualified professionals is so important.

PRACTICE

Practice is the process of learning what is needed to achieve the desired result—acquiring the skills and applying the underlying mechanics and techniques to achieve proficiency. In voiceover work, the practice phase begins with the initial read-through; having any questions answered by the producer; doing a character analysis; doing a script analysis; working on timing, pacing, and delivery; locking in the correct pronunciation of complicated words; and possibly even recording a few takes to determine how the performance is developing. This phase of practice is an essential step to discover problems in the copy or interpretation and correct them as quickly as possible. If problems are not corrected, they will need to be addressed later during the rehearsal phase.

In the real world of voiceover, there are two aspects to this practice phase. The first is when you are practicing on your own or with a coach to learn basic skills and techniques, and the second is the initial practice read-through at a session as you develop your interpretation. Personal practice should be a life long quest to learn new skills and techniques. The practice phase at a recording session generally lasts only a few minutes.

REHEARSAL AND PERFORMANCE

Rehearsal begins once all the details of the performance are worked out. The choices for character, attitude, voice placement, vocal texture, delivery, and timing are set and committed to during practice. The process of perfecting the performance progresses through a series of takes as choices are tested and modified. Each take is subject to refinement by direction from the producer, director, or engineer. Every rehearsal, or recorded take, has the potential of being used as the final performance, either in whole or in part.

Once an aspect of the performance is set, it should be rehearsed in the same manner, as much as possible, until adjusted or modified by the director. When the delivery on a line is set, don't vary it too much in the takes that follow. Set the tone of the delivery in your mind so that you can duplicate it as you polish the rest of the copy.

Eventually, every line of copy will be set to the liking of the producer. In some cases, a producer may actually have the voice actor work line-by-line, getting just the right timing and delivery on one line before moving on to the next line. Later, the engineer will assemble each line's best take to create the final track. This process is considerably different from acting for stage or film

Theatrical and film actors practice their lines as they work on their blocking and staging. The director gives them some instruction, but for the most part, actors are in the practice phase as long as they are working with a script. By the time they are ready to put down their scripts, they are at a point where they know what they are doing on stage—and rehearsal begins.

As they rehearse, the director makes adjustments and polishes the performance, most often in terms of blocking and staging. Finally, there is a dress rehearsal where all the ingredients of the show—music, scenery, props, lighting, special effects, actors, and so on—are brought together. The dress rehearsal is normally the final rehearsal before opening night and is usually considered to be the first complete performance. There is no such thing as a dress practice! Some theatrical directors even consider the entire run of a show as a series of rehearsals with an audience present.

As voice talent, we're fortunate if we receive the script a day or so prior to recording. Quite often the time we have for practice and rehearsal is very limited. The fact that all three elements may occur simultaneously means that it is essential that our use of technique be instinctive.

Never assume you have perfected a technique. There will always be something new, more, or different that you can learn to expand your knowledge. There will always be new techniques for you to try and use. There will always be a different way you can approach a character or piece of copy. There will always be new trends in performance style that require learning new techniques. To be an effective and versatile voice actor, you need to be aware of the trends and be willing to learn new techniques.

The Elements of a Voice Acting Performance

There are many aspects to voiceover performing, most of which must be learned over time. It is through the mastery and application of specific skills and techniques that a performer's unique style and business acumen is developed. And, as with any profession, the use of only a few, highly refined, skills and techniques may be the foundation of a performer's voiceover style. In today's world of voiceover, there are only two paths to success: either be the best you can be in a specific niche or be extremely good and as versatile as possible in multiple areas. Whichever path you choose, mastering technique is the name of the game. This is one of the reasons why I recommend continued training and development of both performing and business skills. The remainder of this chapter will cover a wide variety of skills and techniques that apply directly to voiceover.

LESS IS MORE

When understood and applied, this simple concept is one of the most powerful things you can do to create believability in your performing, and it works well in just about every aspect of the business from marketing to production.

Just because you love what you do does not necessarily mean you are good at what you do. In voice acting, accuracy with pronunciation or an obvious presentation does not necessarily create the highest level of believability. You will find that you can often create a greater level of truth and honesty in a character by simply holding back a little (or a lot). Some professionals refer to this as "letting go of your voice," "making it real," or "being conversational." It may be that speaking a bit slower, a bit softer, altering the phrasing, or being somewhat more relaxed might be just the thing to make that emotional connection with the listener. If your character has a specific regional sound or accent to his or her voice, you may find that softening the edge makes your performance more effective.

Less is more is a technique often used by filmmakers to create tension and suspense or as a form of misdirection to set the audience up for a surprise. For example, in the Steven Spielberg film "Jurassic Park," the initial appearance of the T. Rex was not accompanied by a huge roar. Instead, the tension of the moment was created by ripples in a simple cup of water, implying the approach of something huge and menacing.

The same technique of minimalizing in your voiceover performance can create a moment of dramatic tension, or wild laughter. It often has to do with the character's attitude, the twist of a word, the phrasing of a sentence, the pace of the delivery, or simply a carefully placed pause.

When performing in a conversational style, this technique is often best applied simply by reducing the volume or loudness of your voice to roughly one-half of your normal delivery. This *half voice* delivery creates a greater intimacy with the listener which can draw them into the story being told.

Understanding and applying less is more is an acquired skill, much like comedic timing. It requires a mastery of the craft of voice acting to a point where you are not thinking about what you are doing, and your delivery comes from someplace inside you. Although some people seem to have a natural instinct for interpretation and using the less is more concept to create a believable performance, most acquire this skill through experience.

MORE IS MORE

As powerful as the less is more concept is, there are times when a script simply calls for taking your performance a bit "over the top." To create a believable illusion of reality, you may occasionally need to present an attitude or emotion that feels slightly exaggerated. This *more is more* idea is common in commercials and character voice work for animation, cartoons, and video games.

More is more works in voiceover because the only thing the listener has for creating a scene in their imagination is the sound of the voice. It is interesting to note that a "real life" conversation can often lack the energy necessary to effectively communicate in mass media. "Real life" conversations work in real life because a genuine relationship usually exists between the speaker and the listener. This relationship does not exist in a voiceover performance. Yet, as voice actors, we must speak the words in such a way that implies the existence of that relationship to the listener. A common method of achieving the perception of a "real life" conversation is to take the interpretation and delivery a notch or two above authentic reality. When performed correctly, this strategic use of more is more can create a stronger, and more visual, sense of reality than if the words were spoken from a completely realistic perspective.

The trick to using more is more effectively is to be careful that you don't take it too far over the top or you stand the chance of breaking the illusion of reality with a delivery that sounds forced.

PERFORMANCE DYNAMICS—PACING, VOLUME, RANGE

Performance dynamics are the fundamental elements of vocal variety and lay at the heart of any voiceover performance. When you understand and apply the dynamics of *pacing, volume,* and *range,* you will be able to make any vocal presentation interesting and captivating.

Pacing refers to the variations of speed in your delivery. It is closely related to the rhythm and timing of the copy and to the tempo of your delivery. Pacing is how fast or how slow you are speaking at any given moment. I'm sure you've heard commercials or other voiceover that is delivered at the same pace throughout. There is no phrasing, no pausing for impact, absolutely nothing that makes an emotional connection. Only intellectual information being delivered often at a rapid-fire pace. Or you've heard people who ... seem ... to ... take ... for ... ever ... to ... say ... what's ... on ... their ... mind.

In most cases a steady pace without phrasing is boring and uninteresting, if not downright hard to listen to. There are some exceptions in projects for which a steady or slow pace may be necessary to the effective delivery of information, as in an educational or training program. However, in most cases, slowing down or speeding up your pacing to give importance to certain words, phrases, or ideas will make a big difference in your presentation and make your performance far more interesting.

Within two or three read-throughs, you should be able to find the pace and phrasing that will allow you to read a script within the allotted time and in an interesting manner. Some directing cues that relate to pace are: "pick it up" (speed up), "stretch" (slow down), "fill" (you have extra time), and "tighten" (take out breaths or pauses between words).

Volume, or *dynamic range,* refers to the variations in the loudness of your delivery, and is how soft or how loud you speak at any given moment. Just as volume changes in a piece of classical music keep things interesting, dynamic range in voiceover directly relates to the believability of a performance. Performing a script at the same volume throughout is much like speaking at the same pace throughout. Both result in loss of credibility in the mind of the listener, because real people change how fast and how loud they speak depending on how they feel about what they are saying. The dynamic range of a performance is directly related to attitude and tone—from soft and intimate to loud and aggressive.

Vocal range, or *vocal variety,* refers to a performer's ability to put variety into the performance by adjusting the pitch and placement of the voice to maintain interest. You've, no doubt, experienced a seminar or lecture at which the speaker spoke in a monotone, resulting in the audience tuning out and losing interest. Vocal *range* covers the spectrum from your lowest pitch to your highest pitch. Voice actors for animation require a wide range from which to create many characters. You have a normal vocal range for speaking in everyday conversation, and you can speak at a lower or higher pitch when necessary or when you are expressing an emotion. Practice speaking at a slightly lower or higher pitch and notice how a small change in vocal range can result in a big shift in interpretation.

Listen to the way people talk to each other and you will notice a wide range of speaking styles. Excitement, enthusiasm, awe, sarcasm, pity, wonder, sorrow, cynicism, and sadness are all expressed in different ways by different people. The variations in the way a person expresses herself or himself reflect that individual's *vocal range*.

Observe how you instinctively adjust your *pacing, volume,* and *range* in your everyday conversations. Practice altering your dynamics as you speak to your friends or at work, and notice how they pay more attention to what you have to say.

Be aware, however, that performance dynamics can be easily misused, forced, or overdone. The secret to understanding these dynamics is in the interpretation of a script. What is the writer's objective? Who is the intended audience? How should the words be spoken to achieve the maximum emotional and dramatic effect? How should the intellectual content be delivered so the listener can understand and use it?

When combined, the dynamics of voice acting serve to help create drama, humor, and tension in a performance. When effectively used, they go hand-in-hand to result in a performance that inspires, motivates, and is believable.

ARTICULATION

Complex sentences are an everyday occurrence that every voice actor must deal with. Words must be spoken clearly and concepts communicated in a way that can be understood. Voice acting, and effective communication in general, is a blend of intellectual and emotional information delivered in an interesting and understandable manner. Unless a specific speech affectation is called for in a script, it is generally unacceptable to stumble through words or slur through a piece of copy. *Articulation* refers to the clarity with which words are spoken. Most common problems with articulation are the result of *lazy mouth*, or the tendency to not fully use the muscles of the tongue, jaw, and mouth when speaking. Good articulation, or enunciation, can be especially tricky when copy must be read quickly.

The script we worked with earlier works well as an articulation warm-up exercise. Read the following copy, this time making sure that your articulation is crisp and clear. Don't worry about getting it in "on-time," just focus on making every word clear and distinct. For the purpose of the warm-up exercise, you'll want to force yourself to over -articulate —and don't forget to speak the ends of every word. (See "The Cork" exercise on page 44.) After doing this exercise, your conversational articulation will sound natural, but will actually be more clear because your vocal instrument is warmed-up.

> Come in today for special savings on all patio furniture, lighting fixtures, door bells, and buzzers, including big discounts on hammers, shovels, and power tools, plus super savings on everything you need to keep your garden green and beautiful.

When the same letter is back-to-back in adjacent words such as the "s" in "hammers, shovels" and "plus super," it's easy to slide through the words sounding the letter only once. In a conversational delivery, it's fine to tie those letters together, but for this exercise speak the end of each word clearly. It is also easy to drop the letter "d" from words like "and" and "need," especially when the next word begins with a "t," "d," "g," or "b." The letter "g" on words, such as "big," can sometimes be swallowed resulting in the phrase "big discounts" sounding like "bih discounts." The suffix "ing" can often be modified when in a hurry, causing words, such as "lighting" and "everything," to sound like "lightin" and "everythin." With good articulation, the ends of words are clearly heard, but not overenunciated and suffixes are properly pronounced.

The "s" and "z" sounds should be clearly distinct. The "s" in "door bells" should have a different sound from the "z" in "buzzers." The consonant "s" should sound like the end of the word "yes," which is primarily a non-vocalized release of air over the tongue. To properly pronounce the more complex "z" sound, the tip of the tongue starts in the "es" position and a vocalization is added. Say the word "buzz" and hold the "z." You should feel a distinct vibration of your tongue.

Plosives are another articulation problem area. Plosives are caused by excessive air rushing out of the mouth when speaking letters such as "P," "B," "G," "K," and "T." When this sudden rush of air hits a microphone's diaphragm, the result is a loud "pop." Plosives can be corrected by turning slightly off-axis of the microphone, by using a foam windscreen, or placing a nylon "pop filter" in front of the mic. To feel the effect of plosives, place your hand directly in front of your mouth and say "Puh, Puh, Puh" several times. Turning your hand to the side will show you how the blast of air is reduced when turning off-mic.

To achieve a conversational and believable delivery, it is often necessary to violate some of the basic rules of crisp articulation. However, it is important to understand and to master the correct way to do something before you can effectively do that thing incorrectly and make it believable. In other words, you've got to be good before you can do bad, believably. When speaking in a conversational style, be careful NOT to over-articulate.

An important aspect of articulation is the ends of words. It is common in every-day conversation to drop the ends of words, and we instinctively fill in the missing sounds as we listen. But in voiceover, those ends of words are important and need to be heard. As you begin to work with copy, learn to listen to yourself to hear if you are dropping the ends of words. The technique of *Linking* on page 119 is a good way of correcting this problem.

DICTION

Diction is defined as the accent, inflection, intonation, and speaking style dependent on the choice of words. Diction is directly related to articulation, the clarity of your delivery, the correct pronunciation of words, and the sound of a character's voice. One of the best ways to improve your diction is to simply slow down as you speak and focus on your enunciation and clarity. Diction is important in all voiceover performances—you really do want to say the client's name correctly and clearly.

When creating a character, your diction becomes even more important. Aspects of a character voice may include a specific accent, vocal range, tempo, rhythm, attitude or other characteristics of a specific speaking style. It is vital that your words be understood.

As you develop your character, listen to yourself closely to make sure you are speaking clearly and that all aspects of your delivery are appropriate for the character and the story being told. As with articulation, Exercise 9: "The Cork" on page 44, can help with diction.

TEMPO AND RHYTHM

All voiceover copy has an ideal tempo. *Tempo* refers directly to the speed at which the words are spoken. A performance may be delivered at a constant tempo or at a varying tempo. You speak at a comfortable tempo when you are in conversation. When performing, your delivery tempo may be slower, faster, or about the same as your normal, conversational tempo.

Voiceover copy also has a built-in rhythm. *Rhythm* is an aspect of phrasing and is closely related to tempo. Combined with tempo, rhythm gives a voiceover performance its sense of musicality. It is the flow of the words, the way the words are organized in sentences, and the placement of importance, or value, on certain words. Rhythm is also directly related to the emotional content of the copy. Poetic copy has an obvious rhythm (or meter). The rhythm of narrative copy is a bit more challenging to find, but it is there. Dialogue copy has a distinctive rhythm, which often includes a sort of verbal syncopation, gradually, or quickly, building to a punch line. Just as you speak with your own personal rhythm, the characters you create for a voiceover performance will each speak with their own rhythm. It may be choppy, staccato, smooth, or even vary throughout the delivery. The delivery styles for promo and trailer voiceover each have their own unique tempo and rhythm. Finding the proper rhythm is critical to an effective and compelling performance.

TIMING IS EVERYTHING

The combination of tempo and rhythm in a performance is known as timing. *Timing* also refers to interaction between characters or the manner in which pauses between words or lines of copy, and general phrasing are handled. As a voice actor, where you place a pause or a beat can create tension, humor, or drama in a performance. How quickly does one character speak after another finishes a line? Do the characters step on each other's lines? Is there a long silence before a character speaks? Does a character speak with beats between words or extended vocal sounds within words or at the end of words? These are all aspects of timing.

Watch TV sitcoms to study tempo, rhythm, and timing. Study the interaction between characters and how they deliver their lines. Listen for the jokes, and how a joke is set up and delivered. Watch the physical characteristics of the actors as they work together. What are their gestures? What facial expressions do they use when they deliver a joke? What expressions do they have when they react to something? How do they express emotion and dramatic tension? Use what you learn to help develop tempo, rhythm, and timing for your performances.

The combination of tempo, rhythm, and timing works differently for different media. Theater has the slowest tempo and rhythm, then film, followed by television and finally, radio with the fastest tempo and rhythm. In some ways, radio can be performed at almost any rate, but generally a radio performance is faster than the same copy performed on-camera for television or film. Because radio uses only one of the senses, the rhythm, timing, and pace are set a bit faster to create a more real and believable interaction between characters. The faster tempo of radio gives the copywriter and talent an opportunity to quickly establish and develop an interesting story that will grab the listener's attention and hold it while the message is delivered.

If you have a natural sense of timing, you are ahead of the game. Timing cannot be taught. It can only be learned through personal experience. You may find it helpful to work with a coach or attend voiceover workout sessions where you will discover the many facets of performance timing. As you become comfortable working with various scripts, and performing styles, timing becomes automatic.

PHRASING

One of the most common challenges when working with a script is to determine the proper delivery speed and variety. How quickly or slowly should you speak? And how will you adjust your phrasing or pacing to add variety to your delivery?

Phrasing in voiceover is very much like phrasing in music. It refers to the overall flow of your delivery; the variations in tempo, rhythm, and timing as you speak; and the subtle nuances of your tone of voice. More specifically, phrasing relates to the way you say certain words or sentences in terms of which word or words are given importance. For example, a short statement—"I would like some more, please!"—can be phrased in several different ways. The first word "I" can be given the most importance to give personal emphasis. By the same token, changing the tempo, and giving the word "would" the greatest value can give an entirely different meaning to the phrase. Breaking the phrase into two sentences by putting a period after the word "some" can result in yet another completely different delivery.

Try this exercise to discover different ways to express this simple phrase. Read each line at different tempos and rhythms, giving importance to the word in bold:

I would like some more, please!
I **would** like some more, please!
I would **like** some more, please!
I would like **some** more, please!
I would like some **more**, please
I would like some more, **please!**

SUSTAIN TO SLOW DOWN AND ADD INTEREST

An aspect of phrasing is sometimes referred to as *pulling words*. This technique focuses on *sustaining*, or stretching, specific sounds, words, or phrases. Sustaining an entire phrase can usually be achieved simply by slowing down the overall delivery of a sentence. But a phrase can be made more interesting by sustaining only the beginning, middle, or end of some words, rather than an entire sentence.

Experiment with this line of copy to get a sense of how you can elevate the interest level of a line by sustaining certain sounds. Start by delivering the line as written, at a steady pace without altering the tempo or rhythm:

> So, you're thinking about buying a new car? Maybe you know something about cars, maybe not.

Here's how this phrase might be written to indicate sustaining sounds:

> Ssssooooo ... you're thinnnking about buying a new carrrr? Mmmmaybe, you knooow something about cars, mmmaybe not.

By sustaining the beginning, middle, or end of a word, or even an entire word, you can create anticipation for what will come next. Adding natural vocal sounds to the phrasing can add even more interest, realism, and believability to the character.

Although pulling lines can help to create a more compelling delivery, it takes up valuable time, and most voiceover projects don't have time to spare. So this technique is generally used in a shortened form, for a specific character's speaking style, or only when necessary.

Phrasing and *sustaining* are both elements of tempo, rhythm, timing, and pacing in that they refer to the way in which words are spoken within a sentence or paragraph. But, even more than that, phrasing allows you to make the words more real by adding compelling emotional content.

THEE AND THUH, AE AND UH

Few words in the English language are used improperly more often than the little words "the" and "a." When used correctly, these words can help add power and emotion to your delivery. Used improperly, your message may sound awkward, and might even create an impression of your being "uneducated." Here are a few quick rules to keep in mind when you see these words in a script. Keep in mind these rules are not set in stone, but are only guidelines. Ultimately, whatever sounds best in the context of your performance, or the way you are directed, is the way you should go:

Basic Rules for "the"

1. Pronounce stressed as "thee" (long ē):
   - When "the" precedes a vowel: *Thē English alphabet has 26 letters.*
     Exception: pronounce as "thuh" if the word starts with a long "U" as in "thuh university" or "thuh United States."
   - When "the" precedes a noun you wish to stress for emphasis (replacing "a" or "an"): *Yes, that is **thē** book you gave me.*
   - When "the" precedes a word you wish to indicate as unique or special, or is part of a title: ***thē** place to shop, **thē** King of France.*
2. Pronounce conversationally and unstressed as "thuh":
   - When "the" precedes a word that begins with a consonant: *The kitchen cabinet is empty. The car ran out of gas. The dog chased the cat.*
   - When "the" modifies an adjective or adverb in the comparative degree: *She's been exercising regularly and looks the better for it.*

Basic Rules for "a" and "an"
1. Use "a" before words that begin with a consonant, "an" before words that begin with a vowel: *a lifetime of choices, an extreme sense of duty.*
   - Words that begin with a vowel but are pronounced with the consonant sound "y" or "w" are preceded with "a" ("uh"): *a European farmer, a united front, a one-room school.*
   - Words that begin with a consonant but are pronounced with a vowel sound are preceded with "an": *an SST (es es tee), an F (ef) in English.*
2. Pronounce stressed as "ae" (as in "hay") (long ā):
   - When "a" is intended to emphasize the next word in a singular sense or is referring to the letter "A": *That is **a** singular opportunity. The letter **A** is the first letter of the alphabet.*
   - The pronunciation of "a" in its stressed form (ae) will be relatively rare for most voiceover copy as it is not generally conversational. However some technical copy may require this pronunciation to properly convey the message or instructions for training purposes.
3. Pronounce unstressed as "ă" ("uh") when:
   - "ă" precedes a consonant: a *horse*, a *new car*, a *cat*, a *TV set.*
   - Your character is speaking conversationally or casually.
   - This unstressed form of "ă" ("uh") is used in most situations.

ATTITUDE

What is it that you bring to the performance of voiceover copy? Are you happy? Sad? Angry? What is the mood of the copy? How do you visualize the scene? What experiences are there—in your personal history—that you can tap into to help make the words real and your performance believable? Answer these questions and you will have your personal attitude. Answer these questions in terms of your script, and you will have your character's attitude.

Attitude is the mindset of the character in the copy. It gives a reason for the words, and motivation for the character's existence and behavior. When you read through copy for the first time, find something in the words that you can relate to. Find an emotional hook. Bring something of yourself to the copy as you perform and you will create more effective characters, a strong suspension of disbelief and a believable illusion of reality.

SENSE MEMORY

Every moment of your life is stored in your memory. And every emotional experience has a physical tension associated with it that might reside anywhere in your body. There is also a sensory experience associated with the emotional experience that is closely linked to the physical tension.

Your five senses are some of your most valuable tools as a voice actor. Constantin Stanislavski, founder of "method acting," developed this tool to help actors create believable characters, and most acting schools today teach some variation of the technique. To truly master the technique of *sense memory* you may need to take some acting classes which involve creative exercises in which you tap into your senses of sight, touch, taste, sound, and smell.

It is said that all creativity originates in the sensory organs. So, to fully utilize your creative voice-acting abilities, you will need to develop skills for recalling and utilizing sensory memories. Once the basic concept of *sense memory* is understood, you can apply this technique to become a better communicator and achieve some amazing results. Here's how:

Close your eyes and think back through your life to a time, event, experience, sensation, or feeling that is similar to what your character is experiencing and hold that memory in your mind. Make the memory as visual as you possibly can. With that memory held in your mind, recall how your senses were affected by what took place. Was there a special smell? A certain sound? Did something taste odd, or especially good? Did you see something unusual? Do you recall touching something in your memory?

As your memory becomes more visual, observe where in your body the physical tension for that memory is being held: neck, shoulders, chest, stomach, legs, arms, and so on. Recall the physical tension, body posture, facial expression, and hold onto it. Keep that memory firmly fixed in your imagination. Now, open your eyes and allow your character to speak the words in the script, in a sense filtered through your experience.

Although mastering this technique may take some time, even doing just the basics will put you well on your way to becoming a successful voice actor. Many voice actors either don't utilize this technique, don't understand how to use it, are simply not aware of it.

SUBTEXT

All copy has within the words, an attitude. Your job is to find it and exploit it. One way to find the attitude is to uncover the thoughts or feelings behind the words. This is commonly known in theater as *subtext.* Subtext is what sets your character's attitude and establishes, or shades, the meaning of what is said. It is the inner motivation behind your words. Subtext allows you to breathe life into the words in a script and into the character you create.

Using your sense memory to unlock emotional hooks is a technique for setting attitude. Now take that process a step further and define the attitude in words to arrive at the subtext. For example, let's say you have this line: "What an interesting fragrance." If the thought behind your words is "What is that disgusting odor? You smell like something that's been dead for a week!," the perceived meaning will be quite different than if your thought and/or feeling is "Wow! You smell amazing! That perfume you're wearing makes me want to be close to you." Each of these subtexts results in a different mental and physical attitude that comes through in your voice.

What you are thinking and feeling as you deliver your lines makes a tremendous difference in the believability of your character. You have a subtext in your everyday conversations and interactions with others. The idea here is to include a subtext as an integral part of your performance. Decide how you want the listener to feel or respond to your character—what emotional response do you want to produce? To get the desired response, all you have to do is internalize the appropriate thoughts and feelings as you perform. Acquiring the ability to quickly discover subtext may take some practice. There are many tools in this book that you can use to help reveal the meaning behind the words in a script.

For some copy, creating a believable character can be challenging, even with a well-understood subtext. The problem may lie in the subtext itself. If you have chosen a subtext that is weak or unclear, try changing the subtext to something completely different, using an entirely different set of emotional hooks. You will often find that by shifting your subtext, your entire performance attitude, delivery, and sometimes even the character will change.

TONE

Closely related to attitude and subtext is tone. Occasionally referred to as "tone of voice," the *tone* of your performance is the sum total of *pacing, volume, range, articulation, diction, tempo, rhythm, phrasing, attitude,* and *subtext.* It is important to be consistent throughout your performance. Do not change your tone mid-copy. If you are doing a soft, intimate delivery with a friendly attitude, maintain that tone from beginning to end. If your attitude is fast-paced and agressive, keep that attitude and tone throughout.

Tone can also refer to the quality of your performance. If you change tone as you read, you will fall out of character and your levels on the audio console will fluctuate, which will drive the engineer and producer crazy. To maintain a consistent tone, do not drift off-mic. Keep your head in the same position relative to the microphone from start to finish. Working close to the mic gives a warm, soft tone, while backing off as little as a few inches gives a cooler, more open, tone for straighter, more direct reads.

Occasionally a script is written that calls for a complete change of attitude and tone in mid-copy. If there is a logical motivation for your character to change attitude, then it would be out of character to maintain a consistent tone throughout the copy.

PAUSE FOR IMPORTANCE

A *pause* is much more than just a beat of silence between words or phrases. It is an aspect of phrasing and timing, and a powerful tool you can use to take a voiceover performance to an entirely new level. A pause in your delivery can be any length from a fraction of a second to a few seconds, depending on the context of a script. You pause instinctively in normal conversation whenever you are thinking about what you'll say next. It's almost possible to hear the thought or the intention of importance that takes place during even the shortest pause. A pause implies that something big is coming and builds tension and suspense in the mind of the listener. When you pause, whatever follows is automatically perceived as being more important. And that's exactly what we want to achieve by using this tool.

Learning how to use a pause effectively can take some time, but once understood, the concept can be used to help create humor, drama, tension, suspense, and emotional response.

Another way to look at a pause is in terms of *timing*. Comedic timing requires just the right amount of time—or beat—between the set-up of a joke and its punch line. If the timing is off, the joke isn't funny. The same is true in voiceover. Timing is everything.

Improper use of a pause can result in an uneven or choppy delivery, or in a delivery that sounds as if the script is being read. If there is nothing happening in your mind during the pause, those beats of silence are little more than empty holes in the phrasing. To be effective, there must be something happening that fills those holes. There must be thoughts taking place that are in alignment with the wants, needs and feelings of your character. Those thoughts won't be verbalized, of course, but their mere existence will be heard in your tone of voice, attitude, and overall delivery.

The following phrase will give you an idea of how you can use a pause to create value and importance. Begin by just reading the line slowly and deliberately to get an understanding of its meaning and to come up with some initial delivery choices. Now deliver the line out loud as one continuous thought—no pauses.

Everything in our store is on sale this week only at Ponds.

Since there is no punctuation to give you hints as to the delivery, you're on your own to find the most effective way to say the phrase. Delivering the line as one continuous stream of words is certainly a valid choice, but it may not be the strongest. Now, deliver the same phrase, this time experimenting with placing a pause or two in your delivery. Use each hyphen in the lines below as a cue for a beat or brief pause in your delivery. Notice that no matter where you place a pause, the words in bold will instinctively be spoken with greater value. A change in tempo or rhythm, or even a shift in facial expression will further enhance the meaning of the phrase. Be careful not to emphasize the words in bold. Instead, just notice how your inflection and interpretation changes as a result of the pause.

Everything in our store—**is on sale** this week only at Ponds.
(the event receives natural emphasis)

Everything in our store—**is on sale**—**this week** only at Ponds.
(the event and time receive natural emphasis)

Everything in our store is on sale this week—**only at Ponds**.
(the location receives natural emphasis)

Everything in our store is on sale—**this week only**—**at Ponds**.
(the time and location receive natural emphasis)

The only way you'll find the most effective delivery when using the pause is to experiment with the many possibilities in every script.

107

HOLD THAT THOUGHT—USING THE ELLIPSIS

Interruptions are a way of life. You experience them every day. You might be in the middle of saying something really interesting ... and then someone breaks in or cuts you off before you finish what you are saying. Or you might be talking about one thing ... and suddenly change to a different topic in mid-sentence. Interruptions also happen in voiceover, especially in dialogue, but they also often occur in single voice copy. The challenge for the voice actor is to make the interruption sound real and believable.

In a voiceover script, an interruption is usually indicated by the ellipsis, or 3 dots (...). The ellipsis can also indicate a pause or beat in the delivery, a bridge between phrases or to replace a comma or other punctuation. There are three common situations in which the ellipsis is used to imply an interruption:

1) The ellipsis implies a thought in the mind of the speaker, usually indicated by a slight pause in the delivery. In this situation, the thought is often vocalized.
2) The ellipsis indicates an interruption by another person, indicated by an abrupt stop mid-sentence.
3) The ellipsis indicates a continuation of a thought following an interjection by another person. In this case, the ellipsis is used at the end of one line of copy and the thought continues after the other person's interjection.

This short example demonstrates all three uses of the ellipsis:

Boss:	Peterson ... we seem to be having some problems in your division. What do you have to say about that?
Peterson:	Well, sir, I ...
Boss:	Now, listen up, Peterson. We need this taken care of right away ...
Peterson:	*(just above a whisper)* Today?
Boss:	Understand?

The vocalization of thoughts implied by an ellipsis is rarely scripted. It is up to the voice actor to determine if vocalized human sounds will enhance the delivery to help make the words real. In the above example, a simple "uh," "um," or a throat clearing after the word "Peterson ..." might make the Boss's first line more real.

The trick to making an interruption sound real is to continue the thought beyond the last word to be spoken. Much like a pause, if the line is simply read as written, the performance can easily sound like the words are being read, or the interaction between characters may sound "off" or artificial. However, if the thought is carried beyond the last word, the interruption becomes real and natural.

To continue the thought, all you need to do is make up something your character might say that is appropriate to the context of the script. Write it on the script, if you like, but at the very least, keep the complete thought in your mind as you deliver the line, and be prepared to speak the words. Completing a thought will enable you to create a believable delivery of the words. This concept works well in a variety of situations.

Let's take another look at the conversation between Peterson and his Boss. The Boss begins with a self-interruption of his own thought. When Peterson speaks, he continues his thought until interrupted. By completing the thought "Well, sir, I ..." you will set the tone, attitude, and pace for your delivery of the line.

> Boss: Peterson ... *(hesistant, vocalized throat clearing)* we seem to be having some problems in your division. What do you have to say about that?
> Peterson: Well, sir, I ... *[continued thought, unspoken: I've taken steps to get things back on track. Vocalized "uhhh" at interruption[*
> Boss: Now, listen up, Peterson. We need this taken care of right away ... *[Takes a beat for scripted interjection of next line.]*
> Peterson: *(just above a whisper)* Today? *[delivered during the beat.]*
> Boss: Understand?

When the moment of the interruption occurs, simply hold the thought and let the interruption happen naturally. The continuation of the thought is often more realistic if verbalized, especially in a dialogue performance. If the other actor is a bit late with the interruption, no one will ever know, because you kept the thought going. If you are the actor who is interrupting, you need to make sure you deliver your line with the appropriate energy and attitude, and that you are cutting off the other person in a way that sounds like a real conversation.

When the ellipsis is used to indicate a scripted interjection, it is important that the timing be correct. The first person speaking must allow for a natural beat, or pause, as he speaks both parts of his line. The beat must be just enough so that the actor speaking the interjection can speak her line in a very natural manner. If the timing is off, the conversation will sound stilted or awkward, and will lack authenticity.

THOUGHT PACING—ANOTHER USE OF THE ELLIPSIS

Thought pacing is another tool that makes your character real! When you see ellipses in a script, you have an ideal opportunity to reveal the thoughts of your character. Not only can you keep the initial thought going until you are interrupted, but you can also make your character more real by vocalizing sounds during the ellipses. For example, as I've mentioned, in the above script, Peterson might interject unscripted responses during the ellipses, and the Boss might even put in some "umms," or "uhhs" to add believability.

Another aspect of *thought pacing* is to ad-lib natural, conversational, responses while delivering a script. This will most often occur in a dialogue script, but ad-libbed human sounds can also be quite effective in the delivery of a single voice script. The proper use of thought pacing can literally bring a script—and your character—to life.

IMITATION

It has been said that *imitation* is the sincerest form of flattery. This may be true, but as a voice actor, you want to be unique. Mimicking the delivery style of an experienced professional can be an excellent way to learn the pacing, inflection, and nuance of a particular voiceover niche. But be careful that your imitation of other voiceover performers is for the purpose of developing your own unique style. If all you can do is mimic someone else's style, dynamics, or attitude, you are doing nothing unique.

Be yourself, and find the uniqueness of your voice. That's what will get you work! Only mimic other voice talent or actors in an effort to learn their techniques. Then adapt what you learn to your personality and style. If you insist on imitating other performers, it could take a long time for you to find your unique voice-acting personality and your signature voice.

RESOURCES

Scan this response code, or visit the AOVA Extras section at **VoiceActing.com** to listen to audio descriptions of numerous techniques that can help you develop your unique style.

In this Chapter

Techniques

7

Techniques for Developing Style

The techniques covered in this chapter are intended to help you quickly discover the most effective, or appropriate, choices for delivering a line of copy, a phrase, or an entire script. In other words, these are tools to aid you in developing your interpretation of a script. As you work with more and more copy, you will gradually develop a process through which you apply a variety of techniques to ultimately arrive at your performance. The process you develop, and the techniques you utilize, will have a direct effect on your overall performing style.

Before you can begin to understand or apply a technique, you must have, at least, a basic understanding of the fundamental concepts that comprise the craft of performing for voiceover. Many of these core concepts have already been discussed. But when it comes to developing your individual, unique performing style, there are a few concepts that are essential.

Critical Voice Acting Concepts

LET GO OF JUDGMENTS AND INHIBITIONS

An important part of developing your process for interpretation and performance, is to experiment with your choices out loud, exactly the way you intend to perform the lines. This means you can't hold back just because you are afraid of what someone nearby might think. Always keep in mind that you are an actor, and as an actor, your job is to perform. And in order to create a great performance, you must rehearse the way you will be performing.

Be careful not to make the mistake of rehearsing silently or at a whisper. Unless you test your choices out loud, you can't possibly know exactly what your performance will sound like. Your delivery might sound great in your head, but the minute you start performing on mic, it will almost always come out of your mouth sounding completely different from what you had in mind.

One of the keys to success in voice acting is to let go of any judgments, inhibitions, and concerns you might have about what you are doing. Leave your ego outside. Allow yourself to become the character in your script. If your delivery needs to be loud, and you are concerned about disturbing those around you, go someplace where you can be alone to work on your performance.

The director in the front row of your mind is not there to judge you, but should be considered a coach and an advocate whose sole purpose is to make your performance better. There is an important difference between being critically analytical about your performance and being judgmental.

Judgmental thinking would be:

- •"The way I delivered that last copy was just horrible! I'll never be able to do these lines right."
- •"I just can't get into this character!"
- •"I can't do this kind of copy!"
- •"I shouldn't feel embarrassed when I do copy like this."

Analytical, or critical, thinking would be:

- •"I didn't like the way I delivered the copy—it just didn't seem real."
- •"I know I can be more effective than that last read."
- •"What can I do to make my character more believable?"

Judgmental thinking usually approaches the subject from a negative point of view, stops you in your tracks, and prevents you from discovering the solutions you need. Critical (analytical) thinking is constructive and helps move you toward solutions that will make your performance more believable. Of the two, judgmental thinking comes naturally to most people, while critical thinking is a learned skill.

When you leave your ego, judgments, and inhibitions in the car, you'll be open to critically analyzing your script to achieve the best possible performance. Chapter 11, "The Character in the Copy," will give you some tools and techniques for doing this.

TAKE THE "VOICE" OUT OF "VOICEOVER"

While developing your interpretation, don't just read your copy. Have a conversation with the listener. Talk *to* your audience, not *at* them, always striving to motivate, persuade, or move the listener to action. Remember that even if you are the only person in the booth, the *other* person is always there. Visualize the perfect person to hear the message, and talk *to* them. Talking *at* your audience will sound like you are either reading the script, selling the message, or acting. All of these perceptions are ineffective and ultimately result in the listener disconnecting from the story.

Only by taking the voice out of voiceover—in other words, creating a completely believable and compelling conversation—will you be able to draw the listener into your story. Although we refer to the craft as voice acting, or voiceover, the reality is that you are a storyteller. Remember:

- Use drama (*emotional hooks*) to attract and hold attention.
- Talk in phrases, not word by word.
- Don't read—tell, don't sell.
- Don't act—be authentic and real at all times.
- Let the content and subtext of the copy determine your dynamics.
- Have a conversation with the listener.
- Talk out loud to yourself to find hidden treasures in your delivery.
- Experiment with different attitudes, inflections, and emotions.
- Take out the punctuation marks in the script to make the copy flow more naturally and conversationally.
- Have a mental attitude that allows you to create a feeling of reality and believability. If you believe your character is real, your listener will.

INTERRUPT – ENGAGE – EDUCATE – OFFER

Regardless of the type of voiceover script you might be working with, your job as a voice actor is to effectively communicate the message, often attempting to reach the listener on an emotional level. The challenge is in figuring out how to do that.

We can borrow a basic concept of marketing and apply it to our voiceover work to result in a powerful tool for creating an effective delivery. Whenever we want to communicate something to someone else, we need to do four things: 1) we need to get their attention, 2) we need to keep their attention, 3) we need to give them the information, and 4) we need to give them an opportunity to respond or act on what we've said.

In marketing, this is the process of *interrupt, engage, educate, and offer.* This process should not be confused with advertising. Although an advertisement might include these four components— and some of the best ads do—advertising is more about creating an interrupt and making a message memorable through repetition. Marketing is more about creating a unique aspect to the message that will make it memorable without repetition.

So, how do we apply this concept to voiceover? Glad you asked!

As you peruse your copy, searching for the various elements discussed so far, take a close look at the first sentence or two. How can you speak those words in a way that will instantly take the listener's mind off of what they are thinking and swing their attention towards you? Your interpretation of those first few words creates the *interrupt*—and there may be dozens of ways to do it! You might achieve it with a whisper, an emotional subtext, through tempo, or by speaking with an attitude in your tone of voice. Every script will be different, and there may be only a few ways that will work well with any given script. Many of the techniques explained earlier are specifically intended to help you to create a powerful Interrupt.

Now that you've got the listener's attention the real work begins. In order to keep them listening you've got to *engage* them in the message. A well-written script will help, but the real secret to successful engagement is in the nuance and subtlety of your interpretation. You can't just be reading the words. And if you sound at all like you are acting, or in any way phony, all credibility and believability will be lost. This step of engaging the listener requires a deep understanding of your character's role in telling the story. This component is critical to an effective voiceover performance because it gets the listener involved and invested in the story.

Once the listener is invested in listening to the message, important information can be delivered to *educate* them. This part of a script is usually pretty obvious. It's the description and price details, or the explanation of how something works. It's often nothing more than raw, uninteresting information. But you can't let it sound like that. You've put a lot of work into getting your listener invested in what you have to say. Don't throw it all away now! By the time you get to the educational part of your story, your delivery needs to have evolved in such a way that the flow from interrupt through engagement and into education is imperceptible.

The final step in this process is the *offer.* This could be a tag delivered by a different voice, or it could simply be an address or phone number. The idea of the offer in marketing is to provide a safe and low-risk way for the audience to take the next step in the sales process. In advertising, this is referred to as a *call to action*. As with the other three components, the way you deliver the offer will be directly dependent upon the context of the script and your choices in how the story will be told.

These steps of *interrupt, engage, educate*, and *offer* must be positioned in that order for the communication to be effective. Once the first three elements are presented, the sequence can be repeated and mixed up in any order. There may be multiple Interrupts, multiple Engagements and several injections of Education. The Offer may even be presented several times, or only once at the end. A properly written script will use this structure.

Unfortunately, many inexperienced copywriters don't understand basic marketing and advertising concepts and will leave one of the components out completely, or worse—begin the script with the offer. This sort of poorly-written copy is all too common. As a voice actor, it will be your job to bring the words to life—regardless of how they are written. When you master the various ways to incorporate *interrupt, engage, educate,* and *offer* into your delivery style, you will be far ahead of most other voice actors who will still be struggling with their basic interpretation.

It is only through a complete understanding of the story in a script that you will be able to discover the most effective punctuation, phrasing, attitude, character, emotion, subtlety, nuance, and the meaning of words in the context of telling the story. You can't change the words in a script, but as a voice actor, you have a tremendous amount of flexibility in determining how those words might be spoken.

NEVER PLAY COMEDY FOR THE LAUGH

Comedy is a common approach to communicating a message, especially in advertising copy. People relate to humor and are intrigued by an oddball character delivery, non sequitur statement, quirky personality, or out-of-place situation. All of these things serve as *Interrupts* or *Engagements* that consistently grab or hold the listener's attention. But they only work when the listener believes that what they are hearing has a sense of truth and reality.

When playing a comedic role or performing a comedic script, many beginning actors will tend to "go for the joke, or "play the comedy for the laugh." This rarely works, and when it does, it only works when "playing for the laugh" is a component of the character's personality or behavior.

"Playing for the laugh" will ultimately tip the hand and kill the joke resulting in a performance that isn't funny. At best, going for the laugh will dilute the message. At worst, it will completely antagonize the listener. Playing for the laugh is, technically, over-acting and simply does not ring true in the mind of the listener.

When you are working with a script that is clearly written for comedy, you will be far more effective to play the role for the truth and reality of the moment. Play the comedy as though whatever is being said is "simply the way it is." Now, that's funny!

Shortcuts that Trick Your Brain

Over the years, your brain has developed some very specific and predictable ways in which information is perceived and interpreted. It

 is because of this predictability that we can utilize some clever techniques that effectively "short-circuit" our normal brain processes so we can achieve our desired results in a performance. You'll be amazed at how effective some of these shortcuts are!

THE 2-4 SHORTCUT

When you speak conversationally with a fairly relaxed delivery, the result is that certain words are often pronounced in a manner that is not totally accurate. Regional accents and dialects will reveal a wide variety of how certain words are spoken. For example, the word "tomorrow" is often pronounced as "tahmarrow," or "tamarreh." "Forget" becomes "fergit," "our" becomes "are," and so on.

When you want to speak with the standard non-accented American English to correctly pronounce words that have a "to" or "for" in them, simply replace the "to" or "for" with the numeral "2" or "4." Your brain is trained to say the numbers as "two" and "four," so as you are reading, your brain sees the number and you automatically speak the word more precisely.

RESPELL WITH SOUNDALIKES

The same basic idea as the *2-4 shortcut* can be used for other words as well. When you find you are mispronouncing a word, or need to speak with clearer diction, you can simply respell the word phonetically or using a different word that has the sound you want. For a word like "our," change the spelling to "hour." One student of mine had difficulty speaking the word "cellular" when used in the context of a script discussing cellular telephones. By simply changing the spelling of the word on his script from "cellular" to "sell-ya-ler," he was almost immediately able to deliver the lines perfectly. This little trick fools the brain and works with most sound-alike words. The possibilities are unlimited, and using this trick can truly be a life saver when working with technical or medical copy.

LINKING

A common problem is the de-articulation, or dropping, of the last letter or sound of a word. This condition is occasionally referred to as *lazy mouth*, and is simply the result of poor diction. Although it may be OK for general conversation, this can present a problem for recorded projects. When the last sound of a word is not spoken, or is spoken too softly, the word can get "lost in the mix" when combined with music or sound effects.

To correct for this, most people will mistakenly adjust their delivery to be overly articulated or over-enunciated. The result is an artificial sound that is not authentic. In some cases, where the character naturally speaks in a "lazy" style, this de-articulation of the ends of words can be completely appropriate. However, for most voiceover copy—especially copy that will eventually be mixed with music or sound effects—the delivery must be spoken with clear diction. Here's a way to do that without resorting to over-articulation.

The technique is called *linking*, and it's a trick that comes from the world of singing. The idea is to take the last letter of a word and attach that letter to the beginning of the next word. For example, the phrase "… and everyone was there" might sound like "an everyone was there," with the "d" not spoken on the word "and." To use the *linking* technique, the "d" on "and" is moved to become the first letter of the word "d-everyone." So the adjusted line will sound like "an deveryone was there."

Advanced Techniques

As with most things in life, voiceover work has many levels of skill and techniques that range from very simple to very difficult. The following techniques fall in the "Advanced" category, not because they are especially difficult, but, rather, because these concepts are most effectively applied after achieving a certain level of skill with other, fundamental processes and performing techniques described earlier in this book.

MAKE THEM THE ONLY WORDS

Occasionally the way a paragraph is written can be troublesome, resulting in difficulty finding an effective interpretation. When you notice that you're throwing away the end of a sentence, or that your inflections are the same for every line, reduce the script to the one line of copy giving you trouble. Make that one line the entire script and deliver it out loud to hear how it sounds. Say it a few different ways and choose the best interpretation. Then put the line back into the context of the script to hear how it works with the full text. This trick will usually make a big difference.

REMOVE OR CHANGE PUNCTUATION MARKS

Copywriters use *punctuation marks* because a script is originally written grammatically correct for the eye, to be read. However, we don't use punctuation marks when speaking in conversation. Part of our job as voice talent is to take the words "off the page" and make them real and believable. If you work the punctuation marks, your delivery will usually end up sounding like you're reading.

One of the best ways to create an illusion of reality in a performance is to remove or change the punctuation marks. Instead of instinctively pausing at a comma, or stopping at a period, try ignoring the punctuation to create a contiguous flow of words. Let the words and phrasing guide you through your telling of the story.

Removing the punctuation marks doesn't mean literally going through the script with white-out, although I do know of some voice actors who actually do that. What it does mean is performing the copy in a real, believable, and conversational manner. A real-life conversation is punctuated with pauses, changes of inflection, dynamics (soft, loud), emotional attitude (excitement, sadness, and so on), vocalized sounds (uh-huh, hmmm, etc.), and many other subtleties. To create a sense of reality, voiceover copy should be delivered the same way. Let your delivery dictate the punctuation— not the other way around.

Just because there is a comma in the script, it doesn't mean you have to pause or take a breath! Just because there is a period, doesn't mean you can't deliver the line as a question or as an exclamation. What would your delivery sound like if you changed a comma to a dash? What if you put a comma at a different place in the sentence? What if you read a sentence ending with a question mark as an exclamatory statement of fact? You have an almost infinite number of possibilities for delivering any line of copy.

Allow the scripted punctuation marks to guide you, but be careful not to take them too literally. Sometimes, a simple change of punctuation can make a big difference in the interpretation, thus improving the performance. Allow the lines of a script to flow into one another as they would if you were telling the story to another person—not reading it. Take the punctuation marks out of your performance and your performance will be on its way to being more believable.

Occasionally, you'll get a piece of copy that just doesn't make sense because the grammar or punctuation is wrong or grammatically incorrect. The writer may understand what she wants to say, and even how the words should be spoken, but because it isn't punctuated properly for the eye, the words are pretty much meaningless. It then becomes your job to figure out what the correct punctuation should be so you can give the words meaning. For example, punctuate the following phrase to give it meaning[1]:

that that is is that that is not is not is that it it is

There is only one correct way to punctuate this line of copy to give it meaning. When you get the correct punctuation, the phrase will make sense in its written form as well as when you speak it. Most copy will also have one punctuation that works best for the eye, but there may be multiple options from which to choose when those words are spoken. You'll find the correct punctuation for the above line of text at the end of this chapter.[2]

Changing and removing punctuation marks as you perform is a way of making the words your own to truly take them "off the page." This tool can help you find the inflection, energy, and dynamics you are looking for as you begin to make the critical choices for delivering your copy.

REVERSE TEXT TO FIND INFLECTION

Occasionally, it can be challenging to find the best way to deliver a line of copy. This often happens when an inexperienced copywriter writes a script for the eye and not for the ear. Sentence structure for the written word is often quite different than for the spoken word. A trick I call *text reversal* can often help. The basic idea is to simply reverse the sentence structure to discover a different way of inflecting the words. Once found, put the sentence back as written, and deliver with the newly discovered inflection and energy. It works just about every time! Here's an example of common writing for the eye:

Created to bring you the ultimate home theater experience, our showrooms are stocked with the latest high-tech equipment.

By reversing the two parts of the sentence, you may discover a better way to inflect the words.

Our showrooms are stocked with the latest high-tech equipment, and are created to bring you the ultimate home theater experience.

Once you've found an inflection you like, deliver as written, but keep the new inflection.

RIDE THE ELEVATOR TO TWEAK YOUR TIMING

Commercial scripts are often written with too little, or too much copy. It's just a fact of life. Also, we may discover that the choices we make for our character result in a delivery that is too slow or too fast. We need to be able to adjust our delivery so that we complete the copy within the specified period of time. Sometimes this challenge can only be resolved through script revisions. But, more often than not, we can easily adjust the tempo of our delivery without affecting the meaning or intentions of our delivery.

The common way to think of this adjustment is to simply speed up or slow down the delivery tempo. But thinking in these terms can have an adverse effect in that the words may sound rushed or unnaturally slow. A better, and much more practical, way to think of adjusting speed is to imagine that you are riding in an elevator. To speed up your delivery, simply imagine that you and the person you are speaking to get on at the same time, and that they are getting off at the next floor. You must tell them what you have to say by the time the elevator doors open. When you need to slow your pace, give yourself an extra floor or two for telling your story.

Changing the way you think about how you speak the words in a script can completely change the believability of your voiceover performance.

SUBSTITUTION: CHANGING CONTEXT TO FIND ATTITUDE

Changing *context* is yet another way to look at your script from a different perspective. This simple trick, that I refer to as *substitution*, might make the difference between a flat delivery and one that lands on target. This trick is similar to reversing the text, except that instead of reversing the sentence structure to find alternative choices, only certain words are changed, while leaving the overall sentence structure intact.

When you have problems with a line, you can completely change the sentence to something that you understand and relate to. It's OK to change the words because this is only a process for you to discover choices. Once you've found a meaningful interpretation, go back to the script and use the same delivery style. For example, this probably won't mean much to you:

> The GMS 5502 and the H-27-R hybrid transducer were successfully tested during a trial period in October of last year.

So, let's change it to something like this:

> The red cherries and the yellow lemon were successfully eaten during a lunch break last week.

The new context doesn't need to make any more sense than the original script. But by using *substitution* to change the context to something you easily understand, you will be able to create a meaningful delivery. Now all you need to do is apply your chosen delivery to the original script.

ADD A WORD OR TWO

As a general rule of thumb, you will want to deliver a script as written. However, the underlying job of a voice actor is to bring the words to life by creating a believable character who delivers the message in an interesting and compelling manner. Sometimes the way a script is written just doesn't lend itself to an effective rhythm. This is often true of lists in which every item of the list tends to have the identical inflection resulting in a monotonous rhythm.

To create greater interest and a more compelling rhythm try *adding conjunctions* between items in a list. This can give each item greater value and, depending on the intonation of your delivery, effectively convey a specific attitude or emotion such as excitement or frustration. For example, here's how a typical list might be written:

> Your burger comes with two patties, tomato, lettuce, cheese, onion, ketchup, mustard, and pickles.

Adding conjunctions will allow you to "play" with inflection, pacing, and attitude as you speak, making each item important in its own right. You will also be able to more effectively build interest throughout the list by creating the impression that you are thinking of each item just before you say the words:

> Your burger comes with two patties, and tomato, and lettuce, and cheese, and onion, and ketchup, and mustard, and pickles.

Adding words will almost always add length and time to your performance, which may require you to make timing adjustments in other parts of your delivery. A more advanced use of this technique is to add words silently as you deliver a line of copy. Not speaking the added words can be a bit tricky, but the effect can be very powerful as a means for creating an emotionally charged delivery.

This technique should be used judiciously as many producers will want you to deliver the script exactly as written.

SUBTRACT WORDS

Just as adding a word or two can enhance your delivery, the same can be true if you *subtract* a word or two. This technique can speed up your delivery by making statements more terse and abrupt. By removing the "and" that usually sits between the last two items of a list, the overall tone of the delivery can instantly take on a sense of authority.

> Your burger comes with two patties, tomato, lettuce, cheese, onion, ketchup, mustard, pickles.

BREAK THE RULES OF LOGIC

Logic dictates that we deliver a line of copy with proper sentence structure, articulation, grammar, and an interpretation based on our understanding of the text. Many of the most effective techniques for creating a believable character and compelling delivery require breaking the rules of logic. *Breaking the rules of logic* can have a powerful impact on your delivery.

Here's yet another nifty trick for keeping the listener's attention: Break a single word into two or more words. In most cases, we logically deliver a word the same way regardless of the context of the script. Breaking a single word into its component parts can result in an enhanced understanding of the underlying meaning. For example, speaking the simple phrase "Absolutely amazing!" will have a certain level of impact. However, the meaning will be completely different if you restate the phrase by treating each syllable as a separate word: "Ab so lute ly a maz ing!"

This technique won't work in every situation or with every script, but when you need to draw importance to a specific copy point this tool can be incredibly effective.

BREAK THE RULES OF GRAMMAR

Copy is written grammatically for the eye. Even when a script is written in the style of a specific character, the text will often tend to be written grammatically correct and may even include syntax that is not consistent with the character you create. *Break the rules of grammar* by dropping words, adding words or sounds, rearranging words, changing punctuation, and altering the rhythm or tempo to create more compelling characters.

A basic premise of all voice acting is that you must do whatever it takes to bring the words to life. If the character you create speaks in a specific manner with an accent, attitude, or incorrect grammar, then you need to present that in your performance. In other words, *character has precedence over copy.* Of course, your producer may want you to deliver the copy in a certain way which may stifle your creative efforts, but that's the way this business works. This concept is covered in more detail in Chapter 11, "The Character in the Copy."

WORK BACKWARDS

This is a quick trick to quickly get a sense of the big picture of a story or script. It can help you to quickly get an idea of the copywriter's intent, the target audience, the client's message, and some solid clues about your character and the story in the copy.

The idea is to scan the script from the end first, working your way up to the first line of the script. The end of a script is where the resolution or non-resolution of conflict occurs and is usually the point where a character's attitude or true motivation is revealed. It is also where the most important part of the message usually resides.

Many times, simply reading the tag or the last few lines of a script will give you a very good idea of where you need to take your performance for the entire script. It doesn't work all the time or with all scripts, but when it does work, it can be a tremendous time saver.

FIND EMOTIONAL HOOKS

These are the words or phrases that carry an emotional impact. Recall, from past experience, a similar emotion (*sense memory*). Notice that the memory of the emotion creates a certain physical tension someplace in your body (see "Create Tension" on page 167.) Observe where the tension is located in your body and what it feels like. Hold this sensation as you deliver the copy, re-experiencing the emotion or feeling. Now speak from that place in your body, fully expressing the emotion. This technique helps to make your performance more believable and your character more real.

MEMORIZE THE FIRST LINE

This is a neat trick given to me by fellow VO coach, Marc Cashman, to quickly achieve a conversational delivery. The general idea is to *memorize* the first sentence or two of a script and pick up reading the text from the second or third sentence. The process of memorizing the first few lines allows you to internalize the words, context, and interpretation so that when you begin reading you will already be in a conversational delivery. Memorizing the first few lines also makes it easier to stay in character and sustain attitude throughout your performance. Even though you may have the first line or two memorized, be prepared to adjust your delivery if asked to do so by your director.

USE MUSIC AS INSPIRATION (MUSIC MATCH EXERCISE)

This advanced technique isn't for everyone, and it's definitely not a quick fix or something that will work in all situations. However, for those sessions when you have some time and are stuck trying to figure out a delivery attitude or you are facing a challenge developing a character, delivery tempo, or rhythm, this idea may serve you well.

The general idea is to use *music* as a tool for developing your interpretation or character. Music can be a powerful motivator and an inspiration at an emotional level. The ancient Greeks considered music as the study of invisible, internal, hidden objects. Your interpretation of a script is largely based on your personal, internal, hidden responses to the words in the script, so it's only natural that music can help trigger those responses to help you discover energy, attitude, emotion, and much more.

Begin by finding a piece of music that fits the mood, tone, or energy of the script. Instrumentals will often work best, but vocals may give you some ideas for phrasing or voice characterization.

As you listen to several pieces of music you may find that each piece of music you listen to will give you additional ideas or inspire a new interpretation. Let the music be your guide for making a variety of choices with your delivery. Test your performance choices by rehearsing the script as the music plays in the background. Focus on matching your delivery to the mood, tempo, rhythm, and tone of the music. You'll quickly discover that if you let the music guide you to your character, everything about your performance will change depending on the music you are working to. An upbeat music track will result in more smile, a quicker pace, and a brighter performance. A slower, dramatic music track will result in a more intense, dramatic, and emotional performance.

Finally, rehearse your script without music to confirm that your choices are strong and effective. By testing your performance against a variety of musical styles, you'll be better prepared to make valid choices for your performance when you record your auditions and paid session work.

Of course, the music you rehearse with will never actually be used, so you can feel free to use your favorite instrumental CDs or downloaded files. Movie soundtracks are excellent for this technique because of the wide range of emotions and dramatic content. If you want to work with the same type of music that commercial producers use, you can visit any of the numerous online music libraries. Although these music libraries sell their music downloads, there is no charge for auditioning, or listening to the music. It's relatively easy to select a genre and start listening to music as you work with your script.

Because your job as a voice actor is to provide dry voice tracks to your clients, I don't recommend purchasing any library music. Of course, if you have the talent for providing complete production services, having some library music on-hand can certainly be a benefit.

There are literally dozens of online music libraries and the easiest way to find them is to simply enter an Internet search for the keywords: *production music library*.

USING PROPS

Quite often a voiceover script will describe a procedure, gesture, or other physical action. Most of the time, simply miming the described action or pretending to hold the item will help to create the reality of the moment. However, sometimes, it can be more helpful to actually hold something physical in your hands that represents the item you are talking about.

My recommendation is to not use props unless absolutely necessary. However, should you choose to use a physical prop, just be aware that they can make noise and inhibit other physicality which can adversely affect your performance.

As with any other performing technique, props will work better for some people and will not work at all for others.

---

[1] Keyes, D. (1995). *Flowers for Algernon.* Harcourt (reissue).
[2] Here is the proper punctuation for the line on page 121:
  That that is, is. That that is not, is not. Is that it? It is.

In this Chapter

8

Microphone Technique

Your New Best Friend

This might seem an odd place for a technical discussion of microphones. But the simple fact is that, next to your room acoustics, your microphone is the single most important tool in your voiceover arsenal. It is critical that you have more than just a working knowledge of this vital piece of equipment. How you "work" your microphone can have a huge impact on your performance.

Microphone technique is a subtle but powerful way of enhancing your character or the emotional impact of your delivery. Mic technique refers to how you use the microphone to your advantage while in the booth.

MICROPHONE BASICS

Before you can use a microphone effectively, it is helpful to first have a basic understanding of how these marvelous instruments work. The basic purpose of a microphone is to convert acoustical energy (sound waves) to electrical energy that can be manipulated and recorded. There are several designs for microphones, *dynamic* and *condenser* being the most popular and most functional for voiceover work.

Dynamic mics use a moving coil attached to a diaphragm (much like a loudspeaker in reverse) to convert acoustic energy to electrical energy. Dynamic mics are relatively

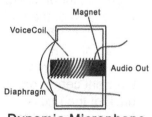

Dynamic Microphone

inexpensive and rugged. Sound quality is generally better with the more expensive models. Simply plug your mic in to the appropriate equipment and start talking.

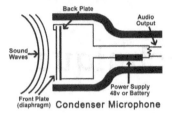

Condenser Microphone

Condenser mics use two fixed plates very close to each other, but not touching. A constant voltage is placed across the two plates, provided by a phantom power supply (usually from a battery or external power source). As sound waves strike the front plate, a change in the electrical energy is the result. Condenser mics are more expensive, far more sensitive, and more fragile than dynamic mics. Because a condenser mic's front plate moves faster than a dynamic mic diaphragm, the sound quality of a condenser mic is brighter and "crisper" than that of a dynamic mic.

MICROPHONE PICK-UP PATTERNS

A microphone's pickup pattern determines how a microphone "hears" sound waves. The two most common pickup patterns are *omnidirectional* and *cardioid* (*unidirectional*). Of these, the most common type of microphone for voiceover recording is the cardioid. Omni and cardioid mics can be either dynamic or condenser.

Omnidirectional mics pick up sound equally from all directions. Because of this, they are not recommended for high-quality voice recording. They are generally less expensive than cardioid mics, less susceptible to handling noise, and are less susceptible to "popping."

Omnidirectional Mic

©Shure.co.uk

Cardioid mics (also called unidirectional mics) come in a wide variety of designs, but virtually all of them pick up sound best from directly in front of the mic. The sound pick-up fades as you move off-axis of the front center of the mic. The back of the mic is the point of maximum sound rejection.

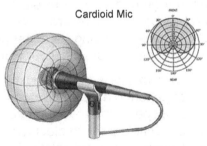

Cardioid Mic

©Shure.co.uk

MICROPHONE PLACEMENT AND COPY STAND POSITION

In a recording studio environment you will generally be standing or seated in front of a music stand (copy stand) with a microphone on a boom at about head level. Adjust the copy stand to eye level so you can see the entire script without having to tilt your head down. Tilting your head can affect your sound by constricting your throat and cause you to move off-mic.

Studio microphones are very sensitive and often have a "pop" screen positioned between the mic and your mouth. The pop screen serves two purposes: 1) it prevents blasts of air from hitting the microphone's diaphragm, and 2) it prevents condensation of moisture from your breath from building up on the microphone diaphragm. Over time, moisture from your breath can affect the microphone's diaphragm, dulling its sound. If properly positioned, a pop screen will not be needed for preventing breath pops, but still may be advisable for blocking condensation.

It is a myth that the microphone must be directly in front of your mouth. Microphones really don't care where they are in relation to your mouth. Six inches off to the left will pick up your voice exactly the same as six inches directly in front of you or six inches above your mouth (at about eye level). You should always position yourself so you are talking across the microphone and never directly into it. Speaking directly into the mic can blast the diaphragm. Although this is rarely harmful to the mic, the resulting "popping" sounds can be a serious problem for the recording and

Mic at eye level, approx. 8" from mouth, 4" off to right and aimed down to mouth.

can be difficult or impossible to fix later on. In some cases, even use of a pop screen may not completely eliminate breath pops from an incorrectly positioned microphone.

Studio microphones are usually *cardioid* (directional), and most engineers position the mic off to the side or perhaps in front of the performer, above the copy stand at about forehead level with the mic aimed towards the mouth. The acoustics of the voice booth are *dead*, meaning there are no reflected echoes. The result is a very clean sound with no "pops." See "Working the Microphone" later in this chapter for more about using your mic.

Microphone placement is simple for a single performer, but becomes more critical when there are several performers in the studio, each with her own mic. In this case, the engineer strives to obtain maximum separation from each performer to minimize how much of each actor's voice is picked up by the other microphones.

As a starting point, position yourself so your mouth is about 6 to 8 inches from the mic. You can easily estimate this by extending your thumb and little finger; place your thumb against your chin, and the mic at the tip of your little finger. This is not a critical distance, and your engineer may adjust the mic closer or further from you. If you are working in your own home studio, you should experiment with different mic positions to discover the best placement for your voice. You may want to change the mic placement depending on the sound you want for a specific script.

For more about microphone pickup patterns and how to choose a mic that's right for your, click on this response code to listen to a demonstration.

LET THE ENGINEER POSITION THE MICROPHONE

When working in someone else's studio, always let the engineer adjust the mic to where you will be standing or sitting. Do not move or adjust the mic yourself. The same goes for the pop screen. After positioning your mic and returning to the control room, the engineer will ask for your level, and may ask you to physically change your position relative to the mic. You may be asked to *move in* on the mic (move closer), or *back off* a bit (move a bit away from the mic). These physical adjustments should be minor, and are intended to produce the right sound for your voice. If you are popping, you may be asked to change the angle of your face in relation to the mic, or to turn slightly off-mic to prevent your breath from hitting the mic.

In your personal home studio, you will, of course, have complete freedom to position your mic to sound your best. Experimentation will reveal the best mic placement for your home studio.

WORKING THE MICROPHONE

While performing, keep your head in a constant relationship to the microphone. The rest of your body can move as much as you need to, provided you aren't making any noise. But your head must remain relatively stationary. If your position drifts too far off-mic, your voice will appear to fade in and out. This drives engineers crazy because the overall volume of your performance is constantly changing. Even with the best equipment, moving off-mic is extremely difficult to deal with simply because a change of just a few inches can result in a very noticeable change in the *room tone* or ambience picked up by the mic.

Be aware that condenser mics will pick up everything! If your clothing rustles, it will be picked up. If your stomach gurgles, it will be picked up. Mouth noise will be picked up. Dynamic mics are much more forgiving and less susceptible to picking up room noise.

USING PROXIMITY EFFECT TO YOUR ADVANTAGE

As you physically move closer to a cardioid microphone, your voice increases in lower frequencies (bass) and the overall tone of your voice will be warmer and more intimate. This phenomenon is called *proximity effect* and is a common characteristic of all directional microphones. As you move away from a cardioid mic, the mic picks up more of the natural ambience of the room. This results in a more open sound, which is cooler and less intimate. Don't be afraid to experiment, but do let the engineer know what you are doing because he or she will need to adjust recording levels accordingly.

NEVER BLOW INTO OR TAP A MICROPHONE

Condenser microphones are delicate and often *very* expensive. Blowing into a any microphone can cause severe damage. When testing a mic or giving a level to the engineer, always speak in the actual volume of your performance. When the engineer asks you to read for levels, consider it an opportunity to rehearse your performance.

Tapping the mic, although not usually harmful, is annoying to most engineers. It's good to keep the studio engineer on your side; they control how you sound and have complete power in the control room. Remember basic studio etiquette—don't touch the equipment, unless, of course, it's yours!

HOLDING THE MICROPHONE

You will rarely need to hold the mic during an actual session. However, it may be necessary at times and it will usually be with a handheld mic. Here's how to properly use a handheld mic.

Once again, the common myth is that the mic needs to be directly in front of the mouth. If you hold your mic in this position, you will be almost guaranteed to have lots of "pops" and breath noise in your recording.

Incorrect: Mic in front of mouth will pick up breath.

The correct handheld mic technique is to hold it vertically or at a slight angle, with the top of the mic at chin level, about an inch

below the lips and slightly away from the chin, not touching the face. In this position, you will be speaking across the top of the mic rather than directly into it. Talking across the mic minimizes breath pops. You can test for proper mic placement with this exercise: Say "puh, puh," expelling a blast of air with each "puh." Slowly raise a finger from below your chin up to your lips and you will know where to position a mic to avoid being hit with your breath.

Correct: Talk across mic held below mouth.

If you need to hold the mic, do not play with the cord. Just let it hang. Wriggling the cable can result in handling noise that can adversely affect your recording, even though you may not hear anything.

Using Headphones

Can you record your voice without using headphones? Of course! But would you want to or, more importantly, should you? There are good reasons to argue both sides of the question of whether or not to use headphones. Your headphones are every bit as much a tool in your studio as your microphone and, as with your microphone, there is a correct way to use your headphones, and an incorrect way. And whether you use headphones or not may depend on the type of voiceover work you are doing.

Unlike music recordings, the end product of most voiceover work is heard over speakers rather than ear buds or headphones. Monitoring under headphones removes room acoustics from the listening experience and, since music is commonly listened to under headphones, many music recording engineers are beginning to mix under headphones to create the best possible sound for the listener.

In voiceover work, headphones serve a similar, yet slightly different purpose. By wearing headphones, you will be able to clearly hear yourself as you are delivering your lines. This auditory *foldback* of your voice will accurately reflect how your microphone hears you, and will often allow you to hear subtle mistakes that might go unnoticed if you aren't wearing headphones. You will be able to hear any flaws in your room acoustics, and it will also allow you to effectively apply certain microphone techniques for achieving warmth, presence, or avoiding breath pops.

Another benefit of wearing headphones—especially if you are recording in a professional studio—is that the many studios are not set up to allow for talkback over speakers, so headphones become a critical aspect of communication.

A third benefit happens when you are doing rolling punch-ins or working to a playback. Headphones allow you to hear what you are working with, without the microphone picking up the playback audio.

Some voice talent feel that headphones are a distraction and prefer to work without them. This is often because headphones tend to isolate a performance and the foldback audio puts the focus on the actor's voice, rather than on their performance.

WHAT KIND OF HEADPHONES ARE BEST?

There is no rule that says you can't take your favorite headphones to a session. It's done all the time. The important thing is that you treat your headphones as another tool for use during your performance of voiceover.

Keep in mind that your headphones need to accurately represent your voice as it will be recorded. This is the only way you will truly know that you are sounding your best. Ear buds and many consumer headphones will emphasize lower frequencies, often producing a very warm and sometimes "boomy" sound, which might sound very nice, but may not necessarily be an accurate representation of your recording. These, of course, can be used to monitor your recordings, but you should at least be aware of the consequences. When it comes to using headphones to monitor your recordings, you don't necessarily get what you hear.

Comfort is another important aspect to keep in mind when selecting your headphones. As your voiceover work increases, you may find yourself spending many hours at a time under headphones. The last thing you want is to have sore ears or a headache caused by uncomfortable headphones.

One final consideration is listening volume. When using ear buds or some consumer headphones, the tendency is to turn up the volume. Monitoring at a too loud a level can cause your ears to fatigue, requiring you to turn up the volume even more. Loud monitor levels can also result in high frequency hearing loss, which can adversely affect the way you hear your recordings. If you don't already have a favorite pair of comfortable headphones, you might want to put a sample recording of your voice on an MP3 player and take it with you as you test different models of headphones. You don't need to spend a lot of money on headphones, but you should be satisfied that the headphones you choose are comfortable and will accurately represent your voice recordings.

The Seven Core Elements

In this Chapter

9

The Seven Core Elements of an Effective Performance
(AKA: The A-B-Cs of Voice Acting)

Acting is Acting is Acting ... Sort of

If you've watched any TV, seen a movie, or sat through a play, you are, no doubt, aware that not all acting is equal. Some actors are brilliant, some are so-so, and some ... well, just don't belong on stage or in front of the camera. So, what is it that makes the difference between a brilliant performance and one that gives new meaning to the word mediocre?

The answer lies largely in the talent and ability of the actor to understand and apply the dozens of techniques and skills necessary to create a compelling and believable performance. If the actor has not mastered the essential elements and techniques of performance, the audience will sense that something is wrong.

Over the many years of teaching voice acting workshops, we've boiled down the essence of acting for voiceover to Seven Core Elements that we refer to as *The A-B-C's of Voice Acting*. Traditional acting classes for stage, film, and television teach many of these concepts, but not quite the way you'll learn here.

Take a look at the title of this chapter again. I'll wait.

You'll notice that the title includes the words *effective performance*. Voiceover work is not about what most people think of as "acting" or performing. To be effective, an actor in any genre must create a sense of drama. Merriam-Webster defines *drama* as "a situation or series of events in which there is an interesting or intense conflict of forces." In other words, drama is what gives a performance the appearance of believable reality. Any actor can deliver words from a script, but to be effective, an actor must develop a sense of the drama. All drama contains elements of conflict, humor, mystery, emotion, and feelings. Drama also creates tension, suspense, and anticipation for what will happen next.

As you learn how to apply the concepts in this book, and more specifically, in this chapter, you will begin to learn how to create compelling, believable, and real characters in the mind of your audience. That's what an effective performance is all about.

So now the question you should be asking is: "How do I create drama?" The answer is simple in concept but complex in execution. The answer is: "You must make choices and you must commit to those choices." The Seven Core Elements of a performance are all about making choices.

It Starts with Pretending

A voiceover performer is an actor—period. It doesn't matter what the script is for. It doesn't matter if the copy is well written or poorly written. It doesn't matter if you are delivering the copy alone or with others. You are an actor when you stand in front of the microphone.

It is truly a rare individual who is born with natural acting ability. For most people, acting skills take time to learn and master. Acting is not difficult; it's just that as we've grown, we've simply forgotten how to play. As a child, you were acting whenever you pretended to be a fireman, a princess or anyone else you created in your imagination. Pretending is where it starts. But there's a lot more to it than that.

Voiceover performing—or, more accurately, voice acting—is an opportunity to bring out your inner child. Regardless of the copy you are reading, there will always be some sort of character in the words. To be believable, that character must be brought to life. To do that effectively, you must start by becoming a master of pretending.

By definition, the word *pretend* means "to give a false appearance of being." So, if you are strictly pretending, you are not being real, but the objective of all acting is to create the illusion of reality. Learning how to pretend believably (or act) allows you overcome this apparent contradiction so you can step outside of yourself, using what you know as you move down the path of creating that illusion of reality.

The major problem most people have in performing for voiceover is in creating a believable illusion of reality while reading from a script. Reading is a left-brain, linear process, while performing is a right-brain, non-linear, process. The tendency is to "read" the words, rather than allowing the words to become real by pretending to be the person speaking the words.

This is where the Seven Core Elements of an Effective Performance come in. By applying these seven elements, you will be able to take your acting from simple pretending to creating a completely believable reality.

If you remember nothing else from this book, the following concepts will take you further in voice acting, or any other performing craft, than just about anything else. You can also apply these ideas in any area of your personal or professional life to achieve a high level of communication skill. These techniques do not have to be done in sequence. In fact, most of the time one element will help define another. As you work on your performance, begin by making choices in whichever element seems to be a good place to start, but be sure that you include them all.

A = AUDIENCE:
Core Element #1

When you have a conversation with someone, you know who you are talking to. As a result, you speak conversationally and in a manner that is appropriate for your topic of conversation.

When you are working from a script, you need to determine who you (or, more accurately, your character) is talking to? Decide on who will be hearing the message—the ideal person who needs to hear what you have to say. Different styles of delivery are appropriate for different audiences. In most cases, the copy will give you a good idea of who the ideal audience is. It may be helpful to ask the producer who he or she is trying to reach, or you may need to make a choice based on your gut instincts. By knowing your audience, you will be able to figure out the most appropriate and effective way to speak to them.

The most important thing to remember about your audience is that no matter what the script or project may be, you are *always* talking to *only one person*. Attempting to *shotgun* your performance, by trying to connect with many people at once, will generally result in the listening audience losing interest and becoming uneasy with you as a performer. There is a very subtle difference between focusing attention on an individual versus focusing on a mass of people. You've no doubt experienced seminars where the speaker just doesn't seem to reach the audience, and yet there are others where everyone is hanging on the speaker's every word. In the first instance, the speaker is most likely "shot-gunning" their message in an attempt to reach everyone in the audience. In the second, the speaker is getting eye contact with individuals in the audience—one at a time, and has a crystal clear idea of the ideal person who needs to hear the message. When you focus your attention on one person, and speak with honesty and sincerity, everyone listening will feel drawn in, as though you are speaking only to them. This is an incredibly powerful technique that many voice talent simply don't understand or apply.

For the following line of copy, make some choices as to who the one, ideal person who needs to hear the message might be:

> Some people think they're a mistake! But most people think they're delicious! OK ... so they've got a big seed and they're green ... Avocados are still my favorite fruit. Great in salads ... or all by themselves. Get some today.

Here are some possible choices:

- A shopper in a grocery story also looking at avocados
- Someone who has never seen an avocado before
- A grocery clerk who is carefully stacking avocados
- A customer in a restaurant ordering a meal with avocados

The choice you make for your audience will help determine your tone of voice, your attitude, and the overall approach to your performance. Focus your attention on speaking to just one person as though you were having a conversation with them. Describe the person you are speaking to in as much detail as possible and give him or her a name. Use a photograph to get the feeling of having eye contact with a real person. Doing this may help make your delivery more conversational and believable.

Here's a tip when choosing your one-person audience: Don't choose to be speaking to someone you know. The reason for this is that you have a relationship with that person that will color your interpretation of the words. When you select someone you know as your audience, the speaker of the words becomes *you* and it will be considerably more challenging to create a believable performance when reading from a script intended to be spoken by a character who is not you. Choose someone you do not know as your audience.

It's entirely possible that the original choice you make for your audience may not be the best choice and you will need to change it. There may be many reasons for this, but regardless of how it happens, you will need to make an *adjustment* and make a new choice.

B = BACK STORY:
Core Element #2

In voiceover, a *back story* is the specific event that takes place immediately before the first word of copy. It is what the character in the script is responding to. The back story is the reason why your character is saying the words in the script. If the back story is not clearly defined in the script—your job, as an actor, is to make one up! This is a very important aspect of performing from a written script because the back story sets your character's motivation, attitude, and purpose for speaking.

Acting coaches will often refer to a back story as "the moment before." Technically, a back story consists of the character's entire life experience that has brought them to the moment in time for the story in the script. For voiceover work, that's too much information, and we don't have the time to deal with a long, involved story leading up to the first word of the script. So, I suggest that you define a back story in specific terms that can be described in a single sentence. It must be something very immediate and powerful that has caused your character to speak. It can't be a vague description of a scene—it must elicit a specific response.

In some scripts, the back story is pretty obvious. In others, you'll have to make up something. Either way, the back story is essential to the development of your character. By understanding what brought your character to this moment, you will know how your character should respond. This, in turn will make it much easier for you to sustain your character and effectively communicate your character's feelings, attitudes, and emotions as he or she interacts with the audience and other characters.

For the following line of copy, make some choices as to the specific event that occurred, or words spoken immediately before this statement, and to which this statement is in response:

> Some people think they're a mistake! But most people
> think they're delicious! OK ... so they've got a big seed
> and they're green ... Avocados are still my favorite fruit.
> Great in salads ... or all by themselves. Get some today.

To discover the back story, look for clues in the script that reveal specific details about what is taking place. Use these clues to create your own idea of what took place *before* the story in the script. This is the essence of your back story, and this is what brought your character to this moment in time.

Here are some possible choices for a back story for the first line:

- The person you are speaking to has asked you what this big green thing is with all the bumps. You respond with the first line of the script.
- The person you are speaking to has mentioned that they absolutely love avocados. You respond with a silent lead-in "I love them too, but, you know ..." followed by a short pause, then the first line of the script.
- The person you are speaking to is ordering a meal and is uncertain about whether or not to add avocado by saying "... would you recommend avocado?" You respond with the first line of the script.

Any given script may have several opportunities for a back story—possibly for every line, and occasionally even within a line. For each of those back story opportunities a very short phrase or one-word lead-in may help to *bridge* transitional thoughts or lines of copy to help add reality to the delivery. When you bridge lines of a script in this way, what you are actually doing is adding a thought process to your performance, which is a direct reflection of how our minds really work when we are having a conversation. For example, a bridging back story for the line "OK ... so they've got a big seed and they're green ..." might be this: The person you are speaking to says "I've heard avocados have a huge seed!" Obviously, we don't have time to actually verbalize or deal with these bridge lines in real time. Simply writing the word or phrase on your script or holding it in your imagination will usually be enough to trigger the thought process and thus create a sense of reality.

One way to use a back story to your advantage is to create a *lead-in line*, or *pre-life*, as discussed on page 67. To review, this is simply a verbalization of the back story to assist you in creating a believable response. For example, if you are speaking to someone who has never seen an avocado before you might create a lead-in line like: "So ... you've never seen an avocado before? Well ..." and then begin the script. A lead-in line is not intended to be spoken out loud, but, rather, should be said silently to set up the intonation and attitude of the words that will be spoken.

Each of these choices will have a different effect on your approach to the performance, including intonation, rate of delivery, attitude, dynamics, and underlying meaning (or subtext). As with the other choices you'll be making, one of these may be more suitable than the others. The only way you'll know which choice works best is to test them. When you make a choice, commit to it until either you or your director determine that the choice needs to be adjusted.

C = CHARACTER:
Core Element #3

For every voiceover performance, you will need to determine who is speaking the words in the script. This is your role in the story, or more accurately, this is the character you will be playing. In most cases, you will find clues about your character within the script itself—in the way it is written, the phrasing, or even in the way certain words are spelled. If you are lucky, the copy writer provided a short description of your character.

As you begin working on your performance, define your character in as much detail as you like—the more detailed, the better. How does your character dress? What does the character's voice sound like? Does the character speak with an accent, dialect, or have any speaking quirks? Does the character exhibit any sort of attitude or personality quirks? How does the character move? How does the character think? What is the character's lifestyle? How does the character interact with other characters in the story, known or unknown? In what ways does the character respond to events that take place during the telling of the story? How does the character feel about the product, service, or subject of the script? The more details you can come up with, the more believable your character will be to you and to your audience. Every script has a character, regardless of how poorly the script may be written or what the content of the script may be. Your job is to find that character and give it life.

Just as in life, scripted characters have feelings and experience emotions about the stories they tell. And, just as in life, characters respond, evolve, and express emotions during the course of their stories. Learn how to reveal those emotions and feelings through your voice and you will create believable characters. Chapter 11, "The Character in the Copy," will explain many ways for you to do this, and you will find additional tools for creating and documenting characters in Chapter 16, "Mastering Character Voices."

For the following line of copy, make some choices that will clearly define and describe the person speaking:

> Some people think they're a mistake! But most people
> think they're delicious! OK ... so they've got a big seed
> and they're green ... Avocados are still my favorite fruit.
> Great in salads ... or all by themselves. Get some today.

Here are some possibilities for the character who is speaking these words:

- A grocery clerk stocking the shelves
- A shopper (talking to another shopper)
- An avocado grower or farmer
- A waiter or waitress in a restaurant
- A person speaking to a friend about fruits and vegetables

As with the other choices you make, your choice and definition of the character you are playing will have an impact on every aspect of your performance. Your other choices may affect your choice of character, and, of course, your choice of the character may require that you adjust some or all of your other choices. If you commit to each of your choices until you determine a choice is not working, you will be well on your way to creating consistent, interesting, and compelling characters.

D = DESIRES:
Core Element #4

All characters have wants and needs! Theatrical actors will refer to this aspect of character development as the character's *objectives* or *intentions*. *Desires*, *objectives*, and *intentions* all refer to what your character ultimately wants as a result of his or her words and actions. Use whichever term works best for you, but for the purpose of this alphabetical mnemonic, "D" for *desires* works best. A-B-C-O, just doesn't seem right! Some actors mistakenly use the term *motivation* when describing their character's wants and needs. However, a character's motivation is more accurately related to the *back story*, which gives the character a reason for responding. The character's *desires* refer to the outcome of the character's words and actions.

The character always wants something very specific from speaking the words. It may be simply to enlighten the listener with a valuable piece of information, it may be to entertain, or it may be to instruct the listener in the fine points of operating a complex piece of machinery. Whatever it may be, your character wants, needs, and desires to accomplish something from speaking those words. If that desire is not clearly explained in the context of the script—use whatever information is available to make it up.

Here's a quick test: What does the character in the following script want and need (desire) as a result of speaking these words?

Come up with a half-dozen or more choices of your own before reading further.

> Some people think they're a mistake! But most people think they're delicious! OK … so they've got a big seed and they're green … Avocados are still my favorite fruit. Great in salads … or all by themselves. Get some today.

Here are some possibilities for the character's desires and the words that might be clues to the ultimate desire:

- Establish curiosity (Some people think they're a mistake!)
- Tease to create interest (… they're delicious …)
- Add a touch of humor (… so they've got a big seed …)
- Intrigue the listener (… they're green …)
- Provide important information (they're a fruit and taste good in salad)
- Create urgency (Get some today.)

As you can see, there are many possibilities. There is really no single, correct way to interpret or deliver any piece of copy. As an actor, you need to make a choice as to what might be the most appropriate message that your character wants to communicate. And there may be more than one. As with your other choices, the only way you will know what works best is to test them when rehearsing the copy.

There are no wrong choices. But there are choices that may be more effective than others in terms of communicating the message. One key to choosing your character's desires is to consider the interaction between your character and the one-person audience. Also, be wary of choosing a desire of "selling." People love to buy, but they hate to be "sold." Choosing a desire of helping by providing important information that allows the listener to make an educated decision to buy will almost always be best.

E = ENERGY:
Core Element #5

Voice acting comes from your entire body.
If only your mouth is moving, that's all anyone will hear.[1]
Cory Burton

There are three distinct levels of energy in every performance: psychological energy, physical energy, and emotional energy. All three must be present. Leave one of these out and your character will lack a sense of truth and honesty.

PSYCHOLOGICAL ENERGY

Think back to a time when you said one thing, but what you really meant was something else entirely—and the person you were speaking to somehow knew exactly what you meant. We've all done this at one time or another. In fact, this is the basis of all sarcasm. The thought you hold in your head can directly affect the way the words come out of your mouth.

Try this: Say the phrase "That's a really nice hat." You most likely just spoke the words without any objective, intention, or desire, so it probably sounded pretty flat and uninteresting. Now hold the thought in your head that the hat you're looking at is the most incredible hat you've ever seen, and on the person you're talking to, it looks amazing! You want them to know how excited and happy you are that they have found a "look" that works for them. Say the phrase again and notice how different it sounds.

"That's a really nice hat."

Now, change the thought in your imagination to be that you are very jealous to see the other person wearing a hat that is exactly like your favorite hat. Your desire is to outwardly compliment them on their hat, but on the inside you really don't think it looks very good (even if it does). You're not happy, and you want them to know it without really saying it.

"That's a really nice hat."

The words are exactly the same in both situations, but the thoughts you held in your mind were different. The result is that the perceived meaning of the words is different.

In theater, the term *subtext* is used to refer to the underlying personality, and unspoken thoughts of a character that define the character's behavior and reveal what they really believe. *Psychological energy* is simply another way to understand *subtext*.

Psychological energy is a powerful concept when applied to voice acting. In voiceover, the sound of our voice is all we have to communicate the message in a script, and we need to use every tool available to create a believable reality. Applying psychological energy to a performance allows you to emulate the thought process of your character, which in turn allows the words to sound honest, real, and authentic.

The trick to using psychological energy properly is to keep the true belief just under the surface and to not reveal it during the performance, except through subtle intonation and behavior. By keeping the true belief hidden behind the words, it allows other characters to respond more appropriately, and it keeps the audience curious. This is especially important if the true meaning is in direct opposition to the textual meaning.

Although the concept of psychological energy may sound relatively simple, putting it to work as part of a voiceover performance may take some practice. Once you've mastered this aspect of a performance you'll be well on your way to creating consistently believable characters and highly effective performances.

PHYSICAL ENERGY

Physicalize the moment ... and your voice will follow.
Bob Bergen (based on teachings of Daws Butler)[2]

I think it's pretty safe to say that when you are in conversation with someone, you are not standing or sitting perfectly still, without moving. OK, maybe some of you reading this don't move, but most people use much more than just their mouth when talking. Facial expressions, body language, physical movement, and gestures are all part of the way we communicate when speaking to others. I'll bet you move your body even when you're talking on the phone.

Have you ever noticed that your physical movements are a big part of the way you speak? You use *physical energy* to give power to the thoughts and emotions that lay just under the surface of the words you speak.

Physical energy is absolutely essential in any voiceover performance. When you move your body with appropriate energy to support the emotions and thoughts of the words you speak, the result can be a totally believable performance.

A mistake many beginning voice actors make is that they will stand perfectly still and stiff-as-a-board when they are in front of a microphone. Their hands will hang at their sides and their faces will show no expression. Their performance will be flat and uninteresting, with often an almost monotone delivery. Once they start moving, everything changes. Words come to life, we can hear how the character feels, and we are actually drawn in to the drama of the story.

Unfortunately, for some, the idea of putting physical movement to words while reading from a script is much like walking and chewing gum at the same time—it can be a challenge to learn how to do it. Fortunately, it is an easily acquired skill. Usually, lack of movement is the result of nervousness or comes from a feeling of discomfort or insecurity from being in an unfamiliar environment (often called "mic fright"). But the simple truth in voice acting is that you <u>must</u> move. It is one element of a performance that is essential to creating compelling and believable characters.

EMOTIONAL ENERGY

> *Life will give you what you need.*
> *Situations are your tools.*[3]
> Christina Fasano

Understanding how your character feels about a situation, thing, product, event or person is an aspect of *subtext*. It's part of what lies just below the surface of the words and directly affects tone of voice and attitude. Your character's emotional energy is different from psychological energy in that psychological energy deals with the thoughts behind the words, whereas *emotional energy* is the expression of the feelings and emotions that underscore the thoughts. The two go hand in hand.

Using the hat example, consider how your character feels emotionally about the discovery that someone else has the exact same hat they have—and that they look great wearing it. Your character might feel devastated, frustrated, angry, happy, proud, or even excited. A full range of emotions is possible, but the most appropriate emotion will be determined by looking at the overall context of the story—understanding the big picture. Based on your choices as to how your character behaves and speaks within the context of the whole story, you will better understand the how and why of the character's feelings and emotional responses.

Keep in mind, that as actors, our job is to create a sense of reality, so any expression of emotion that is *over-the-top* might destroy any chance of believability. The best way to use emotional energy is to keep the emotions just under the surface. Start by allowing yourself to recall how you felt emotionally in a similar situation and observe where you hold physical tension in your body for that response. Then, base your performance from that feeling and the tension in your body.

By using a personal experience the emotional response will have truth and honesty, which will support the thoughts held in your imagination, which, in turn, will result in a more authentic and believable performance.

The essence of how the three levels of energy affect your performance can be summed up as:

- Change your thoughts—it will change the way you move, which will change the sound of the words you speak
- Change your physical movement—it will change the way you feel, which will affect the sound of the words you speak
- Change your emotions—it will change the way you sound

For the following line of copy, make some choices as to how your character might think (psychological energy), how he/she might move and where tension is held in the body while talking (physical energy), and how he/she feels about the subject (emotional energy).

Some people think they're a mistake! But most people think they're delicious! OK … so they've got a big seed and they're green … Avocados are still my favorite fruit. Great in salads … or all by themselves. Get some today.

The important thing to keep in mind when it comes to *energy* in your performance is to remember that all energy must start with a thought and move through physical movement before the emotion can be effectively communicated.

F = FORGET WHO YOU ARE AND FOCUS: Core Element #6

Acting is all about listening and forgetting who you are.[4]
Shirley MacLaine

A key principal of acting is to "get out of your own way" so the character or role you are playing can emerge and appear real to your audience. It sounds simple on the surface, but this idea may be confusing to some people. After all, isn't it an actor's job to figure out how a particular role should be played? Doesn't the actor need to be present during a performance? Aren't there a whole bunch of techniques that an actor can use to make a role believable? And doesn't all this mean that an actor needs to put a lot of thought into their performance?

Although all of these things are true to some degree, they are all just parts of the process of creating a performance. They are not the performance. The reality of all acting is that the role you are playing is *not* you. The secret to excellent acting is to do everything that needs to be done to understand the story, character, relationships, responses, moods, attitudes, dynamics, and energy; apply the appropriate acting techniques to give meaning to the story, breathe life into the character, and "take the words off the page"; then put all of that behind you as the real you steps aside to let the character come to life. And to do all of this invisibly without giving the appearance that you are "acting." If there is any part of the real you that is apparent in a performance, it is you "doing" the character—not the character being authentic. You're thinking too much about what you need to do, or you're giving too much importance to the techniques you are using. In other words, when you put too much effort into the process of creating a performance, your acting becomes apparent and the performance will suffer, often by sounding as though you are "reading" the script or over-acting.

One of the most difficult things for any actor to learn is how to forget who they are so the character can become real. The reason this is often a difficult task is because, as human beings, we have an ego that can cause us to second guess ourselves or stand in the way of what we know needs to be done. We can be a master of performing techniques and still be in our own way on an unconscious level. Often the only way we know it's happening is when our director asks us to make an adjustment in our performance.

Learning how to get out of our own way is, for most of us, an acquired skill that can take many years to master—or it can be achieved in an instant. This is one of the reasons acting is a craft and not a skill. A skill is a specific talent or ability, while a craft is the application of multiple skills to achieve a specific end result. Mastering any skill or craft takes time, patience, and dedication.

Listen to your director, listen to your instincts, listen to the unspoken words to which your character is responding, listen to the other actors in the studio, listen to everything. It is only through listening that you will be able to *focus* on doing what needs to be done to create the reality of the moment. When you are fully focused, you will discover that you no longer need to think about what you are doing. The characters you create will almost magically come to life. The second you allow yourself to drift off focus, or start to think about what you are doing, you will fall out of character.

If you don't fully grasp the idea of *forget who you are and focus*, don't be concerned. Many very successful actors and performers don't fully understand this concept and may never experience what it is like to truly forget who they are and get out of their way. For most actors, the experience is erratic at best, happening only occasionally. Achieving this state of performance on a consistent basis usually comes only with consistent work and study over a long period of time. The best I can say is that when you achieve this state of performance, you'll know it! It will feel as though you are outside of yourself observing your performance. Sort of like an "out-of-body" experience, except that you have complete control. This is the state of performance we strive for.

G = GAMBLE:
Core Element #7

Be willing to gamble. Be willing to take a chance.

If you are going to succeed in voiceover, you must be willing to risk. Every performance requires that the performer be willing to step outside of their comfort zone to do or be something that most people would feel uncomfortable doing or being. It could be as simple as making an announcement at a party, standing on stage in front of an audience of thousands, or standing all by yourself in front of a microphone in a voiceover booth.

The reason many people are unwilling to risk, is simply because of fear. By definition, fear is simply "being afraid of something." A practical, rational fear might be one of being struck by a car if you walk across a highway of fast moving traffic. There is clear evidence of what would happen in that situation, which totally justifies the fear. It make complete sense to be afraid of walking into busy traffic.

However, most fears are unsubstantiated, having no practical or physical evidence to establish a foundation for the fear. A fear is often the result of our internal negative self-talk. These "voices in our head" will tell us we cannot do something, that we aren't good enough, that we aren't competent, that what we want will never happen, and on and on. Our voices can literally stop us dead in our tracks, preventing us from taking even the slightest risk that could lead to achieving our life's ambitions.

My favorite definition of the word "fear" is "false expectations appearing real." This definition allows us to understand fear for what it really is. When you realize that there is no evidence to support something you might fear, you can more easily work through the fear and do it anyway. You will begin to realize that your voices are only trying to protect you from the unknown. And, because the unknown is just that ... unknown ... there is no evidence to support any outcome, one way or another.

Quieting the voices in your head, and thus removing or reducing the fear, is actually quite simple in concept. Your voices are part of your unconscious mind that are helping you to deal with situations that exist outside of your comfort zone. The important thing is that the voices must be acknowledged. If you don't let your voices know they have been heard, they will just persist and get louder. But when you acknowledge your voices, and simply say "Thank you for sharing, but I'm going to do it anyway," over time, they will begin to quiet down. It will take consistent effort, but you really can quiet your voices. When you quiet your internal negative self-talk, you will find that you will be much more open to rationally evaluating potential risks and that you will be more willing to take those risks that can move you forward without experiencing fear. You may actually discover that you begin to seek out opportunities in which you can stretch your abilities by overcoming your fears. The process can be very enlightening.

All performing is about risk. You risk the chance of not being liked, you risk making inappropriate choices, you risk the chance of not being believable, you risk the chance of not being hired again, you risk many things on many levels.

All performing is about taking a chance on an uncertain outcome. You may never know exactly what the producer or director is looking for in your performance, if your performance truly meets their needs, or how your performance will ultimately be used. Even though you may not know, you must be willing to take a chance, based on experience and observation, that what you do will be the best bet for a successful outcome.

All performing is a *gamble*. You are gambling that the choices you make for creating your character and delivering your lines will bring the character and the story to life.

Building your business as a voice actor requires a willingness to risk. You'll risk your money as you build your home studio, invest in your marketing, produce your demo and study to master your craft. You'll risk rejection when you audition, when you call prospective clients, and when you think you've come up with exactly what a script needs—and the producer doesn't think so.

If you are not willing to take a risk, performing as a voice actor is probably not something you should pursue any further. Just stop reading right now and give this book to someone who is willing to take the risk of doing something they have never done before. A simple truth of this business is that, with relatively few exceptions, you cannot achieve any level of success if you insist on being only you as you read a script.

Voiceover is a craft based on creating compelling characters in interesting relationships. The only way you can create a character that is not you is to be willing to *gamble*, or risk that you can do what needs to be done for a believable performance.

It's completely natural to be reluctant, or fearful, of taking a risk when the outcome is known. But there is a huge difference between taking an educated risk versus one that is unfounded. Gambling on your performance is *not* about winning or losing. It *is* about using the tools of your trade, your experience, your training, and your many performing and business skills to create more certainty for an otherwise uncertain outcome. In other words, by understanding risk and allowing yourself to take the gamble, you can stack the deck to improve the odds for a masterful performance and successful voiceover career each time you stand in front of a microphone.

This book is about giving you the basic knowledge that will enable you to take an educated risk if voiceover work is something you truly want to pursue.

---

[1] Burton, C. (2003). *Scenes for Actors and Voices by Daws Butler.* Bear Manor Media.

[2] Bergen, B. Warner Bros. voice of Porky Pig and other characters—www.bobbergen.com.

[3] Fasano, C. (1999). Lyrics from the song "Welcome to the Workshop," *Spiritually Wet,* published by FWG Music.

[4] MacLaine, S. in an interview by James Lipton, *Inside the Actor's Studio.* Bravo Television Network.

In this Chapter

10

Wood Shedding and Script Analysis

The Director in the Front Row of Your Mind

Every script is written for the purpose of communicating something—selling, education, entertainment, or expressing an emotion or feeling. No matter how well-written a script might be, it is not the words in and of themselves that convey the message, it is the way in which the words are spoken that ultimately moves the audience. It is the details of the performance that lie behind the words—the nuance, the emotions—that allow a performer to bring a script to life. And behind every performer, there is a director.

You may not realize it, but somewhere in your mind there is a director. Allow your director to sit front row, center in your mind—in a big, overstuffed chair—so he or she can objectively watch your performance to keep you performing at your best.

A voiceover performance is theatrical truth—not real-life truth—and your internal director is the part of you that gives you silent cues to keep you, or rather, your character, real. As you work with copy, you will find a little voice in your head that tells you, "Yeah, that was good" or "That line needs to be done differently." The director in the front row of your mind is the result of critical thinking. He or she is the part of you that helps you stay in the moment, and gives you focus and guidance with your performance. Think of this director as a separate person (or part of you) who is objectively watching your performance from a distance, yet close enough to give you cues.

In time, your internal director and your performance will become as one—a seamless blending of director and performer resulting in a truly professional dramatic artist, without any conscious effort. This mastery of self-direction is the level to strive for.

But there is a catch! As with most things in life, you must learn to walk before you can run. When performing voiceover, a mastery of performing skills is only the beginning. You must also learn how to dig deep into a script to uncover the truth that is hidden behind the words. This is a process commonly known as *script analysis*, or *wood shedding*.

"Wood Shed" Your Copy

The term wood shedding comes from the early days of American theater. As theatrical troupes traveled to new frontiers in the early West, the only place they could rehearse and work out their performances was in a woodshed. The term stuck and it's still in common use today.

From the moment you first read any script, you will instinctively develop an interpretation. Sometimes your gut instincts and choices will be dead-on accurate. At other times, you may struggle as you try to figure out what the story is all about, your character's role in telling the story, and the best way to tell the story. The character you create may ultimately be defined as simply an "announcer" or spokesperson doing a hard-sell sales pitch or, perhaps, a "friendly neighbor" telling her story about a great new product. In other cases, the character you need to define may have a complex personality with a range of emotions. For almost every script, you'll need to do some sort of basic analysis to uncover the information you need for an effective performance. The process you use may be very simple, or it may be a complex analysis of every detail in the script. As your skills develop, you will most likely change the way you wood shed a script.

Let's review some of the key elements that can help you determine the many aspects of how you tell the story.

- **The structure of the copy** (the way it is written)—Is the copy written in a dialect style? Is the wording "flowery" or expressive in some way? Is the copy a straight pitch? What is the pace of the copy? What is the mood of the copy? What is the attitude of the character speaking the words?

- **Know the audience**—Identifying the target audience is a good way to discover your character. Experienced copywriters know that most people fit primarily into one of several clearly defined categories or personality types. The words and style they choose for their copy will be carefully chosen to target the specific behaviors and characteristics of the public they want to reach. Specific words and phrases will be used to elicit an emotional response from the target audience. Your character may be defined in part by the words spoken to convey a thought, or his or her attitude may be clearly expressed within the context of the copy.

- **What is the back story** (the moment before)?—What happened before the first word of copy? The back story is the specific event that brought your character to this moment in time and to which he or she is responding. This may or may not be obvious. Every script has a back story. If a back story is not defined within the context of the script, make one up.

- **Who are the characters?**—Who is your character and how do other characters, known or unknown, interrelate with your character and each other (as in a dialogue script)? This interaction can give solid clues about your character.

- **What is the scene?**—Where does the story in the script take place? What is the environment? Temperature? Understanding the big picture of the script will reveal a tremendous amount of information that will help you discover the most effective performance.

- **What does your character want?**—Your character has a specific purpose for speaking the words in the script. What is the underlying want and need of your character, and what is ultimately achieved by the end of the script?

- **How does your character behave or move?**—The writing style or context of a script will often reveal how your character moves and behaves as he or she responds to various to other characters or situations occurring in the story.

- **Are there any comparisons in the copy?**—Does the story include a contrast or comparison between two or more items or ideas? If a contrast or comparison exists, how many different ways can you speak the words in a way that makes the comparison clear to the listener?

- **What is the conflict?**—What happens in the copy to draw the listener into the story? Where is the drama in the story? Is the conflict humorous or serious? When you discover the conflict, your performance will be much more interesting and compelling. Almost every script contains some form of conflict.

- **How is the conflict resolved ... or not?**—How is the product or message presented through the resolution or non-resolution of conflict? Does the resolution of the conflict indicate a change in attitude, behavior or energy in telling the story? If the conflict is not resolved, how does the story end? Is there a logical conclusion? Or does the story end by leaving the listener to arrive at their own resolution?

There are many other clues in the copy that will lead you to discover the character and the best way to tell the story. As the performer, you may have one idea for delivering a script and your client or producer may have another. If there is any question about your character or other aspects of the message, you would be wise to discuss it with the producer.

Wood shedding is about getting to the essence of the message or story. What core, underlying emotional need is being satisfied? Convenience? Comfort? Friendship? Satisfaction? Hunger? Using your wood shedding process to put this into one sentence or less will help to reveal the ideal tone of voice and attitude for the script.

Creating a Performance Road Map: Analyzing and Marking a Script

One of the first things you should do as you begin working with a script is to quickly analyze it; *wood shed* it, searching for clues to help you create a believable character and effective delivery.

As you begin working with voiceover copy, you may find, at first, that it might take you a few minutes to make the choices about your character and other aspects of the copy. However, as you gain experience, you will be able to do a thorough wood shedding in the time it takes you to read through the script once or twice.

The Script Analysis Worksheet on pages 164 and 165 can be used when working with any piece of copy. The worksheet is another tool you can use when breaking down a script to define the *Seven Core Elements* of a performance. If you find a sequential, linear process beneficial, you may find the worksheet helpful.

Once you've done this process a few times, it will become automatic and you won't need the worksheet any longer. By answering the questions on the worksheet, you can quickly learn everything you need to know about a script and your character. If an answer is not clear from the copy, then make it up. You won't be graded on your answers, I promise. The answers you come up with will give you critical information you can use in developing effective characters and delivery. They are simply a way for you to make practical choices for the script you are performing. For you to maintain a consistent performance, it is important that you stick with the choices you make in your script analysis. If something isn't working for you, of course, you can change your mind. But any new choices or changes should only be made to make your performance and your character more real and believable.

TO MARK OR NOT TO MARK

Through experimentation, you will find a form of script analysis that works for you. You may find that it is very helpful to mark your script with notes, lines, and boxes designed to chart your path through a performance. Or you may find it completely unnecessary to mark your script in detail, and instead only make minor notations as needed. Whatever works for you is what you should use.

If you find you are paying too much attention to your notations as you read a script, or if your script has excessive markings, you are probably over-analyzing the text. This can result in a script that is hard to read or a delivery that is unfocused and sounds like you are reading. The more you think about what you are doing, the less you are truly in character. As you develop your personal process for script analysis and notation, and your performing skills improve, you will most likely find you need to mark your script less and less. .

Regardless of your individual process, or how much you mark your script, the basic *wood shedding process* will remain the same. As you analyze a script, you will want to look for key words and phrases that reveal attitude and emotion, and give clues about your character and how your character responds to information, situations, and other characters. Notice the context of the copy and how the message is presented. Look for places where you can add variety by using the dynamics of pacing, energy, attitude, tone of voice, and emotion. Look for natural breaks, shifts of attitude or emotion, and transitions in the copy. Look for *catchphrases* that reveal your character's attitude, emotion, or feelings.

By the time you read a script through once or twice, you should be able to make some solid choices for your performance. You should know who the one person is you are speaking to (the *audience*); who you are as the speaker (your *character*); and what you are responding to, or why you are speaking the words in the script at this moment in time (your *back story*).

MAPPING YOUR PERFORMANCE

Marking your script with specific notations can help you create a map of how you will deliver it. These markings are your personal cues to guide you through an effective performance of the copy.

Practice marking magazine or newspaper articles or short stories and you will quickly find a system that works for you. In a short time, you will refine your system to a few key markings which you can use regularly to guide you through almost any script.

Here are a few suggested markings and possible uses. Adapt, modify and add to them as you like:

- Underline (_____)—emphasize a word, phrase, or descriptive adjectives
- Circle (O)—key elements of conflict in the script
- Box (□)—the peak moment in the copy—put a box around the words or phrase at that point in the copy
- Highlight (�) or different color underline—resolution or non-resolution of conflict
- Arrow pointing UP (➚)—take inflection on a word up
- Arrow pointing DOWN (➘)—take inflection on a word down
- Wavy line (~~~)—modulate your voice or inflection
- Slash or double slash (//)—indicate a pause

One of the most common markings is to simply underline a word that needs to be made important. This works fine in most cases, but there may be times when you want to make sure you say a word correctly. Try underlining only the syllable of the word that needs emphasis. For example: <u>de</u>fense or de<u>fense</u>.

The degree to which you mark your script may vary from project to project, but it will certainly help to have a system in place when you need it.

Wood Shed Your Script to be More Believable

Just as you have a personality, so does the character written into every script. The character for a single-voice script is often simply that of an announcer or spokesperson delivering a sales pitch, or communicating basic information. But, even this "announcer" has a personality that is appropriate to the copy. He or she needs to be perceived as a real person talking to another real person.

For all types of copy, finding the personality of the character you are playing allows you to lend authenticity to the role which gives the character life and helps make your performance believable. Your performance must include variety, tension, conflict, and sincerity. It must also be easy to listen to and be in a style that the audience can relate to. Making your performance believable is what voice acting is all about.

CHARACTER ANALYSIS: Core Element #3

The role you play in a voiceover performance may be defined simply by the manner in which the words are written, or the context may be vague, leaving it up to you to create something. Scripts written for specific or stereotyped characters may have some direction written on the script for the purpose of helping you to understand the writer's vision of the story. Phrases like like: "read with an English accent," "cowboy attitude," or "edgy and nervous," or references to other actors who have the "sound" the writer is looking for may are common. It will then be up to you to create an appropriate attitude and voice for that character.

In theater, this process of defining the attitude and personality of a character is called a *character analysis*. As a voice actor, you need to know as much about the role you are playing as possible. The more details you include in your character analysis, and the more you understand your character, the better you will be able to take an attitude and personality to "become" that character for your performance. Or, to put it another way, the more you understand the character in your copy, the easier it will be for you to find those emotions, attitudes, and personality traits within you that you can use to create your character and bring life to the words in the script.

The target audience, the mood or attitude of the copy, the writing style, and any descriptive notes all give you valuable information about your role. As with other parts of the wood shedding process, character analysis is something that will become automatic in time. Once you know what to look for, you will soon be able to define your character after reading through the copy once or twice.

Voice acting does not require the same sort of in-depth, detailed character analysis that might be necessary for a theatrical performer. However, to be believable, you do need to have a good idea of the character you are portraying. Here are some things to look for and consider as you read through your copy to define your character:

- Who is this character talking to? (target audience)
- What is the environment for the copy? (mood)
- What is the character's age? (young, old, middle-aged)
- How does the character stand? (straight and tall, hunched over, arms crossed, hands on hips, etc.)
- Where is the character from? (geographic region, country)
- Does the character speak with an accent or in a dialect? (If so, what would be the country of origin? A poorly done dialect or accent can have negative results unless done as a parody or characterization.)
- How would the character dress? (business suit, or casual)
- What do you know (or can guess) about the character's economic status? (financially well-off, struggling, etc.)
- What is the overall mood or attitude of the copy? (fast-paced, slow and relaxed, romantic feel, emotional, aggressive, etc.)
- What is the pace of the copy? (Slow-paced copy often calls for

a relaxed type of character while fast-paced copy demands a character with more energy.)

- From the context of the script, what do you know about the way your character moves? (energy)
- What is the product or service? (The subject of the copy often dictates a specific type of character.)
- What is the character's purpose, or role, in the script? (protagonist, antagonist, delivering the message, part of a story script, comedic role, that of straight-man)
- What life events or actions brought the character to this moment in time? (theatrical back story)
- What is your character responding to? (back story)
- What does the character want from telling the story? (desires)

Finding answers to questions like these will help you develop a visual image of your character that will help you to instinctively know what is needed to deliver the copy effectively and believably. You will know, for example, if the character needs to speak quickly or slowly, with an accent, or with an attitude.

Creating a visual image of your character and the environment in which the conversation is taking place will help to develop the necessary tension for drama. The tension here is not between characters, but rather a physical tension located somewhere in your body. It is this tension that will allow you to bring energy to the words and give life to the character in the copy.

Discovering the character in the copy may appear to be a lengthy process, but, in fact, it happens quickly once you know what to look for. Character development is further discussed in Chapter 11, "The Character in the Copy."

FIND THE BACK STORY: Core Element #2

All copy has a back story, also known as "the moment before." There are two definitions for back story: the first is theatrical back story, which refers to the life experience of the character that brought him or her to the moment of the story. The second definition of back story is what we use in voiceover: that is, the specific event or action to which our character is responding.

No matter how you define it, the back story is the result of the wants and needs of the character that provides the motivation for the words, actions, and reactions to what happens throughout the story.

In theater, the back story, or what brought a character to this moment in time, is frequently unveiled during the course of the performance. With voiceover copy, there is rarely enough time to reveal the back story or provide much character development. A radio commercial must tell a complete story with a beginning, middle, and an end—and with fully developed characters from the outset—all in a very short period of time.

In a dialogue script, you will often be able to figure out the back story with ease simply because the interactions between characters are written into the script. It is these interactions and responses that reveal clues to the back story and the relationship between characters.

It can be more of a challenge with a single-voice script in which there may be few, if any, clues that reveal what brought your character to the point of speaking the words in the copy, or even why, or to what your character is responding. If a back story is not clear from the copy, make one up! After all, you are an actor and you do have permission to pretend.

The idea is to create a believable motivation for your character. The back story will reveal your character's wants and needs at this moment in time, and that information will help guide you in your delivery. The fastest way to do this is to figure out what your character is responding to with the first few words of the script.

Define the back story and what the character wants in just a few words. Keep it concise, believable, and real.

UNVEIL THE CONFLICT

Conflict is an essential part of dialogue copy, and is often also present in a single-voice script that tells a story. Conflict rarely occurs in information-based copy in which the message is less of a story and more of a sales pitch or instructional in nature. Conflict creates drama, and drama holds interest.

A dialogue script without conflict will be boring and uninteresting. On the other hand, a dialogue script with a well-defined conflict can be funny, emotional, heartwarming, and informative—all at the same time. Look for the primary conflict in the script. Usually, this will be some difference of opinion, a crisis, an impasse, or some other obstacle. Define this primary conflict in a few concise words.

Now look for any complications that support or exaggerate the conflict. These are often secondary or minor conflicts that serve to add meaning and importance to the primary conflict.

Follow the development of the conflict to reveal its peak moment, or climax. It will usually be found immediately prior to the resolution or non-resolution of the conflict. The *peak moment* is often the point in the copy where the advertiser's name is mentioned or the purpose of the commercial is revealed.

Script Analysis Worksheet

Answering the following questions, based on the copy, will help you discover the audience you are speaking to, your character, and any special attitude you need to incorporate into your performance.

Who is the advertiser or client? _____

_____

What is the product or service? _____

_____

What is the delivery style?
- ☐ Fast and punchy ☐ Conversational/friendly ☐ Relaxed/mellow
- ☐ Single voice   ☐ Dialogue/multiple   ☐ Character/animation
- ☐ Authoritative   ☐ Business-to-business   ☐ Narration

Who is the advertiser/client trying to reach (target AUDIENCE)? Determine the age range, income, gender, buying habits, and any other specific details that become apparent from the way the script is written. Who is the "other person" you are talking to? Visualize this individual as you perform the copy.

_____

_____

_____

Find important key words or catchphrases where the use of dynamics of loudness or emotion will give value and importance. Look for the advertiser's name, product, descriptive adjectives, and an address or phone number. These elements may need special attention during your performance. Underline or highlight the words or phrases you want to make important.

What is the message the advertiser/client wants to communicate to the target audience? What is the story you are telling through your performance? What is the USP (unique selling proposition)?

_____

_____

How does the story (plot) develop? For dialogue copy, find the setup, the conflict, and how the conflict is resolved or not resolved. Discover how the plot flows. Are there any attitude changes with your character or others? Plot development is critical to effective dialogue copy. Determine your role in the plot and how your character develops.

_____

_____

Use up and down arrows to indicate copy points for changes in inflection or attitude.

What is your role (CHARACTER in the story) in terms of how the story is being told? Do a basic character analysis to define your character's age, lifestyle, clothing, speaking style, attitude toward the product or situation in the script, etc. What are your character's motivations? What are your character's WANTS and NEEDS (DESIRES) at *this moment in time*? What happened immediately before the copy to which your character is responding (BACK STORY)? Be as detailed as you can in order to discover your character.

How does your character relate to any other characters in the script, or to the audience in general? Is your character an active player in telling the story (as in a dialogue commercial), or is your character that of a narrator imparting information to a captive audience (as in a single-voice "spokesperson" commercial)? What can you do to create a bond between your character, other characters in the script, and the audience?

What can you do to make your character believable? Any special vocal treatments or physical attitudes?

Does your character have any unique or interesting attitudes, body postures, or speaking characteristics (speaks slowly, fast, with an accent, squeaky voice, etc.)? If so, identify these.

Study the copy for pauses that might be used to create tension or drama, and for places to breathe. This is especially important for industrial copy, which frequently contains long, run-on sentences with technical terminology. Mark breaths and pauses with a slash mark (/).

Find the rhythm of the copy. All copy has a rhythm, a beat, and timing. Discover the proper timing for the copy you are reading. Dialogue copy has a separate rhythm for each character as well as an interactive rhythm.

Look for transitions in the script (similar to attitude changes). These may be transitions from asking a question to providing an answer (common in commercial copy), or a transition between the attitudes of your character.

Look for key words you can give importance to, and that will connect you with the audience. Personal pronouns, such as "you," "our," "my," and "I," may be written into the script or simply implied. If connecting words are implied, find a way to make that implied connection through your performance (without actually saying the words).

DISCOVER THE RESOLUTION OR NON-RESOLUTION OF THE CONFLICT

In commercial copy, it is through the resolution or non-resolution of the conflict that the message is expressed. Sometimes ending a commercial with an unresolved conflict can create a memorable impression in the mind of the listener. An unresolved conflict leaves the end of the story up to the listener's imagination, and that can be a very powerful motivation for action. For example, a radio commercial we produced for the high-end toy store, Toy Smart, presented a conflict between a mother and her "child." As the story developed, the mother tried to coax her "child" to eat his green beans with less than satisfactory results. This conflict resolved when the "child" turned out to be the husband who said "I'll be happy to eat all the green beans you want, as long as you put them with a T-bone steak!" However, at the very end of the commercial, the husband had one more line, which left the conflict in a state of non-resolution: "What do I get if I eat all my brussels sprouts?" This left the resolution of the conflict to the imagination of the listener and created a memorable impact moment in the commercial.

Look for details in the copy that give clues as to how the message is actually communicated. Are there a series of gags, jokes, or a play on words that lead to expression of the message? Do characters in the copy shift roles (reversals)? Is there a list of information that ends with an unusual twist? Does the story take place in an unusual location? Is there something in the story that appears to be out of context with what is taking place? Is there a personality problem or physical limitation with one or more of the characters? How are these resolved—or not?

DISCOVER THE UNIQUE SELLING PROPOSITION (USP)

In all advertising, at some point during the course of developing a story line, the primary benefit will be revealed. Something will be stated that positions the company, product or service as being uniquely better than or different from the competition. This is the advertiser's *positioning statement.* It could be a sentence, a paragraph, or, in some cases, the entire message.

But somewhere within that larger statement will be a singular concept or idea that sets the product, service, or company apart from its competition. This singular "idea" is the *unique selling proposition,* or USP. It might be a descriptive adjective, a complete sentence, or simply a short slogan and it's usually not hard to find.

As you wood shed your copy, pay particular attention to the USP. Not only is it important in terms of the overall message, but when you understand the uniqueness of whatever it is you are talking about, that knowledge, alone, can shade your entire performance. Your understanding the unique aspect of the message will open up opportunities for you to communicate on a much deeper emotional level. And when you reach your audience on an emotional level, they will be much more likely to remember the message and take action.

MAKE THE COPY YOUR OWN

As you analyze a script, remember that there are no right or wrong answers to the questions you ask, and there are no good or bad choices. Use your imagination and bring something of yourself into the copy. The idea is to create a believable character and situation for the copy you are reading. Bringing your personal experience into the character you create will aid in making him or her real to the listener.

Use what you learn from the copy and the tools at your disposal to make the copy your own. If you have a naturally dry and sarcastic style, you may be able to apply that trait to your character to make it unique. If you have a bubbly speaking style, that trait might give a unique twist to a character. Don't be afraid to experiment and play with different approaches to performing a character.

On the surface, "making the copy your own" may appear to be a contradiction. After all, according to Core Element #6, *Forget Who You Are and Focus*, one of our objectives is to get out of our way to allow the character to become real. But bringing part of your own personality or attitude to your character can actually make it easier to create an interesting and compelling performance.

CREATE TENSION

It is important to be specific when defining a scene or character and to commit to the choices you make. Using specific terms creates tension in your body that can be heard in your voice. Without tension you will be unable to create drama, which is essential for capturing and holding the attention of the listener.

To create tension in your body, begin by observing your feelings and emotions as you read the copy. Allow your senses to be open to experience whatever sensations might appear and make a mental note of where that sensation occurred in your body. As you begin to add life to your character, recall the memory of the sensation you just experienced (*sense memory*). Focus on placing your voice or performance at that place in your body. This technique may be somewhat difficult to master at first, but keep working at it—the result is truly amazing once you have the knack of doing it.

LOOK FOR QUESTION MARKS IN THE COPY

Question marks are opportunities for dramatic punctuation. I'm not referring to the punctuation mark—?. I'm referring to words or phrases in the copy that give you the opportunity to ask a question. If the copy specifically asks a question, you should make that clear with your performance either through an upward inflection typical of asking a question, or making it clear that the question is rhetorical through your tone of voice. Question marks that do not ask questions are usually found in sentences that describe or explain something. Someplace in the sentence there will be an opportunity to answer the unasked question.

Find those opportunities, ask the questions, and figure out your own answers to the questions. This wood shedding technique can be incredibly useful to bring your character to life because the answers you come up with are part of the character's knowledge or history, which helps make the character real.

One of the secrets to using this technique is to break down your search for question marks to single words or very short phrases. The more precise you can be with the questions you ask and the answers you come up with, the more subtext you will be creating for your performance. Your answers really do not need to have anything to do with the context of the script. The important thing is that you have some sort of subtext for the words as you speak them.

Look for the questions in this 30-second radio script and come up with some answers. As you work through the script, notice how the questions you ask and the answers you arrive at affect your character and interpretation of the story.

> Have you ever started a relationship and then discovered the truth? I was thinking about working with an agent to sell my home, but then I found out about their high commissions! Not my idea of a great relationship. Then I discovered MyOpenHouse.com I can get my home listed with an agent and save up to 40% on their commission. It's like the best of both worlds—professional help, and a really low commission. MyOpenHouse.com. Now that's a relationship I can live with!

Now, let's break down that script to see where some possible question marks in the copy might be present:

Have you ever started *(what does it mean to get started?)* **a relationship** *(What kind of relationship?)* **– and then discovered the truth?** *(What truth? And HOW DOES IT FEEL to discover that kind of truth?)* **I was thinking about working with an agent** *(what kind of agent?)* **to sell my home,** *(What kind of home?)* **but then I found out about their high commissions!** *(How high?)* **Not my idea of a great relationship.** *(What is a great relationship?)* **Then I discovered MyOpenHouse.com!** *(How does it feel to make a great discovery?)* **I can get my home** *(What does "home" mean to you?)* **listed with an agent,** *(What is that like?)* **and <u>save</u> up to 40% on their commission.** *(How does it feel to save that much?)* **It's like the best of both worlds – professional help,** *(What does "professional" mean to you?)* **and a really low commission.** *(How does that feel?)* **MyOpenHouse.com. Now that's a relationship I can live with!** *(How long will this last?)*

You can take this process as far as you like, even to the point of asking questions about every word in the script. As you choose the answers to the unasked questions, you will create the foundation of your character's attitude and personality, and a context for your performance. Commit to the answers you come up with and use them to give your character life. However, be prepared to modify your answers as your character develops and you receive direction.

Tips for Wood Shedding

- Develop your wood shedding skills so they become automatic.
- Look under the surface to discover the subtlety and nuance of copy.
- Don't settle on your first choices.
- Always experiment and test different options for delivery of a line.
- Explore emotion, attitude, pacing, rhythm, tempo, and so on to reveal alternative choices.
- Look for key words and catchphrases.
- Mark your script with a pencil. It is inevitable that at least some of your choices will change.
- Be careful not to over-analyze your script. Over-analysis can result in a flat delivery.
- Find a way to deliver the first line in a way that gets the listener's attention and evolve your telling of the story using the *interrupt, engage, educate*, and *offer* concept.
- Look for the Unique Selling Proposition in advertising copy.

In this Chapter

 Scan these response codes for more information or visit the AOVA Extras section at **VoiceActing.com**.

Penny Abshire—Characters in My Pocket

11

The Character
in the Copy

How Will You Play the Role?

Are you a voice actor? Or are you a voice talent? There's a big difference! These seemingly similar references to our craft are, in reality, radically different approaches to performing and working with a script.

When you are performing a voiceover script as a voice actor, you are playing a role, no different than if you were playing a part in a stage play or movie. That's why this craft is called *voice acting!* Unless you are telling your own personal story, the words and situations are not yours—they are those of a character who may be substantially different from you. To play the role of any character believably requires training and developing the ability to detach personal beliefs and attitudes from those of the character being portrayed. This is the essence of all acting.

On the other hand, there are many talented individuals who make a good living from performing with their voice, but who have little or no training or acting ability. For these individuals, or "voice talent," the opportunities for voiceover work will be limited simply because they are seen by casting directors and producers as only being able to do one thing or have only one sound.

The focus of this chapter will be on the voice actor who, by definition, has studied the craft of acting and has developed the ability to create a variety of believable characters.

THE TWO TYPES OF ACTORS

Whether you work behind a microphone, on stage, on television, or in film, there are two distinctly different approaches to performing and creating characters. One is where the actor develops a strong and highly identifiable performing style that is at the foundation of every role. The style may be one of a specific voice characteristic, physical appearance, performance rhythm, underlying attitude or body movement. I refer to actors in this category as *celebrity actors*. When these actors perform, we have no doubt in our mind that we are watching that person perform. We become involved with their performance, in part, because their acting style is completely appropriate for the roles they choose to play. In other words, no matter what the role, their characters are believable, largely because there is some aspect of the character role that is very similar to the actor. Some film actors I would place in this category are Jack Nicholson, Christian Slater, Adam Sandler, Tom Cruise, Keanu Reeves, Cameron Diaz, and Jennifer Lopez.

Many highly successful voiceover talent frame their performance through an interpretation of each script based on skill and instincts developed over many years. Although many of these performers have the ability to create a wide range of vocal styles, emotions, and attitudes, their performance comes more from who they are, than by creating a unique character for each role they play.

Some acting courses teach that the actor should bring as much of his or her self to the performance as possible, and design their performance on how *they* would handle the situations, based on personal experience and interpretation. If you are merely "being you" as you perform a script, even on an extended level, then your performance may risk sounding like **_you_** doing the words, and there may, or may not, be anything unique or special about your performance. Now, you may be an excellent reader with a talent for interpreting or spinning a phrase, or you may posses an incredible vocal resonance and command when you speak, but if you are personally attached to the words of the script, you are not truly acting by creating a character.

The other approach to performing is one in which a wide range of acting skills and abilities is developed which allows the actor to literally create many different emotions, attitudes, and personalities that are outside of who they really are. Actors who have mastered this approach literally become the character they are playing. As we watch or listen to them, we see the character they have created, not the person they are. I refer to these actors as *character actors*. I consider Jim Carrey, Jodie Foster, Drew Barrymore, Tom Hanks, Dustin Hoffman, Meryl Streep, and Robin Williams all excellent examples of actors who truly become the characters they are playing. In the world of voiceover, many of the best known and highest paid voice actors have developed the ability to create a variety of uniquely different voices and personalities for the characters they play.

Both approaches to voiceover work are completely valid, and both offer potential for success. However, it's important to understand the differences because your individual abilities may direct you to follow one path or the other. Not everyone working in voiceover is a voice actor. For example, if you have very strong personal or religious beliefs, you may discover that it is very difficult to separate yourself from those beliefs in order to create a believable character that has opposing beliefs or attitudes.

No matter how hard you might try, you may not be able to create a sense of truth as you speak the words. If this is true for you, then the path of mastering performing skills as an actor may not be for you. You must follow a different path, with different training that will give you the skills to base your interpretation and performance of a script on who you are. You will need to develop a deep understanding of your innermost self, and you will need to learn how to tell a compelling story from the perspective of *you* as the story teller. You will need to learn how to be a masterful reader of stories, rather than a creator of characters who tell their stories.

The ability to read a script with a powerful interpretation is no less a skill than that of a voice actor creating and playing a believable character. In voiceover, performers with these heightened reading and interpretive skills commonly refer to themselves as voice artists or voice talent. Those who develop the skills for creating compelling characters can accurately refer to themselves as voice actors. Both performing styles are common, but the trend in most areas of voiceover has been moving toward voice acting.

THE DILEMMA

A common dilemma with performers just learning the craft of acting is the thought that they are "lying" or being "untruthful" when they perform the role of a character who expresses thoughts, ideas, beliefs, or opinions that may be radically different from their own. Or they feel guilty when they are getting paid to read a script for a product they don't believe in. By definition, the term "actor" simply means *playing the role of a character.* There is nothing in the definition that implies that the performer is lying, cheating, or being dishonest in any manner. In fact, the underlying precept of all forms of acting is that it is the actor's job to create a believable reality of the moment for the character he or she is playing. The dilemma occurs because the neophyte actor is confusing their personal beliefs with those of the character they are playing. Without a disconnect of personal beliefs, it is extremely difficult to create a believable and compelling character. This disconnect, or momentarily forgetting who you are, is essential and necessary in all forms of acting, including voice acting. And, in some situations, it can be difficult to achieve.

So, as a voice actor, should you take any job offered to you, regardless of the message or its ultimate purpose? Of course not! Your personal beliefs, ethics, and philosophy should certainly be factors in choosing your performance material. All scripts are not right for all voice actors. Even if you are a highly skilled reader, there will be many scripts crossing your desk that are not appropriate, either for your style of delivery, or in their content. Ultimately, it is up to each individual performer to choose the jobs they will accept. As with anything else in life, some choices will be better than others.

Your Best Tool is Your Own Personality

Whether you approach your voiceover work as a voice actor or as a voice talent, the best tool you have to define a character or discover an interpretation is your own personality. When you know yourself, you can tap into parts of your personality to more effectively tell the story and give life to the character in the copy.

Personality analysis is a subject that has been studied for thousands of years. Hippocrates developed a system for defining personality, which placed individuals into four personality types with dominant (sanguine and choleric) and recessive (melancholic and phlegmatic) traits. The Hippocrates system of personality analysis was very restrictive in its definitions of personality types but it did provide a basic structure within which people could be placed.

More recently the psychologists of our world have developed highly refined methods of determining specific personality types. Some of their studies have shown that personality is largely a result of the chemical makeup of the brain. Cultural upbringing and conditioning further contribute to personality development.

There are many excellent books available that will help you discover some fascinating aspects of your personality. Many of these books are written as aids to improving relationships or developing self-awareness. Three excellent personality books are: *Please Understand Me: Character and Temperament Types* by David Keirsey and Marilyn Bates (1984); *Are You My Type, Am I Yours* by Renee Baron and Elizabeth Wagele (1995); and *Dealing with People You Can't Stand* by Dr. Rick Brinkman and Dr. Rick Kirschner (2002). Another approach to understanding personality types is through the *Enneagram*. There are many books on this subject, among them, *Personality Types: Using the Enneagram for Self-Discovery* by Ross Hudson and Don Richard Riso (1996). These books look at personality types from different points of view and offer some fascinating reading.

An advertiser's understanding of who buys their company's products is crucial when it comes to a marketing campaign. Your understanding of yourself is equally necessary when it comes to creating a character that will effectively communicate the message in the advertiser's copy. The best way for you to learn more about yourself is to ask questions and find the most appropriate answers. Based on your answers, you will be able to determine some of your dominant and recessive personality traits.

Most studies of personality type start with several basic categories, then divide those into subcategories. Every person has characteristics in several categories, but certain areas are dominant, and others are recessive. The following simple questions will give you an idea of some basic personality differences.

- Do you respond to problems emotionally, or do you think about them before responding?
- Do you have a strong need to express yourself creatively, or do you prefer quiet activities?
- Do you avoid unpleasant emotions (including fear), or are you inclined to take risks?
- Do you rely on your instincts for information, or do you rely on what you see and hear?
- Do you seek approval from authority figures, or do you rebel?
- Do you play the role of a nurturer, or do you treat others in a detached manner?
- Do you express anger readily? Are you accommodating and out of touch with your anger, or do you see anger as a character flaw?
- Do you prefer literal writing or a more figurative writing style?
- Are you more realistic or speculative?
- Do emotions impress you more, or do principles?
- Are you attracted to creative, imaginative people, or to more sensible, structured people?
- Do you tend to arrive at events early, or are you generally late?
- Do you do things in the usual way, or in your own way?

- Do you feel better having made a purchase or having the option to purchase?
- Do you operate more from facts or from principles?
- Do you find it easy to speak to strangers, or is this difficult?
- Are you fair-minded or sympathetic?
- Do you prefer planned activities or unplanned activities?

Your answers to these and other questions will only scratch the surface of your personality. When you gain an in-depth understanding of who you are, you will be ahead of the game when it comes to creating a marketable style. When you understand yourself, you will be able to tap into some of the core elements of your own personality as you create a unique character. Discovering the essence of who you are is the first step in developing acting skills that will allow you to create believable and compelling characters.

THE TWO BOXES

In our VoiceActing Academy Workshops, I teach the concept of *The Two Boxes.* You and the character you are playing each live in a box. You are very comfortable within the walls of your box. Your box contains all of your life experience, belief system, habits, behaviors, attitudes, emotions, feelings, knowledge, wisdom, and more. The box your character lives in contains all the same stuff you have in your box, only it's those of the character—not yours. The character's box may be larger or smaller than your box, and the character you will portray is very comfortable within the walls of his or her box.

You need to understand the real you and how you exist in your box before you can fully understand how your character exists in his or her box.

As an actor, your job is to climb out of your box and into the box of your character. You bring everything from your box with you except the box itself. You separate yourself from the confines of the walls of your box as you enter the box of your character. Everything you bring with you is available as tools that can be used to help bring the character to life.

If your character's box is larger than yours, you need to be aware of this in order to allow yourself to behave believably as the character. Learning how to do this may be uncomfortable at first, but that's only because your comfort level is relative to existing within your box and you've not yet grown comfortable in a bigger or smaller box. The path to becoming comfortable in the character's box is through the use of the many acting and performing techniques you've learned from this and other acting books, acting classes, and improvisation classes.

Once you've climbed into your character's box, you need to let go of the real you and experience how the character you are portraying lives and behaves. There will always be a part of you there to make your character real. In a very real sense, when you create a character, you are tapping into that part of you where the character lives.

This is the commonality between you and the character. It's the stuff you brought with you from your box that also exists as the same, or very similar, stuff in your character's box. Those things in your character's box that are different from anything in your box must be created through your performance. But in order to achieve this, you must know what they are, and have some way to create them. This is why basic training in acting and performing technique is an essential part of the study of voice acting.

A mastery of this process results in a truly believable character that you can create on demand without thinking about what you are doing. This is what Core Element #6, *Forget Who You Are and Focus* is all about.

Theater of the Mind

Voice acting is *theater of the mind*. You do not have the advantage of props, flashy lighting, wardrobe, makeup or scenery. All you have are the words on a piece of paper, and your individual creativity. From the words alone, you must create an illusion of reality in the mind of your audience. In order for you to create a believable illusion, you need to know what is going on in the mind of the character you are playing. To learn what is going on in the character's mind, you need to fully understand the script. You also need to know your character's role in the story, and his or her relationships to other characters, objects, and the product or service.

To create effective theater of the mind, your performance must reflect real life, exhibit some sort of tension, contain something the listener can relate to, and have a sense of honesty and a ring of truth. These are all elements of good theater and should be incorporated into any voice acting performance, regardless of the type of copy or the length of the project.

When creating a character for your performance, keep in mind the following basic elements of good theater:

- Interesting characters with wants and needs "at this moment in time"
- A story or sequence of events that builds and leads to a climax
- Conflict in one or more forms

- Resolution or nonresolution of the conflict, usually in an interesting or unexpected manner
- Closure in which any loose ends are satisfactorily resolved

Uncover these elements in a voiceover script and you will be able to understand your character better.

An Exercise for Creating Real Characters

Visualization is a powerful technique that can help bring your characters to life, and this exercise will do just that! The first time I used this exercise in my workshop, the result was amazing. We witnessed a total transformation and the student, who was having difficulty finding the proper voice and attitude, was able to create a completely believable character that she did not know existed within her. As I've mentioned before, for a character in a script to be "real" to a listener, everything about the character must flow through you just as if you were the character.

Once understood, the following visualization process can take as little as only a few seconds to a minute or so. However, as you learn this technique you may want to spend some additional time relaxing your body and mind prior to doing this exercise. Of course, in an actual session you won't have much time for a lengthy visualization, but by then the process should be second nature.

Define your character in as much detail as you possibly can, including physical appearance, clothing, hair, posture, mannerisms, and other features. Begin by thoroughly wood shedding your script and making choices for your audience, back story, and character. Visualize this character in your imagination. This character description and image will become important later on, so don't skimp on the details.

You may find it helpful to do this as a guided visualization by scanning this response code, listening to the audio file in the AOVA Extras section at **VoiceActing.com**, or recording the script yourself. Take your time with this, and don't rush it. The clearer and more vivid the visualization, the better the results, and the more believable your character will be.

At first glance, this visualization may seem a bit unusual. However, when you give it a try, you may be surprised at what you are able to come up with, not only with physical changes, but also with the sound of your voice that results from creating a believable character.

Visualization Script for "Creating a Character"

With your character in mind, close your eyes and take a slow deep breath through your nose. Fill your lungs completely. Exhale slowly through your mouth to relax. Repeat with another long deep breath ... and slowly exhale. Don't forget to keep breathing.

Imagine yourself standing in front of the microphone, or in the voiceover booth. See yourself in your imagination—it's as though you are observing yourself from across the room. Create the image of yourself as clearly as you possibly can, in whatever manner works for you. When you have a sense of seeing yourself standing in the room, take another long deep breath ... and slowly exhale.

Now, imagine the character you will be playing coming into the scene in your imagination. See the character walking in. Notice how the character is walking. Observe the posture and physical movement. Notice what the character is wearing: What do the clothes look like? What kind of shoes is your character wearing? Is your character wearing glasses or jewelry?

As you observe this scene, see yourself look at your character's face. Notice any facial details, color of the eyes, appearance of the skin. Does your character appear to present any sort of attitude or have interesting facial expressions? When you have a clear image of the character in your imagination, take a long deep breath ... and slowly exhale.

Now, as you are observing the two of you in the room, imagine seeing the real you step out of your body and come to the place from where you are observing. As the real you steps out of your body, imagine the character stepping into your body. Everything about the character is now reflected in your body: The character's posture, the way the character stands and moves, the character's physical appearance, facial expressions, and mental attitude. Everything about the character is now expressed through your body, mind, and voice.

Allow yourself to fully experience this transformation. Notice any tension in your body. Be aware of how you feel as this character—physically, mentally, and emotionally. When you have a sense of the transformation, take a slow deep breath; exhale, maintain the physical, emotional, and mental state; open your eyes, and begin speaking the words in your script.

Making Your Characters Believable

FIND THE MUSIC

There is *music* in your daily conversations, and there is a great deal of music in any voice acting performance. Some of the basic elements of music are pitch, tempo, rhythm, volume, quality, and intonation—all of which are present in every sentence you speak.

It is the music of your performance that will convey the subtlety and nuance of the meaning behind the words. Find the music in the way your character speaks and you will create a believable character. Chapter 16, "Mastering Character Voices," explains in detail how to find and sustain interesting and musical character voices.

STUDY OTHER PERFORMERS

Study film and television actors. Observe how they deliver their lines and interact with other characters. Listen to the dynamics of their voices. Notice that most actors use a lot of vocal variety and inflection. They also move and express emotion physically as well as verbally. Mimic what you see other actors do and how they speak so you can get the experience of what they are doing. Study their techniques and apply them to your style. You will soon find the point where your stretch becomes uncomfortable. To grow as a performer, you need to find a way to work past that boundary.

STRETCH YOUR BOUNDARIES AND BE WILLING TO RISK

Be willing to experiment and risk moving beyond your comfort zone (Core Element #7, *Gamble*). Practice the techniques to develop the skills that will make moving outside of your comfort zone easier. Don't worry about how you will appear or sound to anybody! As a voice actor, your job is to perform the copy and your character in the best manner possible. Leave your inhibitions, personal judgments and self-conscious attitudes outside the studio door.

Stretch beyond what feels comfortable. It is better to stretch too far than not far enough. It is easier for a director to pull you back after setting a character that is too far out there, than it is to stretch you further. Remember, there is no right or wrong way to perform. Everything you do is simply a choice. Each performer is unique and different techniques work better for different performers. Do what works best for you to make your performance real and believable.

As you stretch your abilities, you will probably feel uncomfortable at first. Remember to be non-judgmental and to not worry about how well you are doing. Each of us has an individual concept of some point at which we feel we would be going too far, or over the edge. Practice taking yourself just a little bit over that line until you begin to feel uncomfortable. Then take yourself a little bit further. The more you move beyond the point of discomfort, the faster you will develop the ability to create any character.

You must be willing to risk total failure. Intend to perform to the best of your abilities. Become the character and do whatever it takes to make the character real, even if that character is an extension of your own personality. Remember that you are uniquely you, and that you are interesting just as you are. Also remember that the people you are working with have insecurities of their own and may actually know less about the business than you do. Know that you know what you are doing. If you never risk, you can never learn. Use each audition or session as a learning experience. Keep an attitude of always being in training.

MAKE EVERY TIME THE FIRST TIME

Make each and every performance seem as if it is the first time. It is very easy to get sloppy by take 27. Take 28 should sound as fresh and real as take one—only better. Unless your director tells you otherwise, you should maintain the same energy and attitude for each take. Use the director's guidance as a tool to help you focus in on your best performance. Add a little spin to a word, or shift your emphasis here or there with each take, but keep your energy and attitude consistent. This becomes very important to the editor who needs to put the final project together long after you have gone. Variations in your performance energy can stand out very clearly if you are not consistent, and make the editor's job a nightmare.

CHARACTER HAS PRECEDENCE OVER COPY

As you learn how to create believable characters, you will discover that your characters may want to say and do things in a certain way. After all, if the characters you create say things exactly the way you do, what would be the purpose of creating the character?

To be real, each character you create must have its own personality, mannerisms, thought processes, and speaking style. Every subtlety and nuance of your character contributes to its believability. Forcing your character to say or do something that is not appropriate will instantly take your performance out of character.

Scripts are often written with a specific attitude, phrasing, or delivery style in mind, yet what the writer had in mind may not be what ends up being recorded. Provided your delivery is *in character*, it is perfectly acceptable, for example, to contract or un-contract words that aren't written that way. This is closely related to the idea of changing or removing punctuation marks and other techniques intended to help create a more natural and conversational delivery.

Your objective as a voice actor is to bring your character to life, and you should strive to do whatever is necessary to create that reality. You can't change the words in the script, but you can change the way you say the words. The way your character speaks will always have precedence over the written script. This will be true until the director tells you otherwise.

ACT PROFESSIONAL

Play the part! Enter a studio—yes, even your home studio—with the attitude of a professional there to do a job and with the confidence that the character you create will be exactly right. Be friendly, cooperative, and ready to work. Making money does not make you a professional. Acting professionally makes you money. When you act like a pro, the people hiring you will believe that you are a pro and they will respect you. Remember that this business is all about creating believability in the mind of the audience. When you enter a studio, your first audience will be the people who hired you. Make them believe you are good at what you do and prove it with your performance.

Become the child you once were! Pretend! Play! Have fun!

Tips for Performing All Types of Copy

When you become the character in the copy, you will be believable to the audience, and a suspension of disbelief will be created. When the audience suspends their disbelief in what they hear, they become more open to the message. This all starts when you discover the character in the copy.

- Don't overanalyze your copy. Overanalyzing can cause you to lose spontaneity and cause your delivery to become flat and uninteresting.
- Rely on your instincts, and trust the director in your mind to guide your delivery to keep it on track, conversational, and real.
- Learn how to listen to yourself (self-direct) as you perform.

- Tell the story. All scripts tell a story. Storytelling is always about relationships. To be believable, make the relationships appear real.

- Make your character believable and unique by adding something of yourself. Let your imagination run wild. If you believe in the reality of your performance, the audience will believe.

- Don't become so focused on your character that you lose sight of the story, the drama, and the relationships between characters and conflict.

- Internalize the wants and needs of your character, both physically and emotionally. Find the place in your body where a tension develops. Hold it there to *set your character*, and deliver your lines from that place. Use your imagination to create a vivid reality of the scene, situation, relationships, and conversation in your mind.

- For your first read-through, go very slowly with a very flat delivery. Avoid the temptation to inject interpretation. Just read the words to get a sense of the story, phrasing, and complicated words.

- Play it over-the-top as you rehearse. Use more attitude, dynamics, or energy in your delivery than you think may be necessary. You will gradually learn to hear what is too much and too little. It's much easier to pull back than to push you further out.

- Underplay, rather than overplay. Louder may not be better. Pull back, speak more softly, and be more natural. Remember, "less is more."

- Keep your posture in a stance consistent with the character and the choices you have made in regards to how your character stands, moves, and behaves. Maintain this attitude throughout your performance.

- Find the music in the copy. All copy has a tempo, rhythm, dynamics, and other musical qualities. Speak as quickly and as quietly as you would if you were talking to someone in a real conversation.

- Allow your character (even if that is you) to speak the words. Learn how to get out of your own way.

- Stay in the moment. Pick up cues. Interact with other performers. Don't let your lines become separated from those of the other performers. Listen to yourself, the director, and other performers and respond appropriately (*listen and answer*).

In this Chapter

Scan these response codes for more information or visit the AOVA Extras section at **VoiceActing.com**.

Single Voice

12

Single Voice Commercial

Commercials are <u>Not</u> About Selling

IT'S ALL ABOUT THE STORY

Single voice copy is written for a solo performer who will deliver the entire message, with the possible exception of a separate tag line which may or may not be voiced by a different performer. Because there is only one character speaking, any interaction is implied, either between the character speaking and any unheard other characters or between the performer and the listener. The most often thought of form of single-voice work is commercials. However, the vast majority of single voice work is in narration.

Radio and television commercials are all about the advertiser's story. A well-written commercial will put the advertiser's message or product in the context of a compelling story that will motivate or inspire the listener to take the desired action.

Advertising copy writers will write a commercial script to reach a specific demographic group or *target audience*. This group is usually referred to by gender and age range, for example: women, 25–35 or men 30-45. However, your performance must be focused on speaking to only one person. Knowing the broader demographic can help, but the fact that the copy writer and you, as the actor, have differing intentions, can be somewhat confusing. If you ask the writer or producer specifically who you are speaking to (the one person), she will probably not know what you are talking about or may reply in terms of the demographic group. You need to be able to quickly determine your audience based solely on the script and, if you are lucky, any additional information the producer might provide.

The target audience of a single-voice script can usually be determined pretty easily; however, sometimes it can be a challenge to define the character speaking. Well-written copy that clearly tells a story makes the character you play and the audience easy to define. Poorly written copy that contains only information in the form of facts and figures can make this difficult.

Whether it's a radio commercial or a corporate training video, consider single-voice copy as a story you are telling. Begin by making sure you fully understand the story. Then find your inner storyteller and commit to the attitude and style choices you make. Deliver the copy from a set point of view by finding the subtext (how you think and feel) behind the words you speak and express it through your voice. Study your script closely to determine if it was written to match a current trend.

One key to effective single-voice delivery is to use the basic dramatic principle of having a conversation with another person. Make the other person the ideal person who needs to hear what you have to say. Another key is to find the appropriate attitude or style. Both of these can be effective interrupts and engagements when done properly. Make your conversation natural, believable, and candid, speaking to only one person at a time. Shotgunning, trying to speak to several people at once, tends to make your delivery sound more like a speech than a conversation, although that may be appropriate for some types of copy.

TELLING THE STORY IN TIME

Commercials, by their very nature, need to be delivered within a specific time-frame with the most common broadcast lengths being :10, :15, :20, :30, and :60 and Web advertising, infomercials and other marketing messages can be of any length. If you are voicing a spot message for broadcast, your goal should be to deliver the script about one-half to a full second shorter than the length of the commercial. This allows time for production value like music and sound effects. Of course, if your delivery runs too long or short, there are editing techniques and digital time compression processes that can be used. But if you understand your body's internal timing, you should be able to deliver any script in the allotted time.

In previous chapters, I've covered many ways to wood shed a script and dozens of techniques for bringing the words to life. Now, I'm going to suggest something radically different: Try performing your script completely cold the first time through. Don't analyze the script and don't perform with any pre-conceived notions. Just let the words guide you through your interpretation. Read the script slowly, word by word, without inflection or dynamics and without any concern about timing. Well-known voice acting coach, Patrick Fraley refers to this technique as *reading like a first grader*. The idea is that as you slowly work your way through the script, you will instinctively get a sense of the story and how to tell it. You will also discover complex phrases and difficult words. Once you've got that, you can begin a more thorough script analysis to hone your performance.

SCRIPT FORMATS

Although there are a few common formats for commercial copy, there are no real standards. There can be many different written references to the performer, such as VO, ANNCR, or TALENT—and all may be used interchangeably. You may also see references to music, SFX (sound effects), and even directorial cues, which are not to be read by the performer. The format may be single or double-spaced and may or may not include a separate column for video and other instructions. Read everything on the page in order to fully understand the message and your character's role. Then quickly run through your Seven Core Elements to set your choices.

Tips for Performing Single-Voice Copy

- You are a storyteller, and stories are always about relationships. Find the relationships in the story you are telling.
- Analyze the copy for character, mood, attitude, conflict, rhythm, and so on. (See Chapter 11, "The Character in the Copy.")
- Look for the message, image, feeling, or unique quality that the advertiser wants to communicate to the listener. What separates this product or service from its competitors?
- Find the subtext, thoughts and feelings behind the words.
- Determine who the one perfect audience is and why she should be listening to what you have to say.
- Speak conversationally, having the expectation of a response. Talk <u>to</u> the other person, not at him or her. Don't "read".
- Determine the creative strategy that will enable you to build dramatic tension and allow for expression of the message. Use sense-memory techniques to locate tension in your body and speak from that place.
- Deliver the first line of copy in a way that will interrupt the listener's thoughts and bring them in to listening to your story.
- Be careful not to telegraph the message or send a message of "here comes another commercial."

Single Voice Scripts

As you work with the following scripts, you might find it interesting to read through the script before reading the copy notes.

Come up with your interpretation for attitude, pacing, character, and performance, and then read through the notes to see how close you came to what the producers of these projects intended. You'll find more scripts in the AOVA Extras section at **VoiceActing.com** or by scanning this response code. Scanning the response codes adjacent to the following scripts with your smart phone or other device will play an MP3 audio file.

FUNERALL

Title/Media: "Funerall" Demonstration :30
Style: Movie trailer, high energy and exciting
Talent: Larry Davis
Copy Notes: VO coach, talent and producer Marc Cashman produced this commercial to demonstrate how the same copy can be delivered in different ways to have a completely different impact. Explore several approaches to the script on your own, then listen to Larry Davis demonstrate his versatility as a voice actor performing three different versions. Scan the response code to hear all three versions back to back.

> In a world …
> … where people die every day …
> … there's one company …
> … that's changing the face of death!
> FunerALL.
> From coffin to crypt to cremation, we do it all!
> Delivering customer-driven solutions to the funeral service profession.
> Giving you the tools to reach your full market potential.
> With technologically advanced revenue streams …
> … that build your bottom line.
> FunerALL.
> Changing the face of death … one body at a time!

PAYCHEX TODAY

Title/Media: "New Car" Radio :30
Style: Young 20-something with mild excitement
Character: Real person, mid-20s
Talent: Jon Allen, James Alburger
Copy Notes: A slow economy can make it difficult to make ends meet. This message is intended to provide an option for those who are employed, but may need a little extra cash from time to time. No announcing or acting. Must sound real and believable.

VO: I didn't know what to do! I finally found the car I was looking for, but the guy who was selling it would only take cash and I was between paydays. Man, I'm glad I remembered Paychex. Since I have a job, I could borrow $1,000 from Paychex until I got my regular paycheck. You gotta see my car!

TAG: Call toll free 877 PAYCHEX, that's Pay Chex, with an X. No matter how bad your credit is, if you have a job you can borrow up to one thousand dollars until your next pay day, guaranteed. 877 Pay Chex. That's Pay Chex with an X. Always borrow responsibly.

LIBERTY TRUST

Title/Media: "Boise" Radio :30
Character: Laid back male or female
Talent: James Alburger
Copy Notes: This spot requires a relaxed, story teller delivery to show the value of working with a bank that puts its customers first.

Scott Carlson didn't spend his vacation in Boise with his in-laws this year! People like Scott expect a little more out of life … and they get it by being smart with their money … and working with a bank that knows how to help. These days it can make a difference. Between the kind of fun-times you've always dreamed of … and a weekend in Boise.

Expect more from your bank. Visit a Liberty Trust office near you. Open seven days a week. Liberty Trust. We want to help.

In this Chapter

Scan these response codes for more information or visit the AOVA Extras section at **VoiceActing.com**.

Multiples - Dialogue

13

Multiples & Dialogue

Types of Dialogue Copy

THE CONVERSATION

As with single-voice copy, dialogue copy involves a conversation between two or more characters. The primary difference with dialogue copy is that your one-person audience is present in the script.

Unlike most single-voice copy, dialogue usually involves a story with a specific plotline and interaction between two or more characters. It is important for you to understand the whole story, not just your part in it. If you limit your understanding to just your role, you may miss subtle details that are vital to effectively interacting with the other characters, or for creating the dramatic tension that is so necessary for giving the characters life and making them real to the listener. When two or more characters are having a conversation, I refer to it as *interactive dialogue*.

Another form of dialogue is one in which the characters are not talking to each other, but are instead speaking directly to the audience in turn. A conversation is still taking place, but in this case, it is more one-sided with each actor sharing a portion of the overall delivery. I refer to this type of dialogue as *shared information*. This is very similar to a single-voice delivery, except that in this type of performance each character is interacting primarily with the audience, but must also respond appropriately to the other character sharing information.

In the area of multi-voice ADR (automatic dialogue replacement) and looping, the dialogue lines may be adlibbed and a scene may involve many voice actors. Regardless of the structure, all dialogue requires excellent listening, timing and performing skills. Interactions between characters must be believable and timing must be correct for a dialogue performance to be accepted by the listener.

COMEDY

Comedy is a very popular form of dialogue copy. It is not the words on the page that make a script funny; it is the intent behind the words. In part, comedy is based on the unexpected—leading the audience in one direction and then suddenly changing direction and ending up someplace else. Comedy is often based on overstating the obvious or placing a totally serious character in a ludicrous situation. Comedy can also be achieved by creating a sense of discomfort in the mind of the audience.

Think of a comedy script as a slice of life—with a twist. Playing lines for laughs will never work. Laughs come only when the audience is surprised.

Rhythm and timing are essential with dialogue. A natural interaction between characters, overlapping lines, or stepping on lines, gives a more real feeling and helps set the rhythm and pace of the story. Pauses (where appropriate), and natural vocal embellishments can add naturalness.

Ask the producer or director before taking too many liberties with any copy; this is especially true with comedy dialogue. If the producer understands comedy, you may be given the freedom to experiment with your character and how you deliver your lines. Ultimately, your character should have precedence over the copy and certain ad-libs or other adaptations may be necessary to create the illusion of reality. Say your lines in a natural, conversational way, appropriate to the situation, and the comedy will happen.

To be effective, comedy dialogue must have a sense of reality, even if the situation is ludicrous and the characters are exaggerated. The following tips and suggestions will help you perform comedy copy effectively.

Tips for Performing Comedic Dialogue Copy

- Be real. Keep your character spontaneous and natural. Use a back story or lead-in line to help get into the moment.
- Find the dialogue rhythm. The rhythm for a comedic script will be different from that of a serious script.

- Humanize your character by adding natural sounds, such as "uhh," "yeah," "uh-huh," "mmm," etc. These sounds help give the feeling of a real, natural conversation. Ask before making copy changes.

- Find the *subtext*—what's going on behind the words. This is especially important with dialogue. If your character is that of a normal person in a ludicrous situation, you need to have a subtext of normalcy. If your thoughts anticipate the punch line, it will be communicated through your performance.

- Stay in the moment, listen and answer. Respond authentically to the other characters or situations that occur, expecting a response.

Dialogue and Multiple-Voice Scripts

You'll find more scripts in the AOVA Extras section at **VoiceActing.com** or by scanning this response code. Scanning the response codes adjacent to the scripts that follow with your smart phone or other device will play an MP3 audio file.

NATURE LIFE

Title/Media: "Bears" Radio :60
Target Audience: Natural food enthusiasts
Style: Conversational
Characters: Two male bears in dialogue plus 1 female host
Talent: Tom Daniels, James Alburger, Penny Abshire
Copy Notes: This is a very fast moving conversation. The characters should not be over the top, but should be believable.

Host: We're here at the National Forest with our hidden microphone to eavesdrop on a rare conversation between two grizzly bears. Let's listen in …

Bear 1:   You know, Harve, I don't get it … I've been gaining weight. I watch what I eat … I've even tried giving up hikers …

Bear 2:   Murray, I know a new way to lose weight.

Bear 1:   Stop! No more diet programs. I can't stand being hungry all the time! I get very grouchy and the wife really hates that.

Bear 2:   This isn't a diet program. Ever heard of Nature Life cereal? I … borrowed a box from some campers last week… it's really good.

Bear 1:	Isn't that the stuff that looks like twigs and leaves? And Humans eat it?
Bear 2:	Murray ... Just because Humans eat it doesn't make it bad! Besides Nature Life cereal really tastes great! Best part is ... it fills you up so you aren't hungry all the time. And when you aren't hungry ...
Bear 1:	I don't eat as much! Hey, I'd lose weight then, huh? But I'm real particular about things being natural.
Bear 2:	Murray, Murray ... Would I recommend something that wasn't 100% natural with no additives? I may be wild life, but I do have my standards!
Bear 1:	Huh ... Nature Life ... I'll try it. But ... I'm not giving up hikers ... completely.
Host:	Nature Life cereal. At a store near you.

SAN DIEGO TOURISM

Title/Media: "Summer" Radio :60
Target Audience: Men and women who travel
Style: Real person, conversational
Characters: Wife and husband plus tag announcer
Talent: Penny Abshire, James R. Alburger, Paul Bellantoni
Copy Notes: This radio spot is part of a larger campaign of radio and television ads to promote tourism in San Diego. Keep the conversation real and believable. No acting or announcing.

(SFX: Interior of a car. Cars passing. Freeway traffic)
Husband: Ahh, summer in Southern California. Great weather ...

Wife: Long days ...

Husband: What could be better?

Wife: Well, we could be going in the opposite direction.

Husband: Hey. Did I miss my exit!!??

(SFX: Big "U" turn, motor revs, tires screech, horns honk)
Wife: I'm impressed ... An eight lane U-turn!

Husband: Thanks.

Wife: What I meant was that we could be going away from the traffic and the crowds, instead of toward them.

Husband: Did you have any special direction in mind?

Wife: Yeah. That way ... San Diego.

(SFX: Swoosh of car passing)
Husband: I suppose you want to go see him again. That big gorilla.

Wife: Actually, I was thinking about Shamu ... But we could go to the zoo too. Then we could go sailing, lie on the beach ...

Husband: See a play, try out all those great restaurants ...

Wife: Explore the Gas Lamp District ...

Husband: Spend a lazy afternoon by the pool ...

(SFX: Swoosh of car passing)

Wife: You know, it would take us a week to do all that.

Husband: Let's go.

(SFX: Big "U" turn, motor revs, tires screech, horns honk)

Wife: There are people who would say you're impulsive.

Husband: Yeah. But they're not on their way to San Diego.

Wife: Yeah.

(SFX: Swoosh)

Anncr: Turn your summer around. Plan your San Diego vacation now. Visit San Diego dot com.

CHEAP TIMES

Title/Media: "Memories" Radio :60
Target Audience: Thrifty shoppers
Style: Conversational, real people, could be characterizations
Characters: 1 male, 1 female or possibly 2 M or F plus tag VO
Talent: James Alburger, Penny Abshire, Paul Bellantoni
Copy Notes: This is a friendly, competitive dialogue in which the two participants are one-upping each other with reminiscences of the good old days when things were cheap.

Male: You know, you just don't get much for your money these days. What with gas costing what it does—I can hardly afford to drive to the store, let alone buy anything. Why can't things be as cheap as they used to be?

Female: I remember back when a loaf of bread only cost a quarter.

Male: Well, I remember when things were so cheap you could get a whole meal for under a buck.

Female: Yeah? Well, my mother was so cheap she used to feed our family on 75 cents - and have leftovers the next day.

Male: MY mom used to make spaghetti out of ketchup and shoelaces! We ate it ... and we liked it.

Female: That's nothing. My dad was so cheap, he used to get free black bananas from the store and he'd tell us they were from France, and really rare! And we believed him.

Male: You think that's something? My mom was so cheap she used to make our underware out of used gunny sacks.

Female: Oh, now you're just making stuff up!

TAG: Remember when things really were cheap? Well, they are again! Visit CheapTimes dot com for great deals on the things you need today ... or remember from yesterday. CheapTimes dot com. Great stuff. Cheap prices.

SUNLAND BANK AND TRUST

Title/Media: "The Memo" Radio :60
Target Audience: Adults who save and invest
Style: Conversational, real people
Characters: 1 male, 1 female plus tag
Talent: James Alburger, Penny Abshire, Paul Bellantoni
Copy Notes: JB should have a sense of authority, but he really doesn't have a clue. His tone should be somewhat stern, but conversational. PW really runs the business, but lets JB think he does. Her tone needs to be very conversational and supportive yet slightly condescending.

ANNC: Sunland Bank and Trust presents The Memo.

(SFX: Door bursts open into bank ambience)

JB: Ms. Pepperwill ! ! ! ! !

PW: Yes, J.B.? **(from a distance)**

JB: What's the meaning of this memo?

PW: **(approaching)** About your golf membership?

(SFX: Footsteps approach under above lines)

JB: No, this new investment plan for businesses.

PW: Oh, Sunland Bank's "Wall Street Business Fund Limited" account.

JB: You say it'll take customers away from First Enormous Bank.

PW: Sunland Bank listened to what their customers wanted ...

JB: Hmpf

PW: ... And gave it to them.

JB: That's very disloyal, Ms. Pepperwill.

PW: Just facing facts, sir.

JB: Facts?

PW: The "Wall Street Business Fund" is insured by the FDIC, it's completely liquid and you can even write checks.

JB: Yes. **(He's saying "So what")**

PW: And it's tied to the "Wall Street Journal" prime rate.

JB: What ! ! ! **(incredulous, quickly he starts to panic)**

PW: Businesses get prime minus 2.75 or 3 percent, depending on their balance. So they know their interest rate will reflect the market.

JB: **(He panics)** What's our rate tied to?

PW: You know ... **(She's happy, pleasant, believes her boss)**

JB: Huh? **(Quickly, he's bewildered)**

PW: **(Same attitude)** Your lucky coin ... heads we raise the rate, tails we don't.

JB: Never mind. There must be a catch to that wall street business fund.

PW: It is a limited time offer.

JB: Thank goodness! **(Out of breath, terribly relieved)**

ANNC: Don't trust your business to a flip of a coin. Open your "Wall Street Business Fund" account today. Minimum balance $25,000. Other restrictions apply. Call or visit Sunland Bank and Trust for details.

(SFX: Coin hits and spins)

In this Chapter

Scan these response codes for more information or visit the AOVA Extras section at **VoiceActing.com**.

14

Industrials:
Long Form Narration

Telling a Different Kind of Story

Sales presentation, marketing videos, in-house training tapes, point-of-purchase videos, film documentaries, telephone messages, and many other projects all fall into the category of corporate and narrative. Frequently, these scripts are written to be read and not spoken.

Writers of industrials—corporate and narrative—copy are often not experienced writers, or usually write copy for print. There are exceptions to this, but overall you can expect copy in this category to be pretty dry. Corporate and narrative copy is often full of statistics, complex names or phrases and terminology specific to a business or industry. These can be a challenge for even an experienced voiceover performer.

As you perform a corporate or narrative script, you are still performing a character telling a story, just as for any other type of copy. You should know who your character is, who you are talking to, and what you are talking about. You also need to find a way to create an image of knowledge and authority for your character. What is it about your character that gives him the authority to be speaking the words? Is your character the owner of the company, a satisfied customer, the company's top salesperson, or a driver for one of the delivery trucks? To create an image of credibility, figure out an appropriate role for your character and commit to your choice.

A corporate or narrative script for a video project might have several performers on camera. These are often professional actors, but sometimes include employees of the business. There also may be several voiceover performers for different sections of the script.

Many scripts in this category are written for a single voiceover performer, but occasionally two or more performers will alternate lines or voice different sections. There may also be some interactive dialogue sections of the script. The complexity of a corporate script will vary greatly depending on the intended purpose, the content, the length, and the budget for the project.

A rapidly growing genre of long-form narration is in the area of medical narration. These projects are loaded with incredibly complex phrasing and words that can be difficult to pronounce. The narrator's tone of voice must be one of knowledge, expertise and authority. These projects include web learning, medical procedure instruction, drug introductions and more. Many medical projects can be an hour or more of recorded content.

It is often very challenging to deliver a script of this nature in a conversational manner, but it is possible. Facts, numbers, unusual terms, and complex names all contribute to a presentation more like a lecture than a conversation. However, the information is important, and the audience must be able to relate to the presentation as well as clearly understand what they hear. If the presentation of the information (your performance) is interesting and entertaining, the effectiveness of the communication will be much better.

Although medical and technical narration is one of my personal specialties, I've asked Julie Williams to offer some suggestions for working in this genre of voiceover. Julie is a voiceover actress and coach with thousands of credits. She is the author of "How To Make Money in Voice-Overs Even if You Don't Live in NY or LA, Proven Voice-Over Techniques," and is one of a handful of voiceover coaches who teaches medical narration with her "Medical Mumbo Advanced Narration Workshop."

The Challenges of Medical Narration
By Julie Williams
(**voiceoverchocolate.com - voiceoverinsider.com**)

Medical Narration is its own animal. It's a VO genre that presents unique challenges, but also offers great rewards.

One of the greatest rewards in Medical Narration is repeat business. Once a client finds a talent who can confidently and competently rise to the challenge, he usually comes back time and time again. It's not easy for clients to find someone who can do medical narration well. In fact, I've noticed that even many seasoned voice actors and actresses—not to mention some prominent coaches who have decades of experience—do not do a very good job with medical narration!

Why? Perhaps because they focus too much on pronouncing difficult terminology correctly—as if that were the big challenge of medical narration. It's not. Sure, pronunciation can literally be a mouthful, but that's easy to remedy. Find out how to say the words and practice saying them until they roll off your tongue like a fluent language.

The real challenge in medical narration is telling the story. And for good reason. In many medical narrations the terminology is so difficult, and the subject so foreign, that even the narrator can't see the story! How can you tell a story you don't know? Yet if the words are spoken in such a manner that the story is not told, the narrator loses the credibility in the eyes of the most important listener, the audience for whom the script was written. Whether it be doctors learning about a disease, students exploring biological processes, or patients being instructed on how to use a medical device, presumably, the audience will understand what is being said— even if the narrator doesn't! And to that audience the narrator is supposed to be the expert! He or she is the one teaching the information!

So, how can you know the story? There are a number of techniques we practice in my Medical Mumbo workshop (where we use the most difficult medical copy you've ever seen in your life!) But for starters, don't let the words get in the way. Don't get so wrapped up in the medical mumbo that you can't see past it to the underlying message—the story.

HOW TO APPROACH YOUR MEDICAL SCRIPT

- Go through the script and make a note of every word or term you don't know
- Do some legwork to figure out how to pronounce the terms
- Go to **m-w.com** and look up the word
- Ask a doctor, librarian, or other medical person who may know the correct pronunciation
- Ask the client
- When in doubt, do two takes of that part, pronouncing it two ways so the client can choose
- Read the script for the story
- If you don't know the story, break down the copy until you do
- Tell the story (don't "announce" it!)

Tips for Performing Corporate and Narrative Copy

The following tips and suggestions will help you with corporate and narrative copy in general.

- Talk to the audience on their level, not at them, even though the script might be full of facts, statistics, and unusual names or phrases. You must know who you are talking to.
- Take your time delivering the copy. There is rarely any time limitation for corporate and narrative copy.
- Be clear on the facts and pronunciation of complex words. These are important to the client and need to be correct and accurate. You must sound like you say these words every day.
- Slow your delivery or pace in sections where there is important information; speak more quickly in other parts of the script.
- If you are alternating lines with another performer, and the script is not written for dialogue, be careful to not overlap or step on the other performer's lines.

Corporate and Narrative Scripts

LIGHTING STORE (LightingStore.ca)
Project Type: Web video
Narrator: Penny Abshire (PennyAbshire.com)
Notes: Voiceover narration for web video marketing is a growing part of the voiceover world. This video was produced as a marketing video and introduction to Canada's only on-line lighting store. Direction was to be friendly, conversational and friendly.

Welcome! Come on in – we're so happy you're visiting us today. Take some time and look around. We know you'll like what you see.

You know, when you flip those light switches in your home – it isn't just to chase away the dark. When the warm light surrounds you, it illuminates the very heart of your home.

Whether your taste is contemporary, modern or traditional, finding the right lighting fixture will express your personality as well as bring warmth to your living area. And we make it so easy. Just pick up the phone and a personal designer will help you find exactly what you're looking for. So you'll never feel lost or overwhelmed with having to make all the decisions alone.

We'll be right there with you – every step of the way.

Sometimes you want quality, sometimes you want service, sometimes you want both. And that's what you'll get here at the Lighting Store.

 RAPIDaccess: How to use the Interface
Project Type: Web Instructional Video
Narrator: James R. Alburger (JamesAlburger.com)
NOTES: This narration is for an instructional video demonstrating how to use the RAPIDaccess user interface. Delivery should be conversational and somewhat authoritative, demonstrating an understanding of the interface.

Hi, and welcome to this demonstration of RAPIDaccess, the ATM for SolidWorks Enterprise PDM. In this demonstration I will introduce the end user interface and highlight some of its basic functions. I will show several methods to listing files inside of a vault and how to filter those results. I will also demonstrate how to open files, save files locally, and list past revisions.

First, I will launch RAPIDaccess by double clicking on the desktop shortcut, which has been provided by my EPDM administrator. RAPIDaccess takes care of connecting to the server using the security protocol and provides the simple user interface that you see now.

The RAPIDaccess window can be resized or maximized to suit user preferences. Also, column widths can be widened, if necessary. RAPIDaccess will remember the window size and column widths between sessions. Simply double clicking in the header area will return the window to its default settings. The user interface is divided into three sections. The top section is used to generate and filter a file list, the middle section displays the results list, and the bottom section includes action buttons and a status bar.

Starting in the top section, the file name text box first user input box is used to enter either a specific file name or a wildcard string to search for. In this example I will type the wild card string *5-5 followed by an asterisk into this box. Pressing enter or clicking on the Search button will query the vault and generate a file list matching the search criteria. I can now simply open one of the resulting files from the list by double clicking on it.

This example queried the entre vault, but let's say I wanted to search in only a specific project. This can easily be accomplished by skipping the search box and selecting a project from the pull down list. Notice that when a project is selected a wildcard character is automatically entered into the search box. I can now simply press the enter key to see all of the selected project's files. I could have also narrowed the search further by adding additional characters in the search box.

The description text filter allows me to narrow a file list down further by showing only those files that include matching text within the file's description.

For example, I'll type the word 'assembly' and then click on the apply button. Notice only files with the word assembly in their description are now listed. Clicking on the remove button restores the original search results.

The file list area contains some useful notifications and features such as highlighting recently released files making them stand out for quick recognition. Also, columns can be sorted by clicking on any of the column headers, once for ascending, and again for descending. The fourth column can be customized to show any variable in the vault. Ask your EPDM administrator for a list of available variables.

The bottom section of the RAPIDaccess window contains action buttons and a status bar. The first button opens the tool's settings window which will be covered in a different video. The help button d shows simple user instructions. Clicking on the Excel button will open the file list in a new Microsoft Excel worksheet. The new worksheet is formatted to match the file list exactly as it is shown in RAPIDaccess, including the file order and the recently released highlight color. It is also setup with Freeze Panes and column filters to make it immediately more functional.

Continuing with the action buttons, the next one is the Open button which can be used to open one or more selected files. Next is the Save Locally button. After selecting a file in the list I can click on this button and be presented with a standard Windows "Save As" dialog box. Notice the revision of the file is automatically added to the end of the file name and that the default save location is the current user's desktop folder.

Next is the Past Revisions button. After selecting a file, I can click on this button to open another window that lists all the past revisions available for this file. To demonstrate one of the best features of RAPIDaccess, I will select two past revisions of this file and open them simultaneously. Notice I didn't have to save anything locally to use this very valuable function.

The last button does exactly what you would expect, it closes the RAPIDaccess window.

That concludes this quick demonstration of the basic end user functions of RAPIDaccess, the ATM for SolidWorks Enterprise PDM.

For additional information, more demonstrations, to inquire about a trial license, or to purchase RAPIDaccess for your company, please check out our website ... zero wait dash state dot com forward slash RAPIDaccess: www.zerowait-state.com/RAPIDaccess.

Thank you for watching. We hope to hear from you soon.

In this Chapter

 Scan these response codes for more information or visit the AOVA Extras section at **VoiceActing.com**.

Hillary Huber—A Bit About Audio Books (3e/4e)

15

Audio Books

Telling the Long Story

THE AUDIO BOOK CHALLENGE

Audio book narration is a voiceover world unto itself. It is highly specialized and different from every other area of voiceover, both in terms of performing and obtaining work. Unless you have a history of successful audio book projects, your compensation will be comparatively low, compared to some other areas of voiceover. Basically, you won't be doing audio books for the money, but rather, you'll be narrating audio books for the love of it.

Audio book narration is much more than simply "reading" a book out loud. It requires exceptional reading skills and outstanding story telling skills with an ability to quickly adapt in real-time to different vocal placements or attitudes for multiple characters during a scripted conversation. You will need to be able to differentiate every character in the story and accurately reproduce each character's vocal attitude or placement every time that character appears in the story. There are a variety of processes for achieving this, including color coding the lines for each character and developing a chart or spreadsheet that breaks down the characters, their attitudes and their vocal characteristics.

As an audio book reader you will read a book, on average, three or four times. The first time through is to get a sense of the story. The second time through is for the purpose of identifying and marking the scenes, characters, emotions, and story dynamics; and starting to develop the voice treatments for each character. The third time through is usually the recording session, or perhaps a final read to rehearse the delivery, in which case the fourth time through would be the session. If you don't enjoy reading, audio book narration may not be right for you.

To say the least, audio book narration is challenging! However, as challenging as it may be, audio book narration is one of the fastest growing areas of voiceover.

As an audio book narrator, you'll spend many long hours in the studio recording your telling of the story. In most cases, your delivery must be precisely accurate, word-for-word as written. If you are working directly for an author, you may be allowed to take some liberties with your narration, such as contracting words or making minor phrasing adjustments to make the "read" more conversational or to adjust the text "for the ear."

A typical audio book recording session will last about four to five hours per day. Most *readers* recommend taking frequent breaks and speaking continuously for no more than 50 minutes at a time. For the most part, the session goes nonstop, and the same process will repeat for as many days as it takes to complete the project—and that could be one or two days or up to several weeks. And even when you think your recording is complete, you may be called back to the studio months later for *pick-ups* to replace some lines or re-track a page or two. When this happens, you need to be able to match the original delivery both in delivery style and vocal quality.

Remember that the microphone hears everything. Even a slight change in position can result in a change in the quality or consistency of your performance. Wear clothing that doesn't make any noise, move silently, and learn to take shallow breaths. Many audio book readers work from an electronic tablet, but if working directly from the book or from a paper script, page turns should be done as quietly as possible. If a sentence at the bottom of one page continues to the next, complete the sentence at the bottom of the page, pause, turn the page, then pick up with the next sentence. Don't try to do a page turn in mid-sentence. Changes in your delivery style, vocal placement, or bad edits will all result in your voice becoming a distraction to the listener.

FINDING AUDIO BOOK CLIENTS

Some of the larger audio book publishers will hire major celebrities and record in a conventional recording studio. However, the trend for most start-up and independent audio book publishers is to hire independent voice actors to record in their home studio.

Marketing yourself as an audio book narrator requires some special skills and knowledge. As an independent audio book narrator, you will be expected to deliver a high-quality recording that is ready for publication on **iTunes.com**, **Audible.com**, audio CD, or other electronic media. This means you'll be handling every aspect of your recording, including quality control and editing. Quality control simply means that you have a system in place for making certain you don't skip words, mispronounce words, and that your delivery and timing are appropriate for your telling of the story. Some readers will hire an assistant to "proof" their narration, while others will simply spend the additional time proofing their read as they edit.

There are some companies that specialize in producing audio books; they do everything from arranging for the recording rights and booking the performers to handling distribution. You can contact these companies directly regarding work as an audio book narrator. Some will record at their facility, while others may be open to having you simply provide the completed and edited recordings.

In an effort to open the audio book industry to more authors and narrators, **Audible.com** created the Audio book Creation Exchange. With ACX, the audio book genre of voiceover has been given specific standards of practice for performance and recording quality. Today, thousands of voice actors are vying for work as audio book narrators with ACX projects through **acx.com**.

Some audio book voice actors will take on the roles of both talent and producer by finding a book that they think will be marketable, arranging for recording rights from the author or publisher, preparing a production budget, and pitching the book to an audio book publisher with themselves as the performer. Developing an audio book project in this manner can create an income stream from several different areas.

One of the best ways to learn about audio books is to begin by studying acting and other performers who narrate audio books. Then find a voiceover coach who knows the audio book business, and who offers a class in audio book narration. You'll find additional information about the audio book industry at the Audio book Publishers Association website, **audiopub.org**. Audio book work can be tiring and exhausting, but if you enjoy reading and storytelling, it can be very enjoyable and gratifying.

An Internet search for "public domain books" will bring up many sources for books that are in the public domain and available for production. You'll also find links to more scripts in the AOVA Extras section at **VoiceActing.com** or by scanning the response code for these scripts.

For more about Audio Books, scan this response code to read Hillary Huber's "A Bit About Audio Books" from the fourth edition of this book.

Tips for Performing Audio Books

- You must have excellent reading skills. You may be reading several pages without a break.
- You must be an exceptional story teller with an ability to create distinctions between characters and narrator.
- You must have a thorough understanding of the story and the interrelationships of the characters in it.
- The overall audio book style is more of reading out loud than of talking conversationally to one person. The conversations happen between the characters in the story.
- Be prepared for long hours in front of the microphone and in editing your recordings.
- You must have an excellent home studio and a thorough understanding of your equipment and the audio book production process.

Audio Book Scripts

THE TIME MACHINE (from Gutenburg.org)
H.G. Wells—Chapter 1
Reader: George Asteri (GeorgeAsteri.com)

As a Shakespearean trained actor, George Asteri has a story telling style that is captivating and very comfortable to listen to. One challenge of reading a classic in literature is in dealing with the sometimes awkward phrases while maintaining a consistent sense of the story.

The Time Traveler (for so it will be convenient to speak of him) was expounding a recondite matter to us. His grey eyes shone and twinkled, and his usually pale face was flushed and animated. The fire burned brightly, and the soft radiance of the incandescent lights in the lilies of silver caught the bubbles that flashed and passed in our glasses. Our chairs, being his patents, embraced and caressed us rather than submitted to be sat upon, and there was that luxurious after-dinner atmosphere when thought roams gracefully free of the trammels of precision. And he put it to us in this way—marking the points with a lean forefinger—as we sat and lazily admired his earnestness over this new paradox (as we thought it) and his fecundity.

"You must follow me carefully. I shall have to controvert one or two ideas that are almost universally accepted. The geometry, for instance, they taught you at school is founded on a misconception."

"Is not that rather a large thing to expect us to begin upon?" said Filby, an argumentative person with red hair.

"I do not mean to ask you to accept anything without reasonable ground for it. You will soon admit as much as I need from you. You know of course that a mathematical line, a line of thickness *nil*, has no real existence. They taught you that? Neither has a mathematical plane. These things are mere abstractions."

"That is all right," said the Psychologist.

"Nor, having only length, breadth, and thickness, can a cube have a real existence."

"There I object," said Filby. "Of course a solid body may exist. All real things—"

"So most people think. But wait a moment. Can an *instantaneous* cube exist?"

"Don't follow you," said Filby.

"Can a cube that does not last for any time at all, have a real existence?"

Filby became pensive. "Clearly," the Time Traveler proceeded, "any real body must have extension in *four* directions: it must have Length, Breadth, Thickness, and—Duration. But through a natural infirmity of the flesh, which I will explain to you in a moment, we incline to overlook this fact. There are really four dimensions, three which we call the three planes of Space, and a fourth, Time. There is, however, a tendency to draw an unreal distinction between the former three dimensions and the latter, because it happens that our consciousness moves intermittently in one direction along the latter from the beginning to the end of our lives."

"That," said a very young man, making spasmodic efforts to relight his cigar over the lamp; "that ... very clear indeed."

"Now, it is very remarkable that this is so extensively overlooked," continued the Time Traveler, with a slight accession of cheerfulness. "Really this is what is meant by the Fourth Dimension, though some people who talk about the Fourth Dimension do not know they mean it. It is only another way of looking at Time. There is no difference between Time and any of the three dimensions of Space except that our consciousness moves along it. But some foolish people have got hold of the wrong side of that idea. You have all heard what they have to say about this Fourth Dimension?"

"I have not," said the Provincial Mayor.

"It is simply this. That Space, as our mathematicians have it, is spoken of as having three dimensions, which one may call Length, Breadth, and Thickness, and is always definable by reference to three planes, each at right angles to the others. But some philosophical people have been asking why *three* dimensions particularly—why not another direction at right angles to the other three?—and have even tried to construct a Four-Dimension geometry. Professor Simon Newcomb was expounding this to the New York Mathematical Society only a month or so ago. You know how on a flat surface, which has only two dimensions, we can represent a figure of a three-dimensional solid, and similarly they think that by models of three dimensions they could represent one of four—if they could master the perspective of the thing. See?"

 KNOW THY NEIGHBOR
Author: Anton Scheller (AntonScheller.com)
Narrator: Lynne Darlington (LynneDarlington.com)
Additional Voice/Engineer: Jeff Clement

For some stories, it's easy to go "over the top," and that might actually work … sometimes, but most of the time your story telling will be far more effective (and scarier) when the narration is held back a bit. Lynne Darlington is a professional voice actor with a history of voice work for commercials, narration and audio books. Her reading of "Know Thy Neighbor" is a good example of a casual telling of a scary story that effectively uses the "less is more" technique.

I don't usually talk much to my neighbors. There are just three apartments in our house, but I can't remember the last time I talked to Jude and Stella. I wasn't exactly surprised that they moved out. And it's not like I expected them to invite me to their farewell party, but couldn't they at least have left a note?

Well, anyway, now there is Ken. From the glance I got into his apartment, he even kept most of their furniture. The only new thing was a painting. It was leaning against the old sofa when I peeked in. It looked like an ancient map, composed of ochre and beige patches that seemed to be marking countries. Thinking about it, he didn't just keep the furniture; Ken even dressed a bit like Jude.

It's strange that I never really got to know Jude and Stella. It was one of those weird neighbor relationships where we greeted each other in the hallway. Occasionally we even promised to meet up for a beer. But somehow I never made the first step – and neither did they.

Ken is different. He came right on the first night, but I was already going out on a date. Actually, he came nearly every night. But as things often are when a new relationship starts, what with the dating and the usual stress at work, I always had a reason to decline.

In the beginning, Ken came frequently to ask for stuff. With a big grin on his face, he would stand in my doorstep and ask for scissors or packing tape. He even borrowed my kitchen utensils "to prepare food for a few weeks." From the smell of it, he must use a camping cooker – maybe the gas company didn't connect him yet?

I offered to let him use my kitchen, but he always declined. Such a polite man.

But even though Ken is nice, I have to say he is a bit too persistent. Since around the middle of last week, he comes every night once or twice, or even thrice. He always invites me to come down to his apartment. First he asked me to watch sports, but I told him that would bore me. He looked a bit sad and tried again a few hours later, but by then I was too tired to even be polite.

But his reasons kept getting weirder. He invited me for a movie, but I thought that was a bit too intimate for a new friend. Then he asked to cook me a meal, but I had other plans. And, to be honest, I got uncomfortable because he asked so often. Maybe he was just lonely and looking for new friends in a new town?

"Go down the street," he said, "and when you can see the face of the fat cashier, turn left."

He continued.

"When you get past the poster for the strip club, the one that all the men shyly glance at, turn right. The shop is the only one with two people behind the counter; the married woman and the young man that is laughing eagerly at her jokes."

His descriptions weirded me out. But when I actually walked along the street, his words still ringing in my ears, I saw it all happening. The moment the fat cashier came in my view, there was a narrow path between two houses – a shortcut I had never noticed before.

[… more]

The full script is available in the AOVA Extras area at **VoiceActing.com** or by scanning this response code.

In this Chapter

Scan the response codes below for more information or visit the AOVA Extras section at **VoiceActing.com**.

Deb Munro—Inside Anime (3e/4e)

Lani Minella on Celebrity Voices (unpublished)

Lani Minella—Video Games (3e)

16

Mastering
Character Voices

*A good actor can do a thousand voices
because he finds a place in his body for his voice
and centers his performance from that place.*
Charles Nelson Reilly

Vocalizing Characters

Most genres of voiceover require the voice actor to create a character and, logically, a voice for that character. A forced voice is rarely the most effective, is difficult to sustain, and can actually cause physical damage to your vocal cords. The most effective character voices are those that originate from your normal voice and slightly exaggerate the attitudes, emotions and other traits of the character being portrayed, or take a small quirk or idiosyncrasy and blow it out of proportion through a shift in placement, texture, tempo or rhythm. Character voices for animation and video games often further exaggerate those unique personality traits, taking them to an extreme.

Over the past few years, the trend in feature film animation has been to apply very real, human characteristics and voices to animated characters. Although there is still a place for the occasional wacky voice, the vast majority of animation work has moved to a more conversational style sourced from the actor's natural voice.

ANIMATION, GAME AND OTHER CHARACTER VOICES

Understanding the character and story are extremely important in character voice work. Many factors affect the voice, so the more you know about the character, the easier it will be to find its true voice.

Consistency is also extremely important in this type of voice work. When you find the character's voice, lock it into your memory and keep the proper physicality, attitude and quality of sound throughout your performance, adapting your character's voice when the mood of the story changes. The important thing here is to avoid allowing the sound of your character to drift. To make your character believable and real to the audience, the quality of the voice must not change from the beginning of the script to the end and it must, in some way, be different from your natural voice. Achieving excellence in this aspect of the craft requires specialized knowledge and a mastery of performing skills.

Most animation voice actors have a repertoire of several voices. A typical session may require voicing three characters before lunch, three more after lunch, and then going back for pick-ups on some of the first set of characters. This sort of schedule means character voice actors must be extremely versatile and must be able to accurately repeat and sustain voice characterizations. These demands make animation and video game work a challenging niche to break into, and one of the most creative in voiceover.

In addition to voices and sounds for animation and games, character voice work can also include dialects, foreign and regional accents, and even celebrity impersonations. Special accents and dialects require an ability to mimic a sound or attitude that is familiar to a portion of the listening audience. Usually, this mimicking is a stylized interpretation and doesn't necessarily have to be 100 percent accurate, unless the character is represented as being authentic to a region or culture. Many times, the best accent is one that reflects what a community "thinks" the accent should sound like, which is often not the real thing. However, when authenticity is required to give the character believability, vocal accuracy is important. Most of the time, however, a slight exaggeration of certain regional vocal traits tends to give the character attitude and personality. Personal familiarity with the culture, region, or dialect is also helpful.

Celebrity voice impersonations are often the most challenging because the celebrities are usually well-known. The voice actor's job is to create a voice that offers recognition of the celebrity, yet hints at being just a bit different. Celebrity impersonations are usually done in the context of humor in which some aspect of the celebrity's personality or vocal styling is exaggerated or used as a device for communicating the message. In most cases, if a producer wants an extremely accurate celebrity voice, he will hire the celebrity. It may cost more to hire the actual person behind the voice, but the increased credibility is often worth it and hiring the real person will circumvent any potential legal issues.

In the case of dialogue replacement, accuracy of the celebrity's voice is important. The voice actor will usually be replacing short lines or sections of dialogue when the original actor is unavailable.

THE SIX ELEMENTS OF CHARACTER VOICE

Pat Fraley is one of the most amazing voice actors I've met. He's not only a consummate performer—in just about every area of voice work—but he's also an excellent, and very generous, teacher. Pat understands character voice work better than most professionals. He's one of the top 10 voice actors for animation, having performed more than 4,000 different cartoon voices. He's narrated dozens of audio books, and voiced thousands of commercials.

Just as I've broken down a performance to its *Seven Core Elements*, Pat breaks down a character voice to its six critical elements.

Pat Fraley's Six Critical Elements of a Character Voice
© Patrick Fraley, 2006
PatFraleyTeaches.com

With any artful endeavor, you will find two words that are important to define: Form and Content. What is the *form* of a character voice? The way this applies to character voice is that the *form* is the *sound* of the voice. The *content* is the thinking and feeling, the psychology of the character. The Six Elements of a Character Voice are all about the *form*. What makes up the form of a character voice? Like everything else, there's a finite amount of elements.

These are the six elements: *Pitch, Pitch Characteristic, Tempo, Rhythm, Placement,* and *Mouth Work.*

Pitch (Higher or lower than your own?)

Pitch Characteristic (Gravelly? Breathy? Husky? Constricted?)

Tempo (Faster or slower than your own?)

Rhythm (Syncopated? Plodding? Loping?)

Placement (Nasal? Back of Throat? Normal?)

Mouth Work (Accent? Lisp? Tight lips?)

The first element is *Pitch*. Pitch relates to the musical notes of the character's voice. Is the character's voice higher than your own? Is it lower? Or perhaps the character goes both higher and lower, showing a wider range. Thus far we've dealt with Pitch and it has been assumed that the characteristic of the pitch was clear.

The second element deals with the specific characteristic of the pitch, *Pitch Characteristic*. Pitch Characteristic is the dynamic of the pitch, or coloring. If Pitch were a noun, Pitch Characteristic would be its adjective, as it describes the nature of the pitch. It is clear? Is it gravelly? Is it hoarse? Is it breathy? Is it constricted? Is it cracking? Velvety?

The third element is *Tempo*. Tempo refers to the character's general rate of delivery. There are three possibilities: (1) Does the character speak faster than you? (2) Slower than you? (3) Or does the character vary or have a wider range of tempo than you?

The fourth element is *Rhythm*. Vivid characters go about getting what they want, and they go about getting it in the same way, over and over. There is a pattern to their behavior. This pattern shows up in the way they speak. Character Rhythm is defined as a repetitive pattern of emphasis in the way the character speaks which emerges from the thinking and feeling of the character. It's kind of a vocal thumb print.

The fifth element is *Placement*. Placement refers to where the voice seems to be coming from or where it's placed. When I think about placing my voice in my nose the sound takes on a whole different dynamic. I feel a lot of air coming through my nose. It sounds a whole lot different than when I place my voice in the back of my mouth. How about if I think of creating the voice in my throat? Distinct sounds? The trick is to learn how to *stay* in the placement all the time for any given character.

Because placement happens in and around the mouth, it has a kind of relationship with our sixth and final element, *Mouth Work*. Mouth Work refers to anything done in and around the mouth to affect the character. The kind of affect that comes to mind is accents. But also, having tight lips affect the way we sound, stretching your mouth to one side and talking, or the way a character pronounces their "S"s.

So that's all the ingredients it takes to bake up the form of a character voice—no less, no more: Pitch, Pitch Characteristic, Tempo, Rhythm, Placement, and Mouth Work.

Finding Your Voice

Begin creating a character's voice by doing a thorough character analysis to discover as much as you can about him or her (or it). Based on the copy, make the decisions and commit to who you are talking to and if your character has any special accent or attitude. Finally, decide where in your body the character's voice will be placed.

Visualize the voice coming from a specific location in your body and work with the copy until the voice feels right, using choices about the character's physical size and shape to help you localize the voice. Use the "sweep" (Exercise #10, page 44) to find a suitable pitch for your character voice. Once you have found a pitch, use placement, pitch characteristics, tempo, rhythm, and mouth work to create a unique sound. Here are some possible placements:

top of head (tiny)	under tongue (sloppy)	nose (nasal)
behind eyes (denasal)	diaphragm (strong)	chest (boomy)
top of cheeks (bright)	loose cheeks (mushy)	throat (raspy)
front of mouth (crisp)	back of throat (breathy)	stomach (low)

Practice different voices with different attitudes. Use computer clip art, comic strips and other drawings to get ideas for character voices. You may find that a particular physical characteristic or facial expression is needed in order for you to get the proper sound and attitude. Remember: *Physicalize the moment and the voice will follow.* Record a variety of voices and characters, then listen to what you've recorded. If your character voices all sound the same, you'll need to work on your character voice skills.

The Character Voice Worksheet

In animation, you must be able to recall a voice on demand. The Character Voice Worksheet on page 221 is just one of many good ways to document the characteristics of each voice you create. The worksheet is divided into four parts: (1) Accessing and recalling the character voice, (2) Placement, (3) Physical characteristics, and (4) Other notes.

Accessing and recalling the character voice:
- Give your character a name for quick recall,
- Define age, gender, attitude, physical attributes, energy level,

- Create a *key phrase* that will allow you to return to the character. You will know the phrase is correct when it sounds natural.

Placement:

- Determine where in your body you are positioning the voice.
- Choose appropriate pitch, pitch characteristics, tempo, rhythm, and mouth work to contribute to the reality of the voice.
- Understand the character's emotions and feelings.

Physical:

- Determine how your character stands and moves in space and time. Experiment with facial expressions, physical gestures, and speaking quirks, including how your character laughs.

Other Notes:

- Include any additional information that will help you recall your voice.

Each voice you document is what Pat Fraley terms a *starter.* This is a core voice from which you can create many more simply by adjusting some of the characteristics. Start with a defined voice, then experiment with changing the pitch and altering pitch characteristics. Change the tempo and rhythm as you work with the voice, or see what happens as you adjust the voice placement or slightly modify the mouth work—and voila, you've got a new character. Scan this response code to hear Penny Abshire demonstrate how she creates and documents her characters.

Tips for Character and Animation Copy

Character voice work can be challenging, but lots of fun. Use the following tips and suggestions to help find your character's voice.

- Understand your character and the scene. In animation, you must often use your imagination to make up what you are reacting to.
- Discover who the audience is and understand how the audience will relate to the character.
- Maintain a consistent voice throughout the copy and be careful not to injure your voice by stretching too far. It is better to pull back a little and create a voice that can be maintained rather than push too hard for a voice you can only sustain for one or two pages.

The Character Voice Worksheet

Sketch or pic of character

Character name: _____

Age: _____ Height: _____

Gender: _____ Body type: _____

Character source (where did you get the idea?): _____

_____

Describe primary energy: _____

Key phrase: _____

Appearance (hair, clothing, etc.): _____

Placement (location of voice in your body):

Vertical pitch: _____

_____ Abdomen _____ Chest _____ Throat _____ Eyes

_____ Adenoid _____ Nasal _____ Face _____ Top of head

Horizontal placement: _____

_____ Front of face/body _____ Centered _____ Back of head/body

Pitch Characteristics: _____
(raspy, gravelly, smooth, clear, smoky, edgy, nasal, de-nasal, nervous, breathy, tight, etc.)

Vocal Dynamics—Phrasing/Pacing (musicality of your character's voice):

Tempo: _____ Fast _____ Slow _____ Moderate _____ Varying

Rhythm: _____ Smooth flow _____ Staccato _____ Melodic

Attitude—Tone of Voice: _____

Emotion: _____

Volume (loud/soft/varied): _____

Physicalization (how does your character move in time and space?):

Stance: _____ Walk: _____

Quirks: _____ Laugh: _____

Body: _____ Hands/arms: _____

Mouth work: _____ Dialect/accent: _____

Associated color, sound, or taste: _____

If your character was real, who or what might it be like?

_____

Other notes: _____

_____

- Be willing to exaggerate attitudes or personality traits for the sake of finding the voice.
- If a drawing, photo, or picture of the character is available, use it as a tool to discover the personality of the character.
- Find the place in your body from which the voice will come.
- Experiment with pitch, pitch characteristics, tempo, rhythm, placement, and mouth work to discover the most appropriate vocal delivery for your character.
- Experiment to take on the physical characteristics of the character.

Character, Game and Animation Scripts

Find a suitable voice and delivery for each of the following characters. Use the six elements of character voice: *Pitch, Pitch Characteristics, Tempo, Rhythm, Placement, and Mouth Work* to create a believable voice. Do a quick "A-B-C" (*Audience, Back Story, Character, Desires*, and *Energy*) for each line of copy to discover clues about your character. Explore any relationships that may exist in the copy or in the drawing. Experiment with different voice possibilities and add layers of *emotion*, *attitude*, and *physical movement*.

You'll find more about character voice work in the AOVA Extras section at **VoiceActing.com** or by scanning this response code.

©Timothy Abshire

Character Name: Ganbaatar (a warrior)
Attitude: Strong, powerful, demands blind obedience, loves violence

Copy line 1: I am Ganbaatar, leader of the village of Terduk. Bow before me.

Copy line 2: It is true. I have many wives. But this … is the mother of my first born son who will inherit my kingdom.

Copy line 3: The path I follow is one of obedience and obligation. It is my destiny. You may choose to follow, but know the journey will be difficult. There shall be no dishonor if you choose to leave … now.

Character Name: Dilbert D. Duck
Attitude: Cocky, arrogant, smart aleck

Copy line 1: Am I the ONLY duck who hates the rain? Really???

Copy line 2: Noah, buddy, wait ... I was just kidding! There's still room ... right?

©Timothy Abshire

Copy line 3: Open the door sweetie. I promise I won't quack around any more.

Character Name: Herbert Hare
Attitude: Optimistic, friendly, helpful

Copy line 1: Can you see me? I can see yoooouuuu.

Copy line 2: With these glasses, no one will ever notice my teeth.

Copy line 3: May I help you out? ... Which way did you come in?

©Timothy Abshire

©Timothy Abshire

Character Name: Lewy the lips
Attitude: An alien collector with a heart of gold. Pretends to be tough, but really likes needlepoint. Soft tone, emotional, sucker for a good sob story

Copy line 1: Ya got that stuff ya owe my boss? I know ya do! So why not just give it to me and save yaself some pain.

Copy line 2: Ya like my teeth, huh? Pretty, huh! Thanks ... I just got 'em capped. Wadda ya mean, ya don't like the color?

Copy line 3: Ya ever been squeezed so hard your eyes pop outta yer head? Yeah? Me either.

Character Name: Quexxityr
Attitude: Sarcastic, disbelieving, irritated, annoyed

Copy line 1: They said ... let's make a quick stop on Earth for takeout! Now, THIS happens!!!

Copy line 2: Don't be fooled ... space travel is NOT all it's cracked up to be.

©Timothy Abshire

Copy line 3: Really ... I have my papers right here ... someplace ... Just because I'm an alien doesn't I'm illegal.

Character Name: Majizmo
Attitude: Introverted, polite, quiet. Wants to be an extrovert.

Copy line 1: Hello, ma'am. I was wondering if you could direct me to the auditions?

Copy line 2: Must I hold this pose for much longer? My arm is getting really tired.

Copy line 3: I am the Great and Powerful Majizimo! Prepare to be amazed!

©Timothy Abshire

©Timothy Abshire

Character Name: James the Brave
Attitude: Proud, commanding, respectful, always in control

Copy line 1: My mission is a simple one ... I must find the treasure of Nyphoon.

Copy line 2: Stand and defend yourself, villain.

Copy line 3: Stand alert! Keep your eyes open and your wits about you.

Character Name: Sir Phillip of Exanham
Attitude: Ultimate optimist, near-sighted, loyal, thoughtful, not well-connected to reality

Copy line 1: No dream is impossible if you truly believe.

Copy line 2: Why ... this is incredible! With these new spectacles, this Knight can see at night!

Copy line 3: Fear not, my dear Thespian! I'm quite certain my King's army is just beyond that hill. Or ... perhaps ... not.

©Timothy Abshire

Character Name: Lillian (Lil) Valenka
Attitude: Sarcastic, brittle, unfriendly, rigid, not at all feminine

Copy line 1: Remove your hand, sir. Or you shall draw back a bloody stump.

Copy line 2: What makes you think I'd have even the slightest interest in helping you?

Copy line 3: Go! Go! Go! Leave him ... he's as good as dead! Take the case and GO!

©Timothy Abshire

©Timothy Abshire

Character Name: Captain Confused
Attitude: Confused, easily distracted, finds wonder in everything.

Copy line 1: (surprised) Wooooo! I think I found my missing seat belt!

Copy line 2: Base! Come in base ... I think I've found the lost city! Oh? It wasn't lost? 10-4. Never mind.

Copy line 3: Uhhhhh ... Let's see ... If I push this button ... I should go forward! Uh oh ... Didn't mean to do that. Ayyyyeeeeeeee

In this Chapter

Scan this response code for more information or visit the AOVA Extras section at **VoiceActing.com**.

17

Imaging - Promo - Trailer
Voiceover for radio, television & film industries

Radio Imaging

THE RADIO BROADCASTER'S BRAND & SIGNATURE

The term *imaging* refers to the niche area of voiceover work that specifically promotes a radio station's sound or marketing image. The best imaging voice actors come from radio station production departments where they learn first-hand what station imaging is all about. An imaging production is usually fast-paced with lots of rapid-fire, short liners, station call letters, station slogan or USP, punchy music cues, catchy sound effects, and processed voice tracks that define a station's "sound" within its format.

An imaging voice talent will be voicing a station's IDs, promos, sweepers, and liners, and in some cases may even be handling the production. If you don't know what those are, imaging may not be for you.

If imaging is something you are interested in, you'll need to know how radio stations promote themselves, and how your voice will be used as an identifiable part of that promotion process. You'll also need to understand the differences between the various radio formats, and you'll most likely need to produce a separate demo for each format. Imaging formats include: Contemporary Hit Radio (CHR), formerly Top Forty; Adult Contemporary (AC); Hot AC; Urban Contemporary; Alternative; Modern; Jazz; Oldies; Classic Rock; Country; News/Talk, and a few dozen more. Each format has its unique style and associated sound.

Radio is a very itinerant type of work, and most of the top radio imaging voice talent have a background of several years working in many cities and a variety of formats. They also have a solid background in production with an almost uncanny ability to instantly change their attitude and tone of voice to match specific radio formats.

Although there are many imaging voice talent who provide only dry voice tracks, there are many more who can also handle the highly specialized production necessary to create the final imaging spots.

To sum it up ... radio imaging is about promoting the station's image and attitude through your tone of voice and delivery.

Gabby Nistico of **VoiceHunter.com** is an imaging voice talent, a coach, a producer, and represents many of the nation's top imaging voices. For more about radio imaging, scan this response code to read her article from the fourth edition of this book. Gabby's Imaging demo is in the audio section of AOVA Extras.

Television Promo

This category of voice work is for television and film promotion, which is different from radio imaging, although there are similarities. While imaging covers station IDs and programming transitions to establish a radio station's audio brand, *promotion* is generally considered to be advertising for a television station's programming products. *Promo* voiceover work usually refers to television station promos, although it can sometimes apply to radio. *Trailer* voice work, on the other hand, refers to the promotion of motion pictures.

Originally *promo* and *trailer* voiceover work were lumped into the same category because of the similarities of style and purpose for the product. However, as the voiceover world has become more and more niche oriented, the two genres of voiceover work have each become specialties in their own right. Both are essentially storytelling and the differences in style are subtle, but distinct.

Let's discuss promo voiceover first: As with radio, television stations present a specific image in their market. While radio must rely only on audio, a television station has the advantage of adding pictures and graphics to their broadcast image. If you watch much TV, you'll notice that each station has its own look and sound. The pictures, graphics, and voiceover will be consistent for just about everything the station airs to promote its programming and image. This is true for all television and cable broadcasters, from the local station to the national networks.

A network promo voice talent will generally work to an already-edited video with a music track and sound bites that set the tone, pace, and attitude of the promo. The delivery will be one that is involved with the story and characters. For local television stations, promo voiceover will often be done as *dry voice tracks* without the benefit of seeing the picture or hearing the music.

Working as a television promo voice talent can often mean the talent is "the voice," or one of the voices, of the television station. A promo voice talent will voice station IDs, program introductions, program promos (commercials for the station's programming), program VOCs (voice over credits — the "coming up next" voiceover you'll often hear at the end of a program), public service announcements, news opens, news promos, and possibly even station marketing and sales videos. As the voice of the station, you may be asked to voice anything and everything that serves to promote the station. Depending on the station and market, a television station might have two, three, or even more voice talent to handle specific promotional needs. One might voice only news promos, while another might voice the VOCs and program promos. Still another might only voice the radio commercials for the station.

Landing a job as a station promo voice can mean a lot of work on a regular basis. It used to be that you would have to travel to the station's studios to record your voice tracks. However with today's technology, you will most likely be recording at your home studio via ISDN or sending your tracks to the station's FTP website. Promo work is usually recorded on a daily basis, and most promo voice talent are "on call" in the event of a major breaking news story that needs a promo produced quickly.

Network promo voiceover is a completely different animal. At one time the networks hired one person as "the voice" of the network. However, today the major networks will use many different voice talent for different aspects of their promotion. There might be a specific voice talent hired for comedy promos, dramatic promos, political promos, and so on. Most voice talent who are hired to work on promos at the network level have several years of voiceover experience and understand the performing styles for voicing promos.

In most cases, television promo work is about telling the story of the program being promoted or the station sponsored event in a manner appropriate to the story. News promotion, however, can have a "sound" all its own. Daily, topical, promos will often be voiced by the station's news reporters or by a contracted voice actor. Either way, news promos will often have a somewhat detached sound with a sense of drama and urgency underscoring the delivery.

Trailer

Although similar to promo voiceover, trailer work requires a somewhat different form of storytelling. The copy is usually read *wild*, without the benefit of picture or a soundtrack, but the lines must be delivered within a specific time.

While a promo may be delivered with a range of delivery styles from conversational to intensely dramatic, trailer voice work will generally treat almost every word and phrase as the most important, dramatic, or impactful word or phrase ever spoken. The style is often one in which the voice actor is less involved with the characters and moves the story forward with a very dramatic, detached or almost "announcer-y" delivery. A conversational style used for a commercial or narration will usually not be effective for trailer voiceover.

Tips for Performing Imaging, Promo and Trailer

- You are a storyteller, and stories are always about relationships. Find the relationships in the story you are telling.
- Look for the message, image, feeling, or unique quality of the program or station. This can often be determined by listening to the music and sound bites for a promo, or getting a sense of the energy of a radio station for imaging.
- Determine the creative strategy that will enable you to build dramatic tension and allow for expression of the message. Use sense-memory techniques to locate tension in your body and speak from that place.
- Find a way to deliver the first line of copy in a way that will interrupt the listener's thoughts and bring them in to listening to your story.

Imaging Scripts

Note the station format for the liners below. Each radio format has its unique sound and attitude. Some typical formats are below.

Rock: (edgy with an attitude)
- We give you all the classics … all the time! What you do with them is your damn business! Rock 97.3.

AC (Adult Contemporary): (Friendly, conversational)

- There are many radio stations in San Diego ... One for your kids, one for your wife, and even one for that surfer dude next door. But there's only ONE station that's perfect for you ... Hits 104.5, KVAA. The best of the 80s, 90s and today.

Jazz: (hip)

- Smooth Jazz 103.9. The cutting edge blend of smooth sounds, cool jazz and just a hint of soul. 104.5 Smooth FM.

Country: (relaxed, casual)

- Commercials? Naw! More Hit Country music? Yeah! That's how we do it around here. Today's Hit Country starts now on Country 99.5.

News Talk Sports: (authoritative)

- The acknowledged leader in local news coverage, this is KVAA News 103.
- Traffic on the 10s. Weekdays here on Talk Radio 1020.
- Tomorrow the Chargers meet the Raiders in San Diego. Pre-game at 9; Kick-off at high noon on Sports 107.

Promo Scripts

Each of the following is a separate promo. Uncover the tone, mood or attitude of the story and find an interesting way to tell it:

Channel Lineup #1: (With a tone of quirky fun)

Coming up next it's the Klondike Kids followed by Stevie, Stewie and Sid. Right here on Kidz Network.

Channel Lineup #2: (A bit tongue in cheek)

If you need him, you've got a problem! Rod Hammer is on next! He'll try to fix anything! Then it's time for truth, justice and the last piece of popcorn with Priscilla Periwinkle. And it's all right here on Kidz Network.

Channel Lineup #3: (With an air of suspense and drama)

Join us as we take you on a journey through your mind to the limits of your imagination. "Amazing Mind," Wednesday at 9, right here on KAVA.

Sports: (Big and bold with an edge.)

It's a rivalry for the ages. Who will come out on top? The Bolts meet the Blades, Sunday at 4, here on KAVA.

Comedy: (Lots of smile)

Non-stop laughs and silliness. Weeknights, here on KAVA.

News—General: (:30 News Team promo. Serious tone.)

 There's a place for News the right way. There's a place for reporting that's more than the late-breaking story. There's a place for thinking that's seasoned with wisdom and experience. There's a place where your questions are answered with truth and honesty. There's a place where people are more important than politics. The place is KAVA.

Your place for News the right way.

Trailer Scripts

For each trailer, find the underlying tone for the script as you tell the story. Make every phrase the most important words every spoken. Deliver with intensity, but not over the top. Remember that lines in trailer copy are often separated with sound bites from the film.

DRAMA: (serious tone)

Through every crisis.
Through every argument.
Through every disappointment.
A family on the edge of disaster.
Discovers ... the only thing that can save them.
Is the one thing they have in common.
Each other.
Stevie Long ... Reid Shannon ... Susan James ...
Each Other.

MYSTERY, SUSPENSE: (build anticipation)

Just as it seemed to be getting better.
His world fell apart.
Magic was everywhere.
But nothing was real.
Living a lie was his only revenge.
And revenge was only an illusion.
Reese Whitney ... Anton Ross ...
Presto.

COMEDY: (light-hearted with a smile)

He'll do anything to keep his job.
Including inventing the perfect family.
Now he's getting everything he expected and a whole lot more.
And his perfect family is anything but ...
Kevin Thompson ...
Perfect!

SCI-FI, ACTION, ADVENTURE: (dramatic with an edge)

They built it to be their home.
They built it to be their sanctuary.
They built it to last forever.
But nothing ...
Lasts forever ...
10 light years from Earth.
When everything goes wrong.
No one can hear you scream.
From the director of Dark Side.
Where will you be on ...
The Last Day.

FANTASY: (light, friendly, with an air of mystery)

Three thousand years ago, something magical happened.
Today, it's going to happen again.
Magic was his life.
Illusion was his world.
What happens next will turn his world upside down.
Everything he believed to be true will be proven a lie.
And every illusion he created will be real.
What is the difference ...
Between illusion ...
And ...
Reality!

Other VO Genres

In this Chapter

Scan these response codes for more information or visit the AOVA Extras section at **VoiceActing.com**.

More about ADR
James Phillips—PDF (from 4e)

18

Other VO Genres

What is Your Niche?

There are many niches of voiceover work. Previous chapters have discussed the essentials of most of the primary voiceover genres. This chapter will briefly cover a few of the more obscure, but still relatively common niches. Even with this, however, there are still many other genres of voiceover that exist. Fortunately, the basic performing techniques are essentially the same regardless of the genre. Some of the more obscure voiceover niches include talking toys, real estate talking tours, in-store advertising, museum and self-guided walking tours, podcasts, and foreign language dubbing and translation. If you can think of something where you hear the voice but do not see the person talking, you've probably found a VO niche.

One big mistake many entry-level voice talent make is that they want to be a voiceover "jack of all trades." Although it certainly may be possible to develop a high level of skill in a few voiceover genres, the idea of being able to work in every area of voiceover is impractical, at best. Although the basics may be the same, each genre has its unique marketing and performance requirements.

Diversification as an actor is definitely a benefit. However, as you begin to explore your talents and capabilities as a voice actor, you will discover that you are simply better and more comfortable working in some genres than others. You would be wise to find those performing styles in which you excel and focus on developing your business in those areas.

If you'd like to read more about some of the many niches in voiceover, scan this response code or visit the AOVA Extras page at **VoiceActing.com**.

Telephony

Telephony voiceover work includes the broad range of telephone messaging. If you've recorded an outgoing message on your home answering machine or voice mail, you've done the most basic of telephony work. Many businesses will use voice talent for *message-on-hold* (MOH), and *voice prompts*, among others. Scan the response code to listen to some creative outgoing messages. If you have a knack for creative writing and character voices, why not put those skills to work on your own phone message?

A message-on-hold recording is one or more messages, usually with background music, that are heard when a caller is placed on hold. A good MOH script will contain several short messages that focus on a service, product, or benefit offered by the business.

Voice prompts are the automated outgoing messages that provide instructions to a caller. One type of voice prompt simply asks the caller to take a specific action either verbally or by using the phone's key pad, like "press 2 for sales."

Another type of voice prompt takes an outgoing message to the level of creating a virtual person having a conversation with the caller. This is known as *Interactive Voice Response* (IVR). The caller is greeted by a recorded "person" who engages the caller in a conversation that will ultimately get her where she wants to go. The caller responds by speaking the request, and the computer uses voice recognition technology to move to the next prompt based on what the caller said. It's completely automated, but fully interactive. When properly produced, the voice prompts sound completely natural and may even be mistaken for a real person. Ah, technology.

Concatenation is a process in which the voice talent records individual words, short phrases or sounds. Computer technology assembles the appropriate sounds, words or phrases into sentences that provide information or instruction to the caller. Scan the response code to listen to an example of a typical concatenation that you might hear as an automated reminder for a doctor's appointment.

Voiceover in this genre will often require a very conversational style, but will sometimes require more of a commercial sales type of delivery. Telephony voice prompts are increasingly the first contact a customer has with a business, and there are literally dozens of companies who are eager to provide this service. An Internet search for "message on hold companies" will bring up dozens of prospects.

Telephony can be an excellent entry to voiceover work. Scripts are often very short, but the best thing about Telephony work is that the voice talent will often become the signature voice for a business. When working for a large company, this type of voiceover work can also lead to other voiceover work for the company as a narrator for corporate training, marketing videos, and radio/TV commercials.

ADR/Looping

Automated (or Automatic) Dialogue Replacement (ADR) and *Looping* are niche areas of voiceover that have remained hidden secrets for quite some time.

The term "looping" comes from the early days of film sound when a segment of the film was spliced into a continuous loop. A set of white lines was drawn on the film using a grease-pencil, with the lines converging where dialogue needed to be replaced. The actor, watching the lines converge, would begin speaking on cue, matching his original performance.

In today's complex world of film sound, the process is basically the same, except it is now done with a video playback with audio beeps replacing the grease-pencil. The definition of looping has also expanded in that it now also includes recording the natural human sound effects of crowd scenes, non-scripted voiceover, and efforts (the sounds of human exertion in fights, etc.).

Specifically, ADR is the process of replacing dialogue for a feature film or TV program. Original dialogue may need replacing for any of several reasons: the location sound is unusable; the director did not like a line's delivery, even though the rest of the scene was OK; or, profanity needs to be replaced for television or air-travel use. In most cases, the original actor will be brought in to replace their own dialogue, perfectly matching their original performance. However, occasionally, the actor may not be available, so his or her lines may need to be replaced by a sound-alike voice talent who will perfectly match the actor's lip-sync. Most of the major studio feature films will have 50-80 percent or more of the dialogue replaced—and some will ADR the entire film, discarding all of the original dialogue.

An ADR session will usually only have one or two actors in the booth, while a looping session may include a group of up to 20 "loop group" actors. The director will assign actors to a specific task, or to replace a line of dialogue, as needed. The actors may perform individually, or as a group, depending on the needs of the film.

Breaking in to ADR/Looping can be a challenge as it is a small niche of voiceover work. Improvisation and acting skills are essential, as is an ability to perfectly match lip-sync. "Loopers" must be excellent researchers in order to create the realism for specific time periods and locations.

The best way to break in to this part of the business is to find a loop group and ask to start sitting in on sessions. As a loop group director gets to know you and learn about your abilities, they may invite you to participate.

Anime

Anime is a sub-genre of animation and a form of dialogue replacement. Technically, Anime is a form of Japanese animation that has seen unprecedented popularity around the world, including the United States. Anime voiceover requires a conversational style of real-people voice characterization and emotional dialogue. Unlike standard animation, in which the voiceover is recorded first, in Anime, the voice actor will be replacing the original Japanese voice track. This requires exceptional acting skills, an excellent sense of timing, a keen screen-eye coordination, and thorough understanding of the characters and story line.

Anime voiceover is a very small niche and it can be one that is difficult to break into. Although there are a few well-paid "stars" in Anime voiceover, the majority of work in this genre has a reputation of offering a relatively low pay rate. Most voice talent who work in Anime do it because they love the genre. One excellent way to learn the requirements of Anime voiceover is to join one of the hundreds of groups that produce on-line Anime, most of which do not pay for any work done. An Internet search for "fandub anime" will bring up thousands of resources.

Professional Anime voice talent recommend that anyone wishing to enter this area of voiceover begin by mastering their acting skills and study the film genre to have a thorough understanding of the Anime art form.

New Media

Recent advances in technology have spawned dozens, if not hundreds or even thousands, of new opportunities for voiceover work. Doors have opened for providing voiceover for everything from blogging to website audio and much more. The genre of voiceover in New Media, is just that ... "new." This is one of those specialty areas which is definitely not for everyone, but may be the perfect entry for the voice actor who has an interest in this area. As with most other areas of voiceover work, New Media jobs can lead to other, more lucrative work in other areas of voiceover.

Joe Klein is one of the recognized authorities on New Media and how to work as a voice talent in this highly unique genre. For over four decades, Joe has written, voiced, produced and directed literally thousands of product jingles, records, national radio commercials, corporate presentation soundtracks and network promos. During the 1970s and '80s, Joe established a reputation as one of Hollywood's leading voice directors, receiving multiple Clio and International Broadcast awards, and was widely known for the "bigger than life" sound he achieved. Since 2005, Joe has been a leader in providing voiceover content for podcasters, video bloggers and new media networks through his company, New Media Creative.

The following section is edited from the chapter on New Media that appeared in the fourth edition of this book. The full chapter is included in the AOVA Extras at **VoiceActing.com** or by scanning this response code.

JOE KLEIN (Laughlin, NV)
NewMediaCreative.com

A Revolution in Media Content & Delivery

So, just what is this new media thing, anyway?

For those in their twenties, New Media is more than just a familiar term! It's most likely the only kind of media that the majority of those in this demographic consume. For those more "old skool" folks, however, the term has often evoked looks of bewilderment over the last few years.

The term new media refers primarily to newer forms of media content, which, beginning early in the new millennium, were originally being created by alternative and renegade content creators. Falling under the new media genre now is a rapidly growing new breed of alternative content being produced by mainstream media outlets as well, including repurposed versions of the content that appears on traditional media channels.

If you are a voiceover artist or media professional involved in the field, it's time you got a handle on the brave new world of delivering programming, promotion, training, marketing, and a growing number of forms of alternative advertising.

THE VOICE ACTOR'S PLACE IN NEW MEDIA

The ongoing advancement and expansion of new media is unquestioned. Likewise, the migration to new media outlets of current media applications such as commercials, training video, film, television programming, and many other genres of entertainment and business is opening doors to many new opportunities for the observant voice actor. Soon, new media will be the mainstream.

As more and more new media producers are, finally, moving toward "professional quality" production, there is an increasing amount of voiceover work up for grabs. Online commercials and promos, promotional videos, training videos, marketing tools, and instructional and informational media of every shape and form are being produced at a constantly growing rate. Even short form media elements, such as fully produced show opens, closes and promos are being widely used in new media content.

The sheer quantity of content now being produced presents a wealth of opportunities for producers, performers and others involved in the creative process. But, with the opportunities come an unprecedented level of competition to achieve success. Besides competition, the biggest challenge to today's voiceover artist is, and will continue to be, keeping up to speed with the market and all the technologies related to it. Another pressure is on pricing. Intense competition has made pricing an important issue to deal with. Those paying for voiceovers, like other employers, want more for less, so it is more important than ever for a voiceover artist to be more than just an able performer.

Being skilled in the art of pricing and negotiation are now vital. If you don't feel comfortable dealing with these areas, seek out an agent or representation of some kind. But, keep in mind that a growing number of voice actors bite the bullet and negotiate for themselves these days, so paying for the services of a representative may add a cost that hinders your ability to compete. Tips on pricing and negotiation are often topics of conversation on the blogs of voiceover professionals.

Lastly, it is now more important than ever for today's announcers and voice actors to take a direct and active role in marketing and promoting their own services and "brand." Again, extensive use of the Internet and participation in social networks are, increasingly, the keys to success in any profession or business enterprise, and voiceover is hardly an exception. Educating oneself as to where the work is and how to get a piece of it is the key to achieving success!

Remember, it's all about networking in the new online world. See, and be seen. Follow, and be followed. Communicate, and people will soon start to communicate back to you. These days, dialogue leads to success!

I am constantly asked how one can navigate the rapid sea of change constantly occurring in these areas. To be sure, staying on top of the latest developments and innovations in new media and social networking is very much a full-time job in itself. By the time you are reading this, it is a certainty that much of the information offered here will be dated or superseded, and hundreds of new products and services will have come—and gone. The best way to stay current is to go online, search for and then gather the latest information.

Here are a few suggestions that I hope will stay current. To keep abreast of what's going on, there are thousands of blogs online that cover the latest developments and trends in new media, social networking and related fields. As of this writing, a few of the better, and most popular tech blogs are TechCrunch, Gizmodo, Engadget, Technorati and Slashdot. My vote for the best blog covering the world of social networking is Mashable. All of the blogs above also do a good job of covering new media news and views. Of course, all of these blogs have Twitter feeds as well, so you can follow them post by post on Twitter, which, in effect, acts as a headline service for the blogs.

Besides blogs, a good source to stay on top of all things tech and the online world is to regularly listen to podcasts or view some of the thousands of podcasts or online video programs out there. I highly recommend a collection of weekly programs offered up by the TWiT Network, which, as of this writing, can be found at **twit.tv**. TWiT offers several shows about tech in general, the Internet, and several more specialized subjects, such as Google, Windows, Macs, digital photography and much more. You can watch them live as they're being recorded or download them at any time. Another popular online new media network to check out is Revision 3. Both Revision 3 and TWiT are great sources for information about tech, new media and other current topics.

There is definitely way too much information for most of us to consume, so find a few blogs that you like best, and just follow them as best as you can and at your own pace.

As it has always been in the art of voice acting, the new media voice actor's job will continue to be one of communicating a compelling message through the creation and presentation of interesting characters and reads. And, although the fundamental performing skills remain the same, the business model, technology, and marketing methodologies are ever-changing and do require constant monitoring to adapt to trends as they evolve.

There is a new breed of creative new media producers offering new opportunities for voiceover talent to help them deliver their content. As voice actors, it is our job to evolve along with the new media marketplace.

In this Chapter

Getting Paid to Play

19

The Business of Voiceover: Getting Paid to Play

It's Show-biz, Folks!

One thing many people seem to either not realize—or simply forget—is that voiceover is part of show business—and the larger part of show business is business! Before making the investment in time, energy, and money for workshops, training, and equipment to become a voice actor, it is important to have an understanding of what this business entails, how it works, and what is expected of you as an independent business owner.

This chapter will introduce you to the business of voiceover so you will be able to make an educated decision as to whether or not this type of work is right for you. Demos, marketing, auditions, and many other aspects of this business are discussed in detail later in this book.

Acting for voiceover may be one of the best-kept secrets around. You get to be serious, funny, and sometimes downright silly and your voice may be heard by thousands. Voiceover can be an incredible outlet for your creativity and it can often seem like you get paid to play!

To be perfectly honest, voice acting can be very challenging at times. The reality is that you are an entrepreneur running your own business and you can expect all the ups and downs that go along with that. Depending on the type of voiceover work you choose to do and the clients you work with, you may be on call 24/7/365. Vacations may be difficult to schedule and there will be moments when you wish you were somewhere else. You will encounter producers and/or directors who do not seem to know what they are doing and who will test your patience. You will be faced with cramming :40 of copy into :30—and the producer will expect it to sound natural and believable. All of this—and more—is just part of working in the world of voiceover. That's show-biz!

Fortunately, the uncomfortable moments are relatively rare, and the majority of voiceover work is enjoyable and often downright fun. If you really enjoy what you do, and become good at it, even challenging sessions can seem like play, although it may appear to be hard work to everyone else. If you approach voiceover work with a positive attitude, a mindset of teamwork, and an eagerness to help your clients achieve their objectives—rather than as just a way to make money, your likelihood of success will be much greater. To a large extent, your level of success as a voice actor will depend on your mental attitude and how you approach your work.

The Many Hats of a Voiceover Professional

In the "old days," a voice actor would be booked simply as a performer. But times have changed! Today, if you are going to work in voiceover at a professional level, you must not only be an excellent performer, but you must also have functional skill sets in most or all of the following business areas:

- Marketing and branding (advertising)
- Social media networking
- Business management
- Sales and negotiating (for setting and negotiating talent fees)
- Telemarketing (cold calls and phone marketing)
- Copy writing (for promotional materials and web content)
- Talent director (self-direction)
- Audio engineering (recording and editing your voice tracks)
- System design (setting up and using your home studio)
- Acoustician (knowledgeable of room acoustics)
- Accounting (managing your income and expenses)
- Computer skills (Word processing, spreadsheets, etc.)

There are many other aspects of running a business that may also come into play as your voiceover business develops. For example, you may do mass email marketing, in which case you will need to know how to design effective email campaigns and you will need the software or support services for bulk email without landing in the recipient's junk email folder. Or you may decide to create a blog or manage your own website. These would both require some knowledge of how to manage files on the web. In short, you will be wearing many hats and you may change hats many times a day.

Many voice actors also work as on-camera talent or in theatrical productions. After all, acting is acting, and the more versatile you are as an actor, the greater your likelihood of success in voiceover. As you master voice-acting and business skills, you may find yourself developing other talents as well. This diversification can provide income from several sources.

Making Money Doing Voiceover Work

There are only two ways to get paid for voiceover performing: union jobs and non-union freelance jobs. If you are just starting out, it is a good idea to do as much non-union work as possible before joining a performing union. It's sort of like "on-the-job training." Non-union voiceover work will provide the opportunities to get the experience you need and accumulate some recordings of your work.

If you pursue voiceover work as a career, you may eventually join a union, especially if you live in a large market. However, it is not necessary to join a union to become successful. There are many independent voiceover performers in major markets who are earning substantial incomes, even though they are not members of any union. The choice of whether or not to join a union is one that only you can make—and you don't need to make that decision now.

THE UNIONS

Nothing in this book is intended to either promote or discourage union membership. However, joining a performing union is an important decision for anyone pursuing a career in voiceover. If you are just beginning, a basic knowledge of the unions is all you need. As you gain experience, at some point you may want to consider union membership. Much of the information in this section can be found on the SAG-AFTRA website at **sagaftra.org**.

SAG-AFTRA is currently the only union that handles voiceover performers in the U.S. For decades, the American Federation of Television and Radio Artists (AFTRA) handled performers working in electronic media and the Screen Actor's Guild (SAG) handled actors working in film. In 2012, these two unions merged to form SAG-AFTRA. In Canada, voiceover work is handled by ACTRA (the Alliance of Canadian Cinema, Television, and Radio Artists)—**actra.ca**. British Columbia has UBCP (the Union of BC Performers), **ubcp.com**, which is the BC branch of ACTRA. In the United Kingdom, the voiceover talent union is Equity, **equity.org.uk**. Other countries with collective bargaining unions will also have one or more unions that work with voice talent.

The job of all unions is to ensure proper working conditions, to make sure you are paid a reasonable fee for your work, to help you get paid in a timely manner, and to provide health and retirement benefits. The degree to which these are accomplished may vary. Since the focus of this book is on the general craft and business of voiceover, I'll limit the discussion of performing unions to the U.S. SAG-AFTRA union. If you will be doing voiceover work outside of the United States, you should know that many performance unions have agreements or affiliations with unions in other countries, so your original union will be the best place to start. It may be necessary to contact a local talent agent to learn which union applies in your country.

In the U.S., AFTRA and SAG came into being in the early days of film, radio, and later, television. Unscrupulous producers were notorious for taking advantage of the actors and not paying performers a decent wage—some not even paying them at all. So, the unions were set up to make sure performers got paid and were treated fairly.

As the unions grew, Congress decided that it was unfair for a person just working once or twice a year to have to join the union and pay dues every six months. The result was the Taft-Hartley Act, which made major changes in U.S. labor-management relations. In regards to voiceover, this law gives you (the actor) an opportunity to work under the jurisdiction of the union for 30 consecutive days without having to join. You then become union eligible, "vouchered," or "Taft-Hartley'd," and must join the union at your next union job.

What this means is that if you do a lot of freelance work, you can still do a union job without having to join the union or pay union dues. The trick is that the next union job you do, you must join the union, whether it is three days or three years after your first union job. Immediately after the 30-day grace period you have the option to join or not join the union. At the time of this writing, with SAG-AFTRA you can join after working one job as a principal performer, which would include most voiceover work. As a background player, you must work three days under a SAG-AFTRA contract before you can join.

One of the advantages of being in the union is that you are more likely to be paid a higher fee, or scale, than if you did the same job as a freelancer. Although, in some situations, you may be able to negotiate a higher fee as a freelancer, you will not receive any of the benefits of being a union member. Union *scale* is the fee set by the union for a specific type of work. By the time you reach the level of skill to have been hired for a union job, you will most likely be ready to join the union.

One function of the union is to protect your rights as a performer. For example, a voiceover performance for a radio commercial can also be used in a TV spot or for an industrial video. Unless you are a union member, there is little you can do to protect yourself. There are some 400 different union agreements for different types of projects, each of which has a different pay scale. Radio and TV commercials are paid based on the market in which they air and how long they will be aired. Industrial videos and CD-ROMs are handled in other ways. Without the union you are potentially at the mercy of the person hiring you, and your voice may end up being used for projects you never agreed to.

As a union member you agree to work under the principal of *Rule 1*, which simply means that union members agree not to work without a guild or union contract. A union member working in a non-union production cannot be protected if the producer refuses to pay, pays late, makes unauthorized use of the performance, or in any other way takes advantage of the performer. Any legal action taken by a performer working outside of Rule 1 is at the performer's expense, and the union may actually discipline the member with fines, censure, suspension, or even expulsion.

As a member of SAG-AFTRA[1], you are free to audition for any job, including non-union jobs. If you are hired for a non-union job and the employer is not a signatory, the union may contact the producer and have him or her sign a signatory agreement before hiring you. If you are a union member, and are not sure about your employer's status with the union, call the union office in your area.

One way for a union member in the U.S. to work a non-union job is a waiver called a *One Production Only* (O.P.O.) *Limited Letter of Adherence*. This waiver is good for one job only, and the work you do on that job is considered union work. The advantage is that the non-union producer agrees to the terms of the union agreement, but does not have to become a union signatory. The O.P.O. contract must be signed before any session work.

Some producers, for one reason or another, prefer to not work with union performers. Money is usually not the reason. It may be unrealistic demands from an agent, company policy to work only with non-union talent, or a dislike of the paperwork. To get around these and other issues, some agents and production companies will work as a union signatory effectively separating a non-union producer from the union. This is a win-win situation—because the producer does not have to deal directly with the union, the quality of the talent remains high, and union performers have the opportunity to work for a greater variety of clients at a fair level of compensation. Some voiceover performers operate their own independent production companies as signatories and essentially hire themselves. It is also possible for you, as a union member, to handle the paperwork, thus making it more attractive for a producer to hire you.

Joining SAG-AFTRA requires payment of a one-time initiation fee and current dues. The initiation fee can be paid as a single payment or through the Union's member-owned credit union over a 24 month payment plan. Dues are set at a base fee until a minimum income from union work is reached. Above the minimum, dues are a calculation of the base plus a percentage of union income. Visit the SAG-AFTRA website for more information. Most everything you need to know about membership, dues, and member benefits is on the union's website at **sagaftra.com**.

FINANCIAL CORE

Financial core, or *fi-core* is an aspect of union membership in the U.S. that has been and remains very controversial. Fi-core is a level of union membership at which an actor can be a member of a union and still be able to work non-union jobs.

Since the beginning of labor unions, states would make their own laws about whether they would be a "union shop," or a "right-to-work" state. In a Union Shop state, laws were passed that required a person to be a union member and pay dues in order to do union work. Right to Work states allow unions to exist, but membership is voluntary, and the union cannot require a person to pay anything as a condition of employment.[2]

Financial core came about as a result of union members who disagreed with the way their union was using a portion of their dues for political activities. They also disagreed with their union's control over work they could and could not accept. A series of U.S. Supreme Court legal battles beginning in 1963[3] eventually culminated in a 1988[4] landmark decision that changed the way all unions work (not just SAG-AFTRA). In 2001, President George Bush signed an executive order that requires all unions to inform prospective members of their "financial core rights," or "Beck Rights," before they join the union.

The resulting legal decisions for Financial Core require that an individual must first be a union member, and then formally request a change to Financial Core membership status. Upon declaration of Fi-Core status, the union member loses specific membership rights: the right to vote, hold union office, receive the union newsletter, declare their union status, and participate in union-sponsored events, among others. Payment of semi-annual dues is still required, however at a slightly reduced rate. The union determines the portion of dues that are spent for political and other activities that do not directly apply to the union's collective bargaining efforts, and for those at Fi-Core status, that percentage of dues is deducted from the dues payment.

At its essence, Financial Core creates a non-member, dues-paying status that allows a performer to work both union and non-union jobs. Those who favor Fi-Core will mention that the performer regains control over the kind of work they do and their compensation. Those against Fi-Core claim that this membership status seriously disables the effectiveness of collective bargaining. Ultimately, as a voiceover talent, it is up to you to fully research Fi-Core so you completely understand its ramifications when the time comes for you to join SAG-AFTRA.

An Internet search for "financial core" will bring up dozens of websites that discuss both sides of this controversial aspect of union membership.

WHEN SHOULD I JOIN THE UNION?

You may be tempted to join the union sooner than later, believing that union membership will mean higher pay and more credibility as a performer. Although both may be true to some degree, it is generally a good idea to put off joining SAG-AFTRA until you have mastered the skills necessary to compete with seasoned union talent. Producers expect a high level of performance quality and versatility from union performers and it takes time and experience to master the skills necessary to perform at that level. Because the union initiation fee is quite high, joining SAG-AFTRA too soon not only may be an unwise financial expense, but it could have the potential for adversely affecting your voice-acting career. Most voice talent need the seasoning of working lots of non-union jobs before they will be at a level of performing skill and business knowledge that can be considered competitive with professional union talent.

Here are some reasons to consider union membership when you feel you are ready, when you begin getting audition calls for union work, or when you are booked for your first union job:

- Union membership is considered an indicator of professionalism and quality. Producers know they will get what they want in 2 or 3 takes instead of 20.
- Your performance is protected. Union signatories pay residual fees for use of your work beyond the originally contracted period of time.
- You will also be paid for any time over one hour on first and second auditions, and paid a fee for any additional callbacks.

WORKING FREELANCE

Non-union, freelance work is an excellent way to get started in the business, and there are lots of advertisers and producers who use non-union performers. As a non-union performer, you or your agent will negotiate your fee. The fee will be a one-time-only *buyout* payment. There are no residuals for non-union work, including non-union work done at *financial core*. The going rate for freelance voice work can be anywhere from $50 to $250 or more depending on the project, the market, your skill level, and what you can negotiate. For non-union work, or work booked without representation, the negotiated terms are between you and the producer, as are the terms of payment. If you have one, your agent will negotiate your fee and terms for the booking.

If a non-union producer should ask your fee, and you are not sure what to say, the safest thing to do is to quote the current minimum union scale for the type of project you are being asked to do. You can always negotiate a lower fee. If you have an agent, the correct thing to do is to ask the client to contact your agent. A complete discussion of setting rates, negotiating fees, and getting paid is in Chapter 25, "Managing Your Voiceover Business."

Talent Agencies, Casting Agencies, Personal Managers, and Advertising Agencies

The jobs of talent agents, casting agents, and personal managers are often misunderstood by people not in the business or just starting out. They all have different functions in the world of voiceover.

THE TALENT AGENCY

Talent agents are in the business of representing performers for the purpose of getting them work. Talent agencies are licensed by the state and must include the words "Talent Agent" or "Talent Agency" in any print advertising, along with their address and license number. The talent agent works with producers, casting directors and advertising agencies to obtain auditions and negotiate talent fees and booking schedules.

A talent agent receives a commission of 10% to 25% based on the scale they negotiate for their performer and whether their performer is union or non-union. For union work the commission is above and beyond the performer's fee (scale plus 10%). In some cases, the commission may be taken out of the talent fee, especially for non-union freelance work obtained by an agent. For talent agencies to book union talent, they must be franchised by the local SAG-AFTRA union. Contact the union office in your area for a list of franchised talent agents.

Unfortunately, this is not a perfect world, and there are many unscrupulous agents who will attempt to relieve you of your money. If anyone asks you for money up front to represent you or get you an audition, he or she is operating a scam. Period! The same is true for 1-900 numbers that charge a fee for information on auditions and casting. Most of the information is available elsewhere, either for free or a minimal charge. The best thing to do is find a reputable agent and stay in touch with him or her. Even if you are freelance and must pay your agent a 25% commission, the advantages of representation may well be worth it.

Do you need a talent agent to do voiceover work? No. Will a talent agent benefit you in your voiceover career? In most cases, yes. Chapter 24, "The Talent Agent," includes a complete discussion on how to find and work with a talent agent.

THE CASTING AGENCY OR CASTING DIRECTOR

A casting agency is hired to cast the talent for a particular project. They may also provide scriptwriting and some producing services, such as directing talent. They may even have a small studio where some of the production is done. Casting agent fees are normally charged directly to the client and are in addition to any fees paid for the talent they cast.

Most voice casting agencies work with talent agents and have a pool of talent that covers all the various character styles they use. Talent from this pool are used for all projects they work on and they will rarely add a new voice to their pool unless there is an opening or special need. The talent in their pool may be represented by several talent agents. Casting agencies may occasionally hold open auditions to cast for their projects but they are generally not a good resource for non-union voice talent.

THE PERSONAL MANAGER

A personal manager is hired to manage a performer's career. The personal manager attempts to get the talent agent to send the performer out on auditions, and encourages the agent to go for a higher talent fee. Managers usually work on a commission of up to 20% of the performer's fee, which is taken out before payment to the performer and in addition to the agent's commission. Some managers may work on a retainer. Either way, a manager can be expensive, especially if you are not getting work. Personal managers are fairly rare in the world of voiceover, and the voice actors they work for are generally well-established on-camera performers who will only occasionally do voiceover work.

ON-LINE AUDITION SERVICES

In the early days of voiceover, a talent agent was one of the few sources for learning about voiceover audition opportunities. As the Internet has grown a variety of on-line audition services have taken their place in the world of voiceover. Although on-line audition services have matured over the years, they remain a controversial aspect of the voiceover business.

An on-line audition service should not be mistaken for a talent agent. A talent agent earns their money by representing the performer to a client base they have developed over many years and negotiating talent fees. An online audition service does not represent any talent or negotiate any fees. Instead, they will charge the voice actor a membership fee and, in turn, send the performer a seemingly endless stream of auditions. Those auditions will usually be filtered by certain criteria in the talent's profile and will come from producers, often referred to as *talent seekers* or *talent buyers*, who do not pay anything to the audition service.

While an audition received from a talent agent will usually have a specific fee set for the project, most auditions received through these on-line services will have a pay range for the talent fee, for example: $100-$200 for a single script. It is up to the talent to determine whether the audition, project and fee range are appropriate. The talent must also decide what they would charge the producer, within the offered fee range, should they be booked for the project.

This effectively puts the member voice actors in a bidding war for every project. Some on-line audition sites will recommend their members bid a low fee to increase the likelihood of getting the job. Requiring voice actor members to bid against each other is one of the more controversial aspects of most on-line audition services. Another controversial point of contention is that the talent buyers pay nothing for the service.

On-line audition websites operate as a membership service providing an assortment of benefits to their members on an annual renewal basis. Their primary function is to provide downloadable auditions to their members. However, some offer webinars, blog posts and limited training, among other things, while others only offer auditions.

There are currently four types of websites where voice talent can post their information and demos in the search for voiceover work.

The first is a website operated by an Internet talent agent or casting agent. To be listed on these sites, a voice actor must be accepted by the talent agency for representation. These on-line agents operate like any other talent agent—it's just that their talent pool is spread across the Internet.

The second is a free listing site that will usually offer to post the talent's name, a brief description of the talent's services, and a link to the talent's own website. As with most things in life, you get what you pay for, so these free listing sites are often not very well promoted and don't result in much work—if any. The real benefit of listing on these free sites is the fact that Internet search engines are constantly scanning websites to catalog names and links. The more frequently your name is found by these search engines, the easier it will be for someone to find you. Don't plan on getting jobs from the free sites.

The third type of listing website is one where voice talent can receive requests to submit auditions for a fee. These sites are very clear in stating that they do not act as a talent agent, but instead, serve as an intermediary between the voiceover talent and those seeking voiceover performers. They do not take a commission for work obtained by the talent, but they do charge a membership fee for voice talent to gain access to audition requests. Many voiceover professionals refer to these as *pay-to-play* sites.

A fourth type of on-line audition site has begun to appear over the past few years. These sites are usually operated by legitimate talent agents and, although they operate in a similar manner to the other on-line audition sites in that they charge a fee for audition delivery services, these sites will also take a commission from any work obtained through the agency. Although some of these sites are quite popular and may produce impressive results for their members, the fact that they are both charging a fee and taking a commission may put the ethics of their business model in question.

This act of taking two income streams from the same source is commonly known as *double-dipping*, and is illegal in many States. Owners of these sites will say that the membership fee they charge is for services that are in addition to representation, such as web pages, consultation, and management. However, most of these services have traditionally been considered a cost of doing business for an agent and many of the on-line talent agents do include these services as part of their representation. The fact that an on-line agent might charge a membership fee for services beyond those of representing their clients should not be taken as an implication that they are operating illegally. It is only mentioned here so you are aware of how some on-line agents and audition services operate so you can make an educated decision when considering their services. The majority of membership audition websites are legitimate, do not act as a talent agent, and truly do their keep their promise to market and promote the website (and thus the talent) to producers, ad agencies, and other talent buyers.

On many of these sites a voice actor can, as part of their membership, receive a personalized web page with their bio, performing styles, and several demos ready to be heard. Members also receive a continuous stream of audition requests. The web page is a huge benefit for a beginner who doesn't have a site of their own. A website is a powerful marketing tool, and this feature alone may make a membership worth the price, but for an experienced voice actor who has their own site, this may be of little value, primarily because the web page is actually a *sub domain* of the hosting site with little or no direct marketing value for the member.

Another benefit for beginning voice talent is the constant stream of audition requests. Each audition is an opportunity to practice performing skills and experiment with voiceover technique with real-world copy without risking anything. For this reason alone, it can be well worth the membership fee just to get access to a wide variety of scripts. Experienced voiceover performers don't need the practice, and dealing with the vast number of unqualified auditions can be very time consuming.

Although most on-line audition sites truly have the best interests of their members in mind, there are some that seem to cater to the talent buyers who do not pay for the service, rather than to their voice talent members who pay a fee. This has created a great deal of controversy in the voiceover community primarily due to the large quantity of low-end, inexperienced talent buyers; poorly written copy; and low-ball talent fees.

Although many experienced voiceover professionals are members of these services, many members have little or no experience at all. Since there is no direct representation by the audition service, the talent buyer is taking a risk when they book a voice actor solely on the audition submitted. In order to mitigate this risk and provide a more satisfactory experience for both the performer and talent buyer, some on-line audition services will hold the talent fee in an equity account until the client signs off on the work. This has created yet another controversial aspect of these services in that some will charge a fee to the talent for holding the talent fee in the equity account.

Each on-line audition service has its own personality and you may find that membership in one, more than one, or none will be right for you. It is likely that more on-line audition services will appear in coming years. An Internet search for "on-line voiceover auditions" will reveal many resources. At the moment, however, you can learn more about some of these services at the following websites:

- bodalgo.com (Europe)
- commercialvoices.com (North America)
- opuzzvoice.com (North America)
- piehole.co.uk (U.K.)
- producershandydandy.com (North America)
- sunspotsproductions.com (North America)
- studiocenter.com (North America)
- voiceartistes.com (India)
- voice123.com (North America)
- voicehunter.com (North America)
- voiceovers.co.uk (U.K.)
- voiceovers-uk.com (U.K.)
- voices.com (Canada, North America)
- voplanet.com (North America)

Are the on-line audition sites right for everyone? Of course not. It's ultimately a personal decision. While some will find these services valuable, others will find them frustrating and of no help at all. Submitting auditions on-line is a numbers game. The more auditions you submit, the more likely you will be booked. But be prepared to submit hundreds of auditions before landing that first job.

I would suggest, however, that if you decide to join an on-line audition service, you do so with realistic expectations. Treat your membership as a year of real-world training. Use every audition to polish and perfect your performing skills and to master your recording and editing skills. Don't expect immediate results and consider any jobs you get as icing on the cake.

HOW ADVERTISING AGENCIES WORK

Advertising agencies work for companies that advertise, coordinating every aspect of an advertising or marketing campaign. They write the scripts, arrange for auditions, arrange for the production, supervise the sessions, handle distribution of completed spots (spot announcement, or commercial) to radio and TV stations, purchase air time, and pay all the fees involved in a project.

Ad agencies are reimbursed by their clients (advertisers) for production costs and talent fees. They book airtime at the station's posted rate and receive an agency discount (usually about 15%). They bill their client the station rate and get their commission from the station as a discount. If the advertising agency is a SAG-AFTRA signatory, they will also handle the union fees according to their signatory agreement. Since the ad agency books all airtime, they also handle residual payments, passing these fees on to their clients.

Most advertising agencies work through production companies that subcontract everything needed for the production of a project. Sometimes the production company is actually a radio or TV station that handles the production. In some cases a casting agent might be brought in to handle casting, writing, and production. Some larger ad agencies, with in-house facilities, may work directly with talent agents for casting performers.

Ad agencies can be a good source of work. Your agent should know which agencies use voiceover and will send out your demo accordingly. You can also contact ad agencies directly, especially if you are non-union. As part of your marketing, you can telephone ad agencies and let them know who you are and what you do. You will find many ad agencies work only in print or use only union talent. When you call, ask to speak to the person who books voiceover talent.

Most ad agencies have a similar operating structure. Agencies that handle national accounts will, of course, have a much larger staff and the agency operation can be a bit complex. Many small market ad agencies consist of only one or two people who do everything.

In general, here's how an ad agency works: The ad agency assigns an account executive (AE) or on-staff agency producer (AP) to handle a client's account. Sometimes both an AE and AP are involved, but it is usually the AP who knows more about the production than the AE. The AE is more involved with arranging the schedules for airtime purchases. The AP is the person who is generally in charge of selecting talent. The AE is less involved, but often approves the AP's talent choices.

Either the AE or AP may be present during auditions and one or both is almost always present at the session. If the ad agency is producing the spot, they will want to make sure everything goes as planned. If the spot is being produced by a casting agency, someone from that company may also be at the session. Casting agencies are more common for television on-camera productions than for voiceover, but a casting agency rep may be present at an audition or session if their agency is handling the production. And, of course, advertisers are very likely to be at the audition and session to provide their input.

HOW PRODUCTION COMPANIES WORK

As their name implies, production companies are where the work of creating the radio commercial, TV spot, industrial video, video game, or other production is done. They come in all shapes and sizes, from the one-man shop to the large studio with hundreds of people on staff. Most production companies have a small staff of 2 to 10 people, many of whom may be freelancers. Some work out of a studio located in an industrial complex, while others work from home.

Production companies generally work directly for a client, or as a production resource for an ad agency or a corporation's on-staff producer. Many large corporations have their own in-house production facility which might be staffed by company employees or by freelancers.

Although some production companies can be a good source of freelance voiceover work, most work primarily with talent booked through a talent agent by the producer, or with talent hired by an ad agency. Learn which production companies do the kind of voiceover work you want to do, and get to know who the producers and directors are.

There is no, single resource for identifying production companies. For local producers, an Internet search for "production company your city" will bring up many of your local production companies. You can also contact your Chamber of Commerce to learn about local businesses that provide audio and video production services. Many cities have a film bureau that maintains a list of local production companies.

For television and film documentary narration, you can learn a lot by watching the closing credits of documentary, biographical, travel and other programs on various channels on your cable TV system. Many television program producers work with talent agents or from an internal talent roster. Still, it will be beneficial to learn who the companies are, who the producers are, and the types of programs they produce.

Finally, searching the Internet for websites associated with keywords like "production companies," "audio and video production," "voiceover producers," and so on, will reveal many opportunities.

---

[1] Source: *http://www.SAG-AFTRA.org*

[2] Source: *http://www.nrtw.org/d/rtwempl.htm*

[3] U.S. Supreme Court, *NLRB v. General Motors*, 373 U.S. 734, 1963.

[4] U.S. Supreme Court, *Communications Workers vs. Beck*, 487 U.S. 735, 1988.

In this Chapter

How to work in the VO Biz

20

How to Work in the Voiceover Business

Promoting and Marketing Yourself

Getting voiceover work is a numbers game: The more you hustle, the more contacts you will make. The more contacts you have, the more you will work. The more work you do, the better known you will become. The better known you become, the more people who want to hire you, and you get more work. It's not quite that simple, but you get the idea—it truly is a numbers game. This chapter will help get you started on the right track.

If you're just getting started in voiceover, you'll be doing all the work: making the calls, sending the auditions, recording the sessions, handling the billing, and doing the follow-ups. This can seem overwhelming, but if you are organized and know what you're doing you can reach whatever level of success you desire.

Before embarking on an all-out promotion campaign, do your homework and get organized. Make sure your acting skills are up to professional standards, know what you do best and learn what you need to know to run your business, especially in terms of your marketing. As you create your promotion campaign, keep your long-term objectives in mind and continue honing your performing and engineering skills.

But be prepared … it will take some time. Voiceover is not an "overnight success" kind of business. Achieving any degree of success will take an organized, concerted effort on your part, knowledge of your market and competitive performing skills.

There are many good books on marketing and advertising from which you can gain a tremendous amount of information. You can also learn a great deal by taking an adult education or college extension advertising and marketing course. The Small Business Administration (**sba.gov**) offers a variety of classes, services, and business tools that you may find helpful in organizing and running your business. Through these and other resources, you will not only learn some excellent ways to promote yourself, but you will also learn what goes into creating the marketing and promotional copy that you work with as a voiceover performer.

Managing Your Time

As an entrepreneur or sole proprietor voiceover professional you will face the number one challenge facing every small business owner: how to manage your time.

Generally, time is not on your side: your clients will need their recordings yesterday, but you won't get paid until next month. There will be some days when you are extremely busy, and long stretches of down time when it appears that no one is listening to your auditions. It can be frustrating! Still, if you are going to pursue your dream and stay in business, you will need to learn how to manage your time to handle the work when it comes in and run the many other facets of your business at other times.

For most people, time management is an acquired skill. There are literally dozens of time management systems that have been developed and it is important to note that some people will do better with one system than another. For some, the mere task of getting organized just to the point where they can begin learning how to manage their time will be a major accomplishment and the process of time management itself may be a real challenge. For others, time management will seem like second nature.

LEFT VS. RIGHT

The reason for this apparent dichotomy is simple, and it has to do with the way our brains work. The human brain consists of two hemispheres, a left hemisphere and a right hemisphere. The left side of the brain primarily handles linear, sequential processes. The right side deals mostly with non-linear, creative processes. An individual who is left-brain dominant will love working with logic, numbers, and organized structures. On the other hand, for a creative right-brain dominant individual, organized structure is the last thing on their mind. They would prefer to let their creative juices flow and have fun.

In terms of how our brains work, you could consider Left as Logical and Right as Ridiculous. Left-brain dominant individuals are often led to careers in banking, sales, computers, system design, and other jobs that require focused attention to detail. Right-brain dominant individuals are the artists, painters, actors, and musicians of this world. Society needs both types to function, and most of us have the ability to switch between our hemispheres as needed, even though we might be dominant in one hemisphere or the other.

Although most voice actors tend to lean more to being right-brain creatives, it is critical that we develop some left-brain skills if we are to run our voiceover business effectively. These would include basic business procedures, accounting and, of course, time management.

Whether you are left or right-brain dominant, there will be times when you need to quickly shift to a task that requires efficient functioning from the other hemisphere. For example, you may have just completed a series of auditions and now you need to balance your checkbook. Shifting from one hemisphere to the other can sometimes be a challenge, but fortunately there is a quick trick you can use that will make the transition go smoothly.

To move from a creative, right-brain, mode to a task that requires focused attention, get a blank sheet of paper and a pen or pencil. Starting near the top right of the paper, slowly draw a very straight line of 2 to 3 inches from right to left. Now, repeat with another line just below the first line you drew. Continue this process, keeping equal length and spacing between lines, as you fill the paper adding columns to the left. Don't be concerned if your lines aren't perfectly straight or the spacing isn't exact. The object of the exercise is to focus your thoughts on a very specific, linear task. Drawing the lines from right to left is simply a device to subconsciously tell your brain you are moving from the right hemisphere to the left.

To move from a focused, left-brain mode to a creative mode, start at the upper left of the paper and begin drawing a series of circles in a clockwise motion without taking the pen from the paper. Draw the circles in a variety of sizes and don't worry if the circles aren't exactly round. When you get to the right edge of the paper, just keep drawing clockwise circles to get back to the left edge and keep going. The random nature of the circles will move your brain function from a linear mode to a non-linear, creative mode. Drawing clockwise tells your brain to move from left to right.

It may be difficult to believe that you can change your brain functionality by merely drawing lines and circles, but if you put this technique to work, you may be surprised at your increased ability to focus on a task and your increased creativity when performing.

MAKING THE MINUTES COUNT

The tendency of a creative individual is to avoid anything that requires focused attention to detail. However, in order to manage our time effectively, we must pay attention to what we are doing during those 60-second increments of our day. Everyone on this planet has the exact same number of minutes in a day. The difference between success and failure is in how those minutes are put to work. And that's what time management is all about.

Of the dozens of time management systems available, some are very complex, requiring a considerable amount of organization, while others are quite simple. At the heart of every system is a process to break down daily goals into tasks that can be accomplished in small, manageable pieces. But regardless of the system, to be effective, it must be done consistently and its use must become a habit.

Some of the more popular paper-based systems are Franklin Day Planner (**franklinplanner.com**) and Daytimer (**daytimer.com**). These use a binder and a calendar/organizer that can be used to schedule daily activities, although there are computer and smart phone versions available. Used on a regular basis, these systems work extremely well for thousands of business people. However, they do require some organization and regular attention. For some people this type of system simply doesn't work at all.

An online organizer designed for actors and other performers is Performer Track (**performertrack.com**). This is a subscription-based service that provides for management of every aspect of a performer's busy schedule. Auditions, bookings, scheduling, contacts, mileage tracking, and many other functions are included, most of which allow you to better manage your time.

If you are like me, you may be more attracted to, and more likely to use, a system that is very simple. One of the simplest time management systems around was developed by a university student in the late 1980s. It's call the Pomodoro Technique™ and it's a nifty way to get more things done more efficiently.

As with other systems, this begins with a list of tasks. A task is chosen and worked on during a focused 25-minutes (a pomodoro), which is timed using a kitchen timer. Each pomodoro is followed by a short break with a longer break after four pomodoros. Tasks are divided into morning and afternoon sets of pomodoros and progress is documented at the end of each pomodoro session. You can learn a lot more about the Pomodoro Technique™ and download a free Ebook that explains how to use the system by scanning this response code or visiting **pomodorotechnique.com.**

To get yourself up to speed, there are a few basic time management principals that you can begin to use that will ease you into any of the structured systems.

- Begin each work day by making a list of tasks for that day.
- Work on tasks in short, focused increments. Only one task at a time and try to avoid or minimize interruptions.
- Move tasks not completed to the next day's list.
- As tasks are completed, check them off your list.
- Set aside a specific time of day when you will focus on your auditions. Do this at the same time every day.
- Set aside a specific time of day to check your email.
- Set aside a specific time of day for making outgoing calls.
- Be flexible enough with your schedule to allow for bookings, incoming calls and minor interruptions.

One interesting addition to the classic "to do" task list is to simultaneously create a "to don't" list. These are things you do on a regular basis that are repetitive, waste time, keep you from being productive, or are simply bad habits that you want to change. As you go through your day checking off items on your "to do" list, you'll also see your "to don't" list, which will reminder you to stay focused.

If you do nothing more than implement some basic time management concepts into your daily life, you'll be doing more than the majority of small business owners, and you will see results.

Business Basics

NEVER UNDERESTIMATE THE VALUE OF DUMB LUCK

During an interview at one of our VoiceActing Academy events, Robert Concha, owner of Theatron Productions in San Diego, made the following point: "Dumb luck plays a big part in this business." This simply means you can never tell where the next opportunity might present itself. You might be on vacation and the person next to you on the plane might be a corporate producer looking for a narrator for their next training video. Or, you might overhear a conversation while standing in line at the bank.

Wherever and whenever those opportunities pop up, you need to be prepared. The difference between those who are successful and those who are not is often the ability to recognize the opportunities when they present themselves and the preparation, skill and discipline to self-promote (or, as Robert says, "BS your way into the job") and the ability do the job professionally when you are booked.

Actors of all types seem to have a tradition of "BS-ing" their way into landing work. What usually happens is that the producer or casting agent will ask if the actor can do a specific thing, like tap dance, sing, or do a character voice. The actor, because she wants the job, will of course answer with a resounding "Yes!". Then the actor goes home and calls every friend they have to find out how to do what they were just hired to do.

The important thing to note here is that you must be able to deliver on what you say you can do. And you will only be able to quickly learn a new skill if you already have a strong foundation and expertise in related skills.

The key is to be prepared—both with the skills of your performing craft and with your business skills. You might be able to "BS" your way into a VO gig, but if you can't perform up to the client's expectations, you may have a short-lived career as a voice actor.

NEVER UNDERESTIMATE YOUR ABILITY TO BE ABLE TO DEAL WITH PEOPLE

Inevitably, a situation will occur where you are given a direction that is confusing, unclear, or just plain contradictory to everything you understand about your role. Or you might be working for a client who treats you in a demeaning manner. In either case, you might be working for a client who doesn't know what they are doing, or they might simply be a jerk. This can even happen when working for some of the top ad agencies or big-budget clients.

You must be able to communicate with the director as clearly as possible, so you are both on the same page. If you don't understand a direction, ask for clarification. Don't just say "I've got it." when you have no idea what the director is asking you to do. You must be able to understand what the director means, which may not be exactly what he says. If you are given a line read, you must be able to duplicate the attitude and inflection exactly. A lack of communication skills can result in frustration for both you and your client.

Another aspect of communication during a session in which you have a director is that you will generally not be aware of the conversations taking place in the control room or on the other end of the phone line. In his one-man show, Bob Bergen, the voice of Porky Pig, tells a story about one of his early recording sessions during which he noticed that there were long periods when the control room mic was off and he could see the engineer, producer and director actively discussing things. He wondered what was going on, so one day he hid a small tape recorder under his jacket in the control room. Sure enough, during a long silence Bob could see the control room crew actively waving their arms, pointing, and apparently arguing. From Bob's point of view it looked like they really didn't like his performance. However, when he listened to the hidden recording, what he discovered was that the guys in the control room were arguing about what they were going to have brought in for lunch.

If they're not taking about lunch, the direction you receive may be the direct result of last-minute changes or adjustments necessary to bring the project into time. Regardless of the reasons, you should accept each new direction with a professional attitude and an eagerness to meet the director's request as best as possible. Keep your personal opinions to yourself. If you have a valid idea, wait for an appropriate opportunity to suggest it. And know that that opportunity may never present itself. Develop the ability to work with people and maintain a professional attitude at all times.

Producers, directors, engineers and clients will remember you when you give them a positive experience during a session. Your communication skills and ability to gracefully follow direction will contribute greatly to that experience. Some studios, agents, and producers actually keep lists of performers who cannot follow direction or who are argumentative. Those performers are not likely to be asked back. You do not want to be added to any of those lists.

MAKING CONTACTS WITH PROSPECTIVE CLIENTS

Sales calls are an art form all their own. This primer will give you some basic ideas, but you should also consider some additional study on the subject of sales and marketing.

You will need to spend a fair amount of time on the phone, contacting potential clients. Know what you want to discuss before making any calls. Know your niche, what you do best, who you are marketing to, and be specific about the type or types of voiceover work you are promoting. If you are trying to get into animation voiceover, it's not appropriate to call ad agencies or discuss your expertise with telephone messaging.

Before calling, do some research on your prospects to learn how they use voice talent. When you call, let your professionalism speak for itself and show your prospect that you understand their needs and how your voice work can be of benefit to them. Be careful not to be in a rush to sell your services. You'll be much more successful if you engage your prospect in a conversation to let them get to know you, and for you to gather additional information about how you can help them. Have some prepared notes to look at so that you don't forget anything important during your call, and be prepared to answer any questions that might arise during the conversation.

Needless to say, your business cards should be printed, your demo produced, your email template prepared and follow-up letters ready to mail before you begin making calls, and you should have a system in place for cataloging prospects and following up.

Remember, you need to talk to someone who is directly responsible for hiring voiceover performers. If you do not have a contact name already, tell the receptionist the purpose of your call. She will most likely direct you to that person, or refer you to someone who might know to whom you should speak. If you can't get connected right away, try to get a name to ask for when you call back. If you get voicemail, leave a clear and concise message that includes your phone number at the beginning and end. It's a very good idea to write out your message so you know what to say when you are forwarded to voicemail. Keep it conversational so you don't ramble or sound like you are reading as you leave your message.

It may take a few follow-up calls before you connect with someone. If you already know how the company you are calling uses voiceover, your conversation should be of an introductory nature. If you don't know, your call should focus on how voiceover work might be used to benefit their business. Either way, the call should be more about them than you. You probably will find some companies that have not even considered hiring an outside professional for their voiceover needs. Undoubtedly, you will also find many that are not interested in what you have to offer. Remember, this is a numbers game, so don't let yourself get discouraged.

Offer to send a copy of your demo to those who are interested. Follow up by mailing your demo with a letter of introduction. It is amazing how many people never follow up a lead by sending out their promo kit. You will never get any work if you don't follow up.

FOLLOW-UP

You will need the following basic items for follow-up:

- A cover letter on a professional-looking letterhead
- Business cards
- Labels and envelopes to hold your print materials and demo
- A voiceover client list detailing any session work you have done
- A website you can refer prospects to for additional information about you and your services, and where they can listen to your demo
- Your demo as an audio CD for mailing and as an MP3 file for posting on your website and emailing.

First impressions are important, and the more professional you look in print, and sound on the phone, the more your prospect is likely to consider you for work. If you use color in your logo or graphics design, you should consider using special paper designed for color ink-jet or color laser printing. With appropriate computer software and a good printer, you can design a simple form letter that can be adapted to your needs.

You will need several different versions of your letter of introduction, depending on whether you are following up from a phone call, or if the follow-up is from a personal meeting. Your letter may also need to be adjusted according to the type of voiceover work you are promoting to a given prospect.

Keep your letter to no more than three or four short paragraphs in a formal business style. Personalize the heading as you would for any business letter. Thank the person you spoke to for his or her interest, and for the time spent talking to you. Remind them of who you are and what you spoke about. Let the company know how you can help them, how quickly you can work, and how they can contact you. Also, mention in the letter that you are enclosing your demo. Be sure to include your website and email address in your letter. The following is an example of a typical follow-up letter to production companies that would promote narration services:

Dear Mr. Client:

Thank you for taking the time to speak with me yesterday, and for your interest in my voiceover work.

As I mentioned during our conversation, I am available to help your company as a voiceover performer for in-house training, marketing presentations, and radio or television commercial advertising. I am enclosing a list of some recent projects I have voiced and a copy of my demo. You can learn more about me and listen to more of my work at **JamesAlburger.com**. This will give you a good idea of the types of voiceover work I do that can be of benefit to you. I have a professional home studio and can deliver projects within 24-48 hours.

I look forward to discussing how I may be of service to you. Please feel free to call me anytime at 123-456-7890 or send an email to email@address.com. I look forward to working with you.

Sincerely,

Unlike the other performing arts, in the world of voiceover, a résumé is not a requirement. Most talent buyers are more interested in what you can do for them now, rather than what you have done in the past, but a list of clients can be helpful, especially if they are recognizable names. If you have an agent, include the agent's name and phone number in the letter. In larger markets your agent's number should be the only contact reference. In smaller markets you may want to include your own number as well as your agent's.

When sending a CD, your agent's name and phone number should be included on the label. When sending an email, your agent's information should be in your signature line.

You do not need to mention your union status or fees. Your union status should have been established during your phone call, if that was an issue, and if you are in a union, it should be noted on your demo CD label or in your email signature. Your fees are something to be negotiated either by your agent, or by you, at the time you are booked. If it comes up in a conversation, just tell the person that your agent handles that, or that you cannot quote a rate until you know what you will be doing. If they insist, quote the current SAG-AFTRA scale for the type of work they are asking about. At least that way you will be quoting a rate based in industry standards. If you are booking yourself as non-union, freelance talent, mention that your fees are negotiable.

During your initial call, you should have set up a timeframe for any follow-ups. After sending your thank-you letter and demo, call your contact at the scheduled time to confirm that the package was received. This helps to maintain your professional image and serves to keep your name in their mind. Don't ask if the person has listened to your demo. That's not the purpose of your call. If they bring it up, fine, but you should not mention it.

Before completing your follow-up call, ask if there are any projects coming up in the near future that might take advantage of your talents. If so, and if the company is considering other voiceover talent, be sure to make yourself available for an audition. Phrase your conversation in such a way that it is clear how your services can help them. This puts you in a position of offering something of greater value to your potential employer, rather than just being someone asking for work.

Once you have established a list of possible employers, you will want to stay in touch with them. Consider sending out a brief note or postcard every six months or so and on holidays. The purpose here is to keep your name in front of the people who book talent.

Perhaps the only rule for follow-up is to be consistent and persistent. Maintain a professional image, keep your name in front of your prospects, and you will get more work. Here are some ideas for follow-up reminders:

- Thank-you card (after session, meeting, or conversation)
- Holiday and seasonal cards
- Birthdays and anniversaries (if you know them)
- Current projects you have done
- Generic reminder postcard
- Semiannual one-page newsletter updating your activities
- Special announcement about upcoming projects

REACHING THE PEOPLE WHO BOOK TALENT

Many large companies have in-house production units, while others hire outside production houses and work with agents. There will usually be someone who is in charge of coordinating promotion and advertising that may require the use of voiceover performers.

One problem in reaching people who use voice talent is figuring out which companies are likely to need your services. Some possibilities are:

- **Watch local TV and listen to the radio.** Look for local advertisers who are doing commercials with voiceover talent.

- **Call advertisers and ask who coordinates their radio and TV advertising.** Radio stations frequently use station staff for local commercials, and will not charge their advertisers a talent fee. You need to convince these advertisers why they should pay you to do voiceover work when the radio station does it for free. This can be a real challenge! When talking directly to radio advertisers, you need to put yourself in a class above the radio DJ. Some advertisers like the celebrity tie-in by using station talent. Others may simply prefer to spend as little as possible on advertising. You can get work from these people, but you may need to educate them so they understand the value of using you instead of doing it themselves or using a DJ for their commercials. You may find that they have other uses for voiceover talent for which you would be far more qualified than a DJ.

- **Contact your local chamber of commerce.** Get a list of the largest companies in your area. Many of them will use voiceover performers and some will do in-house production.

- **Check the local newspapers.** Call advertisers that you think might be likely prospects.

- **Use resource directories.** Many cities have a resource directory or a service bureau that can provide you with specific information about businesses in the area. Or, your chamber of commerce may be able to provide this information.

When you contact a non-broadcast business that has a production unit, start by asking to talk to the creative, promotion, or marketing department. You should talk to a producer or director. Don't ask for advertising or sales, or you may be connected to a sales rep. If you ask for the production department, you may end up talking to someone running an assembly line.

Television stations can be a good source for bookings. They use voiceover for all sorts of projects, many of which are never aired. At a TV station, the production department handles most audio and video production. Some TV stations may even have separate production units for commercials, station promotion, and sales and marketing projects. Start by asking to talk to the production manager, an executive producer, or someone in creative services. You may end up talking to someone in the promotion department, because a promotion producer frequently uses more voiceover talent than anyone else at the station.

Recording studios usually will not be a good source for work, simply because most recording studios specialize in music recording. Usually, those that produce a lot of commercials work with performers hired by an ad agency or client. Some studios do a limited amount of producing and writing, and may book their voiceover talent from a pool of performers they work with regularly. In most cities, there are at least one or two studios that specialize in producing radio commercials. Use good judgment when sending your demo to recording studios. You might be wasting your time, but then, you never know from where your next job might appear. Some studios will recommend voice talent when asked.

Of course, contacting advertising agencies directly is another good way to reach the person who books talent. At an ad agency, the person you want to reach is the in-house agency producer (AP). Some ad agencies may have several in-house producers, and some agencies have account executives (AE) who work double duty as producers. If there is any doubt, ask to speak to the person who books or approves voiceover talent.

There are no hard-and-fast rules here. As you call around, you just need to try to find the correct contact person. Once you connect, use the basic marketing techniques described in this chapter to promote yourself.

How Social Media Networking Can Help Your Voiceover Business?

The phrase Social Media Networking has become the buzz of the decade. This one concept, alone, has probably opened more doors for voiceover work than anything else.

Dave Courvoisier is a voice actor, a television news anchor and one of the top authorities on using Social Media Networking in voiceover. His blog is one of the best resources available for keeping up to date on what's new and "happening" in the world of voiceover. At the time of this writing, Dave is a board member of the World

Voices Organization (**WorldVO.org**) and has been a seminar presenter and co-host at several of the VoiceOver International Creative Experience (VOICE) conventions (**VoiceConvention.com**). To put it simply, Courvo (as he is known by most in the voiceover world) is the go-to guy when it comes to using Social Media to promote a voiceover career.

Dave Courvoisier
(CourVO.com & Courvo.biz/blog)

THERE'S VALUE IN SOCIAL MEDIA NETWORKING

Social Media is not a passing trend. 10 years of non-stop growth of FaceBook, YouTube, Twitter, LinkedIn, and many other online networks proves that.

Your presence as a voice actor on these digital platforms is not necessary for voice-acting success, but here are three reasons why they may be of value to you in your freelance business marketing efforts.

- They're free (and effective),
- They build & extend your brand,
- They establish valuable relationships.

Technology has changed the essence of voice-acting in the last decade, but talent and technology alone will not bring you clients. Current wisdom states that our business demands roughly 80% marketing so you can use your talent and technology in the other 20%. Technology also enables the phenomenon of social media, but human nature gives it vitality, character, and potential. Those same three human factors come to life in your marketing ... and social media amplifies them.

While traditional avenues of mailings, cold calls, customer follow-up, and prospecting for clients are not dead, Social Media accelerates the process online, on your computer, and in your hand-held device in ever-increasing proportions. In a very real sense you almost can't afford NOT to be present on Social Media.

So, can Pinterest help your Voice-Acting business? Quite possibly. But if you find it does not fit your style, there are only about 70 other apps, programs, platforms, and online forums that will fit your style.

WHICH ONES SHOULD I BE ON?

Where the people are.

- **FaceBook** is now, and for the foreseeable future, the 800 lb. Gorilla of Social Media. (1.4 billion world-wide)

- **Twitter** confounds many, delights plenty, scares news outlets, and is totally different than FaceBook, but it is also growing extremely fast. (more than 500-million)

- **YouTube** almost as American as Apple pie, and as ubiquitous as shoelaces, YouTube is the 2nd most popular search engine in the world next to Google (and also owned by Google) (4-billion views per day, 1-billion users)

- **LinkedIn** The serious sibling in the Social Media family, and perhaps the best place for you to find work (more on that later) (260-million users)

- **Google+** At 300-million users and growing strong, this platform is feature-rich and is also run by Google, which is desperate for it to succeed.

- **Pinterest, Instagram, Tumblr, RebelMouse, AboutMe** and literally hundreds of others (some with multiple millions of users) are also-rans, but can play their role in certain areas. For instance, MailChimp, which is an online email newsletter service, has 4-million customers and is free, but I'd hardly call it a social media platform.

WHERE DO I START?

With the basics. It is highly recommended that you review this section even if you already have an account open.

- Make your profile as complete as possible without going past your comfort level. For instance, do you want your phone number, address, email, and website URL for all to see? ... or just your website? Or a combination of the above?

- To the extent possible keep your information consistent across all the platforms. Some sites may be more visual (Pinterest), and others more business-like (LinkedIn), but your demo website is the same, and so is your email address, right?

- Use a good headshot picture. There's a lot of debate about this in the world of voice-acting, and voice-acting is maybe the ONLY profession I can think of where the argument has merit. For instance, if your mainstay of work is the voice of a 6-yr-old boy, and then a picture of you as a 40-something, graying man pops up, you can imagine how that will spoil the mental image of potential clients (real-life story). But for the rest of us who do ELearning, commercials, Corporate Tutorials, Audiobooks, etc., your headshot answers every person's natural curiosity as to what you look like. They're going to go on FaceBook anyway and look it up, so put your best "face" forward and beat them to the punch. Everybody has a good side. Pay some bucks to get a decent headshot, Photoshop it if you need to, then use that same head-shot on all the social media platforms. It can be the consistent, recognizable face of your brand.

- If you are still against using a head-shot, a logo is acceptable. It's not very personal, but a good brand logo can say a lot about your business and you. Most Social Media platforms want to put your face or your logo in a square-shaped template rather than rectangular (landscape) orientation

- ESPECIALLY on LinkedIn, complete your profile to the max. The site will lead you through this, and it behooves you to carefully choose (a) representative keywords, (b) authentic work/education history, and (c) current and reliable contact information. Why? Because LinkedIn pays special attention to those keywords, and your name will come up in appropriate searches when someone is looking for "Explainer video voiceover", or "corporate presentation voice actor".

- Unless you want your persona online to be obtuse for a reason, the honest and genuine approach is best. Don't embellish, lie, pose, or lead people to believe you are something you are not. It's too easy for people to verify your true nature online. Social Media is a practice in transparency. To the extent you can, be sincere and straightforward in your profile. That doesn't mean you can't be fun, or show your personality. Everyone has flair, but flair for the purpose of putting forward a false person will eventually work against you. If you're going to be obtuse for a reason, at least do it consistently.

OK, MY PROFILES ARE ALL SET-UP, NOW WHAT?

Be present. Participate. Answer others' posts. Contribute. Pay it forward. Offer links. Post pictures and videos. Get involved in conversation threads. Create relationships. Ask questions. Watch for others to answer. Answer THEM. Follow (or friend) others, and encourage others to follow (friend) you.

Despite the American obsession to amass large numbers of followers, it's not the quantity, but the quality of your relationships online that will bring dividends.

JOIN GROUPS

Most social networks allow for groupings. They may go by different names. On FaceBook and LinkedIn, it's "groups". On Google-Plus it's "communities". On Twitter it's "lists".

The groups typically offer various levels of public/private access—even "hidden" in some circumstances. With these groups, you can petition on your own to join, you can be invited, and you can be endorsed or promoted to join by someone in the group. In these Social Media platforms, groups exist for every conceivable interest, passion, hobby, industry, business, and niche. If you don't see one for you and your interest, you can start one.

All of the big social media networks have a big selection of voice-over groups. Join one. Join several. This is where the meaningful interaction with colleagues and even prospective clients takes place.

I would especially encourage you to join groups on LinkedIn (more than 650,000 groups exist there), that represent a target audience for your services. This may take some time, but luckily, LinkedIn has some wonderful search tools using keywords, regions, business, demographics, etc.

For instance, if you are seeking work in the area of explainer videos, you may start your search using terms (online services like **wordtracker.com** can help you with this) that relate to this niche industry. Once you've found the groups where explainer video writers and producer hang out, join and begin by just lurking. That way you can discover the tenor of the group, and the level of formal or casual activity there. Eventually, you may want to start contributing to the conversation when you feel you have something valuable to add. In time, people will come to recognize that you are a narrator of explainer videos, but not because you've beaten them over the head with a lot of promotional language touting your services … rather because you've offered insights into the process of doing explainer videos from the narrator's perspective.

Mining social media for client prospects is a marathon, not a sprint.

One other note. On LinkedIn, you can directly approach individuals in groups who may not necessarily be first-order or direct connections in your contacts. This is one of the true advantages of LinkedIn groups.

TIPS FOR NET ETIQUETTE & USE OF TIME ON SOCIAL MEDIA

People tend to say things through the veil of social media they would often not say to your face. That can be good and bad. The bad can be terribly rude, and the good can be enabling and supportive. There are limitations to the written word that fail to convey the nuances of intonation, body language, and innuendo. Sarcasm and humor works sometimes, and emoticons help, but generally, social media writing should be unambiguous and straightforward. Don't be lacking in personality, just be very clear.

In general, three topics tend to be lightning rods for controversy: Religion, Politics and Mac vs. Windows. Feel free to say what you want ... just be ready for polarized responses.

If a conversation turns contentious, temper your temper and use equanimity (stability, calmness). No one EVER wins a flame war online. Sometimes they go on and on. Sometimes (rarely, it seems) all sides are willing to engage positively, that's when the conversation can be edifying. Often, though, the thread falls to name calling and ugliness. That's the time to withdraw to a one-on-one message, or leave the conversation altogether.

Some people reach near addictive behavior when it comes to social media. Indeed, the visual and written content can be terribly alluring (especially endless YouTube videos), so it's good to set clear in your mind and in your business plan what you plan to use Social Media for, and how much time each day you are going to allocate to the various networks.

Many people who feel they've had success on social media hold to the following rough structure:

- Take to the Social Media platforms in small chunks of time throughout the day, instead of visiting for one long session in the morning or evening.
- Use a smart phone or tablet to quickly update your participation in valuable conversations when you have brief pockets of time.
- Depend on email notifications to keep you abreast of activity in groups & continuing threads.
- Take advantage of add-ons, browser extensions, and plug-ins to filter and automatically file certain flagged messages into waiting folders.
- If you find you still can't control the amount of time you're spending on social media sites, then plan to use a laptop that is unplugged. When the battery runs out ... time's up!
- If you find you have no stomach for Twitter, Facebook, and Google Plus—that it all seems too frivolous and a waste of time—then you might want to focus on the more business-like LinkedIn platform.

SHOULD I UPGRADE TO A PAID ACCOUNT?

In most cases, no. FaceBook and Twitter are always free anyway, but a vast array of third-party programs are typically for-profit services that start with free, and offer tiered services on a monthly plan. If you find one of these services extremely helpful to the point where you're relying on them, you may want to begin a subscription. LinkedIn offers a richer, full-featured experience for a simple upgrade. With that comes better searches, more notifications of who has viewed your profile, and some other perks.

FINAL RECOMMENDATIONS

Many previous stand-alone internet services are incorporating (integrating) social media features. So what was once a simple online accounting program now might draw in material from your customer relationship management software, your email contact list, and a newsletter service like Constant Contact. These digital inter-program relationships are to your advantage. For instance, online photo storage place Picasa or Photobucket now allows for sharing of your content on Facebook, Twitter, Pinterest and so forth.

Tools that can greatly enhance your social media experience include a smartphone or tablet, a cloud storage service (DropBox or Skydrive), and a ubiquitous note-taking or memory-management program like One-Note, Evernote, or SpringPad.

As you can see, the amount of time spent on marketing, research, Social Media and other promotional and marketing efforts can be daunting. If you take it in small steps, and in an organized manner, you will, in time, develop a consistent and effective marketing plan.

Working Internationally

The voiceover marketplace is truly International in scope, even if you are working from a home studio in the middle of Montana. Using the Internet and some creative marketing, it is very possible to have clients around the world. Global voiceover work can take many forms: working in one country with clients in other countries, living in a foreign country serving clients in your native country, living in a foreign country providing voiceover to clients in that country either in your native language or that of the country in which you are working, or any combination of these.

Many on-line booking websites offer voice talent who are fluent in many languages, and who are heard around the world. Websites like

Bodalgo.com, Piehole.co.uk, and **TheVoiceRealm.com** all have rosters consisting of hundreds of International voice actors and promote their services to a wide range of major global clients.

Although, technically, working internationally is relatively easy to do, most voiceover professionals who work globally will recommend that marketing for International work be reserved until the voice actor has a strong client base in their own country or native language.

Andy Boyns is an actor who truly lives the dream. As a British expat living in Turkey, Andy was faced with an interesting dilemma: How to work in voiceover in a country where he did not speak the language. It's taken some time, but Andy now speaks fluent Turkish and is now working full time as a voiceover and on-camera actor. When he first learned about the VoiceOver International Creative Experience (VOICE) convention, he knew that, financially, he could not afford to attend. But he also knew that the education he would receive and the networking connections he would make meant he could not afford not to attend. He developed a number of networking strategies that paid his way to the convention. In the ensuing years, Andy has established himself as a prominent voice talent in Istanbul.

Andy Boyns (Istanbul, Turkey)
AndyBoyns.com

Working as a Global Voice Actor

"Globalization" and "localization" are two concepts that artist you should embrace and love. Why? Because wherever you are now you can record for a project in your native language for use almost anywhere in the world: for a local client, or someone on the other side of the globe.

Your "native" language can be defined as the language you have been exposed to and used since birth (since my son's "mother tongue" is Turkish, and his "father tongue" is English, one could say he speaks two languages like a native, so I prefer that term).

Globalization leads companies to promote themselves around the world, reaching ever expanding markets; localisation responds to the need for a project to be accessible as if the production were uniquely made for a particular place. So, an audio production of Company X, in city Y and country Z will almost certainly be in the language of country Z, and possibly also in languages D, E, and F. This necessitates the collection of appropriate voices, and while someone may do a passable read in a foreign language, the person who will generally cope best with the nuances of a text is the native speaker.

This is great news for all voice artists who can record and send via the internet, as all can literally develop an international business.

The Art of Voice Acting

Some production companies, studios, or particular projects prefer to work directly with a voice talent face to face. This is where the role of the foreign native voice artist comes in to its own.

My introduction to foreign native voiceovers came during a visit to the London headquarters of BBC World, Bush House, in the early 1980s. As a teenager I was both surprised and slightly confused when my friend explained that she was booking voice artists of many nationalities. Little did I know then that several decades later I would be booked for work as a foreign native voice actor in what has become my adopted home of Istanbul, Turkey.

So what is it like working as a "foreign native", an expat/ expatriate? What sort of work can be found living in a "foreign" market? How does one find work? Can one build a career as a voice actor? What are the rules, and the challenges?

If you have ever lived "abroad" you will recognize immediately that some things are the same the world over, and others are very, very different. The performance techniques discussed elsewhere in this book and the need to behave both professionally and ethically with clients are universals. As for type of work and how to find it, well I reckon that there are no hard and fast rules, and as with the expat lifestyle, you should learn to expect the unexpected! This may also be a global truism for success, but as a "foreigner" you can create opportunity in ways that the locals might find more difficult.

The type of work available depends on your success at developing the right connections, and for me this is the golden nugget of voice work. This is a people business – when I started, my knowledge of the local language was severely limited, but through the help of my personal network my workload slowly increased. Initially work happened to be focused mainly on company videos, and adverts, as these were the most common format produced at the time in my native tongue (English). While the types of regular production opportunities are likely to vary immensely, I've found it amazing that almost anything is possible: documentaries, audio books, e-Learning, telephone message on-hold, desktop and tablet applications, presentations, announcements, viral content for web, etc. I have yet to voice a video game in English, but having recently discovered a couple of companies which produce games, I most certainly hope the opportunity will arise. By personally meeting the local producers, I've opened up possibilities for them to think about.

In all likelihood the top casting agents will have a roster of foreign voices, so this is another means to finding work. While they are likely to be connected with some of the better commercial opportunities, an agent may also require exclusivity, so you need to weigh up whether you feel you can better network a wider range of opportunity. While for the first few years I worked through an agent, I have found the freelance route to be personally a more effective way of developing my brand in my present market.

The question of legality is also one which needs to be considered locally – do you have a right to earn money, or do you need a special work permit? Can you hold a day job and organise recording sessions outside your normal working hours? It's always worth speaking openly with clients about your availability. If it's your voice they want, and they need you in the studio, then there's a strong possibility they will work to accommodate you as best they can – be prepared to be flexible and pull your own strings to get out of your day job early if you discover they're on a tight timescale.

The life of a foreign native voice artist is certainly rewarding and fun, but also requires patience, tact, and diplomacy when presented with a translated text which might not strictly resemble the language you know and love. When faced with errors in a script, screaming "This is rubbish! A monkey could do a better translation!", while potentially true is unlikely to create on-going work opportunity. Ask for permission to correct errors, offer to record the original and, as an alternative, what you think is the correct version. To some extent polishing off minor errors are, in my opinion, part of the reason you've been hired as the native "expert". This is a tricky area unless you want to become a translator, which is a totally different profession, and if your knowledge of the original language is not perfect you run the risk of introducing new errors.

Today I make my living entirely from voiceover and production work. When I started (in 2005) all I knew about the industry was that I enjoyed the recording process, from a couple of exam audio scripts I read in the university where I was based. My ability to communicate in Turkish was almost non-existent. Imagine the fun I've had over the years learning how to communicate with sound engineers, how to self-direct, and to be directed. Fortunately my language skills are pretty good today, and in consequence I am much better able to develop new opportunities and clients. It's not just all about having fun, it's all about people, and the fact that you have something unique to add to their productions.

One of the remaining challenges is that of training, and I sometimes envy those who have the opportunity to meet up in local copy workouts. Thanks to the many excellent voiceover groups available via social media, and international events such as the VOICE convention (and the resource you are reading now!) it is possible to somewhat bridge this gap. The secret is to get creative with your networking and, yes, seek out opportunity through the global community. It's all about people.

A Business Plan for Voice Actor You, Inc.

You have probably heard the phrase: "If you fail to plan, you plan to fail." This is as true in voiceover as it is for any other business. You need to have a vision of where you want to be and have some sort of plan as to how you will get there. If either of these is missing, chances are you will not be as successful as you hope to be as quickly as you would like to be. Things will get in your way from time to time, and you will be distracted by just living your life. However, if you have a plan, you will be prepared to work around those obstacles when they jump in front of you.

As an independent professional, you need to look at what you do as a business. With that in mind, my coaching and business partner, Penny Abshire, has adapted a simple business plan that you can use to develop focus on the business side of voice acting. You will wear many "hats" as you operate your business. You are the CEO, CFO, Sales Manager, Marketing Director, Director of Education, and finally, a performer. It is critical to your success that you understand what you are doing for each of your duties and that you have a direction in which you are moving. The "Business Plan for Voice Actor You, Inc." on the following pages is something to which you should really give some serious attention. Don't just skim through this and forget about it. Copy these pages and read through the questions. Set it aside for a few hours to think about how you will plan your career, market yourself, sell your services, learn new skills, and protect your future. Some of the questions will be fairly easy to answer, while others may take a great deal of time and thought.

The time you spend preparing your plan will be time well spent. Refer to your plan on a regular basis and review it about every six months, or at least once a year. Things do change, and your goals and objectives may change. This is intended to be a guide to keep you on track for your career.

Business Plan for Voice Actor You, Inc.

This simple business plan is designed to help you focus on your business and propel you in the direction you want to go. Give each question some serious thought before answering and review what you've written at least once or twice a year.

1. As **Chief Executive Officer**, what is your vision or plan for a career as a voice actor; it should be specifically designed to ensure your growth, profitability, and financial gain?

   _____

   _____

   What change(s) must take place to bring this plan to fruition?

   _____

   _____

2. What strategic alliances are you forming to ensure the achievement of the vision or plan of VOICE ACTOR YOU, INC.?
   a) With whom are you aligning?

   _____

   b) How will this be beneficial?

   _____

3. As V.P. of Quality Control, what are you specifically doing to ensure and/or improve the quality of the service provided by VOICE ACTOR YOU?

   _____

4. As **Chief Financial Officer**, what plans must be made to accommodate the financial and marketing continuity of VOICE ACTOR YOU, INC.?

   Current strategy: Anticipated cost:

   _____

   a) Alternative sources of revenue?

   _____

   b) Probability of primary revenue continuation over next 5 years?
      Excellent___   Very good ____   Fair____   Poor____
   c) Back-up strategy:

   _____

5. As **V.P. of Marketing**, what steps are you taking to seek new or additional target markets for your services?

   a) Local markets?

   _____

   b) Other markets?

   _____

6. As **V.P. of Promotions**, what steps are you taking to complete the following:

   a) Seek representation?

   _____

   b) Collect materials and prepare for demo?

   _____

   c) Demo production?

   _____

   d) Graphic design (logo, USP, business cards, stationery/thank-you cards, etc.)?
      Slogan _____
      Design _____
      Printing _____

   e) On-going promotion (blog, etc.) _____

7. As **V.P. of Sales**, what is the projected revenue for year-end?
      $_____

   a) Is that enough to cover company expenses? ___yes ___no

   b) What about expected revenue growth for next year $_____

8. As **V.P. of Education**, what is the training plan *specifically designed* to ensure the services offered by Voice Actor You, Inc. are equal to, or exceed, industry standards?

   _____

   What is the time-line for implementation of the training program?

   By _____ I will be enrolled in _____ Completion date: _____
   By _____ I will be enrolled in _____ Completion date: _____
   By _____ I will be enrolled in _____ Completion date: _____

   By _____ I will read _____ Completion date: _____
   By _____ I will read _____ Completion date: _____
   By _____ I will read _____ Completion date: _____

   By _____ I will study and/or research _____
   _____ Completion date: _____
   By _____ I will study and/or research _____
   _____ Completion date: _____
   By _____ I will study and/or research _____
   _____ Completion date: _____
   By _____ I will study and/or research _____
   _____ Completion date: _____

9. As **V.P. of Human Resources**, what needs to be done to protect the mental, physical, and spiritual health of the primary employee (*you*)?

_____

   a) Vacation allotment, family leave, and general mental health maintenance?

   _____

   b) Maintaining connection with corporate stockholders? (*family*)

   _____

   c) Your spiritual health?

   _____

10. As **Director of Maintenance**, what adjustments should be made to improve the visual appearance and physical health of the primary employee (*you*), the product, or service?
    a) What do you plan to do?

   _____

   b) When will you get started—*specifically?*

   _____

11. As **Chief Benefits Officer**, what financial planning is in place to ensure your future financial security (*i.e., retirement*)?
    a) What do you plan to do?

   _____

   b) When will you get started?

   _____

12. As **Accounting Department Head**, what steps are you taking to maintain accurate invoicing, recordkeeping, and IRS accountability?

   _____

   _____

   _____

   _____

   _____

   _____

   _____

In this Chapter

21

Your Voiceover Demo

Knowing the basics of how to run your voiceover business is just the beginning. As your business develops, there are many things that will need to come together: your office, your demo, your print materials, your marketing, your website, and more. At times it may seem overwhelming and that you need to have one thing in place before you can start the next. If you take it one step at a time, you will be able to complete everything in due course and you'll be able to do it right the first time. If you jump in too quickly or skip a step, you may find that you hit a roadblock or that your marketing falls flat.

One of the most important parts of your voiceover business will be your voiceover demo. As I mentioned earlier, you might be able to get some voiceover work without a demo, but if you are going to present yourself as a voiceover professional, eventually you will need a professionally produced demo.

Your Professional Calling Card

Your voiceover demo is your best first—and sometimes only—opportunity to present your performing skills and abilities to talent agents, producers, and talent buyers. In the world of voice acting, your demo is your calling card. It is your portfolio. It is your audio résumé. It is, in a sense, your letter of introduction. You don't need headshots, or a printed résumé, but you absolutely do need a high-quality, professionally produced demo. It is the single most important thing you <u>must</u> have if you are to compete in the world of professional voiceover.

Demo Rule #1:
Don't Produce Your Demo Until You Are Ready

HOW WILL I KNOW?

OK, you've just completed several weeks of voiceover training and you're excited about getting started on your new career path. You received lots of positive feedback and encouragement during the workshop, and now you're ready to produce your voiceover demo, right? Probably not!

The single biggest mistake beginning voice actors make is to produce their demo too soon.

The reality is that unless you already have a strong performing background, you are simply not going to be ready for your demo after taking a single workshop—or, for that matter, possibly several workshops or even months of private coaching. You certainly won't be ready for your demo after just reading this book. Mastering your performing skills may take a considerable amount of time.

Producing your demo too soon may result in a presentation that is likely to be much less than is needed to be successful in this business and is simply a waste of time and money. A poor demo can potentially affect your credibility as a performer later on.

Before you even think about having your demo produced, make sure you have acquired both the business skills and good performing habits necessary to compete in this extremely challenging business. Remember that there are a lot of other people trying to do the same thing as you. Anything you can do to improve your abilities and make your performing style just a bit unique will be to your advantage.

Study your craft, learn acting skills, and develop a plan to market yourself <u>before</u> you do your demo. Take *lots* of classes—you'll learn something new from each coach! Acting and improvisation classes will help you develop your performing skills and voiceover classes, workshops, and conventions will hone those skills for the unique demands of voiceover work. If possible, find a voiceover coach who will work with you one-on-one to polish your technique before you go into the studio or, ideally, direct your session. Your coach knows what you do best and how to get the best performance from you.

So, you're probably asking the question: "How will I know when I'm ready to do my demo?" Good question! In her *Demo and Marketing Magic for Voice Actors* workshop and E-book, my coaching partner, Penny Abshire, breaks this question down to four possible answers.

• **The short answer is:** You'll know.

- **The medium answer is:** You'll know after you have the proper training, you've researched and studied other professional voice talent and their demos, know what the marketplace is looking for and feel confident you can deliver at the same level as other professionals doing similar voiceover work.

- **The long answer is:** You'll know when you can be handed *any* script—cold—and, within two or three takes, you can perform that script at a level comparable to other professional talent. You also feel confident that you can get work with your demo that is enough to cover the costs of its production.

- **The best answer is:** You'll know you're ready when you can stop asking yourself the question "Am I ready to produce my demo?" Which takes us back to: You'll know!

HOW DO I GET TO BE THAT GOOD?

The craft of performing for voiceover is, for most, an acquired skill. There are some rare individuals who are natural-born actors, but most of the working professionals in this business started out by mastering their fundamental acting skills and moving on from there.

Of course, you certainly have the option to take some short-cuts and produce your demo without adequate training. I wouldn't recommend it, but you can do it. And you might get lucky.

Remember this: Your performance, as heard on your demo, will be compared to every other demo a producer listens to—and most producers listen to a <u>lot</u> of voiceover demos. After a few hundred demos, it's not hard to separate the great talent from the "good," and the "good" from the rank beginners. Most producers will know within about five seconds. You want your demo to present you as one of the great talent and keep them listening more than five seconds!

To do that, you must become an expert at communicating with drama and emotion before you have your demo produced. Here are some things that will help you get where you want to be quickly.

- **Study acting.** Acting is the key to an effective performance. Learn how to act so your performance sounds natural and believable, and learn how to use your voice and body to express drama and emotional tension.

- **Do your exercises.** Set up a daily regimen for doing your voice exercises. Get into the habit of keeping your voice in top condition. Your voice is the "tool" of you trade—take care of it.

- **Take classes and workshops.** Have an attitude of always learning. You will learn something new from each class and workshop you take or repeat. The voiceover business is constantly adapting and new trends become popular each year. You need to be ready to adapt as new trends develop. Voiceover workshops will give you a foundation upon which you can develop your craft and business.

- **Attend large voiceover events.** Putting in face time at a voiceover convention will not only give you opportunities to learn from some of the top voiceover talent and coaches in the world, but you'll also get to meet and know your peers. Many incredibly powerful voiceover business relationships have been the direct result of meeting at a voiceover convention.
- **Read other books about voiceover.** Every author presents his or her material in a slightly different manner. That different approach might be all it takes for you to grasp a concept. You may also learn new techniques or get some fresh ideas from reading a variety of books on the subject. If you learn only one thing from reading a book, it was well-worth its purchase price.
- **Practice your skills and techniques.** When working on a piece of copy, rehearse your performance with an attitude of continually perfecting it. Have a solid understanding of the techniques you are using as you rehearse.
- **Get personalized coaching.** Every performer is unique and it takes personalized coaching to truly discover and refine that uniqueness. Seek out a qualified private coach to help you become the best you can be before you produce your demo.

A WORD OF CAUTION

The tendency of many people who enter the world of voiceover is that they want to fast-track their training and rush into promoting themselves as "professional" voice talent.

Consider this: Would you be ready to perform at Carnegie Hall after only a week of piano lessons? Would you be ready to perform major surgery after only a single year of medical training? Of course not! It would be foolish to even consider such things. Professional competency in any craft is only achieved after consistent study and considerable experience. It simply never happens overnight. Yet a beginning voice actor will often jump at the opportunity to spend several thousand dollars to take a fast-track voiceover course so they can get their demo produced long before they have acquired either the essential business or performing skills. Production of a demo after only a few days of training inevitably results in a demo that is both costly and unmarketable.

Before you spend the money for a demo, I strongly encourage you to study both the business and craft of voiceover to the point where there is no doubt in your mind that you are ready to get that demo produced.

Demo Rule #2:
Your Demo Must Accurately Represent Your Abilities

Your voiceover demo must be "great!" It cannot be merely "good." To create a great demo, you must make the effort to develop and hone your performing skills. You must know what you do best. Are you best with commercial copy or character voices? Is your expertise with dialogue, audio books, or medical narration? If you don't know, you're not ready for your demo.

Since your demo may directly result in bookings, it is extremely important that you be able to match the level of your demo performance when under the pressure of a session. It is quite easy for a studio to create a highly produced, yet misrepresentative demo that gives the impression of an extremely talented and polished performer. If the performer's actual abilities are less that what is depicted on the demo, the shortcomings will be quickly revealed during a session.

Deborah Lawrence, senior producer for promotions at KNSD-TV in San Diego, once booked a New York voice actor based solely on her demo. The demo included logos from all the major television networks on its label, was well produced and the voice actor had a long list of performing credits that included many Broadway shows. The voice was perfect for the spots.

When Deb arrived at the studio, the voice actor was already hooked up via ISDN from New York. After some chit chat, the session began and that's when Deb noticed a problem. The woman in New York was having serious problems reading the script and after several takes, the session was gracefully brought to an end.

After the session Deb learned that the talent agency in New York had never auditioned the voice actor. She was represented solely on the quality of her demo. Turns out that the voice actor had dyslexia and could not easily read directly from a script. All of her acting experience was based on memorizing her scripts—and she was very good when working from memory. The recording studio that produced this woman's demo had worked their magic to create a killer demo that completely misrepresented the actor.

Your demo must be an accurate representation of your voiceover skills and it should be professionally produced by someone who knows what they are doing. Even if you've assembled a state-of-the-art home studio, without practical knowledge of the business and extensive production experience, don't even think you can put a demo together at home and expect it to sound professional. It is extremely difficult for one person to deal with both the engineering and performing aspects of producing a demo at the same time. You need to be focused on your performance, not your equipment.

You need a director to listen to your performance objectively, help you stay focused, and help get you in touch with the character in the copy. In today's world of voiceover, it is essential that you develop self-directing skills because you may find yourself recording many projects in the privacy of your home studio without the benefit of direction from your client. However, performing effectively without a director, or by directing yourself, is very challenging and it's the last thing you want to do when producing your demo. Although many professional voice actors believe they don't need a director—and can actually perform quite well without one—all voice actors do, in fact, need a director to bring out their best work. The top professionals will tell you that they perform much better when they have a good director to guide them through their performance.

When you go to the studio to produce your demo, you should consider the session to be just like a real commercial recording session. You need to be able to get to your best performance, in three or four takes. If you need more takes to get the right delivery, you may not be ready. Realistically, anything after about the fifth or sixth take should be aimed at fine-tuning your delivery.

Be careful that you don't spend a lot of time over-rehearsing a script. Too much rehearsal can result in locking you into a groove for your performance that may be difficult to break out of. Your copy should be rehearsed just enough so you are comfortable with it, yet can be directed into alternative deliveries.

Versatility Is Your Selling Tool

There are three primary approaches to voiceover demos. The first approach will demonstrate the performer's range of versatility through a variety of examples showing different emotions, attitudes, and characters. This type of demo reveals a wide range of vocal styles, placements, and character voices, and is commonly used to market voiceover for animation and video games.

The second approach focuses on the performer being the most real and natural person he or she can be while demonstrating a range of emotion within the natural delivery of their own voice. This is the most common approach to commercial, narration, IVR, and telephone messaging demos.

The third approach focuses on a specific delivery style, often heard as an attitude or intonation in the phrasing. This is commonly heard in promo, trailer and radio imaging voiceover demos.

Good voice actors can do dozens of voices, emotions, attitudes and characters because they are able to find a place in their body from which to center the character and place the voice—even if the character and voice originate from their natural personality. Other good voice actors have developed a highly defined performance style that is at the center of everything they do. These two basic types of performers are the *character* and *celebrity* voice actors discussed in detail in Chapter 11.

Regardless of which approach is best for you, it is the range and variety of performance in a demo that demonstrate a voice actor's abilities. The essence of who you are needs to be present in every track of your demo. You need to capitalize on your strong points and present them in the best possible manner in your demo. The range of attitudes, emotions, and characters you can express during a voiceover performance is your own, unique, *vocal versatility.* Your strongest, most dynamic, and most marketable voice is called your *money voice.* This is the voice or delivery style that will get you the work. It is usually the first track on a demo and may eventually become your trademark or signature voice. Your other voices are icing on the cake but are necessary to clearly show your range and versatility as a voice actor.

Demo Basics

DEMO FORMATS

One interesting thing about technology is that it is constantly changing. What was in favor yesterday may be out of favor tomorrow. Reel-to-reel and cassette demos are history! The audio CD, the standard for many years, has given way to demos that exist as electronic data files. There is even demo technology that allows for instantly listening to specific elements of a voiceover demo.

Digital audio files of voiceover demos have several major advantages over the audio CD: there is no expense for packaging; the demo can be posted on a website, which makes it immediately available for listening and/or downloading worldwide; files can easily be copied and cataloged on a computer in folders that identify a performer's style, performance genre, or in whatever way works best for a producer or agent. They can be emailed, edited, re-sequenced, renamed, uploaded, and assembled onto a compilation audio CD. For auditioning purposes, it's very fast and efficient to simply open a folder on a computer and click on successive demo files until the right voice is found. Isn't technology wonderful? It's anybody's guess what the future may hold for voiceover demo distribution formats.

Even with the advances in technology, there are still some producers and agents who prefer holding a CD in their hands. Although it may not be as efficient as electronic files, there is something to be said for reading the label of CD and studying the performer's visual marketing image while listening to their demo.

For the purpose of marketing, it is an absolute must that your voiceover demo exist as an electronic file stored in an easily accessible location on your computer. This file can easily be emailed and with the proper computer software you can create "one-off" CDs that can be packaged and mailed if or when needed. Even in this age of electronic files, it's still not a bad idea to have at least a few CDs on hand for those times when they are requested.

Types of Voiceover Demos

Before producing your voiceover demo, it is important that you study current demos of professionals in the area of voiceover you are interested in. As with any business, you need to know what your competition is. One of the best places to study demos is **voicebank.net**. Here, you will find voiceover demos from nearly every major talent agent in the U.S. Click on "Voiceover Talent Agency," choose a category, select an agent, then start clicking on demos. You'll be amazed at what you will learn as you begin listening to some of the top voiceover professionals in the country.

Through your study of the craft and business of voiceover, you will be discovering the delivery style, characters, and performance techniques that work best for you. You will also be making choices as to the types of voiceover work that you are best suited for. Very few voice talent are able to effectively perform in more than a few categories. Animation and character voice actors will rarely work in narration or audio books, but many will do commercials. Audio book narrators may not find telephony voice work to be at all satisfying, but they may do industrial narration or documentary voice work. Find the areas of voiceover work you enjoy the best and are most suited for, and focus on mastering your craft in those areas.

There are no hard-and-fast rules for producing a voiceover demo. Your objective is to effectively reach the talent buyers who hire voice talent in the area of your demo.

Not too long ago, it was acceptable to produce a demo that featured multiple voiceover genres all wrapped up in a two-minute demo. Today, producers want to hear a specific demo for a specific type of work—and they want to hear it quickly. Your demo should feature examples of what you can do that meets, or exceeds, the expectations of those who are looking for voice talent in that area. In other words, your commercial demo should consist of only your commercial delivery style, and your character demo should feature your character voices. There may be some crossover, such as a character voice in a commercial, but you should avoid the temptation to combine multiple demo types into one demo.

Ideally, your demo should be compiled from actual projects you have worked on. However, if you are just starting out, this is not possible. You will need to create your own copy and design a demo that will catch the listener's attention and hold it. Even working professionals will sometimes write original copy to create a demo that really puts their voice in the spotlight. This can be a challenging task, but it can pay off big.

There are several schools of thought as to the type of voiceover demo to produce when just getting started. One is to produce a commercial demo first, because this is the type of demo that most agents will request first. Another is to produce a narration demo first, primarily because this niche represents the largest percentage of voiceover work. Yet another approach is to produce a demo based on a determination of the specific niche area that the voice actor wants to work in. All three are viable approaches and can result in bookings for an entry-level voice actor. You will be likely be most successful if you produce your first demo in the genre and style that you and your coach determine to be your greatest strength.

Voiceover demos are generally produced with the performer's *money voice* at the beginning and end. In-between are a variety of attitudes and styles that reflect the performer's range and abilities. Sequencing will be determined by your producer or engineer.

There are two basic structures for demos. The first is a *compilation demo* with examples of a variety of performing styles. The second is a *concept demo* that combines the demo clips into a logical sequence or story where each clip leads into the next. In both formats, as the demo progresses, there will be changes in attitude, pacing, energy, and character. Concept demos are rare as they are challenging to write, must be thought out very carefully, and fall into one of two categories: extremely good and unbelievably stupid!

COMMERCIAL DEMOS

Even though radio and TV commercials are only about 10 percent of the business, a well-produced *commercial demo* can demonstrate a performer's abilities for nearly every other type of voice work. Every segment should reveal some aspect of the real you through your delivery and the characters you create. There is little demand for accents, dialects, and wacky characters in radio and

TV commercials. Unless you are marketing your natural accent, those voices should be saved for other demos.

Your demo may contain as many as 12 to 15 segments, each of which demonstrates a different emotion, attitude, level of energy, personality trait, or delivery style at a variety of tempos. The copy chosen must be typical of what is commonly heard on radio and TV commercials. This type of demo should begin with your strongest spot and consist of several very short "clips" of about :03 to :010, fully produced to sound like a real-world commercial. The trend over the past few years is for a commercial demo no longer than one minute. However, you might want a slightly longer version of no more than 1:15 to 1:30 for your website or direct marketing.

INDUSTRIAL NARRATION DEMOS

Corporate and *industrial demos* tend to contain copy that is somewhat longer than the copy in a commercial demo. The longer length of copy allows the producer time to more accurately assess your reading and delivery skills for this type of storytelling. It also gives them an opportunity to hear how you handle complex words, concepts, and sentences. As with the other types of demos, your money voice and strongest material should lead the demo, followed by a variety of styles, range, and versatility. Industrial demos offer a good opportunity to use various microphone techniques, a range of delivery speeds, and storytelling techniques to good advantage.

Where the average length of an individual segment for a commercial demo might be 5 to 10 seconds, a segment on an industrial demo might run 15 to 20 seconds, or even slightly longer. You'll need more time to complete the descriptive text for a procedure or technical discussion.

A typical industrial demo will run about 1:45 to 2:00 and will include five to seven segments. As with a commercial demo, your agent will likely ask for a one-minute edited version for their use.

CHARACTER AND ANIMATION DEMOS (INCLUDING GAMES)

Character and animation demos will feature your talents primarily for animation and video game work. They also demonstrate your ability to create marketable voices for believable, "real" characters.

Animation character voice work is probably the single toughest area of voiceover to break into, so both your performing abilities and your character/animation demo must be of extremely high quality.

At its essence, a character or animation demo features voices that are recognized as either "real" people or extreme attitudes, but which are actually voices you create that are different from your real voice. For animation, the characters are often exaggerated or quirky in some way, while video-game characters are usually "real people." Each clip features a different attitude, vocal characterization, or personality. Not all voice talent have the ability to create voices that sound completely different from their normal voice. If you don't have this ability, a character voice demo may not be for you.

Producing animation demos is a specialty area of production. Each segment of an animation demo must sound like it came from an actual show and similar voices should be separated from each other. Most demo studios have music and sound effects libraries, but not all have the proper music and sound effects needed for an animation demo. Call around or visit **voiceoverresourceguide.com** to find a studio that specializes in animation demos and listen to several demos they have produced.

A typical animation or character voice demo will be about the same length as a commercial demo, around 1:00 maximum, and may include 10 to 15 individual, fully produced elements. Again, if you have an agent, be sure to ask what length they prefer.

AUDIO BOOK DEMOS

The format for an audio book demo is far different from all other voiceover demos. An audio book producer wants to hear how you tell a story over an extended period of time.

There are a few important differences between this type of demo and other voiceover demos. Audio book demos are the only type of demo that should include a slate of your name. The slate should be spoken by someone else who simply says your name followed by the word "reader." After this brief introduction, you begin by giving the title of the book and start reading the story. Your choice of material should include a variety of emotions and attitudes. At least one excerpt should include multiple characters in conversation. You'll need to find something unique for each character in the book you are reading for each segment. This can be a challenge for characters of the opposite sex. Usually a shift in energy or attitude will reveal a character far more effectively than a change of pitch. Change-ups of tempo, rhythm, and the use of other techniques can help differentiate the characters as you tell the story.

Practice for your audio book demo by recording yourself reading out loud, finding the drama, emotion, and attitudes for each scene and character of the story. You must develop the skill to be consistent with your delivery style for a very long period of time. Your audio book demo should reveal that consistency.

A typical audio book demo will run from 5 to 12 minutes and may consist of as few as 3 to 5 fairly long segments averaging about 3 to

4 minutes each. Ideally, you should be able to perform each segment of your audio book demo as a continuous read with a minimum of stops and starts. If you find you need to stop frequently, have difficulty reading the text, or need to go back for pick-ups, you may not be ready for audio book work.

IMAGING, BRANDING, SIGNATURE VOICE DEMOS

Unlike other types of voiceover work, those voice actors who work in the area of radio imaging need special knowledge of the broadcasting industry. If you don't have a radio background or thoroughly understand the purpose of imaging and how this aspect of the voiceover business works, imaging may not be for you.

An imaging demo features a single, specific, often "edgy" delivery style throughout the demo. Most imaging voice talent have a separate demo that features a different, specific attitude for each radio format. Also, unlike other types of voiceover work, imaging often presents a detached delivery—more typical of an announcer, rather than the conversational delivery style for commercials, character, and narration.

An imaging demo should be no longer than one minute in length. Although any studio capable of producing a commercial demo should be able to handle an imaging demo, you would be wise to find a producer who knows and produces imaging work. As with animation demos, imaging requires special music and effects that may not be available at all studios.

PROMO AND TRAILER DEMOS

A *promo* and *trailer* demo focuses on television programs and films. This is the only demo in which two genres are commonly combined, but many voice talent will market these separately.

Television promos are essentially commercials that promote a specific television program instead of a retail product. The program being promoted could be a local show, a movie, news program, news feature segment, or other station programming.

A trailer promotes a movie. To properly produce promo and trailer elements for your demo, you'll need to find suitable *sound bites*, or excerpts from television shows or movies that you will wrap around your voice work. As with a commercial demo, the length will be about one to one-and-a-half minutes.

Most movie trailer work is done in Los Angeles, and there are a handful of voice talent who are consistently hired for this type of work. That doesn't mean you can't break in to trailer VO work, but you'll need to find the companies that produce trailers, you'll need an agent to represent you for trailer work, and you'll need a killer trailer demo. Television promo work is usually booked directly by a television station's Promotions Department and can be an entree to trailer work.

TELEPHONY DEMOS

Sometimes referred to as a *message-on-hold demo* (MOH) or *IVR* (*Interactive Voice Response*), this type of demo is pretty basic. It usually consists of one or two examples of outgoing messages, one or two on-hold messages for different types of businesses, and perhaps even an example or two of a concatenation project or interactive voice responses. Examples should include appropriate background music. The idea of an MOH demo is to demonstrate what you sound like delivering information over the phone.

One might think that because a telephone connection has a reduced frequency response (about 8 kHz), an MOH demo should be equalized so it sounds as though it is being heard over the phone. Although this is certainly an option, I would not recommend it primarily because the reduced frequency response of your demo will not accurately reveal the subtlety of your performance. Even though the nuance and detail of your delivery may be lost during an actual phone message, you want your demo to show you at your absolute best. I'd recommend producing your MOH demo at the highest possible quality. As with most other demos, this one will also be in the one to one-and-a-half minute range.

Producing Your Demo

PREPARATION IS THE KEY TO A GREAT DEMO

I've said this before, but this is so important that I'll say it again: do not produce your demo until you are ready, and even when you are ready, have your marketing plan in place before you spend the money on recording your demo with a qualified demo producer. Spending some time on a critical self-evaluation to determine your performing strengths and weaknesses, your vocal style, the market you want to work in, and researching the talent buyers in that market is homework that will save you time and money.

From this point on, I'll assume you know who you will be marketing to, you've got a marketing plan in place, you've mastered your performing skills, you've gathered a number of scripts, and you've either assembled a home studio or are working on that.

Rehearse your copy with an analog or digital stopwatch. Time yourself with each rehearsal, recording yourself if possible, and do a complete analysis for each script. Make notes on your scripts about the character, attitude, and emotional hooks, as well as ideas for music style and sound effects if appropriate. Consider mic placement for each script. Mark off what you believe to be the strongest :10 to :15 of each script. Be prepared to record the entire script during your demo session, and be flexible enough to understand that everything you rehearse will probably change. The work you do at this stage will pay off later.

If your coach is unable, or unavailable, to help with your demo, you should find a director who can assist you with the production of your demo. Hiring a director is like having a second set of ears. It allows you to focus on your performance so you will not have to worry about the technical details of the session. Many recording studios have engineers experienced in directing voiceover.

Above all, when you are in the studio, have fun and enjoy the experience! I encourage you to stay through as much of the production process as you possibly can. Some studios will record your voice tracks and handle the production after you leave. It is not only your right, but your responsibility to make certain your demo is produced to the highest possible standards and completely meets your needs as a marketing tool. Your input will be important for your producer or the engineer to create an effective demo. You take a great risk if you simply leave the production up to the engineer or your demo producer. By observing the production process for your demo, you will learn a lot about what really goes on behind the scenes in a recording studio.

HOW LONG SHOULD MY DEMO BE?

There are two answers to the question of length. The first answer is: if you have an agent, ask what length is preferred by their agency. The second answer is: if you don't have an agent, you'll want your demo to conform to the current conventional length for the type of demo you will be producing, as discussed earlier in this chapter.

In major markets like Los Angeles, Chicago, and New York, you'll find the average length for a commercial demo to be around 1 minute to no longer than 1:30. The trend has been moving toward shorter demos, and some Los Angeles agents are requesting demos as short at :30. Other markets may prefer longer demos between 1:30 and 2 minutes. It will be rare to find commercial demos longer than 1:30 in today's voiceover world, although demos up to 2 or 3 minutes were the standard length only a few short years ago.

WHAT ABOUT PRODUCT NAMES?

Your demo is an advertisement for you, not for the products included in the demo. There are actually two schools of thought on this. Some producers believe that including product names lends credibility to the performer (especially if the spot is one that the performer actually worked on) and that they give a good opportunity for talent buyers to hear how the performer "sells" the client, or puts a spin on a product name. Other producers feel that the most important aspect of a demo is the performer's ability to communicate the message or tell the story, and that product names can actually become distracting or that the use of product names may be misrepresentation if you didn't do the original spot. The reality is that most talent buyers, agents, and producers don't really care if you actually did the spot or not. They want to hear what you can do with the words. They know that most voiceover demos aren't the real thing—and it doesn't matter.

If you choose to include product names in your demo, I'd suggest including only one or two and let your performing abilities shine for the rest of the copy. You can change the client or product name to avoid any concerns of misrepresenting that you actually did a spot.

As you acquire copies of projects you have worked on, you should include a few product names from actual spots in your updated demos. Unless you have actually worked for the clients you mention in your demo, you should never include their logos on your website or in your marketing, and when you do, it should always be only after obtaining proper permission. To do otherwise may be viewed as misrepresentation or a possible copyright infringement.

WHERE DO I GET THE COPY FOR MY DEMO?

There are many approaches to obtaining copy for a demo. Be creative! Although much of what follows is directed toward producing your commercial demo, the same ideas can be applied to any type of voiceover demo.

Some demo recording studios provide the copy and handle all the production. This is fine if you don't mind taking the chance of other people having the same copy on their demos. The only real advantage of having the studio provide the copy is that your demo session becomes more like a real recording session; that is, you won't have the opportunity to see the copy in advance. The downside is that your session may take considerably longer because you will be working the copy cold and relatively unrehearsed. You might also feel rushed when you are "on the clock" to get through all the copy necessary, which could easily affect the quality of your performance. However, the major problem with the studio providing copy is that you can easily end up using copy that is not right for your style. The purpose of your demo is to present your talent in the best possible manner. Performing copy that is not right for you can only work against you, no matter how well the demo is produced.

A better approach to finding copy for your demo is to listen to radio and TV commercials and browse through magazines looking for advertising copy that fits your style. Record commercial breaks and transcribe the ads that fit your abilities, putting each script on a separate piece of paper. Transcribe the entire commercial even though you may end up using only a small portion if that script makes it into the demo.

Technical, news, travel, and women's magazines often have ads that can be easily adapted for voiceover. Most print ads are written for the eye, designed to be read, and include a lot of text that may not be appropriate for voiceover. However, if you think about it, you'll realize that the people who write these print ads are often the same people who write national-quality radio and television ads. Since print copy is written to be read silently, you will usually need to rewrite the copy so it can be used for voiceover. You don't need to completely rewrite a print ad; just take the strongest sections and rework them so they make sense for spoken word.

Look for ads that include a lot of text. Look for ads that target specific audiences: men, women, young, older adults, and so on. Look for products or services that will allow you to perform the copy in a variety of styles: serious, humorous, hard-sell, soft-sell, dynamic, emotional, and so on. Look for key phrases and sentences that have emotional content—these will be your keys to an effective performance. Most important, select only those ads that might actually be potential radio or TV commercials. The tracks in your demo must sound like real-world radio or television spots.

If you have some writing experience, you might write customized material for your demo. But be aware that if you write your own copy, it must sound as though it was written by a professional.

Obtain as much copy as you can and narrow the scripts down to about 30-40 different ads from radio, TV, magazines, and technical journals. Include a variety of content that will reveal your full range of capabilities: slow, fast, dynamic, emotional, character, and so on. Also make sure each script you choose is appropriate for the type of demo you will be producing. This may seem like a lot of copy, and it is, but by starting with many possibilities, it will be easier to choose the copy that best fits your style. By the time you start recording, those 30 or 40 scripts will be whittled down to about 12 to 15.

Be prepared to perform the entire script at your demo session. The reason for this is that you may actually end up with an extremely effective delivery on a segment of the script that you may not have expected. If you only rehearse portions of your scripts, you might overlook an opportunity for a perfect transitional element, or an especially emotional performance.

Thoroughly wood shed and do a character analysis for each piece of copy, making notes on the scripts, if necessary. Practice your performance for each script just enough to become familiar with it. Be careful not to get yourself locked into any specific attitude or character. Keep in mind that your session engineer might direct you into a performance completely different from what you had decided on. If that happens, you need to be able to adapt to the direction. If you can't, or if you find yourself getting stuck in the same delivery for each take, then you may not be ready to have your demo produced.

You have the luxury of being able to prepare and rehearse. Take advantage of it! You will not have this luxury in a real-life studio session. Take at least three clean copies of each script with you to the studio: one copy for yourself, one for the engineer, and the third for your director.

WHAT ABOUT DIALOGUE, MUSIC, AND SOUND EFFECTS?

The purpose of your demo is to feature <u>your</u> voice-acting performance. Including other voiceover performers should be done judiciously. If you include a dialogue spot, make sure that yours is the featured performance and that the other voice is of the opposite gender. This may seem obvious, but you'd be surprised at the number of demos with two voices that are hard to tell apart. Also be certain that the other performer knows how to act. I've heard far too many demos that include a dialogue spot where the second player showed little or no acting ability, or worse, the other performer showed superior acting ability. And don't be tempted to do both voices yourself. Producers want to hear how you work with other voice talent, not how clever you can be performing multiple voices.

The use of music and sound effects is essential to creating a demo that sounds like it contains real-world spots. Don't worry about finding music yourself—this is part of your engineer or producer's job. If used, music must be appropriate for the mood and energy of the message. It is an infringement of copyright to use music from store-bought CDs or downloads, or even arrangements of popular tunes that you perform yourself. Only suitable music from licensed *music libraries* should be used in your demo. A music library is a collection of music created by a company that produces music specifically designed for use in commercial, TV, and film production. Sound effects should only be used where appropriate, and although sound effects are not copyrighted, they must be of high-quality. This aspect of your demo requires a knowledge of audio production and editing that is acquired only through many years of experience. You might have the best recording equipment and software, but if you don't know how to produce and mix professional audio, you would be best to leave the production to an experienced demo producer/ engineer. Attempting to do this yourself will generally result in a demo that is substandard and can leave a bad impression with those who hear it.

WHAT IS THE PRODUCTION PROCESS?

Every demo producer has their own style and process. However, the basics of producing a demo will be pretty much the same regardless of who is producing. The differences will be in the quality of direction, advance coaching and consultation, and how the studio session is handled.

Some producers will do little more than supervise your demo session at a recording studio while others will provide everything needed for a fully-produced demo, including engineering, music, sound effects, and post-production.

Some producers offer a production service that includes script selection, customized copy and pre-session coaching while others will provide scripts from their archives or ask the client to do everything up to the day of the session.

Some producers will take up to two weeks or more to deliver your completed demo while others will complete the project in one day.

The point here is that you should do your homework when it comes to choosing a demo producer. You need a producer with whom you feel comfortable and confident in their abilities to listen to

 you and make you sound your absolute best. The nine-step production process we use for demo production at VoiceActing Studios (**voiceactingstudios.com**) is covered in detail in the AOVA Extras section at **VoiceActing.com**.

HOW MUCH WILL MY DEMO COST?

Your first demo will very likely be the single most expensive part of breaking into the business of voiceover, perhaps equaled only by what you spend on training.

The cost of producing a demo can vary widely from market to market and will depend on the type of demo, the market you're in, and your demo producer. To a certain extent, it will also depend on your performing abilities. For recording studios, time is money, and the faster you can record a high-quality performance (fewer takes), the sooner your demo will be completed and the less it will cost.

Check with your studio to find out what portions of the session or materials will have sales tax applied. If you've set up your voiceover business properly, the entire cost of producing your demo can be deducted as a business expense.

If you're in a major market like Los Angeles, New York or Chicago, you can expect your demo to cost in the neighborhood of anywhere from $1,500 to $4,000. In other markets, you can expect to pay anywhere from $600 to $1,500, or more, for the production of your voice demo. Studios that are known for producing excellent demos will give you a great product, but it will cost more, and in most cases it will be worth it.

You definitely "get what you pay for" when it comes to demo production. However, beware of the *demo mills* that will offer to produce your demo as part of a short—but very expensive—course. The demos produced by these operations will not present you at your best and will rarely get any work.

Although session fees vary, and may be lower or higher, the following breakdown will give you an idea of what you might expect to pay for your demo session at a studio with a rate of $125 per hour.

PRODUCTION ELEMENTS	TIME AND FEES	SUBTOTALS
Studio time (voice recording)	2 hours @ $125/hour	$250.00
Postproduction (editing, music)	4-6 hours @ $125/hour	min. 500.00
Track sequencing and/or dubbing	1.5 hours @ $125/hour	187.50
Music license (for music used)	1 blanket license	400.00
Outside producer/director	1 flat fee	400.00
Materials (CD), including tax		50.00
Total cost (not including duplication)	7.5 hours in studio	$1787.50

WHAT DO I NEED TO KNOW ABOUT RECORDING STUDIOS?

In this age of easily accessible high technology, it isn't difficult to locate a recording studio capable of recording a high-quality demo. An Internet search for "recording studios your town," should bring up the major recording studios in your area. However, there may also be many excellent home-based project studios in your community that are not advertised anywhere. Even though recording services and studios may be plentiful in your area, this does not mean that all studios are able to produce a marketable voiceover demo.

The majority of commercial recording studios are designed for music sessions. The engineers at these studios may be very competent at recording music, but often know very little about producing commercials or directing voiceover talent. Home-based project studios are also often designed to handle the needs of musicians and composers, and may not be suitable for, or capable of, recording quality voiceover work. Even if you have a state-of-the-art home studio, you should seek out and hire a professional demo producer to produce your demo.

When you book a recording studio, you may be assigned an engineer who is not interested in demo production, and may not be skilled at directing voiceover talent. If you are producing the demo on your own, you need to be prepared for this. As the producer of your demo, you need to be ready to guide your engineer through the process and have a good idea of what you want in your demo, including the selection of music and sound effects, and the final sequencing of clips. If your engineer is not capable of directing you, and you haven't hired a demo producer, you'll need to rely on your self-direction skills to get you through. This can be a real challenge because you should be focusing on your performance—not on the details of directing.

HOW DO I BOOK A DEMO STUDIO AND PRODUCER?

You should ask lots of questions on your quest for a demo producer. Just because your coach might produce demos does not mean that you need to hire them to produce yours.

One of the best ways to find a demo producer is to ask other voice talent who produced their demo and what their experience was like. You may be surprised to find that some talent absolutely love their demo, but had a very difficult time working with their producer, while others had an overall excellent or horrible experience.

The following pages contain some tips and questions to ask as you call around looking for a studio to hire to produce your demo, as well as some important basic information about recording studios.

- **Find a studio that records radio and TV commercials:**
  Look for a studio that is experienced in producing commercials or demos. If they also have experience producing voiceover demos, all the better.
- **Does the studio produce voiceover demos?** This should be one of your first questions. You may also have this question answered when you find out if the studio has an engineer who knows how to work with voiceover talent. Even if a studio does a lot of radio commercials, it does not mean that they also produce voiceover demos.
- **Does the studio have an engineer who knows how to direct voiceover talent?** Unless you have hired a director, you will need an engineer who can direct you as you perform your copy. Many studios have engineers who know how to record the human voice, but don't know the first thing about

directing talent for an effective voice-acting performance. When you enter the studio, you need to take off your producer hat and become the performer. Even if you hire a director, you need to find a studio that has an engineer who knows how to produce and direct for voiceover.

- **Ask to listen to other demos produced by the studio or producer:** You'll be investing a lot of money in your demo, so it's important that your producer or studio is willing to let you hear previous work they've done and provide you names of other talent you can talk to. If they are reluctant to release any information, find a different studio or producer.

- **Does the studio have session time that will coincide with your availability?** If you can't book the studio at a time when you are available, you need to find another studio. Many recording studios offer evening or weekend studio time, and may either offer a discount or charge an extra fee for those sessions. You may be able to get a reduced fee for late-night sessions, but you may not be able to get an engineer experienced with voiceover.

- **What is the studio's hourly rate for voice recording?** Many studios have a sliding scale of prices depending on the requirements of the project. Other studios book at a flat rate, regardless of the session. Shop the studios in your area to find the best price for your demo production. Find out if there are any price changes between the voice session and the production session. Some studios will give a block discount for sessions booking a large amount of time. A demo session probably won't fit this category, but it couldn't hurt to ask. If you're working with a studio that charges a package price for demo production, their hourly rate won't matter.

- **Does the studio have music and sound effects libraries?** Your demo will need music and possibly sound effects to underscore your performance. Audio book demos are the only exception to this rule. If you are producing an animation or an imaging demo, you'll need some very specific types of music and sound effects. Many recording studios do not have access to music that can be used in a demo, even though their primary business may be recording music. Find a demo studio that has access to music libraries to underscore your voice tracks, and that are appropriate for your type of demo.

- **Does the studio charge for music or sound effects?** Some studios charge a fee for music used in your demo, while other studios include music as part of a package price. If there is a music use fee, make sure it is a *blanket license* rather than a per use or *laser-drop* license. A blanket license covers all music used in a project for one fee and is considerably less expensive than several laser-drop licenses. Usually, there is no charge for sound effects.

- **What other fees will the studio charge?** What does the studio charge for CD one-offs, digital media, and other materials used in the production of your demo? Are there any additional charges for archiving (backing up and storing) your demo project? What portions of the demo production will have sales tax applied, if any? All of these items will affect the total cost of your demo.

- **How much time does the studio estimate it will take to produce your demo?** You should plan on at least six to eight hours for the completion of your demo, although depending on the type of demo, this could be more or less. Some demo producers will record your tracks on one day and produce your demo over the next several days or weeks, while others do everything in one day. Ask you producer how long you should expect to wait before hearing your demo.

- **What will you take with you when your demo is done?** In most cases, you can expect to leave the studio with at least least one audio CD of your demo. You should also make sure you receive high quality MP3 files of all versions of your demo. These may be delivered on a data thumb drive, emailed to you, posted on an FTP website, or handed to you on a data CD.

- **How will your demo be backed up?** A *backup* is a copy of all the elements of the project, not necessarily in any special order or structure. A lot of work goes into producing a voiceover demo and a project backup is important if or when it becomes necessary to modify or rebuild sections of the original project. It's not necessary for you to keep a copy of your entire project. But you should make sure the studio will keep a back-up copy of your session on file for future reference. If they don't keep archives, you'll definitely want to get your entire session backed up on data CD or DVD-ROM.

Your Demo Recording Session

If you are prepared and ready to work, your demo session can be a lot of fun, and an educational experience. If, on the other hand, you go to your demo session unprepared or without having mastered the necessary skills, your session can be very uncomfortable.

ARRIVE ON TIME AND PREPARED

In the world of recording studios, time is money. Recording studios usually bill for their time whether you are there or not. The lesson here is to <u>be</u> <u>on</u> <u>time</u>! If you live your life in a constant mode of running late, you might want to set your clocks ahead, or do whatever is necessary to make sure you arrive at your session on time, or preferably a bit early. Arriving late for real world sessions will get you a bad reputation in a hurry, and no doubt will cause you to lose work. Arriving late for your demo session will put you under unnecessary stress, costing you valuable time and money.

WORKING WITH YOUR ENGINEER/PRODUCER

Aside from your producer, if you hire one, your engineer will be one of the most important people you work with during your demo session, possibly even working as your director. In any case, it is important that you and your engineer work together as a team. Remain flexible and open to your engineer's suggestions. If you are careful in booking the studio, you will probably have an engineer who knows much more about voiceover work than you do. You can learn a lot from a good engineer and he or she may even become a good contact for work later on.

KEEPING YOUR DEMO CURRENT

Your demo will be useful for at least six months to a year, although you may actually use your first demo somewhat longer. As you begin doing paid sessions, you will want to get copies of your work and update your demo occasionally. You can book a studio to handle your update or you can do the editing yourself. Either way, plan ahead by budgeting for studio or editing time and have a good idea of what you want to do. Send your updated demo to people you have worked for. A new demo is a good opportunity to stay in touch with past clients and to inquire about upcoming projects.

In this Chapter

22

Your Home Studio

A Million Dollar Studio in Your Home

Since the mid 1990s the business of voiceover has gone through a series of major changes, both in terms of how the business works and in the technology used for recording voice tracks.

Early recording equipment was bulky, complicated to operate, and most of all expensive. It used to be that the home studio was relegated to only the serious audiophile or professional musician.

Advances in computer and recording technology have changed all that. Today, the home studio is commonplace. With a decent computer, recording software, and relatively inexpensive equipment, anyone can now have the capability to do what used to require a multimillion dollar facility. And it will fit in a corner of a room at home!

Unfortunately, most voiceover artists are performers and not recording or acoustical design engineers. For many, the technology of a home studio can be intimidating and overwhelming. Still, in today's world of voiceover it is important to know home studio basics and have functional recording and editing skills.

This chapter will, hopefully, ease your concerns about setting up and operating your own home recording studio. As you design your personal home studio, keep in mind that the quality of your recordings will be directly related to the following items in this order:

1. Room acoustics (most important)
2. Microphone selected to make the most of your voice
3. Your recording levels and editing ability
4. Recording software
5. USB Interface to computer
6. Computer or other recording device

The Challenge of Recording at Home

At one time, virtually all voiceover work was recorded either at a traditional recording studio, at a radio or television station, or a professional production facility. If you are working in voiceover today, it is expected that you not only have the ability to record in your own personal studio, but that you also have the ability to deliver the same quality that would be delivered by a multimillion dollar recording facility. This expectation by talent buyers creates a serious challenge for the neophyte voice actor.

Many talent buyers work from the assumption that booking a voice actor who records from their home studio will be "cheaper" than recording the same actor in a conventional recording studio. Although this assumption may have some merit, conceptually, the assumption is, at best, flawed, and at worst, creates an atmosphere of unfair competition with other recording services in your market. When you invest in a home studio, you are effectively going into business as a recording studio. Whether you realize it or not, you are competing with every other recording service in your area, even though your studio's only client might be you. As I've discussed elsewhere, if you give away your studio time, charging only for your talent fee, you are not only undercutting your competition, but you are losing the potential for considerable additional income. This might be great for your clients, but only you can decide if it is a business model that is right for you.

Many voice talent, in order to achieve the "sound" they think talent buyers will hire, will invest a lot of money in very high-end equipment, which is totally unnecessary. The truth is that your home studio needs to be designed to do the best possible job of making you sound like you! To do that, your home studio needs to be acoustically sound with the proper equipment that will reproduce the cleanest and most natural sound of you that it possibly can.

The equipment for your home studio is relatively inexpensive, and the recording software can even be found as a free download. The major challenge goes well beyond the equipment itself, lying in the complexities of creating a studio-quality environment that is competitive and with the performer's ability to deliver a recording with proper signal levels and clean edits.

It's easy to record audio on your computer! Recording audio that sounds like it came out of a major Los Angeles or New York studio is a different matter entirely. It's not difficult to do this, but it will generally require some serious thought, some research, and, depending on how far you want to go, potentially a lot more money than the cost of your studio equipment.

As a professional voice actor, there are several essential aspects of your home studio that you need to fully understand in order to deliver voice tracks that meet professional standards:

- Basic operation, connection, and functionality of your equipment.
- Operation of your recording software, including an understanding of how to make clean recordings, maintain proper recording levels and handle basic editing processes.
- A basic understanding of room acoustics, how it affects your recordings, and how to correct acoustic problems.
- An understanding of the principals and applications of various microphone techniques used to produce different results.
- A basic understanding of outboard (external) audio equipment and devices that may be needed for processing, communication with clients or for delivery of voice tracks.
- A functional understanding of computer file structures, software operation, and various delivery options.

If all of this sounds intimidating, or you feel like it's too much to deal with, you might want to rethink your entry into the world of voiceover or spend some time in further study of what it takes to record at home. Of all the pressures placed on today's voiceover talent, these expectations are completely reasonable and practical. The majority of professional voice actors working from their home studios have developed these skills and deliver high-quality, professional recordings on a daily basis. If you are going to compete with them, you will need to achieve the same results.

Designing Your Home Studio

With today's computer systems, it's a relatively simple matter to put together the equipment for high-quality voice recording. Regardless of the equipment you use, you will have a choice between a system that is completely digital or one that is a combination of analog and digital equipment. As with most things, there's more than one way to configure your home studio recording system, and none is better than another. It comes down to personal preference and ease of use.

An Internet search for "home recording" will reveal many excellent books and websites that thoroughly discuss the subject of building a home studio. If you need an easy-to-read, clear and concise explanation of the various parts of a home studio and how everything works together, my *Voice Actor's Guide to Professional Home Recording Ebook* will answer most of your questions. This downloadable Ebook, available through **VoiceActing.com** is internally cross-linked and loaded with active Internet links to websites with more information about every aspect of a home studio.

Focal Press (**focalpress.com**), the publisher of this book, has several excellent books on the subject of home recording, including: *Project Studios* by Philip Newell and *Practical Recording Techniques* by Bruce Bartlett. The Focal books are intended more for the home music recordist, but they still contain valuable information that can be applied to voiceover work.

The sole purpose of your home studio is to be a facility where you record and edit audio on your computer. The first thing you need to do is locate a quiet place in your home where you can record. I'll cover that in the next section. Next, you'll need to figure out how to get the sound of your voice onto your computer's hard drive. At first glance this may seem a simple task: you buy a gamer's headset mic, plug it into your computer's sound card, open the recording software that came with the computer, and start recording. Although that's the basic process, the reality is that it's not quite that simple.

For starters, a computer headset mic is not acceptable for professional voiceover work. These microphones are designed for online gaming and not for recording, and if you use one for voiceover work, you'll be plagued with pops and other noise issues. As for software, the basic audio recorder that comes with Windows is pretty much useless and the audio software that comes with a Mac can be challenging to learn and use for voiceover recording. For either type of computer, you will need recording software that offers more than what comes with the system. If you want to record on a mobile device or tablet, there are many apps for recording, some of which can do a good job. However, even though there are some decent recording apps, the challenge with recording on a phone or tablet is in connecting a high-quality microphone to the device.

As I mentioned, there are two technologies for recording your audio into a computer: analog and digital. The primary difference between the two is that an analog system uses a microphone or an analog mixer that is connected to the computer's sound card, and converts the audio to a digital signal inside the computer. A digital system converts the audio signal to digital information outside the computer either directly at the microphone or by using a *USB* or *FireWire* digital interface. The digital interface may be a standalone device, a digital mixer, or even a digital USB microphone. USB (universal serial bus) and FireWire both refer to high-speed digital connections between a computer and an outboard device.

Of the two, the least expensive, is to connect an analog mixer to the line input of your computer's sound card. Although most computer sound cards are adequate for the job, the fact that the digital conversion process is happening inside the computer, an electrically very noisy place, may result in some unwanted noise in your recordings. If you are using an analog path to your computer, it would be well worth the investment of a few hundred dollars to upgrade your sound card to a high-end digital converter.

The recommended option is to go digital and do the analog-to-digital conversion outside the computer. You will be completely bypassing your sound card by using the computer's USB port. This can have its advantages and disadvantages. On the plus side is the portability aspect and the relatively low cost of USB interface devices, which makes them ideal if you are recording on your laptop. On the downside, if you have an older computer with numerous USB devices connected (like external hard drives, a web cam, etc.), your computer may have difficulty processing the large amount of audio data being transferred, which can result in mysterious glitches or even a system crash. Faster processors, updated operating systems and new computer designs have vastly improved the efficiency of working with USB interfaces effectively eliminating these issues.

The equipment and software you purchase for your home studio will depend largely on the kind of work you will be doing. If you are only recording voice tracks or practicing your performing skills, you don't need an elaborate digital mixer with all the bells and whistles. A smart phone, tablet, or low-end laptop will do the job nicely for practice, but you might want to consider dedicating a laptop or larger system for your auditions and paid bookings.

The following are basic components for a home studio, each with some comments as to their role in the studio. These components are discussed in more detail a bit later in this chapter, and in the Products/Equipment section at **VoiceActing.com**:

- **Microphone**—You need a microphone that will make your voice sound great. Different mics sound different on different people. It can take some research to find exactly the right mic. To get started, don't buy the most expensive mic you can find. There are many excellent mics available in the $200-250 range and you can even find some very good mics for under $100. A professional mic with have an XLR 3 pin connector that will connect to a USB interface, a digital mixer, or an analog mixer. There are even

XLR-3

USB mics that connect directly to your computer. A condenser mic is usually recommended over a dynamic mic, due to its superior performance. Condenser microphones require a power source, either by battery or *phantom power* provided by a mixer or USB interface device.

- **Microphone cable**—Professional microphones use a 3-pin XLR type cable that connects the mic to a mixer or USB device. The phantom power for condenser microphones travels through the same wires in the cable that carry the audio signal.

- **USB interface**—The cable from your mic or mixer connects to this device, which converts the analog audio to digital audio. It connects to your computer via a USB cable plugged into a USB port on the computer. The better USB devices will have controls for recording volume and for headset monitoring. A good USB interface also provides phantom power for condenser mics. A USB device will replace your computer's sound card as the audio source.

- **Analog audio mixer**—An analog mixer may connect to either the computer's sound card or to the line level inputs on a USB interface. The mixer is used to control the volume for up to several mics or other sources. If connecting directly to the sound card, you'll need some special adaptors, which may be difficult to locate. Many analog mixers include phantom power to enable condenser microphones to work.

- **Digital audio mixer**—As with an analog mixer, a digital mixer is used to control the volume for up to several mics or other sources. A truly digital mixer will convert the incoming audio to a digital signal as soon as it enters the mixer. Other hybrid mixers will functionally operate as an analog mixer and have multiple analog audio output connectors. However, unlike analog mixers, digital hybrid mixers also have a built-in USB port that allows the mixer to be connected directly to your computer. If you are using a digital mixer with built-in USB, you do not need an external USB interface.

- **Recording software**—Virtually all recording software will provide for recording and editing of recorded audio. However, all audio software is not the same. Some are more user friendly than others, and price is not a good indicator of ease of use. Software prices vary from free to several hundred dollars. Regardless of the software you choose, you should make sure it will easily save or convert your recordings to MP3 compressed files. When investigating recording software, make sure you have a basic understanding of how you will record and edit by taking advantage of any free trial offered before purchasing. Some equipment dealers will recommend ProTools because, they say, it is the standard of the recording industry. That is true. However, ProTools is only the standard for traditional music recording studios—not for voiceover recording. It is very expensive, very difficult to learn, requires proprietary outboard equipment (for a high-end system), and is considerable overkill for recording a single voice track. For anyone just getting started, I recommend Audacity. It's free, very simple to use, and does everything (and more) that a voice actor needs. Audacity is available for both PC and Mac from **audacity.sourceforge.net**. To create MP3 files, you will also need to download the L.A.M.E. encoder plug-in from the Audacity web page. The downside with Audacity is that some of its functionality is a bit quirky. Still, for the price and capabilities, it's hard to beat.

- **Microphone stand**—A floor stand with a boom, or a desk stand. Either way, you'll need something to hold your microphone. The most common mic floor stand is a tripod base adjustable stand with a boom attachment. There are also smaller tripod base stands that are short enough to be used as a desk stand. A typical desk stand will have a heavy base.

- **Copy stand** (music stand)—You'll need this to hold your copy so your hands are free for performance and operating the equipment. If you work standing, a collapsible music stand will do the job, but it is usually designed for a performer who is seated and may not have the height adjustment you need. The Manhasset M48 is a much better option: more stable, no knobs to turn, and plenty of height for most uses. I don't recommend using music stands that have knobs to adjust their height or the angle of the paper holder. They might be less expensive, but they can be awkward to use.

- **Headphones**—Conventional stereo headphones or ear buds will work for most voiceover recording. You'll wear your headphones while recording and for other monitoring, if you don't have a set of speakers. You'll want a headset that is comfortable and that reproduces your voice accurately. Some headphones emphasize low frequencies, which will result in a coloration of your voice. Open air headphones will allow much of the room sound to enter your ears, while closed headphones will provide for a more isolated monitoring experience.

- **Speakers**—Although headphones will serve the purpose for monitoring, and even for editing, they can become uncomfortable if worn for extended periods of time. To start your home studio, a pair of good computer speakers connected to your sound card will do nicely. As you bring in voiceover work, you might want to consider upgrading your speakers to some studio monitors. If you are using a USB device for recording, you may need to adjust your software settings so your computer knows you want to use your sound card speakers for playback monitoring. Basic computer speakers are fairly inexpensive. Studio monitors can run into the hundreds or thousands of dollars for a pair of speakers. Professional monitor speakers come in two types: active and passive. Passive speakers require an external power amplifier. Active monitors usually come in a matched pair with each speaker having its own internal amplifier.

- **Stopwatch or timer**—You'll need a way to time yourself as you record. Stopwatches that beep aren't recommended. They're awkward and they make noise. A better choice is an analog 60-second sweep stopwatch, but it will still have a soft ticking sound. Even better, if you have a smart phone, you can download any of several stop watch apps that will do the job. Your software will allow you to check timing after a recording.

- **Acoustic treatment**—Most home studio areas will need some form of acoustic treatment to reduce echoes and unwanted noise. There are many excellent books on this topic, so it will only be discussed briefly in the next section. When designing your home studio, you should be aware that you may need to make some changes to your recording environment for the best recording quality—and that some of those acoustic changes can be expensive.

I recommend that you do some research on the various home studio components before purchasing. You'll find most, if not all, of what you'll need at online audio dealers like: **bhphotovideo.com**, **zzounds.com**, **sweetwatersound.com**, and **musiciansfriend.com**.

Computer stores simply don't deal with this type of equipment, and they don't understand home studios. In fact, most music equipment dealers don't understand the needs of a voice actor and will recommend equipment only in terms of what they know about music recording. Although their advice may hold some value, you may end up spending considerably more than necessary.

Understanding Room Acoustics

This section is not intended to give you absolute solutions to your room acoustic issues, but rather will give you a general understanding of typical acoustic problems facing voiceover actors and some ways to solve them. There are literally dozens of books on how to deal with adverse room acoustics, and an Internet search for "how to fix room acoustics" will bring up thousands resources.

About 90% of the quality of your voiceover recordings is directly related to the acoustics of your recording environment. Your objective should be to record your voice at a quality comparable with that of the best recording studios in the country. OK … that might be a bit lofty a goal, but you do need to be able to record with excellent sound quality.

"So," I hear you ask, "how do I find a place in my home or apartment where I can record my voice and have it sound that good?" You've actually got several options ranging in cost from relatively inexpensive to very costly.

If you've never been inside a major recording studio, you're probably thinking that you don't have a reference point for what a professional studio might sound like. Actually, you do! But it's far more important to know what a professional studio doesn't sound like: It doesn't sound like your living room, your kitchen, your garage, your bedroom, your office, or your bathroom. Although it certainly is possible to locate your home studio in any of these areas, in most cases they simply won't do if you expect to produce high-quality recordings. Or more accurately, these locations won't do if you leave them in their current acoustical condition.

In most homes, all of these rooms have the same inherent acoustic "problems" which fall into two basic categories: 1) reflections of sound waves off hard surfaces, commonly referred to as room reverberation, and 2) transmission of external sounds through walls, floor and ceiling. In order to optimize the acoustical environment, both of these issues must be addressed.

Room reverberation is the common echo resulting from sound waves bouncing off hard parallel surfaces like walls, windows and furniture. A typical bathroom is probably the best example of room echo. Solid hard walls, mirrors, and tile surfaces cause sound waves to bounce all over the place. A slightly less offensive, but still unacceptable, form of reverberation is known as *slap echo*. This form of reverberation is what you'll usually hear when you clap your hands in an empty bedroom. The resulting reflections of sound waves bouncing off parallel walls creates a relatively short and fast flutter echo that may not be obvious until you actually listen for it.

Acoustical transmission of external noise sources can be especially troublesome for voiceover work. The sound of the TV in a room down the hall, your neighbor's barking dog, traffic noise, helicopters, and lawn mowers will all be picked up by your microphone, and usually at the worst possible time.

The one place in your home that most closely resembles the "sound" of a professional recording studio is your bedroom closet stuffed full of clothes. The soft fabrics absorb sound waves, preventing them from bouncing off the walls, floor and ceiling. A room with overstuffed furniture, thick carpet, heavy drapes, and lots of wall hangings will have the same effect of killing reflected sound waves, resulting in a relatively "dead" sound. Another advantage of the bedroom closet is that this area often has only a limited connection, if any, to an exterior wall, thus minimizing transmission of external noise into the closet. The downside of working in a closet is that, unless you have a large walk-in closet, the space can be very confining and often difficult to work in. In many cases it is more practical to work in a larger room.

There are two ways to correct acoustic issues. The first, which can be relatively expensive, is to sound proof the room. Sound proofing ranges from the moderately expensive option of purchasing a pre-constructed booth to serve as your recording space on up to the very expensive option of building an acoustically isolated room within a room. An Internet search for "voiceover booth" will reveal numerous manufacturers of prefabricated booths and even a few sites with instructions on how to build your own.

The second option, which is far more practical for most voice actors, is to sound treat or acoustically dampen the room. Since fully sound proofing a room is neither practical nor cost-effective for most voice actors, this section will only discuss methods for acoustically dampening a room.

Acoustically treating the walls of a room will effectively kill internal reverberations for a "dead" sound and can help reduce external noise. Acoustic treatments can be anything from hanging a few heavy, absorbent blankets to applying acoustic foam or other acoustic material to the walls. The general idea is that you want to create an acoustically non-reflective environment, one in which your voice can be recorded without any reflections from objects or walls. Although fabric wall hangings, blankets, pillows, overstuffed furniture, and other inexpensive acoustic treatments you might have around your home may appear to "fix" many acoustic issues in a room, they still may not create an environment that is ideal for your voiceover recordings. For example, common household blankets and even store-bought furniture moving blankets are not dense enough to provide adequate acoustic treatment.

When it comes to "fixing" room acoustics, many people will first think of acoustic foam. Acoustic foam products come in a variety of shapes and sizes with the most common being a wedge or pyramid design. The purpose of acoustic foam is to both absorb sound and diffuse the reflection of sound waves. The foam is made of thousands of tiny tubes that trap the sound waves while the angular structure of acoustical foam products serves to diffuse the sound. Foam products will dampen a room but may not provide much in the way of acoustic isolation. Acoustic foam can also be fairly expensive.

Blocking transmission of external noise can be a bigger challenge. Obviously, the best way to do this would be to design the room for acoustic isolation from the outset. However, since it usually isn't practical to do this in most homes, other, temporary measures should be considered.

Windows are often the biggest acoustic problem in a home. Single pane windows are almost acoustically transparent. Even double pane windows will allow external sound into a room. Sound transmission only begins to be seriously reduced with triple pane windows, especially when there is at least one pane of a different thickness. However, even the best multi-pane windows will still allow for sound transmission if there is the slightest air gap. To isolate a room, it may be necessary to seal your windows by installing dampening material over the window opening that will block external sound from entering the room.

A wall built for acoustic isolation will usually be framed as a double wall consisting of an exterior wall and a completely separate inside wall. The two walls will be slightly separated and filled with a high R-rated fiberglass insulation between the studs. On the inside of the room, a layer of mass loaded vinyl will be attached to the interior studs and all electrical outlets will be completely sealed. A layer of dry wall will next be installed over the mass loaded vinyl to finish off the interior of the room. This can be a very expensive process. Retrofitting an existing external wall in a home is not practical.

However, it will often be possible to greatly reduce the transmission of external noise by installing mass loaded vinyl over the inside of an existing wall. *Mass loaded vinyl* is a dense vinyl material impregnated with barium salts, which gives it properties of reducing acoustic transmission up to 20db or more. This material replaces lead sheeting which was commonly used in early recording studio construction. Mass loaded vinyl comes in rolls and weighs approximately one pound per square foot. Mounting mass loaded vinyl to the inside wall and completely covering open window spaces can greatly reduce transmission of external noise. An Internet search for "mass loaded vinyl" or "sound proofing" will bring up many sources for this product.

Several years ago, the Hollywood film industry approached one of the nation's largest suppliers of mover's supplies with the idea of developing a furniture blanket that was larger and more dense than the typical moving blanket of the day. The result was the Producer's Choice sound blanket. The large 8' X 7' size, denser material, pre-installed grommets, and affordable price have made these sound blankets very popular for acoustically treating a small room or a movie set.

The concept of the sound blanket was taken to a new level by Vocal Booth to Go (**vocalboothtogo.com**), a subsidiary of the company that designed the original Producer's Choice sound blanket. The company has designed several sizes of very affordable sound booths that are ideal for use in a home studio. Some are free-standing, some can be hung from the ceiling or attached to a wall, and all use the Producer's Choice sound blanket as the key component.

If you are going to try to "fix" the acoustics of an existing room, be careful not to overlook the corners. Corners where walls meet the ceiling or floor are notorious for reflecting low frequency sound waves often resulting in a "boominess" that can seriously affect your recordings. The right-angle corners where walls meet can also create a similar bass reflector. These areas can be dealt with in many ways through the use of acoustic foam, corner bass traps, mounting absorbent material, or even using an overstuffed pillow to effectively eliminate the right angles of the corners.

Don't forget that floors and ceilings are also reflective surfaces. Even if the floor is carpeted, the ceiling can still reflect sound waves that can interfere with good recordings. There are many ways to correct for this including attaching acoustic foam to the ceiling, hanging acoustic fiberglass panels at an angle above where you stand, or even suspending a blanket from the ceiling. With a little imagination you can come up with all sorts of ideas.

Another relatively inexpensive option for room dampening is Dan Lenard's Studio Suit (**vostudiosuit.com**). Dan is a professional voice actor, home studio consultant and studio engineer who set out to develop an affordable solution to improving home studio acoustics. The Studio Suit is made from recycled material and comes in 8' X 5' panels. Similar to Producer's Choice Sound Blankets, each panel has grommets for hanging from the ceiling or a wall.

As nice and convenient as they might be, prefabricated vocal booths, and acoustically treated rooms are not always practical for small homes and apartments. Creating an acoustically dead area surrounding your microphone might work better than trying to treat an entire room. At the very least, it will be less expensive.

Enter the portable vocal booth. These are small enclosures that surround a microphone and provide an acoustically treated space that requires a relatively small footprint compared to the larger free-standing vocal booths. Portable booths use the same acoustic materials used in the larger booths, but are designed to pack into a small space so they can be easily transported by car or even as carry-on baggage on an airplane. They can be an ideal option for a home studio.

When shopping for a portable vocal booth, keep the following criteria mind: ease of set-up/break-down, inside acoustic properties, location of microphone, rejection of outside noise, inside working space, lighting, ability to be mounted on a mic stand, stability, portability, and the ability to hold equipment in transit.

All portable booths are not the same. Acoustic properties will vary greatly depending on the material used and the room in which they are used. Booths made with acoustic foam will tend to have a low-frequency resonance or "boominess;" have very little working space inside; and may require that the microphone be close to the front of the booth, which opens the mic to "hearing" more room reflections than if the mic is placed deeper into the booth.

While most people will use a portable vocal booth while seated, the ability to mount the booth on a mic stand is important for those who prefer to stand while performing. Some so-called portable booths are little more than small acoustic baffles mounted on a mic stand. For others, the center of gravity must be carefully adjusted or the entire unit might fall over if bumped.

The folks at Vocal Booth to Go have designed a portable booth that has a built-in steel table and easily mounts on a standard mic stand with a perfect center of gravity. The booth is made from the Producer's Choice Sound Blankets and provides a clean sound without the boominess that occurs with some of the foam booths. The inside working space is roughly 22" x 22" x 20", which is plenty of room to allow for the microphone to be placed deep into the booth with cables running through the sides. The spaciousness of the booth allows the performer to comfortably work inside the booth, thus reducing the amount of room reflections reaching the mic. The large inside space also provides plenty of room for a script, a tablet computer, and a light. The booth sets up and breaks down in about 30 seconds and has enough room inside to store a mic, cables, and USB interface. And it can be taken on a plane as carry-on baggage.

As with the other components of your home studio, you will likely want to do some additional research before deciding what you will do to make your recording environment as quiet and "dead" as possible. If you're just getting started in voiceover, you should strive for the best room acoustics you can achieve that is within your budget. I would not recommend purchasing a prefabricated voiceover booth or building your own isolation room without first doing a lot of study on the subject of acoustics. Explore other options first. The time to upgrade your home studio environment is when you are generating a substantial voiceover income—not when you are just getting started.

Advanced Home Studio Technology

If you are just getting started in voiceover, you don't need anything more than the basic equipment discussed earlier in this chapter. However, as you begin to work, you'll soon discover that some clients might request a *phone patch, ISDN*, or another technology that will allow them to monitor or record your session remotely. You may never need any of these, but it is still worth knowing what they are and how to use them.

ISDN AND OTHER TECHNOLOGIES

ISDN stands for *Integrated Services Digital Network*. This is basically a hard-wire digital phone line provided by your local phone company that will connect your home studio to any other ISDN studio in the world. It's the next best thing to the client actually being at your home studio. To connect your studio to another studio requires a *codec* (coder-decoder) that will convert your audio to a digital signal that can be transmitted over phone lines. The receiving studio must have a compatible codec in order to receive your audio.

For many years, ISDN was the preferred method for digital audio transmission (and for some studios, it still is) because it allows for real-time, high-quality remote audio recording. However, in recent years, ISDN has steadily been losing favor and many telephone companies are discontinuing or no longer supporting ISDN service.

A number of cost-effective alternatives to ISDN have made their appearance, all of which use advances in Internet technology to provide real-time remote recording similar to ISDN. Some emulate ISDN while others use proprietary technology. Every system requires matching components or software at both ends of the connection. Some of the many contenders to ISDN include: **ipDTL.com, source-elements.com** (Source Connect), **soundstreak.com, audiotx.com, skype.com, luci.eu** (Luci Live), and **connectionopen.com**.

All contenders have a considerably lower cost than ISDN. Depending on location and availability, installation of ISDN phone lines can cost up to several hundred dollars per line and the codec alone can cost up to $3,000. Add to that the monthly service fees and the price of ISDN can add up quickly.

Do you need ISDN—or one of the alternatives? Probably not. Because any digital remote recording scheme will require matching equipment, software, or access to a service provider at both ends and the potential for monthly service fees, I do not recommend investing in any technology of this sort until you have a client base that will support the initial costs and produce a return on your investment. And when you do get that first ISDN booking, there's no need to rush out and install expensive equipment. Most cities have at least one ISDN studio where you can book the session.

PHONE PATCH

Many voiceover talent buyers and producers prefer to direct or supervise their VO sessions from the comfort of their office. In order for them to do this, they need to be able to clearly hear you as you record their script. At the same time, you need to be able to clearly hear them as they direct you through the session. Using a phone patch to your studio is the next best thing to ISDN or its alternatives, and it's a lot less expensive.

Although holding a telephone to your ear will do the job, this is not practical for a voiceover session as the mere action of holding the phone will restrict your physical energy. A telephone headset will do the job nicely and may be the simplest, most cost-effective way to go. Many VO professional use a Bluetooth headset connected to their cell phone with great success. However, ideally, you should be able to connect your home studio directly to your phone system.

A properly configured phone patch system will require an analog or digital mixer with the ability to send your audio both to your computer and to an external telephone hybrid that will interface your mixer's audio output with your telephone system. You will need to be able to monitor the incoming call without your client's audio being recorded. Once installed, your client will call your phone number (or you call them) and you push a button on your hybrid to connect your studio to the phone line. Connecting a phone patch digital hybrid to your equipment can be a bit tricky and is fully explained in *The Voice Actor's Guide to Professional Home Recording Ebook*, available through **VoiceActing.com**.

DIGITAL RECORDING DEVICES

The digital revolution has resulted in recording equipment becoming smaller and lighter while retaining extremely high quality. There are a wide variety of hand-held digital recorders on the market, but only a handful are an option for recording professional voiceover. The smaller, consumer, digital recorders have a built in mic, but no way to connect an external microphone. These often record at a low sample rate so recording quality is poor. Other digital recorders designed for broadcast and professional remote recording applications include the ability to connect 2 XLR mics. These models record at the standard sample rates of 44.1KHz and 48KHz and often have the ability to record directly to MP3 files. As good as they may be at recording, quality can vary and editing is often difficult and inaccurate.

The challenge with any digital audio recorder is in getting the audio file out of the device and into a computer where it can be edited. With professional devices, a simple USB connection to a computer is all that is needed. Some consumer recorders have no way to export files.

The Apple iPad® has become a very popular option for home studio recording partly due to the fact that there are no moving parts to produce sound. A few years after its release, the need for a way to connect a professional microphone and provide phantom power was answered with the **Alesis iDock** and more recently the **Behringer iStudio**. Both of these devices provide a docking bay for the iPad®, allowing for connection of professional microphones, additional audio connections, phantom power, and zero-latency headphone monitoring. Although it is possible, and software is available to record and edit on other digital tablets, the iPad® remains the most popular and functional device for this purpose.

A variety of recording and editing Apps are available for the iPad®, Android devices and even for recording on a smart phone. Yes, there's an App for that.

EQUIPMENT UPGRADES

At some point in your voiceover career you may want to upgrade your home studio. By the time you are ready for this you will have plenty of experience and you'll have a better knowledge of what you might want to upgrade, what equipment or software you might want to add and, more importantly, why. Equipment that is installed outside of your mixer or computer is generally referred to as *outboard equipment*, but much of the signal processing that used to require outboard gear can now be achieved with a plug-in within your recording software. A few of the possible equipment upgrades or additions are listed below:

- **Signal processing**—A signal processor can be any device that modifies or adjusts an audio signal. The most common processors include a compressor/limiter, equalizer, de-esser, noise reduction, de-clicker, signal enhancer, or mic preamp. Some outboard devices include multiple functions while others are dedicated to a single purpose. Most signal processing is also available as a software plug-in.

- **Outboard microphone preamp**—Your mixer or USB interface already includes a high-quality mic preamp. A microphone produces an extremely low electrical output that needs to be boosted (amplified) to a level that can be used by a mixer or other device. An external mic preamp will generally be of a higher quality than the built-in preamp in your mixer or USB interface, but it will also be much more expensive.

- **Powered speakers**—Advances in speaker design have produced speaker systems with the power amplifier built in resulting in extremely high quality audio from relatively small speakers. Most powered speakers are in matched pairs.

- **Additional microphones**—Different microphones can produce different results from your voice recordings. You or your client might want a certain sound for a specific project or type of voiceover work. Careful selection of your mic can help you achieve the desired results and allow you to offer greater versatility with your recording services.

Upgrading your home studio should only be a consideration when you have either a specific need for the upgrade or you have generated enough income to justify the expense.

Managing Your Computer

Regardless of your computer or its operating system, you will need to devise a method for managing your files. There is no single correct or ideal file management system, so this is something you'll

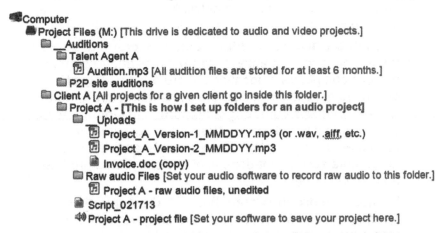

Fig. 22-1: Possible computer file structure. Create folders and sub-folders for all aspects of your recordings using separate folders for different elements. Ideally, put recordings on an external hard drive.

need to work out for yourself. However, I do have some suggestions that you might like to keep in mind as you work out your personal computer management system.

- **Devise a folder system that is easy to work with**—Think of your computer as a file cabinet. You might have a primary folder for each client and subfolders for each project you work on for that client. Within each project's subfolder there might be additional subfolders that hold files for various aspects of that project. The key to a successful and efficient file management system is to thoroughly think it through, even mapping it out on paper, before you start creating folders on your hard drive. This advance planning may reveal potential structural issues or result in some better organizational ideas that you might otherwise miss.

- **Include an "Upload" or "Deliver" folder**—Rendering your MP3 or other deliverable files to a separate folder will make it easier to locate them when burning to a CD-ROM, attaching to an email, or uploading to an FTP site.

- **Use a separate external hard drive for your voiceover projects**—If you keep all of your VO recordings on your C: Drive, you stand a chance of losing everything when your hard drive crashes… and eventually, it will! By using a separate hard drive for your voiceover work, you reduce the amount of stress on your C: Drive, allowing it to work more efficiently for running your system's programs. Using an external USB drive can give you the additional flexibility of moving the drive to a different computer to work on projects. Large capacity portable and network USB hard drives are inexpensive, and the investment will be well worth it.

- **Use remote access or Internet cloud storage to access files**—If you need to access your projects and files from multiple computers or locations, there are a variety of options to choose from. Remote computer control programs like **Teamviewer.com**, **Logmein.com**, and **Gotomypc.com** among others will allow you to share or access your computers from just about anywhere. Do an Internet search for "remote access" for dozens of choices. Some are free and some are paid.

  Services like **dropbox.com**, **box.net**, **drive.google.com**, **onedrive.live.com**, **mediafire.com**, **sugarsync.com**, **pogoplug.com** and dozens more provide cloud storage or synchronization of files and folders between multiple computers (or both). Most have limited free storage with paid upgrades. An Internet search for "similar to dropbox" will give you all sorts of ideas.

- **Master your computer software**—To be seen as a professional, you must be able to handle any computerized business functions quickly and efficiently. Learning how to use your software now will pay big dividends later on.

- **Know in advance how to deliver files**—FTP, CD-ROM, email, and third-party delivery uploads are just a few ways to deliver files. Any of these may be used to deliver files in any format and of any size. CD-ROM delivery requires software to properly burn the files to a disk. Email cannot handle a file larger than about 8–10 MB, and realistically, anything much larger than 4 MB will tend to slow things down. FTP (*File Transfer Protocol*) can be challenging to work with, but is often the preferred delivery method for very large files by larger companies. There are many third-party delivery methods that allow you to upload your files to a server and then notify your client via email with a link to download the files. An Internet search for "file delivery service" will reveal dozens of options, many of which are free and some that can handle files up to several gigabytes in size.

Wearing the Hat of the Audio Engineer

Having a home studio where you can record your auditions and voice tracks does not necessarily qualify you as a recording engineer, nor does it mean that you should even consider handling extensive editing or complete audio production with music and sound effects. If you would like to offer your clients full audio production services, but you know nothing about production, you have your work cut out for you. But that's another book!

At the very least, as a voice actor you will need to master your chosen audio recording software and equipment so you can record pristine audio. Be prepared to spend some time learning how to edit out breaths and adjust spacing between words and phrases. More complex production skills include understanding normalization, and how to adjust the quality of a recording using equalization (EQ), properly utilizing the many features of your software, learning how to use onboard signal processing and how to render high-quality audio in different formats. There are many ways to learn audio production and postproduction skills, and many excellent books on the subject.

As a voice actor, you really only need to know how to record your voice at the highest quality possible. Chances are you may never be asked to provide any extensive postproduction services.

Your home studio is critical to your voiceover business. By mastering the technical skills necessary to build and operate your home studio, you will be in a much better position to build a successful career as a voice actor.

The Mysterious Decibel

You've most likely heard the term *decibel*, or dB, mentioned in terms of audio recording levels, but do you have any idea what it means? Most voice talent don't! This isn't the place to go into a technical discussion of the decibel, but it is important that you have at least a basic understanding of what it is and how to use it. For a thorough discussion of the decibel, click on this response code.

Because the decibel measurement is used in different ways, understanding it can be a bit confusing. I'll do my best to explain this as simply as possible without the technical mumbo jumbo.

Let's start with the basics. Anything that moves has power. Sound waves moving through air have power. Electrons moving through a wire have power. So the question is ... "how do we measure that power and what do we reference it to as a standard?"

The term decibel literally means 1/10 of a Bel, named in honor of Alexander Graham Bell. The decibel is a logarithmic measurement of power used to express physical energy, gain or attenuation in electronics, or a comparative ratio between an input and output. It is usually used in terms of measuring sound in audio electronics or acoustic energy. According to Wikipedia, "A change in power by a factor of 10 is a 10 dB change in level. A change in power by a factor of two is approximately a 3 dB change. A change in voltage by a factor of 10 is equivalent to a change in power by a factor of 100 and is thus a 20 dB change. A change in voltage ratio by a factor of two is approximately a 6 dB change."

Let's use threshold of hearing, which is just above absolute silence, as a reference for zero (0dB). Since we know that a 10-times increase in power is an increase of 10dB, we can measure the comparative loudness of sound in an acoustic environment or in an electronic circuit. Here are just a few common sound levels in dB:

- Threshold of hearing   0 dB
- A whisper   15 dB
- Normal conversation   60 dB
- A lawnmower   90 dB
- A car horn   110 dB
- A jet engine   120 dB
- Threshold of pain   140 dB

The dB levels above are measured in terms of the power of sound waves, or *sound pressure level* (SPL) when referenced to the threshold of hearing. When we talk about measuring audio signals for recording, everything changes.

Measuring power in electronic audio equipment is referenced in terms of voltage and if the signal is audio, an increase or decrease in voltage can refer to a specific change in decibels.

Back in the early days of radio and analog electronics, a standard reference was needed for measuring audio levels. Through a series of calculations, the electronics wizards of the day developed a standard reference level for audio signal measurement. The standardized reference was arrived at by producing a 1KHz sine wave at .775 volts RMS. Don't ask why. The math isn't important. What is important is that you know that the .775 volt RMS signal became the 0VU reference on the old analog VU (volume unit) meters and that, technically, the correct notation for audio measurement is dBu.

The range on the analog VU meters was from -20 to +3, but the actual incoming audio signal could be below -20 or above +3. But 0VU became the optimal audio output level for recording and broadcast. Not coincidentally, that 0VU reference was the equivalent of a specific measurement in decibels, so 0VU also became known as 0dB.

RECORDING LEVELS

As you know, about 90% of your recording quality lies in the acoustics of your recording environment. The next most important thing for making excellent recordings is your recording levels. This simply refers to the volume, or loudness of your recordings as they are represented as a waveform in your software.

The measurement of sound pressure level in dBu is what we are talking about when discussing recording levels, but it is commonly referred to simply as dB after being converted to a digital signal. The optimal record level is for audio peaks to be in the range of -6 to -12db on your computer's digital VU meter. Visually, this is roughly where the wave form on your computer screen fills about 2/3 of the wave form window and just about where the meter begins to change from green to yellow.

All electronic equipment has internal noise that is generated by the mere fact that electricity is running through it. Also, all acoustic environments have a base "noise" level, usually referred to as "room tone". Your room tone level can be as low as -72 or lower in a really quiet room. But most homes are closer to -40 or higher. So, if your room tone level is -40 and your record level averages -15db, there is only a 25dB difference between the two. In order to bring a low recording up to workable levels, it's often necessary to *normalize* the recording. Normalization is a software process in which the computer

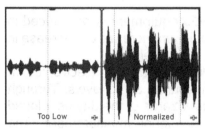

Fig. 22-2: Too low vs. Normalized

scans the recording for the loudest spike and increases the volume of the recording equally so that the loudest audio spike is brought up to a predetermined maximum volume, usually around −1db. When you normalize your recording you are also proportionally increasing all that room noise along with any electronic noise. That's why you'll hear lots of noise (or "hiss") in normalized recordings that started at too low a record level.

If your original record level averages around -6dB and your room noise is −50, you have a 44dB difference between the loudness of your voice and any noise. This difference is called the *signal to noise ratio* (S:N). The greater the signal to noise ratio the quieter the recording. Since

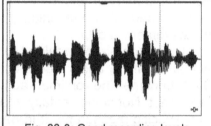

Fig. 22-3: Good recording levels

each change of 1dB is a 10-times change in power, a 44db S:N will be a pretty quiet recording.

If you look closely at your digital VU meter, you'll notice that -12 to -18 is just about the point where the meter color changes from green to yellow. This is the equivalent of the 0VU point on the old analog meter. Analog equipment was designed to have about 20dB of "headroom" above 0VU. So, if -18dB digital is roughly the equivalent of 0VU analog, that means that you have about 20dB of "headroom" above that point where the digital meter begins to change to yellow.

Recording levels that are too high (Fig. 22-4) can also produce some serious problems. Excessive levels are commonly referred to as *clipping*. In the days of analog recording, if you recorded too loud

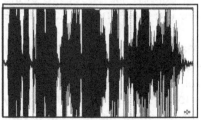

Fig. 22-4: Too hot (clipping)

or too "hot," the audio would simply become distorted. With digital recording, if you record too "hot," putting your level above 0dB, you will actually be losing data. Although there are ways to "restore" missing data, the process is very time consuming and the tools can be very expensive.

Clipping can occur at any of several places in the audio signal path. Your USB interface input volume can be set too high. If you are using a mixer, the input gain trim can be set too high, the input control knob or fader can be set too high, or the master output can be too high—all potentially resulting in clipping in the software.

The best way to determine your optimal recording levels will be to experiment with your equipment and software. Don't worry, you can't break anything. And you will learn a lot about how your equipment and software function.

An Audio Recording & Editing Primer

Sound recording is an art form in its own right. The purpose of this section is not to teach you the finer points of sound recording, but, rather, to give you some insights into how you can record excellent voiceover tracks. Scanning this response code will take you to a video that discusses some of the basics of audio editing.

RECORDING SOFTWARE

Fortunately, all audio recording software is similar in design, so whether you use a PC or a Mac, the basic functionality will be the same. As your voice is recorded digitally in the computer, the software shows a real-time moving timeline with a wave form that represents the amplitude (loudness) of your voice.

If you ask an audio equipment retailer about recording software, most will recommend Pro Tools®, telling you that it is the standard of the recording industry. Although this is largely true, Pro Tools® is extremely complex with a long learning curve and includes features that will never be used by most voice actors. It's really designed for high-end music recording and is overkill for basic voiceover work. You will be far better off starting with trial versions of various software to find what works best for your. Many people start with the free Audacity software (**audacity.sourceforge.net**) and move up to paid software as their skills develop and bookings begin to come in.

BASIC EDITING

Sound editing is an art form in itself and there are many excellent books on this subject. However, it is critical that you understand at least the basics of audio editing if you are going to submit professional auditions and paid work.

The Art of Voice Acting

When you record a script, your phrasing includes an inherent rhythm and timing of beats, inflection, tone of voice, dynamics and more. Many of these elements of your performance can be seen in the recorded waveform, and all of these must be taken into consideration when editing.

Editing is the process of repairing or re-assembling the sequence of the recorded sounds. In other words, if you record a script and make a mistake, you'll need to do a *pickup* to replace the section in which the error was made. If you make a mistake during the pickup, you'll simply record another pickup. When you record a pickup, make sure your tone of voice, levels and inflection are consistent with what you did originally. When it comes time to edit your recording, you'll be removing the parts in error, replacing them with the best pickups.

A common mistake in editing is to overlook the timing or phrasing between words and sentences. If the edit is too tight or too loose, the phrasing will sound wrong. Bad edits are often the result of mismatched timing, not matching inflection with pickups, and removing breaths or mouth noise without retaining the original timing. Always listen to the transition at the original edit point for the timing before making the edit.

Occasionally, adjusting the timing for an edit might result in a gap of *digital silence* at the edit point. Digital silence is a complete absence of sound, and will usually be heard as a drop, or cut-off, of the audio which can be perceived as a mistake. To solve this problem, simply record a few seconds of *room tone*. This is the natural sound of your recording environment with your microphone open and level set at the spot where you would normally record your voice. When you have a gap at an edit point, simply replace the gap with a piece of the natural room tone. When removing breaths or mouth noise, this little trick can also allow you to adjust your timing by shortening or lengthening the beat for a more effective delivery.

Most editing requires a certain level of precision, even for simple voice tracks. For the best edits, you should zoom in on the waveform and make your edit at the point where the waveform crosses the center line (Fig. 22-5). To avoid clicks or audible edits, the waveform should retain its natural flow as it crosses the center line. When you become extremely proficient with your editing, you can replace a single word, part of a word, or even adjust the inflection of a phrase by replacing parts of a sentence.

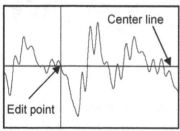

Fig. 22-5: Waveform edit point

SIGNAL PROCESSING

Signal processing is defined as any electronic process that affects the recorded audio signal. This could include normalization, equalization (EQ), compression, limiting, noise reduction, de-clicking, and any number of other processes.

It's not the purpose of this book to explain how to use any of these signal processing tools. The important thing to know is that if you record your auditions or projects in an acoustically quiet area with proper audio levels, you really should not need to do any signal processing prior to rendering your file. More important: if you do not understand how to use a given process or what it does, you would be wise to not use that processing.

The three most common types of audio processing that are misunderstood or misused are 1) *compression*, 2) EQ (*equalization*), and 3) *normalization*.

- **Compression** is a process that balances out the peaks in your recordings, thus smoothing out the overall record levels between low volume and louder sections.
- **EQ (equalization)** is a process that can compensate for problems at specific frequencies. It is similar to the bass and treble tone controls on some audio equipment. EQ can help to compensate for some acoustic issues, but care must be taken to use EQ sparingly. If overused, EQ can severely damage a rendered recording. EQ can also be used to create special effects like the sound of a telephone.
- **Normalization** is the process of proportionally increasing the overall loudness of the entire recording to a pre-set maximum level as determined by the loudest spike in the audio. Normalization is not intended to compensate for poorly recorded audio. This process will increase everything in your recording, including noise. See the section on "Recording Levels" earlier in this chapter for more about Normalization.

Once applied, signal processing cannot be undone after the file is rendered. If not used correctly, signal processing can affect a recording to the point where it becomes unusable. Most producers will prefer a completely unprocessed voice track at proper levels. This allows them to make audio processing adjustments at their end during post-production. However, some clients may request some limited processing. If or when you get this request, be sure to ask for any specific settings they want for the processing.

With the possible exception of normalization, when you apply audio processing to your recording, you are making a subjective judgment about what you think your recording should sound like. This may or may not be what the producer is looking for, and if your choice is wrong, it may affect future work. Your job is to deliver the highest quality, clean, voiceover recording you can deliver, not to demonstrate your subjective opinions through audio processing.

RENDERING

Rendering is the process of compiling all the component parts of a project into a final delivery format. For images, rendered files are commonly .jpg and .png. For audio, rendered files can be any of several formats, including the native formats of .wav and .aiff or any of dozens of other audio formats including .ogg and .mp3. The rendered format is generally requested by the client, depending on the specific needs of the project in production.

All audio high-quality recording software records audio in one of the two primary native audio formats, either .wav for a PC or .aiff for a Mac. Both native formats are standardized to work at either 44.1KHz or 48KHZ as the sample rate for the recording. The *sample rate* is the speed at which analog audio is scanned, or sampled, by the computer as it is converted to a digital representation of the analog signal. 44.1KHz means that any given second of analog audio is sampled 44,100 times. 44.1KHz is the standard sample rate for audio CD and most audio recordings. 48KHZ is generally reserved for video production and is a carry-over from the days of analog video tape. Most audio software will convert imported audio on the fly to the project's sample rate. If you record at 44.1KHZ, you can't go wrong.

In addition to the sample rate, analog audio is converted to digital at a specific bit rate. The *bit rate* refers to the number of data bits (ones and zeros) that are included in each individual sample of the incoming audio. 16 bit means that there is a combination of 16 zeros and ones used to represent each of those 44,100 samples per second. A bit rate of 24 has an additional 8 zeros and ones per sample. The higher the bit rate, the higher the quality of the analog to digital conversion.

The .wav and .aiff native audio formats create very large files, averaging about 10MB per stereo minute. This is great for retaining high quality during editing and production, but is not practical for delivering files by email. When the standards for converting audio and video to a digital format were designed, video was converted to a format known as MPEG, short for *Motion Picture Engineering Group*, the organization responsible for developing the digital conversion standards. Video conversion consisted of two primary components, one for the video signal and one for the audio. To save space in the video file, the audio was stored as a comparatively small file using a method of data compression. As the standards were developed, the audio layer, originally known as MPEG-layer 3, eventually became known as simply MP3 when it was adapted from the video conversion standard to be used exclusively for audio conversion. Audio converted to the MP3 standard is approximately 1/10th the size of the original native format file.

Most of today's auditions and paid projects will be rendered to a compressed MP3 file at 128Kbps. MP3 conversion (or rendering) handles the bit rate in a slightly different way than native files. The bit rate for an MP3 refers to the transfer bit rate at which the file is converted, or more accurately, the degree to which the file has been compressed. The greater the compression the lower the MP3 bit rate, and the lower the quality because more data is being lost in the conversion. An MP3 file with a bit rate of 128Kbps (kilobits per second) is considered to be the standard for MP3 conversion as it is a good compromise of overall quality to file size (roughly 1/10th the size of a native file. Rendering to a higher bit rate (larger number) like 192Kbps or 320Kbps will result in a higher quality MP3 file.

If you render auditions to MP3 at 128Kbps, you'll be within the conventional standard. However, for paid projects, you should always ask your client how they would like you to render your files for delivery.

DELIVERING RENDERED FILES

There is no one, single, best way to deliver your rendered audio files. On-line audition sites will usually ask you to upload an MP3 file through their website. Talent agents will ask for your auditions to be delivered via email or through their website. Clients and production companies may use email, a third party delivery service, or their internal FTP (*file transfer protocol*) upload system. And there are other delivery methods and file sharing services like **sugarsync.com**, **box.com**, **dropbox.com, drive.google.com**, **onedrive.live.com**, **pogoplug.com**, and a few dozen others, all of which establish a direct communication from your computer to that of your client or agent. And, of course, there are those occasions when you might burn your rendered files to an audio CD or DVD for delivery to your client. It will always be a good idea to ask your client how they would like files delivered.

Regardless of the delivery method used, make sure you follow your client's file naming protocol to the letter. Talent agents have a reputation for not accepting mis-named audition files.

In this Chapter

Your Voiceover Identity

23

Establishing Your Voiceover Identity

Present Yourself as a Professional

You've spent a good deal of time studying your craft, and you have made an investment in producing a high-quality, marketable demo. Congratulations ... you're in business. As you begin making contacts for voiceover work, you will be speaking to and meeting professionals who may have been in this business for many years. These people have seen it all, and have little time to waste on an amateur trying to break into the business. Your first impression needs to be memorable and professional.

Managing your voiceover business requires at least some degree of specialized knowledge in an incredibly broad range of activities, even if that knowledge is only an awareness of something you do not know how to do, but which you also know must be done. A professional is someone who knows how to delegate those duties for which they are not an expert. However, the little detail of cost can be a major incentive for a sole proprietor to learn about some of the more esoteric aspects of business management. Chapter 25 will cover many of the more mundane business activities, like setting fees and keeping the books. This section will briefly cover some of the management concepts that will help to establish you in the voiceover marketplace. For more information on any of these topics, an Internet search will reveal many additional resources.

CREATING YOUR BRAND

Presenting yourself as a professional is important when you introduce yourself to agents and talent buyers whether that introduction is in person, through a phone call, in print, or via your website. A coordinated *brand* shows that you mean business, take your career seriously and consider yourself to be a professional. Your brand is the visual and/or auditory representation of who you are and what you do. It sets you apart from your competition in the mind of your clients.

Creating an identity, or brand, for your business is not always an easy thing to do, and it is something you might not want to tackle yourself. Fortunately, there are quite a few talented business consultants and graphic design artists in the business who you can hire to assist you. Even if you hire someone to help develop your brand and design your graphic image, you still need to provide some input. You might even want your advisor and graphic designer to hear your demo to get a better idea of what you do. Branding consultants can get their inspiration from just about anything, so be as thorough as possible when presenting your ideas.

Your visual image is an important part of your marketing campaign and should reflect your individual personality. It can help set you apart from the crowd and ultimately work toward establishing you as a "brand name" in the world of voiceover. It should be consistent in all printed materials and carry through to your website.

WHAT MAKES YOU UNIQUE?

There are two elements of your marketing that can set you apart from others who do what you do. Defining these two components is the first step to creating a strong brand. First is a *UPS,* or *unique positioning statement.* This is a short one or two-sentence statement that clearly defines what you do, for whom you do it, and your unique solution to an urgent need. Writing your UPS can be a challenge because it requires you to fully understand the value of what you do and the critical needs of your clients. This may require some research on your part and a great deal of thought as you hone and refine your statement. It's not as easy as it looks. There are many excellent books and Internet resources that discuss this aspect of business development, and that can help you create your UPS.

The second element is a *USP,* or *unique selling proposition.* A USP is a refinement of the UPS into a short statement. It says: "use our services and you will get this specific benefit." The essence of the USP can then be crafted into a *slogan* that can be anything from a single word to a short phrase. Your slogan, if you have one, along with your visual image, are how most of your clients will come to identify and recognize your unique brand.

Your positioning statement is for you to help give your business focus. Your USP is for your clients to help them remember you.

Here's the unique positioning statement for our coaching and training services website **voiceacting.com**:

We teach powerfully effective communication and performing skills that we've developed over more than three decades of stage, television, recording studio, and advertising experience. We work with people who want to break into the business of voiceover and with business professionals who want to improve relationships with their customers, increase sales, improve their communication skills, create more effective advertising, or become better presenters and performers.

This positioning statement is intended to give us a clearly defined focus on what we do, who we do it for, and the results that can be expected from using our services. It positions us as expert performance coaches and as a business that understands business communication. An orchestra conductor is our logo, representing the process of combining several core elements of communication to achieve effective results. For marketing this aspect of our business, we refine the positioning statement to a single phrase that is more concise, yet conveys the story we want to tell. At first, we successfully marketed our performance coaching under the VoiceActing.com banner graphic and used the USP:

We make you sound great!

The original VoiceActing.com graphic looked like this:

VoiceActing.com
we make you sound great!

As we began to produce the VoiceOver International Creative Experience (VOICE) (**voiceconvention.com**), the world's original International convention for voiceover talent, we realized that, although our positioning statement still conveyed what we did, our USP no longer accurately reflected the way we were perceived by the voiceover community and our clients. In addition to the convention, we had also expanded our services to include a full-service production company, corporate coaching, and had moved the business from a partnership to a Limited Liability Corporation (LLC). We spent a considerable amount of time brainstorming and testing various ideas and slogans. As a result, we expanded the VoiceActing.com brand by adding the VoiceActing Academy, VOICE and VoiceActing Studios. New graphics were designed and a new USP was created for each aspect of our business that we believe more accurately positions who we are and what we do.

The Art of Voice Acting

Here are some examples of our branding graphics:

Second generation VoiceActing Academy with VOICE:
USP: Changing lives, one voice at a time.

Updated brand for website with new USP:
USP: Training and Support in the Craft and Business of Voiceover

VOICE Convention: (three generations of the logo)
USP: Education, Technology, Community

You can create your own UPS, USP, and slogan by taking a close, hard look at what you do, who you do it for, and what makes you different. Only by close examination will you be able to discover what makes you unique from other voice talent in your area. When you discover what that is, write it out in a sentence that describes it clearly and concisely. It should describe who your primary customer is and what they gain from using your services. Use our examples above to get started. This process can take up to several hours or several days and will usually result in numerous variations and possible statements. Once this creative exercise is complete, you'll have a much clearer picture of your role in the world of voiceover. With this understanding in mind, you can now begin to explore various ways of refining the essence of your work into a concise USP and slogan.

As you work on developing your positioning statement, unique selling proposition, and slogan, be creative and let your imagination run wild. Come up with as many ideas as you can and narrow them down to a few that work for you. Pick the best one and use it everywhere. Your slogan and logo are the visual representation of your brand and they should be included in every piece of print material, as an email signature, and on your website.

Here are a few examples:

- *A Penny for your $pots. She just makes cents!* (Penny Abshire)
- *Changing lives one voice at a time* (VoiceActing Academy)
- *Orchestrate your message!* (James R. Alburger)
- *My Voice, Your Way!* (Debbie Munro)
- *Aural gratification guaranteed* (Lani Minella)
- *Guaranteed to round up more business* (Bob Jump)

Building your business as a voice talent can be a daunting task that can be made easier when you understand that you don't have to do everything at once. Take things one step at a time. As you complete one aspect of your business development, begin working on the next. Approach your business development from an organized and structured foundation, much like you have done with your performance craft.

There are dozens of excellent marketing and business development books available that can help you identify your USP and business identity. One of my favorites is a small book by Mark LeBlanc titled *Grow Your Business*. This little book provides the tools and processes to give you the focus to create a powerful defining statement for your business. With that in hand, the world is yours! Mark's website is **smallbusinesssuccess.com**. Another excellent book is "Getting Everything You Can Out of All You've Got" by Jay Abraham.

Setting Up Shop

Today's voiceover world revolves around the voice actor's home studio and office. If you are going to be in this business, you will need to dedicate an area of your home for your studio and office. Of course, your office can be put together over a period of time, and you may already have much of it in place. Your home office will, most likely, be run from the same computer that is your home studio.

The purpose of setting up a formal office area is so that you can really keep yourself in a mindset of handling your voiceover work as a business. The recordkeeping and organizational aspects of a business become increasingly important as you begin generating income from your voiceover work. If or when you join a union, you will want to keep track of your session work and your union paperwork. There are also certain tax advantages to setting up a formal business and you would be wise to consult a tax advisor or accountant on this matter. These topics will be covered in the next few chapters.

As with any business, it is important for you, as a voice actor, to stay in touch with your clients and prospects. Consider some of these necessities for that all-important client communication:

- **A cell phone**—Your cell phone will be one of, if not the, most useful tools you own whether you work exclusively from home or are on the road. It will be an absolute necessity for staying in touch with clients and your agent. There are literally dozens of smart phone Apps that can help you with many aspects of your voiceover business, including even recording directly on your phone and uploading files to agents or clients.

- **An answering machine, voicemail, or service**—If you don't have a cell phone, one of these is absolutely essential. Be sure to check for new messages frequently, especially when you get an agent. There are some interesting virtual phone number messaging services available on the Internet for free or for a minimal monthly charge. Services like Google Voice (**voice.google.com**) can forward calls, take voice mail and even send voicemail messages to your email. An Internet search for "phone messaging service" will reveal many options.

- **Business cards, letterhead and envelopes**—You should consider each contact you make as potential work. Your first impression leaves a lasting memory. Even though we live in a largely electronic world, you should consider professionally designed and printed business cards and stationery as essential ingredients to presenting a professional image.

  A business card is an absolute necessity. As part of your personal networking, you will want to let everyone you meet know what you do. Your business card is the first and best introduction to you and your talent, followed closely by your demo. Always carry a supply of business cards with you and hand them out every chance you get.

  The most important things on your business card are your name and a telephone number where you can be reached, followed closely by your email address and website. The most common problem with business cards is that the telephone number is too small to read easily.

  The second most common problem is too much information on the card. Include only the most important information about yourself on your card. If you are using a slogan or logo, those should be on the card as well. Keep the design clean and simple for best results (see Figure 23-1).

- **Thank-you notes**—A frequently overlooked, yet very important, business practice is the thank-you note. A brief note of thanks is

Figure 23-1: Business card dimensions with sample layout.

often all it takes to leave a good feeling with a producer or client. These little notes can easily be prepared in advance, help generate positive memories of your work, and provide a gentle reminder that you are available. In this electronic age, receiving a printed thank-you note in the mail can have a huge impact simply because it shows that you took the time and effort to make your client know they are special.

- **Newsletters and Postcards**—This form of customer follow-up can be either electronic or sent by mail. As with thank-you notes, newsletters and postcards will have more impact if sent by mail. Content usually includes a brief description of recent projects and clients and any other interesting information. The sole purpose of the newsletter or postcard is to keep your name in front of the talent buyer. If you use email to connect with clients, you might send out a brief update on your activities on a monthly basis.

- **Blogs and social networking websites**—*Blogs* (short for web log) have become a popular, and highly efficient, method for voice actors to communicate with their clients and friends in the voiceover community. Blog subscribers receive almost immediate notification when a new post is added that announces a new client or other news. Most blogs are associated with a website. Social media websites allow for communication on a much broader scale. Dave Courvoisier provides a thorough discussion of how to effectively use social media in Chapter 20.

Print Materials

Even if your marketing will primarily be through your website and email, there are several marketing items you will want to consider having professionally designed and printed, including business cards, envelopes, and stationery. For best results, take your layout to an experienced printer. However, if you are on an extremely tight budget and possess the necessary computer skills, you can use a laser or high-quality, color ink-jet printer to create your own print materials.

Consult with a printing service or paper supply company about paper stock and ink colors. These people are in the business of making printed materials look good and may be able to offer some valuable suggestions. If you do your own printing, choose paper stock that reflects your branding. You can purchase specialized papers and even sheets of preformatted business cards, mailing labels, and CD labels, ready to be loaded into your printer. However, be aware that some specialty papers or perforated paper for business cards may present a less-than-professional image.

Avery is considered by many to be the standard for blank, preformatted labels. Its website, **avery.com**, provides for on-line label design and printing for most of its label paper stock. You can find comparable labels for almost every Avery label design at Label Blank, **labelblankcorporation.com**. You can save a lot of money by purchasing a box of 100 sheets of Label Blank or Avery labels, rather than the smaller packages of 25 sheets that you'll find at most stationery and computer stores.

PHOTOS

One of the nice things about voice acting is that your physical appearance is far less important than your ability to act. No matter how good your demo might be, a photograph is going to give the talent buyer a face to go with your voice. In some respects, you can easily be pigeon-holed or stereotyped as a result of a photo on your demo or website. Many agents and producers will associate a face to a name before they associate a voice to a name. Although not intentional, this can sometimes be a real disservice for the voice actor. My recommendation if you are just starting in this business is to keep your visual image clean and simple without photos, and let your voice do the selling. Later on, as your image, branding, and credibility become established you might consider adding a photo to your marketing materials.

Of course, there are exceptions. If you are also marketing your talents as a model, an on-camera performer, or if you do live theater, a photo is a must. As a multifaceted performer, a photo can work to your benefit because it will tend to associate your versatility with your name in the mind of the talent buyer. Ultimately, using a photo will depend on how you market yourself and which media you use.

If you choose to use a photo as part of your packaging, hire a professional photographer who understands performance headshots to take the picture and make sure the photo reflects your money-voice personality. Your photo is an important part of your branding and should be of the highest quality.

CD LABELS

The era of the audio CD as a distribution medium for voiceover demos has pretty much gone the way of the audio cassette. Individual one-off CDs will, however, most likely remain an option for voiceover demos for some time to come. If you choose to create audio CD demos, you'll want the cover, label, and tray card designs to reflect your professional image and branding. There are several options for labeling and packaging your CD demo. Perhaps the most common form of CD packaging is the familiar plastic jewel case. Alternative packaging options include a clamshell case, basic paper or cardboard sleeve, a slim-line jewel case, and a DVD keep case.

The standard jewel case will provide easy storage and visible access to your demo. The slim-line jewel case has no spine, or edge labeling, and can disappear when placed on a shelf with other CDs. The clamshell case, paper and cardboard sleeves all provide no space for anything other than the CD, and are not recommended. A DVD keep case is not recommended for voiceover demos because it will not fit on the same shelf with other audio CDs. It can be argued that the larger size of the DVD case will make the demo stand out from the crowd, but the reality is that it will usually be stored someplace away from other CDs and can be easily forgotten.

Your jewel case labels should contain the essential information about your demo: your name, catchy slogan (if you have one), logo (if you have one), agent's name (if you have one), and contact phone number (yours or your agent's). The back should include the CD contents, especially if there is more than one demo on the CD. You might also include a short bio or perhaps a brief client list for added credibility. Your or your agent's website and email address might also be included, depending on how you are marketing your demo

The CD itself will also need some sort of label, the simplest being a paper label. If you are duplicating your own CDs you will be using paper labels. Most commercial CD duplicators will use the more professional-looking process of imprinting your label design directly on the CD.

Getting Your Demo Out There:
To Duplicate or Not to Duplicate

One of the things to determine when designing your business and marketing plan is how you will distribute your demo. Within the space of a few short years, demo distribution has moved from reel-to-reel tape to audio cassette to audio CD to electronic data files. In today's voiceover world, your primary distribution will be via an MP3 audio file on your website, sent as an attachment in an email, accessible through an online audition site, or sent from your agent.

When the CD was king, it was often necessary to spend a lot of money for a duplication run of anywhere from 100 to 1,000 or more CDs plus the print material that went with them. In just the past few years, that has all changed! Although the trend today is electronic files as the primary means for demo distribution, the audio CD continues to be found on some agent and talent buyer shelves.

It probably isn't a bad idea to have at least a few audio CDs available for those prospects or agents who might request them. Although you can certainly take the high-end route of CD replication, burning your own CDs directly on your computer is a common and cost-effective method for creating a small supply to keep on hand. Assuming your demo was produced professionally, there is no difference in quality between burning your own CDs or using a duplication service. The advantage of using a CD duplication service is that the final CD will have a more professional look with the label printed directly on the CD.

Because electronic files are so popular as a delivery media for voiceover demos, I wouldn't suggest burning any more than about 25 copies of your demo to start with. These would be reserved for distribution to people you contact who specifically request an audio CD of your demo. When you get an agent, he or she will let you know how many copies the agency needs to keep on hand—if any.

If you've never burned a CD on your computer, it would be to your benefit to learn how to use software designed for that purpose. You'll find a variety of software manufacturers at your local computer store or with an Internet search for "CD burning software." Most software for creating CDs will also burn DVDs. For your voiceover demo, you'll want to use commonly available blank CD or Data CD-R media. DVD media won't play in an audio CD player.

More important than the CD is the MP3 electronic file. The MP3 file originated as the audio portion of a more complex digital video format. The Motion Picture Engineering Group (MPEG) is the organization responsible for developing the standards for digital recording. The original Mpeg 1 video format had several component parts, one of which was known as "audio layer 3." As digital audio recording became popular, this part of the video format was modified to be a standalone format for digital audio. Thus was born MPEG Layer 3 digital audio, or MP3 for short.

An MP3 file is actually a compressed (or compacted) form of a larger .wav (WAVeform audio format) or .aiff (audio information file format) sound recording. Imagine an inflated balloon. The rubber balloon represents the primary digital information and all the air inside represents the redundant, or duplicated data present in the file. An MP3 file can be seen as a deflated balloon. The primary data is the same, but all the redundant data has been removed, thus reducing (or compressing) the size of the file. An MP3 file created at the CD sample rate of 44.1 kHz will be roughly 1/10th the size of the original uncompressed raw audio file.

Most audio recording software can easily create MP3 files, and knowing how to do this is essential if you are going to submit auditions or your demo as electronic files.

Your Website

There once was a time when the Internet did not exist, and no one knew what a website was. I know, hard to believe, but it's true!

For voiceover talent today, a website is an absolute necessity. It's often the first stop a prospect makes to learn who you are and what you can do. A website is your 24/7/365 brochure, available to be visited by anyone, any time, anywhere in the world. If you don't already have a website, I'd suggest you seriously consider learning about the Internet and getting on-line! A website is an invaluable tool in marketing your voiceover talent.

The mere thought of building your own website can be daunting. But, it's really not all that difficult if you have some basic computer skills. Many website hosting companies offer website templates as part of their service. With these, you design your website on-line. It can take some time to add all the bells and whistles, but you can often build a simple site in just a few short hours. There are also several software programs that will allow you to design your own site on your computer. These will offer more options and capabilities than the on-line templates, and allow you to keep a backup of your site on your computer. Their ease-of-use, which is generally reflected by price, ranges from pretty simple, to very complex.

No matter what approach you take for designing and building your website, remember that the purpose of the site is to market you as a voice actor. Flashy animation, glitzy graphics, and clever font styles may look nice, but they may not serve the purpose of branding your voiceover business.

WEBSITE ESSENTIALS

There are many important considerations for putting your website on-line. Here are just a few:

- **URL** (Universal Resource Locator), also known as the *domain name*: This is the name of your website. You want yours to be simple, short, and descriptive. Your domain name must be registered before you can set up an account with a website host. Most hosting companies can help you with registering your URL. Check for availability and register or host through **magicinet.com** or one of many other registrars. Your domain's URL name is associated with an *IP address* (internet protocol) consisting of a series of 12 numbers that identifies the websites location on the Internet. These numbers refer to address or location of the website's *Dynamic Name Servers* (DNS), which are actually the hard drives on which the website exists.

- **FTP (File Transfer Protocol):** This is the means by which a website structure (or file directory) can be accessed on-line. You may be asked to deliver files via FTP to an address given to you by your client. Or, if you are building your site off line, you may need the site's DNS location in order to upload your website files. You can look at your site's URL as the front door of your website and its FTP access as the back door.

- **Site design:** Your website should be designed to reflect who you are and what you do. Carry your branding through to your website to keep your visual image consistent.

- **Email:** Using an email address with your domain, such as "you@yourdomain.com" only makes good marketing sense. Most websites allow for email to be viewed through the website's webmail account, or for email to be forwarded to another address. Avoid using your primary email address as a common .aol, .hotmail, .msn, .yahoo, and similar email addresses that shout "amateur." You can easily set up your domain email address to forward to your generic address, and set your domain address as an additional address so it can be used to send email from within your generic account.

- **Tell your story:** Your website is the perfect place to let prospects know who you are, who you've worked for, and what you can do for them. A one-page site, if well-designed, will present you as a professional. A good example of a single-page site is **pennyabshire.com**. You'll notice that everything you need to know about Penny as a professional voice talent is easily accessible on that one page.

- **Post your demos:** Your demos are your primary marketing tool, and you should absolutely post them on your website. MP3 is the recommended format as it is a fairly small file size and will download quickly. Demos on your site can be text linked to MP3 files stored on your site or they can be set to play within a media player on the site and to offer the file for download. This requires a bit of behind-the-scenes web design, but the benefit is definitely worth the effort. The major difference between a text linked MP3 and streaming audio is that MP3 files must first be downloaded before playing, which can take some time, while streaming audio will play almost instantly. The downside of streaming audio is that the files cannot be downloaded for future reference.

  Another option is to use an off-site media player service like **soundcloud.com**. This type of service allows you to upload your files and create a link to their player that is embedded on your site.

- **Using Photos:** Your voiceover website is about your voice, not what you look like. There are two schools of thought regarding headshots on a voiceover site: one is that giving potential clients a visual image of who you are can result in stereotyping, thus limiting your potential bookings. The other is that a good headshot can help to give your prospects a more personal connection to the "real" you. If you are also an on-camera or stage actor, a good headshot is an essential marketing tool. But if you are exclusively marketing yourself for voiceover, the use of a headshot will be a completely personal choice. If you do choose to include a photo, please make sure it is one that represents you as a professional. Of course, photos of awards you've received, your logo, and even logos of your clients (used with their permission, of course) can all lend credibility to you as a professional voice actor.

Building your own website can be an educational and fun experience—if you have the time and inclination. If you'd rather put your time and energy into developing your performing skills and voiceover business, you might want to consider hiring a web designer to build your site. There are a handful of web designers who specialize in creating sites for voiceover talent. Before hiring any web designer, take a look at their work and ask for referrals. If you expect that you might need to update your site on a regular basis, you may want to consider building your own.

In this Chapter

The Talent Agent

24

The Talent Agent

Finding and Working with an Agent

A common question is "Do I need an agent to do voiceover work?" The short answer is "No, you don't need an agent" but this isn't really the right question to be asking. A better question is "Will a talent agent help me in my voiceover career." For most voiceover talent, the answer is "Yes." If you work without an agent, you are limiting yourself to only those voiceover jobs you can find for yourself, and you will be responsible for negotiating your fees and collecting payments. One major advantage of having representation is that you will gain access to auditions and clients that you might never have met if you were not represented. Your agent will also handle fee negotiations and collect payments. Having a talent agent working for you is definitely to your advantage; however, this does not mean that you *must* have an agent to be successful.

There is a belief among beginning voice actors that landing an agent means they can just sit back and watch the work roll in. Sorry, but it doesn't work that way! The truth is that your agent is only one part of your larger marketing plan. According to Gabrielle Nistico of **vocareer.com**, although an agent will create and distribute marketing materials designed to reach industry professionals, those materials are generally intended to promote the agency, and not an individual talent. It is the voice actor's individual marketing efforts that ultimately promote their unique skills and abilities.

Networking with other voiceover performers keeps you up on current trends, and, if you are non-union, you may get a better idea of the fees other performers are earning. In addition to using social media networking, joining professional associations like Media

Communications Association, International (**mca-i.org**) and on-line sites like **voiceoveruniverse.com, productionhub.com** and others will help to keep you connected with local producers, production companies, and others who may ultimately utilize your services.

When away from your studio, always keep a few demos and business cards with you and be ready to pitch yourself when the opportunity arises. It's a subtlety, but maintaining an attitude of professionalism communicates credibility and integrity.

GETTING THE GIGS

You will probably get your first few voiceover jobs through friends, networking, a coach's referral, a pay-to-play site or some other contact you make yourself. As you begin working, your skills will improve, producers will begin to know about you, and your talents will become more valuable. When you reach the point where you are confident with your abilities, have developed a repeat client base, and are ready for more work, it's time to find an agent. Most professionals have representation, and sooner or later, you should too. So, how do you go about finding yourself an agent?

The first thing to understand is that an agent works for you! Some beginners think it's the other way around. Most agents are very selective about who they represent, and may even give the false impression that the performer is working for them. Not true! It is the agent's job to get you work by sending you out on auditions and connecting you with producers who will hire you. Once on the audition, it becomes your job to perform to the best of your ability. Once a job is booked, the agent negotiates your fee. The day of the agent taking an actor "under their wing" and nurturing them to stardom is long past gone. Your voiceover work is your business and your agent is only there to represent you as your career develops.

As you begin your search, you will find that no two agents are alike. Some handle the paperwork for union work, while others want the performer to handle this task. Talent agents in large markets, like Los Angeles or New York, run their businesses completely different from agents in smaller markets in the Midwest. And working long-distance with an Internet agent is different from working with an agent locally. As with much of the voiceover business, there are no hard-and-fast rules. The important thing is for you to be comfortable with your agent, and that your agent is comfortable with you.

SEARCHING FOR AN AGENT

There are a few things you need to know about talent agents before you start seeking representation:

- A talent agent is not in the business of nurturing you or grooming you to be a professional voice actor. They expect you to have your performing skills in place and ready to go.

- A major-market talent agent may not be interested in you unless you have a track record and an existing client list. Agents are in business to get you booked as often as possible, and at the highest fee possible. They only get paid when you work.

- You may have a great track record, and an incredible demo, but you may be rejected simply because the agency already has other voice talent with the same or similar delivery style as yours. Being rejected for representation is not a personal attack on you or your abilities.

You can start your search for an agent with a simple Internet search for "Talent Agent Your City." Talent agents for major markets in the U.S. are also posted at **voicebank.net**. Another way to find an agent is to go to a theatrical bookstore. Samuel French, Inc. is among the best. See their website, **samuelfrench.com** for store locations in Los Angeles, New York, and Toronto. A keyword search on the site for "agencies" will bring up several resources. You can also contact your local SAG-AFTRA office. Even if you are not a member, they will be able to provide you with a list of all franchised agents in your area. Many agents work exclusively with union talent, although some work with both union and non-union talent.

Another extremely valuable resource for locating talent agents is *The Voiceover Resource Guide* (VORG). A printed booklet is distributed twice a year in Los Angeles and New York as well as a regularly updated website. This handy resource includes agents, demo producers, recording studios, casting services, union rates, voice acting coaches, and lots of other information for voiceover talent. You'll find VORG at **voiceoverresourceguide.com**.

Before contacting any talent agent, you would be wise to visit the agency's website to research the agency and learn about their submission policy. Many agents prefer to receive demos only as electronic MP3 files while others still prefer to receive CDs. Most agents have a procedure for submitting your demo and other information and will often ask that you do not call by phone. You would be wise to follow their submission procedure and wait for them to contact you—which may take several months.

For those agencies that do invite you to call, or that don't ask that you do not call, you may have much better success finding an agent and finding work if you spend some time on the phone. It may take a little research on your part, but the time you spend talking with agents and producers on the phone will pay off later on. Don't expect to get results on the first call. Marketing your talent is an ongoing process and results often come weeks or even years later. Be prepared for rejection.

When sending an email to a prospective agent, be sure to personalize it by including their name in the salutation. Make the subject line something that will get their attention and identifies the purpose of your email. Keep the body of your email short and to the point, and don't forget to include a link to your website either in the body of your email, your signature line, or both. Unless you are asked to submit multiple demos, you should only submit one demo at this time. Your email attachment should be in MP3 format at 44.1Khz, 128Kbps. Do not attach a .wav, .aiff, or any other format unless you are specifically asked to. These raw data formats are simply too large to comfortably send in an email.

Not all agents represent voice actors. You can check the agency's website or call their office to find out if they represent voiceover talent and if they are accepting new performers. Keep this initial call brief and to the point, but be sure to get the name of someone to send your demo to if the agency expresses any interest.

Proper phone etiquette is important when calling a talent agency. Agents are busy people and will appreciate your call more if you are prepared and know what you want. To be perceived as a professional, you must present yourself in a professional manner. To do anything less will only serve to damage your credibility as a business person and a professional voice actor. Here's a very simplified example of an ineffective call to an agent.

AGENT: Hello, Marvelous Talent Agency.
ACTOR: Hi, uh, is there somebody there I could talk to about doing voiceover?
AGENT: Who's calling?
ACTOR: Oh, yeah. My name is David Dumdum, and I'd like to talk to someone about doing voiceovers.
AGENT: This is a talent agency. We don't do voiceovers, we represent talent.
ACTOR: That's what I mean, I want to talk to somebody about representing me.

This kind of call not only takes a long time to get anywhere, but the so-called actor is not at all clear about what he wants to discuss. Even if this performer had a decent demo, the chances of getting representation are poor simply because of a non-businesslike and very unprofessional presentation. When you talk to a talent agent, or any business prospect for that matter, you will have much better success if you keep your conversation at a friendly tone of voice and with a purpose of offering something to the agent that will benefit them. If you are perceived as someone "looking for work," your conversation may be very short, indeed.

Here's a much better way to approach a call. Again, this is a very simplified example, but you'll get the idea.

AGENT: Hello, Marvelous Talent Agency.

ACTOR: Hi, this is Steven Swell. I'd like to know if your agency represents voiceover talent.

AGENT: Yes we do.

ACTOR: Great! I'd like to speak to someone about the possibility of representation. Are you taking on any new clients?

AGENT: We are always interested in looking at new voice talent. If you'd like to send us a copy of your demo, we'll give it a listen and let you know.

ACTOR: That's terrific. Would you prefer a CD or should I send you an email with an MP3 file and a link to my website?

AGENT: We review demo submissions on the last Friday of every month, so you can just send us an MP3 file.

ACTOR: Great! I'll get that to you right away. Should I send that directly to you? *(get the email address and name of who to send the demo to.)*

This performer gets to the point of his call quickly and effectively. He is polite, businesslike, and keeps an upbeat, professional attitude throughout the call. Even though he didn't connect with an agent, he did get a name and has a clear process for submitting his demo.

Narrow down the prospective agents in your area. You can immediately eliminate those who represent only models, print, or on-camera talent. The Los Angeles area has more than 250 franchised agents, and only a handful represent voiceover talent, so in a larger market, you must be very specific in targeting potential agents before making any phone calls or sending out your demo. Smaller markets can have zero to several talent agents, depending on market size. Representation by a small talent agency in a small market can be an excellent way to break into the business of voiceover, but be prepared to move to a larger agency when the time comes. There are also a growing number of talent agents who represent voice talent nationwide, or even worldwide, through the Internet.

Before contacting any agent, prepare a brief and to-the-point cover letter to accompany your demo if you send a CD by mail. This cover letter could also be used as the body of your email if sending your demo as an MP3 file. This is not a résumé. This is a business letter intended to introduce you to the agency and should be no more than a short paragraph or two. Simply state that you are a voiceover talent and that you are interested in discussing the possibilities of representation. Again, depending on your initial contact with the agency, you may be asked to send your demo by postal mail, email, or simply by providing your website.

When sending through the post office, each letter should be an original, and should be addressed to the person whose name you were given during your research. The envelope address may be printed by a computer or by hand. Computer printing gives your envelope a professional appearance, while hand-writing the address can add a more personal touch to your correspondence. Either way, your introductory letter should be computer printed in the format of a business letter. Include any relevant, and recent, performing experience. If you have no experience, you will have better results if you keep your letter to the point of representation and do not mention your lack of experience. Any reputable agent will require a professionally produced demo. For voiceover representation, you generally do not need to prepare a résumé. Agents and talent buyers are more interested in your performing skills and how you work with a script than your training, unrelated job experience, or your home studio equipment. Of course, if you have an existing list of voiceover clients, that information can be of value.

Here's an example of a good cover letter that is short, to the point, gives a professional appearance, provides some important information, and suggests the performer's potential value to the agency. Notice that this example requests action from the agency to arrange an interview.

Dear Mr. Agent:

Thank you for your interest in my demo. As I mentioned during our conversation, I am a voice actor seeking representation. I have been booking myself as a freelance performer for the past few years and have had several successful commercials on the air. I have also narrated a number of corporate projects.

Additional information about me and my background is included on my website at www.JamesAlburger.com. For your convenience, I've enclosed a copy of my current demo.

I believe I can be a valuable asset to your agency, and I look forward to hearing from you so that we can arrange for a meeting to further discuss representation by your agency.

Sincerely,

Once you've been asked to send your introductory letter and demo, <u>do not</u> call to see if your demo was received. It will often do you no good, and may even irritate some agencies. And, if you send a CD, don't expect to get your demo back! Talent agents know you send out demos to other agents in the area. If they hear something they like, they will call you. If you are good, and they're interested, they will call quickly, simply because they won't want to miss out on representing an excellent performer.

Don't be surprised if you don't get a call. There may be many reasons for an agent not accepting you or not getting back to you quickly. Many talent agencies only review submitted demos once a month or every 6 months. Don't expect or ask for a critique of your demo. If an agent is kind enough to critique it for you, use that information to learn how to improve your skills and create a better demo. You may need to produce two, three, or more demos before landing that first agent.

Sooner or later you will find an agent who is interested in talking to you. But be aware, the agent's interest does not mean you have representation. It only means that he or she is interested in learning more about you and your talent, and to determine if you will be a good fit with their agency. When you are selected for representation, expect your agent to request changes in your demo. Your agent knows their clients and the best way to market you to them.

INTERVIEWING AN AGENT

It may take some time, but when you do get a positive response, you may be asked to set up an appointment to meet with the agent. This can be quite exciting. What will you wear? How should you act? What will you say? If you are handling your correspondence via email, you may be asked to call the agent, or the entire process may be done over the Internet.

Remember that although it may appear as though the agent is interviewing you, the reality is that you are interviewing the agent. Handle this interview just as you would an interview for a new job. Dress nicely, and present yourself in a businesslike manner. Be careful to wear clothes that do not make noise. A good agent will probably ask you to read a script as part of the interview. Enter the office with confidence. Play the part of the successful performer. Create your character for the interview just as you would for a script, and act as if you are a seasoned pro and already represented. Your chances of signing with an agent will be much better if your first impression is one of a skilled and professional performer.

Interview all your prospective agents as thoroughly as possible. Listen carefully, and don't be afraid to ask questions. What types of work do they book? What is the average pay scale they get for their performers? What is their commission? For non-union bookings, is their commission added to the performer's fee, or taken out off the top? How many voiceover performers do they represent? How long have they been in business? You can even ask whom they represent and for a list of some performers you can contact.

During your meetings or phone calls, you may find your conversation is about everything except your voiceover work. They will want you to be comfortable so that they can get a sense of you as a person, and you will want to get to know them a bit. You need to decide if you like them and have confidence that the agency will be able to get you work. They need to determine if your skills meet their agency standards and that you can work with them as a team.

Take your time. Don't rush to sign up with the first agent who offers to represent you. Also, if any agent gives you the impression that you are working for him or her, you might want to consider eliminating that person from your list. The agent works for you—not the other way around. If an agent requires a fee of any amount before they will represent you, they may be operating unethically and you should end the conversation and leave. By law a talent agent is only entitled to a commission based on the work they obtain for you. When an agent directly charges you a fee to be posted on their website, or for headshots, or for anything else, they may be *double-dipping,* and that's illegal, or at the very least potentially unethical.

Most talent agents work on a one-year contract. Some agencies request a multiyear agreement, but this can cause problems if your agent doesn't promote you, and you don't get work. If you don't have a good working relationship with your agent, they can literally put your career on hold by simply not sending you auditions. If you are uncertain about the relationship, you may ask for a six-month trial, but if you sense a lack of confidence with the agent, it might be best to simply seek representation elsewhere. Even with a good relationship, it is generally a good idea to renegotiate every year.

A large agency may have many people in the office and represent a large talent pool. A small agency may have only one or two people handling the entire business. It is easy to become a small fish in a big pond if you sign with a large agency. On the other hand, most large talent agencies sign only voiceover performers with years of experience and a solid track record. Your first agent will most likely will be a small agency that can give you more attention and help guide your career.

WORKING WITH YOUR AGENT

Once signed, you should keep your agent up to date on your work. Let him or her know how your auditions and sessions go, and keep the agent current with an updated demo as needed. Calling your talent agent once a week should be adequate, unless he or she requests you call more or less frequently. The key to working with an agent is to stay in touch and ask for advice. They generally know the business far better than you.

One good question to ask your agent is how you should handle work you obtain on your own. Some agents will allow you to handle your own personal bookings without paying a commission. However, it may be advisable when someone directly approaches you for work, that you refer the company or person to your agent, especially if you are a union member. As a professional performer, your job is to perform. Your agent's job is to represent you and negotiate for the highest fee. Although it is generally wise to let your agent handle the negotiations, there may be some situations where it might be best for you to handle the money talk yourself. This is something only you and your agent can work out, but if you have a good relationship with your agent, and the situation warrants, you may have a better chance of landing the job.

I know one voice actor who auditioned for a video game and noticed that the other voice actors who said they had an agent were being passed over for callbacks. With this in mind, he called his agent to discuss the situation. Their mutual decision was that the voice actor would avoid any mention of representation until after he was booked. He handled the negotiations himself and actually managed to get a higher fee than most of the other voice actors booked for the project. After he was booked, he handed the booking over to his agent. Even if you are an accomplished negotiator, your agent is your representative.

As a career grows, it is common for performers to change agents several times. A word of warning, however: Changing agents can be traumatic. You are likely to have a case of the "guilts" when leaving an agent, especially if the person has done a lot to help develop your career. When this time comes, it is important to remember the reasons why you are changing agents. You may have reached a level of skill that is beyond your agent's ability to market effectively, you may be moving to a new part of the country, or you may be moving into an area of voiceover that your agent doesn't handle. On the other hand, you might be changing agents because your current agent is simply not getting you the kinds of jobs you need.

In this Chapter

25

Managing Your Voiceover Business

Setting Your Talent Fee

The first, and most important thing you need to know about setting and negotiating your fee is that <u>you</u> <u>have</u> <u>value</u>. You can do something your client cannot. You have something to offer that is of value to your client, and your client needs what you have to offer. There is something about *you* that the producer believes is right for his or her project. It could be the way you interpret the copy; it could be a quality in your voice; it could be anything. You are the chosen one! Congratulations! If your client didn't want what you have to offer, they would be talking to someone else. You've got the job! All that's necessary now is to work out the details.

Because you have value, you should be fairly compensated for your work. At first glance you may think that a client's proposed budget for voice talent is very reasonable. But be careful not to rush into accepting voiceover work simply based on what the client is offering without first doing a little research. When the script arrives, you may be unpleasantly surprised by the amount of work you really need to do, and as a result, how low your compensation really is. The details of your work need to be clearly defined before you agree to the job.

The second thing you need to know about setting or negotiating your talent fee is that <u>your</u> <u>time</u> <u>is</u> <u>valuable</u>. You've made a considerable investment of time and energy to get to a place where you are ready to market yourself as a professional voice actor. If you expect to ever see a return on your investment, you need to give serious consideration to how you will set your talent fees and how you will work with clients. You need to think like a business person.

If you plan to get paid for your voiceover work (and you should), you'll need to learn some negotiating skills. As a voice actor, you are in business for yourself, and fee negotiation is part of doing business. Even if you have representation, you should still work on your negotiating skills if for no other reason than you will be able to discuss your fees and marketing strategies intelligently with your agent. Since part of an agent's job is to handle fee negotiations, the next few sections of this chapter will address setting fees and negotiating techniques for independent voice talent who do not have agent representation.

Your primary job as a voice actor is to deliver an effective and believable performance. This can be a challenging task when you are placed in a position where you must multitask by running the computer software, making sure your recording quality is up to standards, finding the proper character and attitude, and delivering a performance that meets the client's needs. With a home studio, you're a one-person-shop, and you do it all! It has taken some time for you to learn how to do all of these things.

An often overlooked consideration when setting fees is the investment of time and money in getting started in the business of voiceover. The cost of books, workshops, and demo production can easily add up to several thousand dollars. Add to that the cost of your home office furnishings; business software; office equipment; supplies; business development and marketing; the cost of your computer; your home studio equipment; Internet connection; website hosting; website design services; graphics design; printing; and telephone lines.

It doesn't take much effort to discover the true financial investment you've made in your voiceover business. It is only good business to expect a return on this investment (*ROI*). And, in order to see a return on your investment, you'll need to consider those expenses as you determine your fee structure. There is no easy formula for doing this, but it is something you should consider.

EVALUATE THE JOB REQUIREMENTS

Many experienced producers have a very good understanding of what it takes to record a quality voice track, or produce a complete production. They have been through the production process many times and know what it is like to work with voice talent of all levels of experience. There are many others, however, who have no experience working with voice talent, and have absolutely no idea of what is involved in voice recording and audio production. For a voice talent just getting started, the unfortunate reality is that many first-time clients will be inexperienced and uneducated in the world of audio production, voice recording, and voiceover work in general. As a voice actor, it's not your job to educate your client, but that may be something you'll need to do as part of your negotiations.

Another aspect of voiceover reality is that other producers eager to maximize their profits may be willing to take advantage of beginning voice talent. If you don't know your personal worth, and how to negotiate your fee, it could be a very long time before you begin to see any financial success as a voice actor.

Keep in mind, as you talk to prospective clients, that the fee they offer is not necessarily the fee you will receive for your professional work. Your potential client may have a price in mind, which is based on completely uneducated and unrealistic expectations. You, on the other hand, may have a fee in mind that may be considerably different, based on your knowledge of your investment, your understanding of what it will take to complete their job, and your level of skill. The purpose of a negotiation is to arrive at a level of compensation that is mutually agreeable to both parties. The bottom line in this business is "everything is negotiable." If a prospective client is unwilling to negotiate with you regarding your compensation, you may be wise to reconsider working with that individual.

It is not uncommon for clients booking through Internet audition sites to offer a fee that, at first glance, may appear reasonable, but upon closer examination is little more than minimum wage for a considerable amount of specialized work. Here are two examples of how you can evaluate a potential booking to determine if it will be worth your time and energy:

Example #1: The Trial Transcript

> We have a trial transcript of 2,000 pages double spaced that we need read for an audio book. Contains male and female characters - you would read all parts. Pay is $1,000 +

One thousand dollars—not bad for a few hours of recording time, right? But take a closer look: the project is two thousand pages long. A quick calculation will reveal that this producer is offering only $0.50 per page to record this project! Still, $1,000 is a lot of money! Or is it?

Let's say you estimate that an average completed double-spaced page will take about 1 minute to read. Now triple that because you'll need to edit your recordings and it will take at least an additional 2 minutes of editing time for every minute of completed voice track.

We're now up to 6,000 minutes for recording and editing. Divide 6,000 by 60 minutes and you get 100 hours of work to complete this project. And that's assuming everything goes extremely smoothly.

But wait a minute! You take a look at the script, and you discover the trial had something to do with the biotech Industry and there are lots of technical terms sprinkled throughout the script. Better be safe and add another minute for each page to allow for mistakes and retakes.

Let's be conservative and estimate that it will take about 5 minutes of recording and production time for every minute of completed voice track. We're now at 10,000 minutes—or roughly 166 hours—or about 4 weeks! At their offering fee of $1,000 you'll be making a total income of about $6.00 per hour. The reality is that it will probably take 6 or 7 minutes for each completed minute, so your actual work may be more and your compensation considerably lower. Even if this client is willing to negotiate a higher talent fee, it will most likely not come even close to anything reasonable for the amount of your effort involved. And don't forget that you won't be able to work on anything else while you're recording this epic project. Although 50 cents per page may be a reasonable price for the client, after factoring in your time, it really isn't a very good deal for you. Is your time—and are you—really worth that little?

This example, based on an actual audition request, shows that you must have a very clear understanding of your involvement in a project before you can realistically discuss price. Unfortunately, there are some voice talent who only look at the offered fee and don't take the time to properly evaluate projects like this.

Before you can provide a realistic estimate, or discuss your talent fee with a prospective client, you need to know as much as possible about what you will be doing. You need to know the going market rate for comparable work, and you need to place a value on your time and performing abilities. You may not like the math required to arrive at the numbers, but if you are going to be even slightly successful, you'll need to learn how to do the basic calculations and think on your feet if you are going to negotiate an appropriate fee.

Example #2: The Short Session

Consider this: You've auditioned for, and landed a voiceover job for a 60-second radio commercial for a midsized market. The audition took you 10 minutes to record, edit, and send out. The job will pay $150, and based on the script, you expect it will take you about a half hour to record, edit, and deliver the final project. That works out to $150 for about a half-hour's work, or $300 per hour. Pretty good pay, right? Wrong!

That $150 gig may be the only job that came in that week—or that month. Let's say you spent 10 hours recording and sending out auditions before you got this job, plus another 5 hours on the phone and sending out email. Now, consider what you've spent on phone calls, postage, your website, marketing, training, and everything else that led up to this job.

Just taking into consideration the 15 hours you spent that week, you're looking at a gross income of about $10/hour for that $150 job. But don't forget that the IRS will want part of that income, so you'll actually net something in the neighborhood of $5–$7 dollars/hour for that $150 job.

The point here is that before you can negotiate a reasonable fee for your work, you must know the value of your time and talent.

THINK LIKE AN ENTREPRENEUR

If you haven't already, start right now thinking of your voiceover work as a business. Your objective as a business owner is to make a profit, and to do that you have to be smart about how you use your time and energy, and how you price your services. As voice talent, we may never be able to change the way producers think. However, we can control the way we think about what we do, and we can control what we charge for our services.

When one of my students asks about what they should charge, I suggest they first do some homework. Find out what the best Union voice talent would be paid for the same work. You deserve to be fairly compensated for your work. Even if you're booking your first job, that is no reason for you to undercut your worth. If you have the talent and ability to provide the same quality of work as a veteran voice actor, you should be compensated accordingly.

If you establish a reputation of "working for cheap," you may get yourself into a rut that could be difficult to get out of later on. At the very least, it will be extremely difficult raising your fee for a client you've already worked for at a "bargain basement rate." In voiceover performing, it's always easier to pull you back than to push you out. The same is true with your fees. You can always lower your fees, but it can be extremely difficult to raise them.

SETTING YOUR FEE

As with many things in this world, perception is a very large factor for determining value. The way you perceive your personal value as a voice actor will affect how you determine your fees.

If you are a member of SAG-AFTRA or another performing artists union, your talent fees are set by your union. Through a process of collective bargaining, these unions have determined what are considered to be reasonable performance fees for different types of work. SAG-AFTRA *scale* fees are posted on their website at

sagaftra.org and **voiceoverresourceguide.com**. These posted talent fees are not negotiable and are considered as the lowest level of compensation. Signatory producers have agreed to pay the posted minimum fees, or a higher fee that might be negotiated by an agent. This is one advantage of being a union member—you know in advance what your base talent fee will be for any given type of work. Another aspect of being a union member is that you are automatically perceived by the talent buyer as having a certain level of expertise and professionalism.

If you are non-union, you will need to negotiate your talent fee with your client at the time you are booked. But before you can begin any sort of realistic negotiation, you need to establish a *fee schedule* that outlines your specific fees for specific types of work.

Only you can determine your personal value as a freelance voice actor. The process begins by identifying the type or types of voiceover work you are best suited for. Once you've figured out what you do best, the next step is to identify the market price for comparable voiceover work in those areas. It used to be that you could simply make some phone calls in your city to gauge the current talent fees, but no more. The Internet has changed all that, and your market is now the world. When you submit an audition, you may have no idea what city the producer is in or how your recording will be used, so you may have no real information upon which to base your fee—yet most producers want you to provide a quote for the job you are auditioning. This is why it is important to establish your personal value as a voice talent.

If your performing skills are at a level where you can effectively compete with other professional voice talent—and the fact that you are getting calls for work proves that you are—then why would you consider yourself any less professional than they are? Why should you accept a talent fee of anything less than other professional voice talent?

A common mistake made by many beginning voice talent is to treat their work as a commodity, basing their work solely on price. In an effort to "get the gig," they will lower their talent fee to something they think will be attractive to their clients, without giving any consideration to their investment or the true value of their work. *Low-balling*, or under pricing, your talent fees may get you the job, but the practice does a disservice not only to the voice talent accepting the fee, but to everyone else in the business as well. It tends to lower the bar, which can only result in lower quality work at cheaper prices. To get, and keep, the best clients, you need to develop a high perceived value, and provide excellent work at fair and competitive prices—not the "cheapest" price. You may be better off starting with a higher fee and negotiating to an acceptable middle-ground.

One way to set your personal talent fees is to use union scale as a starting point, even if you are non-union. When negotiating with clients you can, of course, mention that you are non-union and therefore can be somewhat flexible with your talent fee. By starting at union scale, you are telling your client that you are a professional and there is an industry wide value for the work you are being asked to do that needs to be appreciated. Where you go from there is up to you, and it's what the rest of the negotiation process is about. But you've got to start someplace. Here are some considerations as you set your personal talent fees:

- **Your experience and abilities:** How good are you at setting character quickly, finding the right interpretation, seeing the big picture, working as a team player, taking direction, etc? The more skilled you are, the more likely you will be able to demand a higher fee—especially once you have established a name for yourself and are confident with your work.

- **Prior experience and clients:** Have you already done some work for a few satisfied clients? If so, their names may help to establish credibility and thus help to justify a higher fee. Be sure to consider any recent work for inclusion in your demo, but make sure it's good enough in both recording quality and in performance quality.

- **The client's budget:** If you're a non-union freelance voice talent, you'll need to be flexible and decide if you want to work for a minimal fee (which is all that many small or independent producers are willing to pay). Keep in mind that local radio stations will often give away production and voice talent for free just to get an advertiser to buy time on their station, and many independent producers will offer to do the voice work themselves in an effort to save a few bucks. Your challenge as a voice artist is to offer a service that is superior and more effective for the client than what they can get anywhere else.

- **Can you justify your fee?:** This gets back to your abilities. If you market yourself with professional print materials, a dynamite demo, and an awesome website, you had better be able to meet the level of expectations of your client when they book you for a session. If you give the appearance of an experienced pro, but can't deliver, word will spread fast and it may be a long time before you can overcome a negative image. The challenge in setting your fee is to match the fee to your abilities and the market, and still be within the range of other freelance talent, without creating an impression that you will "work cheap" or that you are "overpriced."

- **Consider your market:** Non-union talent fees vary greatly from market to market. In order to set an appropriate fee for your services, you'll need to find out what other voice actors are getting paid in your area or for similar work. In your own city you can call the production department of local radio and TV stations, and advertising agencies to ask what they usually pay for non-union work. However, if the work is out of your city, you may have no other option than to simply decide if the fee offered by a producer is worth your time and energy.

Your training is of less importance than your abilities as an actor. Of course, you must have a great sounding demo, but you need to have the abilities to match. Don't ever think you know all there is to know about working with voiceover copy. Continue taking classes and workshops, read books, and practice your craft daily.

WHAT ABOUT ALL THAT EQUIPMENT?

You do realize, don't you, that if you are recording professional voice tracks on your computer at home, you have a *home studio*? The operative word here is "studio." OK, so your investment in all that goes into a home studio may not amount to the hundreds of thousands of dollars a full-blown recording studio would spend—but the simple fact is this: you've got your own studio! Chapter 22, "Your Home Studio," discusses this in more detail.

From a business standpoint, it makes no sense to set a talent fee that does not at least take into consideration the costs of your studio equipment, office supplies, marketing expenses, training, demo production, and so on. Unless you're performing strictly as a hobby, you'll eventually want to recover all those expenses. One way to do this is to create a separate rate for studio time that you charge in addition to your performance fee.

An hourly fee for studio time is standard practice for virtually every recording studio—and, since you own your own studio, it only makes good business sense for you to use a similar pricing structure. If you have production skills and can offer additional production services, this can be a good way to create an additional revenue stream. Separating out your studio rate and talent fee also gives you some additional negotiating leverage because you can always discount one or the other if needed and still have enough income to make some profit.

However, if you are marketing yourself as strictly voice talent and you have limited production and editing skills, you may not want to separate your talent fee and studio time. It may be more practical to set a slightly higher talent fee that includes your studio time. As a non-union voice talent starting your negotiation at union scale, you'll still have room to adjust your fee if necessary. Of course, your performing skills will need to be at a level where you can justify the higher fee. The important thing to remember is that just because you may be new in this business, it doesn't mean you need to charge unrealistically low talent fees.

BUYOUTS

Projects which are, by nature, limited in their distribution and use, like industrial training programs, marketing videos, documentaries, and audio books can reasonably justify a *buyout* agreement, meaning that the producer pays you a one-time flat fee for your work, and then has the right to do whatever he wants with that recording for as long as he wants—with no further payment to you.

Take a look at the way SAG-AFTRA handles its talent fees and you'll notice that most categories have a time limit for the use of a performance. If a client wants to reuse a performer's work, they pay the talent a new fee called a *residual*.

As a freelance voice actor, you do not need to accept a buyout talent fee for any commercial voiceover work, even though this is the most common type of booking for non-union talent. If you agree to a buyout fee for a radio commercial, there's a good chance you may be hearing that commercial for years to come. Or a portion of the radio voice track may be used for a television commercial, an in-store message, a telephone message, on a website, or any number of other uses—and you'll never get paid a dime beyond your original buyout talent fee.

As a professional voice actor and business person, you can certainly negotiate a timeframe for the use of your performance. If your client agrees to this, you'll need the terms clearly stated in your agreement, and you'll want to create a follow-up system to remind your client of the agreement. Enforcing a reuse clause may be difficult as a non-union voice talent, but if you don't include it in your original contract, you may be leaving money on the table; and you'll have no legal recourse if or when your client reuses your work. Whether or not discussion of a reuse fee is appropriate will depend entirely on the needs of your client, your willingness to compromise, and your ability to "read" your client during your negotiation.

THE AGREEMENT

Every booking is a separate business arrangement with unique time constraints, performance requirements, and payment terms, among other specifications. Whenever you exchange your time, energy, or services for money, the only way you will be protected is if all the details of the business arrangement are detailed in a contract. Depending on the type of project and its ultimate use, you may want to negotiate for certain conditions. For example, if the project is to be sold, you might negotiate a clause that includes a residual payment when sales exceed a certain number of units or you may want limitations on how long your voice track can be used in a commercial, or for which other kinds of media it can be used.

The manner in which your performance can be used, and the duration of its use, are most definitely negotiable points that you should consider and discuss with your client. There are no hard and fast rules here, nor are there any specifically worded contracts available. Every agreement is unique and you'll need to come up with the appropriate wording to describe the terms and conditions for the use of your recorded material. You'll also want to make sure you include adequate controls for tracking any restrictions, and possible remedies for any violations of the agreement.

Your agreement is a contract, and if the project justifies it, you may want to seek legal advice to make sure you are protected and receive the compensation you deserve. Of course, if you have representation, your agent will handle the details of any complex negotiation. The specific details that you might include in your agreement will be discussed later in this chapter.

Negotiating Your Fee

The best way to learn how to negotiate is to do it! If you've never done it, the best way to learn how is to study some of the many excellent books on the subject. A search for "negotiating" on **amazon.com** will bring up hundreds of books on this subject. Find one that looks good to you, buy it, study it, and begin practicing. You'll also find numerous resources with a simple Internet search.

The ultimate purpose of any negotiation is to create an agreement that is acceptable for all parties. Ideally, this agreement should be in the form of a written contract that is signed by both parties prior to the start of any work. Unfortunately, a great deal of voiceover work is booked on only a *verbal agreement*, which is only as good as the paper it's not written on. When you begin work with only a verbal agreement, you take the chance of not getting paid, or of having serious problems of miscommunication, or worse. Always get your agreement in writing before you begin work.

Ideally, an agreement should be received in the mail, but with tight schedules, deadlines, and the popularity of email, this often isn't practical. A faxed document, or a scanned image file attached to an email will work to get things started. In today's electronic age, most courts of law will accept an email agreement as a legal document provided it contains the sender's email address and name.

There are literally dozens of effective negotiating techniques that can be used to maintain high standards and fees for voiceover work. Here are just a few, with only a very brief explanation of how they might be used:

- **Talk about the project:** No matter what you know about a job when you get the call, it isn't enough. One of the first things you should do in any negotiation is to get more information. Ask as many questions as you can, while avoiding any discussion of your fee. When the subject of your fee comes up, divert the discussion by asking more appropriate questions. This requires extremely good listening skills.

- **Get the client to mention the first number:** This can take some skill, but it can often be achieved by simply engaging the client in a conversation and guiding that conversation to a discussion of what they have paid for voice talent for prior work. If your client is comfortable with you, they will often feel safe in talking about what they have paid in the past. At an appropriate point in your conversation you may ask what their budget is for this project and wait for them to answer.

- **Echo ... Pause:** This is a technique for maintaining your fee, or perhaps even increasing it. It has been around for a long time and may not work in all situations, especially if the person you are negotiating with figures out what you are doing. Whether he says so, or not, your client has a number in mind. It's your job to coax it out of him. Let's say he mentions the number $200. You, in a very thoughtful voice, simply repeat the number as though asking a question to verify that you heard it correctly— then stop talking. Be absolutely silent. It may get uncomfortable, but don't speak. At some point the discomfort will be too great and your client will likely come back with something like ". . . well, we might be able to go to $300." At that point, you repeat the Echo and Pause. Usually by about the third time, your client will say something like ". . . $325— that's really all we can afford for this project." You can then use your best acting skills as you say ". . . $325! I can do that for $325."

- **Discount this fee for future work at full fee:** During your conversation, you may find that your client is reluctant to discuss any numbers, or that he truly has only a very limited budget for this project. If that is the case, you can tell him that you base your fees on union scale, but that as non-union talent, you can be somewhat flexible with your rates. If the project appears to be something that might result in future work, you might even offer to discount your talent fee with the understanding that you will be paid your regular fee for future work. When you deliver an outstanding product, your chances of having a new long-term client will be very good. This technique can be a bit risky, so make sure you have your agreement in writing.

The desired outcome of any negotiation is to get paid for your work based on the terms of your negotiation. The challenge today is that the Internet has created an international marketplace. It is common to never meet, or even speak to, your client with everything handled through email. Even with a solid agreement in place, you still have no guarantee that you will be paid when you deliver your voice tracks.

Getting Paid for Your Work

THE DEAL MEMO LETTER

As a freelance voiceover performer, you need to protect yourself from unscrupulous producers (yes, they are out there). The simplest way to protect yourself is to use a written agreement known as a *deal memo*. Even if you are a union member, having a written agreement is a good idea. It protects you and outlines the details of your work. The format for this can be as simple as a brief letter, an invoice, or an email confirmation, to something more formal, such as a multipage contract for services. It's generally a good idea to keep a deal memo as simple as possible. A complicated, legal-sounding document might scare off a potentially valuable employer.

Preparing your deal memo should be the first thing you do when you book a session. A written agreement is your only proof in the event you need to take legal action to collect any money owed to you, or if your performance is used in a manner that you did not agree to. It's a common practice and should be used whenever possible. Make sure you have a signed agreement in hand *before* you begin any work.

The following is an example of a simple deal memo letter. This deal memo includes all the necessary information to confirm the agreement, yet it is presented in a nonthreatening and informal manner. With minor modifications, this letter could be used for either a studio location session or one that you record in your home studio.

Dear Mr. Producer:

Thank you for booking me to be the voice for The Big Store's new radio commercials. As we discussed on the phone today, I will be doing four (4) radio commercials (including up to 6 tags) for $350 per spot as a limited run 90-day buyout for radio only for a total of $1,400. If you later decide to rerun the commercials, or use my voice for television spots or other purposes, please call me to arrange for a new session or to modify our agreement. As we discussed, my fee for each additional tag after the first 6 will be $75 per tag.

You have also agreed to provide me with a recording of the final commercials. I'll call you next week to arrange to pick up a CD or you can send an MP3 file to my email address.

As we discussed, I will need your credit card information, a deposit, or a company PO number to guarantee the session.

I will arrive at Great Sound Recording Studios, 7356 Hillard Ave. on Tuesday the 5th for a 10:00 AM session.

For your records and tax reporting, I will bring a completed W-9. Please make your check in the amount of $1,400.00 payable to My Name so that I can pick it up after the session. Should you prefer that I charge your credit card, please let me know so I can bring the proper paperwork with me.

I look forward to working with you on the 5th.

Sincerely,

Getting paperwork out of the way before the work begins is a good way to make sure that the terms of your performance are understood by all parties and that the producer doesn't try to change the agreement or add additional production after you have done the work. If you are booked early enough for a session at a recording studio, you might want to fax a copy of the agreement to the producer in advance. But you should still plan on having two copies with you when you arrive for the session—the producer is probably not going to bring his copy. Leave one copy for the producer and make sure you have a signed copy before you leave the studio.

If you're recording at your home studio, you can do everything via email and fax. Although an email confirming the details of your work may be considered a legal contract by some courts, it is still a good idea to use your own document and get a written signature.

How to Guarantee You'll Be Paid

Most voiceover work is due and payable upon delivery, but that usually doesn't mean you walk out of the studio with cash in hand or have money in the bank immediately after uploading the files. For many clients, you'll need to send an invoice that states "payable on receipt." Even with that, you may still end up waiting 30 to 90 days before you receive payment. That's just the way some businesses work.

If you don't want to wait to be paid, there are other options available:

- **Insist on clients sending a deposit** for talent fee and studio time to be paid in advance with the balance to be paid on delivery. If your client doesn't pay as agreed, at least you'll receive a partial payment.

- **Ask your client to make payment** through an online payment service like **paypal.com**, **worldpay.com** or any of a several other on-line payment portals. You'll need to set up your own account with these services, which can easily handle credit card payments or your clients can set up their own accounts.

- **Set up a *merchant account*** for your business so you can accept credit cards. Most small businesses can have a merchant account, including individuals operating as a sole proprietor. A merchant account is easy to establish, but it does have a variety of associated monthly and per-transaction fees. If you are only booking occasional work, you would be better off using one of the on-line payment services.

- **Deliver a partial project** (75–80%) or deliver a *watermarked* project for approval, and only send a complete, clean copy upon receipt of payment. A *watermark* is a tone, or sound embedded in your audio that effectively makes the recording unusable, but will allow the client to determine if it otherwise meets their needs.

The specific payment arrangements may be different with each client. If you've never worked with a client before, there is no track record upon which to build trust, so it is reasonable to request a deposit or use one of the above techniques for getting paid. If a client is repeat business, it might be reasonable to invoice them with the payment due net 15 days.

Here's how I work with my clients to make sure I get paid: I have a merchant account so I can accept payment with Master Card and Visa credit cards. I have a stated policy on my website that says I require a valid credit card number at the time of booking to guarantee a session. When booking a session, I take my client's credit card information and run a verification to make sure the card is valid for the amount we've agreed upon, but I do not charge the card yet, unless they wish to pay any deposit on the credit card. Instead, I tell my client that their credit card will *not* be charged the full amount until they have approved my work. Before I send my voice tracks, I'll call my client to let them know the session is ready to deliver and to ask how they would like to make payment.

Since I already have their credit card number, most clients simply ask me to charge card. When the transaction is processed, their payment is electronically transferred to my bank account. If, for some reason their card is rejected (after it was originally verified), or the payment bounces, I have legal recourse and a contract. I have some additional protection in that I don't deliver a clean copy of the work until their payment clears. I have never had a client question this policy, nor have I ever had a problem with a credit card transaction for payment of services. The peace of mind I have in knowing I will be paid for my work makes the discount fees and other minimal charges for maintaining a merchant account well worth the price.

Some clients will prefer to not provide their credit card number. For these clients, I'll request a deposit or payment be sent to my PayPal account. As with a merchant account, PayPal will charge a transaction fee but there are no monthly fees associated with the account. PayPal (and other online payment services) will accept credit cards, but the card number is never revealed to the recipient. These accounts use your email address for payment notifications and associate your online account to your regular bank account. This makes it easy to transfer funds between the accounts and your online history will give you an accurate record of payments received.

Some clients, however, still prefer to pay by company check. If they do, I request a *purchase order* number to guarantee the session. A PO number is a record of transactions that is kept by the company and used to allocate funds for specific purchases. A purchase order number is as good as a contract. I use their PO number as a reference number on my invoice, and my invoice will state "payable upon receipt." If I don't receive payment within a reasonable period of time (as stated in our Deal Memo or Booking Agreement), I'll call my client to follow up on the payment. If it appears that they are delaying payment, I can still charge their credit card, since I don't destroy that information until after I have the money in the bank. Oh, and if your client is in a foreign country, make sure their payment is in U.S. dollars.

CREATE A BOOKING AGREEMENT FORM

I've developed a form that includes a lot of information about the client, the work I'll be doing, the delivery method, my talent fee, my studio charges, and anything else that applies to the project (see

Figure 25-1: Example of a Booking Agreement). I'll fill out the form during the booking conversation and either fax or email a copy of our agreement for them to sign and return. A faxed or emailed PDF copy is good to confirm the session, but I'll also ask that they mail an original to me. The signed agreement and either their credit card information, a PO number, or a deposit constitutes a confirmation of the booking. With that in hand, I'll start recording and complete my part of the agreement.

Note that in my example, there is language that places the contract jurisdiction in the state where you are doing the work. This legal detail may become important if you are working for an out-of-state client who refuses to pay you for your work. By having jurisdiction in your state, you will be able to sue without having to hire an attorney in the state or city where your client lives.

OTHER TYPES OF AGREEMENTS

Some larger companies, such as major radio and TV stations, will not accept or sign a performer's deal memo or contract. These, and other reputable businesses, often have their own procedures for paying talent. If you want the work, you may need to accept their terms. However, you can still insist that you have a written agreement in place and even include a clause that places the contract jurisdiction in your state. If you see something in a contract provided by your client, or if you think something is missing, you have the right to modify the agreement as needed before it is signed. This is usually the final step in any negotiation. With contracts, everything is negotiable until the agreement is signed!

You will be asked to provide your social security number and sign their document before you can be paid. If you are not offered a copy, you should request one for your own records in case payment is delayed. You may need to invoice your client, and you usually will not be paid immediately after your session, but will receive a check in the mail within four to six weeks. If you have representation, this detail will be handled by your agent. However, if you are working freelance, some producers may take advantage of a 30-day payment agreement by basing the payment terms on 30 working days rather than 30 calendar days. This can result in your payment arriving long after you expected it. Some companies will even take as long as 90 days or more before mailing your payment. In some cases, this may be due to your client awaiting payment from their client before they can pay you. But often, this delay is simply so the company can hold funds in their account as long as possible. If you have not received your payment by the agreed upon time, it is up to you to call your client and gently remind them.

Booking Confirmation

Agreement for Voice Talent, Recording and/or Creative & Production Services

Please confirm your booking by signing and returning this agreement by Fax or E-mail.
This agreement for services is between _____ (*Talent*) and the Company or individual named below (*Client*). Your signature constitutes agreement to the terms and fees indicated below. All dates, terms and conditions indicated shall apply until changed by a new agreement. Client agrees that the Laws of _____ (*State*) shall apply to this agreement,and Client agrees to submit to the jurisdiction of _____ (*State*) to resolve any dispute that may arise as a result of this Contract. Services provided under this agreement are not to be considered as "work for hire."
We require a signed copy of this agreement and a Credit Card Number, PayPal payment, or company Purchase Order Number before we can begin your session. We accept payment by VISA, Master Card, Check, or PayPal. Payment in full is due upon completion of services unless noted otherwise.

Today's Date:	_____	Contact Name:	_____
Session Date:	_____	Company:	_____
Session Time:	_____	Address:	_____
On-site or Off-site:	_____	City/State/Zip:	_____
Director (if any):	_____	Phone:	_____ Fax: _____
Phone Patch/ISDN:	_____	E-mail address:	_____
Project #:	_____	Project Title:	_____
Project Details:	_____		
Delivery format:	_____	Delivery Method:	_____

> ➤ **Client copy is due 24 hrs. prior to session. E-mail copy to _____** ◄
> **Our standard page format is 12pt Arial, double spaced, 1" margins all around**

Contracted Services & Rates:

Voiceover Talent:	_____	
Talent Fee per voice for:	Principal: $_____ Secondary: $_____ Tag: $_____ Character: $_____	$_____
Page/Project Rate:	If applicable (incl. talent fee, studio time, and editing/production as requested)	$_____
Estimated Studio Time:	_____ Hourly rate (estimated):	$_____
Music:	___ N/A ___ Library ___Custom/Original License fee (estimated):	$_____
Creative/Writing/Production:	_____ Rate:	$_____
FTP/Matls/Delivery:	___FTP ___CD/DVD ___Other: (Acct. #) _____ Del/Matls. Fee:	$_____
PROJECT ESTIMATE:	**EST.TOTAL CHARGES:**	$_____
DEPOSIT REQUIRED:	___Yes ___No A deposit of this amount is required to guarantee this session:	$_____

Charges here are an estimate only. Actual charges may very and will be itemized on your final invoice.

BALANCE DUE:	**This is your estimated balance due. Payable upon delivery of completed project:**	$_____
COPY OF WORK:	Client agrees that Actor may obtain a copy of the completed work for use in a demo, web site, or in other forms of marketing and/or promotion of the Actor's services.	
CANCELLATION:	Either party may cancel this agreement with at least 24 hours notice by phone or in writing. A minimum $100 session fee plus 50% of above talent fees shall apply to any session cancelled by client with less than 72 hours notice. If cancelled with less than 24 hours notice, the full estimated fee shall apply.	
RE-TAKES/DO-OVERS:	Up to ___ re-takes/corrections to the original project at no charge. A minimum $50 session talent fee, plus studio time, shall apply for client changes after sign-off and delivery of original session. Additional talent fees and/or studio time may apply depending on the revisions required.	
PREFERRED PAYMENT:	___Credit Card ___PayPal ___Invoice ___Check (PO# required for check & invoice)	

A company PO#, PayPal payment, or valid credit card is required to guarantee your session. Deposits may be paid using PayPal or your Credit Card or check in US funds. Your card will NOT be charged until work is approved and delivered. Upon completion, your card will only be charged if that is your preferred payment method, or if an invoiced payment is not received within the terms of this agreement. Invoiced work using your PO Number is due upon receipt, Net 15 days. All credit card information is destroyed upon receipt of payment. Your signature below signifies agreement to these terms and conditions.

___ PO or REF #: _____	Payment Terms: _____
___ Credit Card #: _____	Exp: _____ CVC Code: _____
Name on Card PLEASE PRINT: _____	
Billing Address for Card: _____	
Signature: _____	Date: _____

Please verify the above, sign, date, then return to us to guarantee your session.

Figure 25-1:

Example of a Booking Agreement. A form of this type can be used to gather all the details of a session booking and can also serve as a written agreement, or contract, between the client and voice actor. Using this form for both purposes simplifies the communication process and ensures that the details of the booking and payment are mutually understood. A PDF version of this form is available in the AOVA Extras area at VoiceActing.com.

Another common problem with working freelance is that you can do a session today and be called back for changes tomorrow, but unless you are redoing the entire spot, the producer may expect you to do the pick-up session for free. If you don't like working for free, you should consider including this contingency in your deal memo or booking agreement.

When you are called back to fix a problem, the callback session is technically a new recording session. As a union performer, the producer must pay you an additional fee to return to the studio. As a freelance voice actor, it is up to you to negotiate your fee for the second session or provide for this contingency in your original agreement. Unless the problem was your fault, you should be paid for the follow-up session. The producer must be made to understand that you are a professional and that your time is valuable. You are taking time away from other activities to help fix their problem and you are entitled to fair compensation. A good producer knows this and expects to pay you for the additional work. Of course, if the problem was an oversight on your part, you should do whatever you need to do to make your client happy.

If you didn't include pick-up sessions in your original agreement, try to find out what needs to be fixed before you begin talking about how much you should be paid for the new session. If you are redoing most of the copy, you might want to ask for a fee equal to what you charged the first time. If the fix is simple, you might ask for one-half the original session fee. If you are exceptionally generous, and expect to get a lot of work from the client, you might offer to do the new session for free. If you do negotiate a fee for the follow-up session, make sure you get it in writing in the form of an invoice, a new deal memo, or a copy of their paperwork.

Union Compensation

The purpose of this book is to give you the tools and information you need to build a business and succeed as a voice actor. As with most major industries, unions play a role in establishing working conditions, benefits, and compensation. Joining a performing union is a personal decision that should be based on complete and accurate information from all points of view. I neither encourage, nor discourage union membership, but I do believe it is important to know how unions may have an impact on your voiceover work, whether you choose to not join, join at Financial Core, or join as a Rule 1 member. Most of the information in this section can also be found on the SAG-AFTRA website at **sagaftra.org** and in their print materials. You can find additional discussions on the pros and cons of union membership on many of the voiceover discussion boards and blogs.

By joining SAG-AFTRA, and working union jobs, you will be assured of reasonable compensation for your talents and protection from unscrupulous producers and advertisers. Your union-sanctioned agent will normally handle negotiations for your work and will sometimes negotiate a fee above scale. Regardless of what you are paid, the agent will only receive 10%, and that amount is usually over and above your fee. A performer just starting in the business may make less than scale, but the agent's commission will still be added on top of the performer's fee. The client also contributes to the union's health and retirement and Pension Welfare Fund. For many voiceover performers, the health and retirement benefits are the primary advantage of being union member. However, there is a minimum income requirements before a member can qualify for Health and Retirement benefits.

Residuals were implemented to guarantee that performers are paid for their work as commercials are broadcast. Each airing is considered a separate performance and talent are compensated based on the period of time a commercial is aired. Commercials produced by a SAG-AFTRA signatory have a life span of 8 or 13 weeks. After the original run, if the advertiser reuses the commercial, a new life span begins and the performer's fees, agent commission, and union contributions must be paid again. This happens for every period in which the commercial is used. In radio, residuals begin on the date of the first airing. In television, residuals begin on the date of the recording session, or the "use" date.

If an advertiser is not sure whether the company wants to reuse an existing radio or television commercial, a *holding fee* can be paid. This fee, which is the equivalent of the residual fee, will keep your talents exclusive to that advertiser, and is paid for as long as the spot is held. Once the commercial is reused, residual payments are made just as for the original run. If the advertiser decides the spot has lived its life, your residuals end. At that point, you are free to work for a competing advertiser.

Union recording sessions are divided into several fee categories and specific types of work within each category. For radio and television work, the performer's pay varies depending on the type of work and the market size where the product will be aired. The following is a description of the basic SAG-AFTRA performance fee categories. Although some of the details may change from time to time, this will give you an idea of the broad range of work available in the world of voice acting.

- **Session Fee:** The session fee applies to all types of union voiceover work and will vary depending on the type of work you are doing. A session fee is paid for each commercial you record. For radio and TV commercials, an equal amount is paid for each 13-week renewal cycle while in *use* (being rebroadcast) or if the spot is on *hold* (not aired). Session fees for dubbing, ADR, and looping are based on a performance of five lines or more, and residuals are paid based on each airing of the TV program.

  Animation voice work is paid for individual programs or segments over 10 minutes in length. Up to three voices may be used per program under one session fee. An additional session fee applies for each additional group of three voices, plus an additional 10% is paid for the third voice in each group of three voices performed.

  For off-camera multimedia, CD-ROM, CDI, and 3DO, a session fee is paid for up to three voices during a four-hour day for any single interactive platform. Additional voices are paid on a sliding scale and there is a one hour/one voice session fee and an eight-hour day for seven or more voices. Voices used online or as a lift to another program are paid 100% of the original session fee.

  Industrial, educational, and other nonbroadcast narrative session fees are based on the time spent in the studio. A day rate applies for sessions that go beyond one day.

- **Wild Spot Fee:** Paid for unlimited use of a spot in as many cities, for any number of airings, and on as many stations as the client desires. The Wild Spot *use rate* is paid based on the number and size of the cities where the spot is airing.

- **Tags:** A *tag* is defined by SAG-AFTRA as an incomplete thought or sentence, which signifies a change of name, date, or time. A tag can occur in the body of a radio or television commercial, but is usually found at the end. For radio, each tag is paid a separate fee.

- **Demos:** "Copy tests" for nonair use, paid slightly less than a spot fee. An advertiser might produce a demo for a commercial to be used in market research or for testing an advertising concept. If upgraded for use on radio or TV, the appropriate *use fee* applies.

- **Use Fee:** This fee begins when a commercial airs. Voiceover performers for national TV spots earn an additional fee every time the commercial airs. A standard of 13 weeks is considered a normal *time-buy* that dictates residual payments.

PRODUCT IDENTIFICATION

Radio and television commercials are unique in that they both create an association between the performer and the product. This is most common when an advertiser uses a celebrity spokesperson to promote their product. The viewing audience associates the performer with the product, and the advertiser gains a tremendous amount of credibility.

Product identification can, however, result in some serious conflicts, usually for spots airing in the same market. For example, if you performed the voiceover on a national television commercial for a major furniture store, you may not be able to do voiceover work for a local radio commercial for a competing furniture store. You will need to make sure both spots are not airing in the same market, even though one is for radio and the other is for TV. Conflicts are not a common problem, but they do occur from time to time and usually with union talent. As usual, if you have any questions, the best thing to do is to call your union office.

LIMITED RELEASE PRODUCTIONS

Many projects are never broadcast, such as in-house sales presentations, training tapes, programs intended for commercial sale, and point-of-purchase playback. For most of these projects, performers are paid a one-time-only session *buyout* fee with no residuals. These projects usually have no identification of the performer with the product or service in the mind of the audience, and therefore present little possibility of creating any conflict.

Documenting Your Session

Now that your booking is confirmed with a signed agreement, you're ready to get down to work. You've already got a good idea of what you need to do, you've got a general idea of what will be involved to complete the project and deliver it to your client, and best of all, you are confident that you will be fairly compensated for your work. However, Murphy's Law will inevitably come in to play as some time or another. Anything that can possibly go wrong ... will! And it will happen at the least opportune time.

You need to be prepared for Mr. Murphy and one way to do this is to document the time and details of your work through the use of a Work Order or Session Booking Form (see Figure 25-2: Example of a Session Booking Form).

Session Work Order

Pg: _____ of _____

Client Name: _____	Start Date: _____	Time: _____
Company: _____	Day: _____	Invoice #: _____
Address 1: _____	Terms: _____	
Address 2: _____	Confirmed: _____	
City/St/Zip: _____	Phone: _____	
Project Title: _____	Fax: _____	
Project #: _____	Alt/Cell: _____	
Ref. PO #: _____	E-Mail: _____	

Description: _____

Talent Fee: _____

DATE:	IN:	OUT:	WORK DONE – STUDIO TIME/TALENT FEE:	TIME:	UNIT:	AMOUNT:	OFFICE:

Miscellaneous: **Delivery/Format:**

DATE:	QTY.	ITEM:	AMOUNT:	FORMAT/DATE:	VIA:	AMOUNT:
		ISDN/Phone Patch				
		Outside Studio Fees				
		Travel				
				TRACKING NUMBER:		

Comments – File Name:

Billing:

	RECEIVABLE:	FEES PAYABLE:	PAYABLE CHECK NUMBER – DATE PAID:
Talent Fee:		/////////	
Studio Time:			
Miscellaneous:			
Shipping:			
Sales Tax:			
Other Income:		/////////	
Other Expense:	/////////		
TOTAL:			**Net:**

PAYMENT: Date Rcvd: _____ Check #: _____ Other: _____

Figure 25-2:
Example of a Session Booking Form or Work Order. This form can be used to document recording time and other expenses of a booked project which can then be summarized in your invoice for services. This form and the Booking Agreement should be kept on file for future reference.

You can call the form whatever you like: Work Order, Session Booking Form, Time Sheet, or a name of your own creation. The purpose of the form remains the same, and that is to document the time and processes that comprise the project you have been hired to complete. Virtually every service business uses some sort of documentation for the work they do. As a voice actor, and a good business person, you should do no less.

Everything you note on your Session Booking Form should be directly related to an aspect of the project you are working on, most of which should be part of your chargeable fees. Of course, you can choose to not charge for certain things or bundle items for a single fee, but the idea is that this form will give you a way to keep track of what you did for any given booking.

On the surface, this may seem like extra work or may even appear as completely unnecessary. However, when you document your sessions you will have a reliable negotiating tool for future bookings. For example, you may have contracted for a specific fee, but during the course of recording the project you discover that it actually requires considerably more time to complete, or there were some things that you neglected to include in your negotiations. By documenting the session you will be in a position to discuss those issues with your client when they book you in the future, and you will be better armed to discuss the realistic production requirements with other clients who might wish to book you for similar projects.

Some of the things to keep track of on your Session Booking Form are:

- Rehearsal time
- Copy editing or creative writing (if applicable)
- Consultation calls with your client
- Time spent to research pronunciation
- Time spent casting other voice talent (if applicable)
- Talent fees for other voice talent (if applicable)
- Studio time used for voice track recording
- Studio time used for editing
- Studio time required for file conversion, burning to a CD, or uploading to an FTP site
- Studio time required for pick-ups and subsequent delivery
- Time spent researching music and sound effects (if applicable)
- Music licensing fees (if applicable)
- Postproduction editing and mixing (if applicable)
- Other related items that may come to mind

As you can see, a Session Booking Form can be a very useful tool that can ultimately help you to identify ways to work more efficiently and even help you increase your revenues through a better understanding of exactly what it takes to do what you do. The form in Figure 25-2 is a simplified design based on the Work Order we use at VoiceActing Studios. Our session work order has been refined and honed over more than three decades to a point where it perfectly fits with the way we handle our recording sessions.

Keeping Records

As an independent businessperson, whether you have an agent or not, you need to keep complete and accurate records of income and business-related expenses well beyond just what you do for a particular session. This is not just for your tax records, but also so you have a way of tracking your career as a professional voiceover performer. Consult a tax advisor as to the best way to set up your record-keeping or refer to some of the many books or computer software on the subject.

You will want to keep records of clients you have worked for, what you did for them, and when you did it. When you get called by a producer you worked for last year, you can avoid undercharging by checking your files to see what your fee was last time. You can also use these records for future promotion and reminder mailings. A simple scheduling book can serve the purpose nicely, or you can set up a database on your computer. Personal money management computer programs are another excellent way to keep records. Prices range from under $50 to several hundred dollars.

Under the current tax code, just about any expense you have that directly relates to your business can be deducted as a business expense. Even if you work another full-time job, you can still deduct expenses that directly relate to your voiceover business, providing you are operating under standard business guidelines and not doing voiceover as a hobby. To further establish legitimacy for your business, you may want to obtain a business license in your city, and you eventually may want to incorporate. Setting up a legitimate business entity may have certain tax advantages. A tax advisor can help you with these decisions. The following are some of the things you should keep records of:

- **Income**—Keep separate account categories for income from all sources of income received.

- **Expenses**—The costs of doing business.
  Taxes and deductions: Document anything deducted from

Voice Acting Expense Report

Use this expense report on a weekly basis to track round-trip mileage for classes, sessions, errands, and other business-related expenses.

Week of: _____

NOTE: Attach all receipts to this expense report.

Mileage/Travel/General Expenses:

DATE	DESCRIPTION	START MILEAGE	END MILEAGE	MEALS	OTHER	TOTAL
TOTALS						

Entertainment/Meals:

DATE	PERSON(S) ENTERTAINED	BUSINESS PURPOSE	PLACE	TOTAL
TOTALS				

Figure 25-3:
Sample expense report for documenting business travel and other expenses relating to your voiceover business.

your pay, including income taxes, social security taxes, Medicare taxes, state disability taxes, union fees, and any other deductions from a paycheck.

Demo production: Keep track of payments for studio time, costs and materials, duplication, printing, letterhead, business cards, envelopes, postcards, résumés, CD labels, and travel to/from your demo session studio.

Telephone: Keep track of phone calls made to prospects, your agent, and coaching calls—especially any long-distance charges. You might consider a separate phone line to use exclusively for your business. If you have a cell phone or pager, these costs may be deductible as well.

Website: The costs of registering your URL (domain name), website hosting, and website design are all deductible expenses.

Internet access: The portion of your telephone bill, cable bill, or DSL bill that applies to Internet usage may be a deductible expense. Check with your tax advisor.

Transportation: Keep a log book in your car and note the mileage for all travel to and from auditions, sessions, and client meetings. Include parking fees. (See Figure 25-3: Voice Acting Expense Report.)

Other business expenses: Keep track of postage, office supplies, office equipment, computer equipment, and other supplies. The IRS tends to view computers as personal equipment, rather than business equipment, unless the use is well-documented. Identifying your computer as an "audio workstation" may be a more accurate business description of how your computer is used.

Classes, workshops, and books: Classes, workshops, conventions and books may be deductible as expenses for continued education and training in your chosen field, including travel to and from the workshop or training event.

In-home office: Deducting a portion of your mortgage or rent, and utilities for an in-home office, although legal, may trigger an audit by the IRS. Consult a tax advisor before taking this deduction.

Two excellent resources for software to manage your voiceover business are Performer Track (**performertrack.com**) and Pro Talent Performer (**protalentsoftware.com**). Both are popular with both on-camera and voiceover actors. An Internet search for "contact management software" will reveal many other options worthy of consideration.

Banking and Your Business

You may want to set up a separate checking account for your voiceover business and perhaps use accounting or money management software on your computer. This can help to keep all the financial aspects of your business in one place and simplify your tax preparation. The bottom line is that, as a professional voice actor, you are in business for yourself whether you work another job or not. As a business person it is important that you keep accurate records of your business-related income and expenses.

As with business management software, there are numerous options for financial management. Quicken (**quicken.com**) and QuickBooks (**quickbooks.com**) are among the most popular. Quicken is designed for managing personal finances. QuickBooks has much greater flexibility and is intended for managing business finances.

Voiceover and the Law

As with any other business, there are a great many legal issues that affect the business of voiceover. Contract law, copyright law, entertainment law, local laws, state laws, tax laws … the list goes on and on. Many of the major legal issues that affect the voice actor are addressed in this book. However, this only scratches the surface and the recommendations here cannot be considered legal advice. The legal ramifications of working in voiceover could fill a book of its own.

Fortunately, such a book exists! "Voiceover Legal" was written for the voice actor. Its author, Robert Sciglimpaglia, is an actor for both voiceover and on-camera as well as being a practicing attorney. He is an expert on the law as it applies to voiceover.

Scan this response code to read Robert's chapter from the fourth edition of this book titled: "Shedding Light on the Dark Side of Voiceover." Information on how to purchase "Voiceover Legal" is at **VoiceActing.com**.

In this Chapter

Auditions

26

Auditions

The Audition Process

Auditions are an essential part of the voiceover business. Without auditions, it would be very difficult for performers to get exposure to producers and other talent buyers.

Over the past several years, the audition process has changed from one where the voice talent would go to a studio or other site for a live audition, to one where now the talent will audition via the Internet or email by recording their audition in their home studio. Agents in larger cities will often still handle auditions at their office.

No matter how it's done, the audition process is still the most efficient way a producer or casting person has of choosing the best performer for a project. Once a script is written, copies are sent out to talent agents, casting directors, and on-line audition services. Specific performers or character types may be requested for an audition, and in some cases voiceover talent may be cast directly from a demo or prior work.

Talent agents and casting directors will select performers from their talent pool who they feel will work best for the project being submitted. If a specific voice actor is requested, the talent agent will attempt to book that performer. The *talent* (that's you), is then contacted and scheduled for an audition.

If you are just starting out, you may get the audition call from one of your contacts, through classes, on-line sites, friends, networking, or sending out your demo. You may receive the call several days in advance, the day before, or even the day of an audition. And it may come in an email.

Auditioning from Your Home Studio

The advent of home studios for recording voiceover has made it easy to provide high-quality auditions on a moment's notice. The key to a great sounding audition from your home studio is in two parts: 1) your studio design and equipment, and 2) your performing skills. Acoustics and home studio equipment are covered in detail in Chapter 22, "Your Home Studio."

You have only one chance to make a good first impression. Most auditions will be the first time a producer will experience your sound and performing abilities. If your audition is full of room echo or there's a lawnmower, dog barking, or baby crying in the background, their first impression of you will likely be far less than desirable. These issues must be addressed because when you are booked for a session, you will be expected to deliver a high-quality voice track. It's a myth that the sound quality of your audition is not important, even though this fallacy is taught by some voiceover coaches.

If you have given so little care to the quality of your audition, should a producer reasonably expect anything more from your work if they hire you?

ON-LINE AUDITIONS—PAY TO PLAY WEBSITES

The Internet has spawned a number of specialized websites that exist for the sole purpose of providing talent buyers the opportunity to reach hundreds of voice talent for auditions, and talent the opportunity to audition for hundreds of talent buyers.

The essentials of on-line audition sites is covered in Chapter 19 "Getting Paid to Play." This section will discuss a few aspects of on-line audition sites that directly pertain to recording auditions from your home studio.

Some audition requests are submitted by experienced producers who understand voiceover and who appreciate the time, energy, and money that a serious voice talent has spent developing their skills and business. Their audition requests are clear, specific, and informative. They know what the work will entail, what it is worth, and they offer a reasonable fee, expecting professional results.

Then there are the talent buyers who don't know what they're doing, or who simply want the most work for the lowest price. Many of these producers do not appear to have even the slightest idea of what it takes to create a voiceover performance that will actually get results. Their audition requests are often fragmented, incomplete, or excessively demanding and unrealistic. Here's an example of a typical "low-ball" audition request:

"I need this VO done ASAP. My script is only about a page, so it shouldn't take longer than about 10 or 15 minutes. What you send should be finished with the VO, music, and sound effects tracks. If this works out, I'll have a lot more work for you. I would prefer if you do the spot spec. I will pay on completion, just prior to delivery. I have a budget in mind for this, but I'd like you to send me your prices so I know who will work within my budget range."

One major problem with audition requests like this is that the talent buyer places the voice actor in a position of trying to come up with the lowest bid for the best performance, which can only serve to lower the voice actor's credibility. This producer is probably inexperienced and knows very little, if anything, about what it takes to record a high-quality performance, let alone one that has music and sound effects.

One of my students submitted an audition through one of these member sites and was awarded a job to provide the voiceover work for a radio commercial. It was only after she was hired, and had committed to a fee, that the producer told her they also needed music and sound effects for a completely produced commercial. She was not prepared for this, she is not a production engineer, and she did not have access to the music and sound effects libraries she needed. Yet, because she was eager to please her new client, she was placed in the very uncomfortable position of having to deliver a complex job for a minimal fee. Had she only recorded and delivered the voice track that she had originally agreed to provide, she considered her compensation would have been adequate. However, by the time she completed the production, she had put in many more hours than she had planned and had to spend her own money for production music, all of which resulted in her actual compensation equaling far less than minimum wage. Her mistake was that she agreed to the additional demands of the client, and did not have a clear agreement about what she would provide.

On-line audition sites can work well when you understand how to use them and have the performing and business skills necessary to win the auditions. At the very least, they can be an excellent form of continuing education for honing your home studio skills.

RECORDING A "KILLER" AUDITION

To submit auditions that stand a chance of getting you work, you must know how to properly use your equipment, you must know how to work the microphone (mic technique), you must know how to deal with adverse noise conditions (acoustics), and you must know what you are doing as a performer. In short, you must know how to produce a "killer" audition.

Let's assume you've taken care of all equipment and acoustic issues and that you can record excellent voice tracks. Now what?

The first thing you need to know is that just because you think a script is a perfect match, it doesn't mean your performance is what the producer is looking for. All you can do for any audition is to perform to the best of your abilities, using what you consider to be the best choices for your performance. Then, let it go.

Most talent buyers request auditions be sent as MP3 files without any production, music, or effects. In other words, they want to hear only your *dry voice* at the best possible quality. You may be tempted to use your recording software to "fix" problems by processing the audio with EQ (equalization), or other electronic tools, or you might want to add some music to your audition to give your prospect a better idea of what you can do. I would strongly recommend that you fight these temptations. If your home studio is properly set up and you record with proper levels, you will not need to "fix" your recordings. An audition is not the place for you to demonstrate your production skills or your talent for choosing music.

For most auditions, you simply don't have enough information and may have no idea what the producer is looking for. You are effectively second-guessing the producer in an attempt to come up with a performance that you think will meet their needs. Sometimes, they don't really know what they're listening for, so it may be worth sending two, or at most three, different interpretations of their script.

One of the most important things to keep in mind when auditioning from your home studio is to follow instructions to the letter, especially if the audition request came from a talent agent. If you are asked to *slate*, or identify, your audition in a certain way, do it exactly as requested! If you are asked to name your file a certain way, name it that way. If you are asked to send only one track, don't send two. If you are asked to send your audio at a specific sample rate, you had better know how to do it. If you are asked to upload your audition to an FTP website, don't email it. Producers want to know that you can follow their instructions and take their direction. Read audition instructions carefully, and follow them. If you don't, there's an excellent chance your audition will be never be heard.

WHO WROTE THIS COPY?

It is an unfortunate aspect of the voiceover business that many auditions will arrive as very poorly written scripts. Grammatical and punctuation errors, misspellings, nonsensical syntax, poor sentence structure, and confusing phrasing are commonplace. When you receive a script with any of these issues, your gut instinct may be to change a word or otherwise modify the script to make it "better."

There are several problems with this idea. To begin with, no matter how "bad" a script might seem, you really don't know that the way it is written might be exactly the way the writer intended. If the errors are obvious and extensive, it may be that the script was written in a hurry or perhaps the copywriter is inexperienced, not qualified, or may not be conversationally fluent in writing in English. Or, it could be that the errors are just simple mistakes. It really doesn't matter because your job as a voice actor is to deliver the best audition you can with the script you are given. Your services as a copywriter are not on the table at this stage of the project.

Many inexperienced voice actors make the mistake of thinking that by taking the time to "fix" the copy, they are showing their prospective client that they can work as part of the team, or that their copywriting skills can be an additional benefit to the project. This is flawed thinking because at that stage of the process the client isn't interested in anything you can do beyond your performance of their script. But that's not the worst part.

Suppose you do take the time to improve upon the original copy? You record a brilliant performance of your revised audition script and submit it. The talent buyer is under no obligation to book your voiceover services, and aside from the fact that you were never asked to rewrite the copy, you have just given them an improved version of their script. If they like your revisions, they are under no obligation to pay you for it, and will very likely use it when they book someone else. Because you provided a free rewrite of their original script, you don't even have any copyright to your new version. All your effort will have been to no avail.

Attempting to "fix" an audition script is essentially a waste of your time and energy. Of course, minor corrections might be appropriate for delivering your best work, but the time to discuss major corrections is after you are booked for the recording session. You may be surprised that the final script has been miraculously fixed. Some talent buyers have been known to send out a flawed script as a sort of test to see (or hear) what auditioning voice actors do to handle the errors. It's sneaky, but it does happen from time to time.

As a general rule of thumb, when you get a "bad" script, just do the best you possibly can and leave the copywriting to the client.

UNCOMPENSATED USE OF YOUR AUDITION

So, you've followed all the instructions and you've sent a very good dry voice track recording as your audition. At this point, you don't really know who you're sending your audition to, and you certainly don't have any sort of agreement for compensation should you be chosen for the job. If you've sent out a clean recording, the only thing preventing a producer from using your work without telling you is their personal morals and ethics. The majority of producers maintain high ethical standards and will not use a performer's work without compensation. But there are those unscrupulous producers who will take advantage of a situation.

There are several ways to protect your auditions from being used without compensation, all with the goal of making the audition unusable as a final recording but still providing a good representation of your work. One is to simply send only a partial performance as your audition, leaving out a few critical lines. A similar approach is to change the client name, product name, or phone number. This is not a substantial rewrite, but it does serve to make the audition unusable while giving the producer a good idea of your performance.

Yet another approach to protecting your audition is to use a *watermark* or drop out the audio at certain key words. In its simplest form, a watermark is a beep, tone, or click that is strategically placed to interfere with certain words, thus making the track unusable. At first glance this might make perfect sense as a way to protect your performance, and some of the pay-to-play audition sites encourage its use. However, there is a definite down side to using a watermark.

The only reason to use a watermark is if you suspect that the recipient might steal your work. Producers know this and many consider use of a watermark as a reflection of the actor's integrity. The logic is this: "If this voice actor doesn't trust me to handle their audition with integrity, why should I hire them for this job?" This is simply not a good way to start a professional relationship.

Aside from this negative affect, a watermark can easily be a serious distraction for a realistic evaluation of an audition. No matter how low the volume is set for the watermark, the sound can be distracting and annoying. The result of a watermarked audition can easily be loss of the job. A far better approach to protecting your audition is to simply change a few key words of the script.

The Live Audition

Recording auditions from your home studio quickly becomes second nature, especially as you become familiar with the operation of your equipment and software. When you are auditioning from your home studio, you can take your time and keep recording until you have recorded something you feel comfortable in sending out.

However, a live, in person audition is a completely different experience. Live on-site auditions are becoming more and more rare and are most common in major markets like Los Angeles, New York and Chicago, but they occasionally pop up in other markets.

PREPARING FOR A LIVE AUDITION

As soon as you get the call for your first live audition, you will probably begin to feel butterflies in your stomach. This is a good time to practice some relaxation exercises. You need to prepare yourself mentally and physically for the audition. Just the fact that you were called to audition is a good sign, so keep a positive mental attitude. After all, you have been invited to be there.

Loosen up with your daily stretches and voice exercises. Dress comfortably, yet professionally. Be careful not to wear clothing or jewelry that will make noise. If your audition is close to a meal, eat lightly and avoid foods that you know might cause problems.

Live auditions are usually scheduled, so plan to arrive at your audition about 15 to 20 minutes before your scheduled time. Make sure you leave time for any traffic problems and parking. If you don't plan ahead, you may arrive too late to read for your part, especially for multiple-voice auditions. When in your car, continue with some warm-up exercises and listen to music that will put you in a positive frame of mind. Sing to songs on the radio to loosen up your voice and relax your inhibitions, but don't overdo it. Use your cork.

Always bring several sharpened pencils for making copy notes and changes, and a bottle of water. A briefcase or tote bag containing your supplies, business cards, and several copies of your demo can add that extra touch of professionalism. Don't plan on giving your demo or business cards to the people you are auditioning for, unless they request them—they already know who you are. These are for other people you might meet whom you did not expect to be there.

Act as if you know what you are doing, even if this is your first audition. Watch others, follow their lead, and keep a positive attitude.

WHAT TO EXPECT AT A LIVE AUDITION

When you arrive at the audition, you may find several other performers already there. Also, you may find that several auditions are being conducted at the same time. Find the correct audition and pick up your copy. If the audition is for a large account, someone may be "checking-in" the scheduled performers. In most cases, there will simply be a sign-in sheet at the door and a pile of scripts. Once signed in, you are considered available to audition and may be called at any time. If you are early and want to take some time to study the copy, wait a few minutes before signing in. If you are scheduled for a specific time, be sure you are in the waiting area a few minutes beforehand.

In many cases, you will see the copy for the first time only after you have arrived on site. However with email, fax, and on-line casting services, it is becoming more and more common for audition scripts to be delivered ahead of time. On some occasions, for reasons only the producer can understand, you will have to wait until you are in the booth before you know what you are doing.

BE PREPARED TO WAIT

Even if the audition starts on schedule, chances are that within a short time, the producers will be running late. Have something to read or do while you wait for your turn. Stay relaxed and calm, and keep breathing. This may be a good opportunity to get to know some of the other performers who are there, but only if they are willing to talk to you. Many performers prefer to keep to themselves at an audition in order to stay focused or prepare themselves. Some will see you as their competition while others will not. Always respect the other people who are auditioning. You may end up working with them some day.

Networking can be a valuable tool when used properly—it's often not what you know, but who you know that gets you work. Even though these people may be your direct competition, you may make a connection for work that would have otherwise passed you by.

If the copy is for a dialogue spot, you may find another performer willing to *run lines*, or practice the copy with you. This can be an advantage for both of you, even if you do not do the audition together. However, do keep in mind that interaction with the competition can often be distracting.

Use your waiting time to study the script for your character, key words, target audience, and for anything that is unclear—especially words you don't understand or don't know how to pronounce. Try to get a feel for what they are looking for. What attitude? What sort of delivery? Most of the time, your choices will be clear. Sometimes, there will be a character description on the copy, or some notes as to what the producers are after. If there is a sketch of the character you are to play, make note of any physical features, body language or other characteristics that might be used to develop your performance choices. Note the important words or phrases, the advertiser and product name, where to add drama or emotion, where to pull back.

Mark your copy in advance so that you will know what you need to do to achieve the delivery you want. Rehearse out loud and time yourself. Don't rehearse silently by merely reading and saying the words in your mind. In order to get an accurate timing and believable delivery, you must vocalize the copy.

Be careful not to overanalyze. Read the copy enough times to become familiar with it, then put it aside. Overanalyzing can cause you to lose your spontaneity. Decide on the initial choices for your delivery, and commit to them. But be prepared to give several different variations. Also, be prepared for the unexpected.

Auditions for a TV spot may or may not have a storyboard available. This may be attached to the script, or posted on a wall. It may be legible or it may be a poor copy. A *storyboard* is a series of drawings, similar to a cartoon strip, that describes the visual elements of a TV commercial or film that correspond to the copy. If there is a storyboard for your audition, study it thoroughly. Many TV commercial scripts have a description of the visuals on the left side of the page with the voiceover copy on the right side. The storyboard or visual description is the best tool you have for understanding a video or film project. If you only focus on the words in the script, you will be overlooking valuable information that could give you the inspiration you need to create the performance that gets you the job.

EXPECT TO BE NERVOUS

Nervous energy is only natural, but it is something you need to control. Focus on your acting rather than on the words. Don't waste time trying to suppress or conceal your nervousness. Breathe through it and focus on converting the nervous energy into productive, positive energy for your performance. Many of the top stage and screen actors become very nervous before a performance. It's a common condition of all performing arts. Bob Hope, one of the top comedians of the twentieth century, was known to be incredibly nervous before going on stage. When asked about it, Mr. Hope said he valued his nervousness because he felt it gave him an edge while performing. Adjust for your nervousness by taking a long breath deep down through your body to center yourself and focus your vocal awareness. Chapter 4, "Using Your Instrument," explains how to do this.

EXPECT TO BE TREATED LIKE JUST ANOTHER VOICE

At most auditions, the people there really want you to be the right person for the job. However, if the audition is for a major account in a major city, expect the possibility of being treated rudely by people who just don't care and are trying to rush as many performers through the audition as possible in a limited amount of time. If anything other than this happens, consider yourself lucky. Many times, the people handling the audition are just there to record your performance and have little or nothing to do with the client who will eventually be hiring the actors.

MAKE A GOOD FIRST IMPRESSION

Greet the producer or host, introduce yourself, shake hands, be spontaneous, be sincere, and be friendly. If you are auditioning near the end of a long day, the people in the room may not be in the best of moods. You still need to be friendly and professional as long as you are in that room. Remember, first impressions are important. Your first impression of them might not be very good, but you need to make sure that their first impression of you is as good as possible. Your attitude and willingness to meet their needs will go a long way.

Answer any questions the casting staff or engineer ask of you. They will show you where the mic is and let you know when they are ready for you to begin. Do not touch any equipment—especially the mic. Let the engineer or someone from the audition staff handle the equipment, unless you are specifically asked to make an adjustment.

There will probably be a music stand near the microphone. Put your copy here. If there is no stand, you will have to hold the copy, which may restrict your physicalization. If headphones are available, put them on—this may be the only way you will hear cues and direction from the control room.

Before you start, the engineer or producer may ask you for a *level*. This is so he can set the proper record volume. When giving a level, read your copy exactly the way you plan to perform it. Many people make the mistake of just saying their name or counting 1, 2, 3, ... or speaking in a softer voice than when they read for the audition. Use this as an opportunity to rehearse your performance with all the emotion and dynamics you will use when the engineer starts recording. In fact, in a studio session, many times the engineer will actually record your level test—and occasionally that take, or portions of it, may end up in the final product.

MAKE THE COPY YOUR OWN

Your best bet for getting a job from an audition is to discover the character in the copy and allow that character to be revealed through your performance. Play with the words! Have fun with them! Put your personal spin on the copy! Don't change words, but rather add your own unique twist to the delivery. Don't focus on technique or over-analyze the script. Use the skills of voice acting you have mastered to make the copy your own. If they want something else, they'll ask.

Making the copy your own is an acquired acting skill. It may take you a while to find your unique style, but the search will be worthwhile. Chapter 11, "The Character in the Copy," discusses this aspect of voiceover work.

INTRODUCE YOURSELF WITH A SLATE AND DO YOUR BEST

You will have only a few moments to deliver your best work. Remember, you are auditioning as a professional, and those holding the audition expect a certain level of competency. When asked to begin, start by slating your name, then perform as you have planned.

To *slate*, clearly give both your first and last name, your agent (or contact info), and the title of your audition. You may be asked to slate in a specific order, add additional information, or leave an item out. Many talent buyers only want your name and your agent's name in the slate.

There are two schools of thought on slates: One is to slate with your natural voice. The other is to slate in character or in a manner consistent with the copy. Slating in your natural voice may be like a second audition by giving the casting person a taste of who you really are and what your voice is like. Slating in character provides continuity for the audition. Neither approach is correct in all situations. If you have an agent, ask how they would prefer you handle the slate. For some electronically submitted auditions, you may be asked to *not* include a slate, but you may be asked, instead, to include your name as part of the MP3 file name. Use your best judgment when slating, but always keep it short.

After slating, wait a few beats as you prepare yourself mentally by visualizing the scene, and physically with a good diaphragmatic breath, then begin. Don't just jump in and start reading. When auditioning from home, you have the luxury of editing later on.

At a live audition, you may, or may not, receive direction or coaching from the casting person. If you are given direction, it may be completely different from your interpretation. You may be asked to give several different reads, and you need to be flexible enough to give the producer what he or she wants, regardless of whether you think it is correct. You may, or may not, be able to ask questions. It depends entirely on the producer.

Many auditions are simply intended to narrow down possible voices and the performance is secondary. The copy used in some auditions may be an early draft, while other auditions may provide a final script. Either way, you are expected to perform to the best of your abilities. Do your best interpretation first, and let the producer ask for changes after that. It may be that your interpretation gives the producer an idea he or she had not thought of, which could be the detail that gets you the job. In some cases, you might be asked to simply improvise something, and won't even have a script.

Offering your opinion is usually not a good idea at an audition, but it is something you can do if it feels appropriate. Some producers may be open to suggestions or a different interpretation, while others are totally set in their ways. If the producer is not open to it, he or she will tell you. These are not shy people. At other times, the audition staff will be doing little more than simply giving slate instructions and recording your performance.

The casting person will let you know when they have what they want. Two or three reads of the copy may be all the opportunity you have to do your best work. When you are done, thank them, and then leave. Your audition is over. If you like, take the script with you, unless you are asked to return it.

OWN THE SESSION

This mental mind trick works equally well for on-site auditions, outside studio sessions and home studio sessions. The purpose of this visualization exercise is to put you in a mindset for success.

Begin by observing the environment. If on location, walk across the street or parking lot and observe the building where you will be working. Listen to the birds, study the architecture, notice the trees and observe any traffic. Notice the details. If at home, relax and observe the details of your home studio. Immerse your senses in the sounds and sights of wherever you are.

Next, close your eyes and, in your imagination, see yourself being welcomed by your client and studio staff. Say to yourself positive statements like: "I own this session." "These people work for me." "We're having a great time." Stay in the present tense.

After a moment or two, open your eyes and let it go. Proceed to your session ready to work. You may be surprised at how it goes.

After the Audition

If you do not hear anything within 72 hours after the audition, you can safely assume that you did not get the job. Generally, agents call only if you get the booking or are requested for a callback.

While you are waiting for that call, don't allow yourself to become worried about whether or not you will get the job. Write your follow-up letter and move on. Remember that voice acting is a numbers game, and that if you don't get this job, there is another opportunity coming just down the road.

WHEN THE ACTORS ARE GONE

At the end of the day, the audition staff takes all the auditions and returns to their office where they listen to the recordings and narrow down the candidates. They may choose the voice they want right away, or they may ask for a second audition—called a *callback*—to further narrow the candidates.

A callback session will generally be much more relaxed and you might have more time to work with the script or receive direction from the producer. Don't be surprised if the script has changed.

If for some reason you do not get this job, the producer may remember you next week or next month when another voiceover performer is needed for another project.

After the callback, the audition staff once again takes their collection of auditions (much smaller this time), and returns to their office. This cycle may be repeated several times until the producer or client is satisfied that the right voice is chosen.

BE GOOD TO YOURSELF

On leaving a live audition, you may come up with dozens of things you could have done differently or "better." Second-guessing yourself is self-defeating and counter-productive. Instead of beating yourself up, do something positive and be good to yourself. You've done a your best! You have survived your audition. Now you deserve a treat. Take yourself out to lunch, buy that hot new DVD you've been wanting, or simply do something nice for yourself. It doesn't really matter—just do something special. Then let it go.

Non-Union Auditions

Many union talent wishing to stay true to their Rule 1 agreement believe that they cannot audition for non-union voiceover work. The truth is that any voice actor can audition for any job. If you are non-union, you can audition for a union job. If you land the job, your client can qualify you for the union job under the Taft-Hartley law.

If you are a union member, you can audition for any non-union work that might come your way. If you are booked for the job, there are several things you can do: You can ask the union to get involved to move it to a union job. Or, you can create your own production company as a union signatory and hire yourself as the voice talent. This effectively removes your client from any dealings with the union and keeps the work within union jurisdiction. This topic is discussed in greater detail in Chapter 19, "Getting Paid to Play."

In this Chapter

You're Hired!

27

You're Hired!
The Session

A Journey through the Creative Process

Congratulations, you've got the job! Your audition was the first step—and on average, you'll have submitted about 40–60 auditions for every job you land. The client likes your audition better than anyone else's. You already know the details about the project, they've agreed to hire you at a fee you or your agent has negotiated, and you have a signed booking agreement.

Now, you need to know the details of the session: When does the session start (your *call time*)? Will you be expected to record and deliver files from your home studio? Or will you be going to a recording studio nearby?

The trend in voiceover today, even for top-level professionals, is to record from a home studio. The voice talent may or may not receive direction, so a high level of self-direction skill is essential. The talent may be asked to send the entire recording session, or *raw audio*, or they might be asked to edit best takes or even handle the majority of editing to send only a complete voice track ready for air. In some rare situations, the voice talent might even be asked to handle the post-production by adding music and sound effects. Audio files are then sent to the client for post-production and distribution. In larger markets, like New York, Los Angeles and Chicago, local recording studios are still commonly used for recording voice tracks. When recording in a studio, the talent will leave as soon as the client releases them from the session. When recording at home, the talent will generally move to their next project.

Whether recording from home or at a studio, the process is essentially the same. It's just that if you're recording voice tracks in your own studio, you'll be wearing the hat of not only voice talent, but also that of engineer, office manager and often director. You may have your client on the phone or on a *phone patch* connection to your audio mixer, but you are ultimately in control of both the recording process and your performance. Doing both can be a challenge, and although the focus of this book is not about audio production, it is important that you at least have a basic idea of what's happening on the other side of the glass.

Much of the creative process involves a lot of technology and a high level of creativity from the engineer. As a voiceover performer, only a small portion of the recording process involves you. To give you a better idea of how your performance fits within the whole process, the rest of this chapter will be devoted to walking you through a typical production.

THE PRODUCTION PROCESS

It all begins with an idea! That idea is put into words on a script, which may go through many revisions and changes. At some point during the script's development, thoughts turn to casting the roles in the script. In some cases, a role may be written with a specific performer in mind, but this is usually the exception to the rule. To cast the various roles, the producers listen to demos and hold auditions. The audition process (Chapter 26) narrows the playing field to select the most appropriate voice talent for the project at hand. If your voice is right for the part, and your demo or audition was heard by the right person, you could be hired for a role.

Be absolutely certain you are on time if your session is at a studio or if your client will be on a phone patch. It is much better for you to be early and have to wait than for you to be late and hold up the session. Recording studios book by the hour, and they are not cheap. Basic voiceover session time can cost $100 an hour or more, depending on the studio. Some Hollywood and New York studios book for $300 to $500 per hour. You do not want to be the person responsible for costing the client more money than necessary.

SESSION DELAYS

Time is also of the essence when you are recording. Things can happen very fast once you are on-mic and recording begins. You need to be able to deliver your best performance within a few takes. If the producer or director gives you instructions, you need to understand them quickly and adapt your delivery as needed.

The producer will want your best performance as quickly as possible. In reality, it may take a while to get it. A voiceover session for a :60 radio commercial can take as little as 5 minutes to as much as an hour or longer. But no matter how efficiently things are planned, it seems like there is always something that can cause a delay:

- There may be several voices speaking (dialogue or multi-voice copy), and it may take some time to get the characters right.
- Microphone placement may need to be adjusted or the mic may need to be changed.
- The copy may require major changes or rewrites.
- A session being done to a video playback may require numerous takes to get the timing right.
- There may be technical problems with the equipment.
- The voice tracks may need to be inserted into a rough spot for client approval before the performers can be released.
- The session may be a *phone patch* and the client may request changes that need to be relayed through the producer or engineer.
- Your client may not know what he or she really wants.
- There may be several would-be directors trying to offer their ideas, creating unnecessary delays.
- The voiceover performer may lack experience, and may not be able to give the producer the desired reading without extensive directing.
- An earlier session may have run overtime, causing all subsequent sessions to start late.

Regardless of how long you are in the studio, even if it's your home studio, you are an employee of the ad agency, producer, or client. Present yourself professionally and remain calm. Above all, do your best to enjoy the experience. Keep breathing, stay relaxed, and keep a positive attitude.

WORKING WITH PRODUCERS, DIRECTORS, WRITERS, AND CLIENTS

A voice-actor friend of mine once described a producer/director as "headphones with an attitude." Regardless of the producer's attitude, you need to be able to perform effectively. You must be able to adapt your character and delivery to give the producer what he or she asks for. And you need to be able to do this quickly with an attitude of cooperation.

It is common for a producer, after doing many takes, to decide to go back to the kind of read you did at the beginning. You need to be able to do it! It is also common for a producer to focus on getting exactly the right inflection for a single word in the copy. You might do 15 or 20 takes on just one sentence or a single word, and then a producer will change his mind and you will have to start all over.

Every producer has a unique directing style. You must not let a producer frustrate you. Occasionally, you will work for a producer or writer who is incredibly demanding, or simply does not know what he wants. When working for this type of person, just do your best and when you are done, leave quietly and politely. Later, when you are alone, you can scream as loud as you like.

There are some producers who operate on a principle of never accepting anything the first time—no matter how good it might be. Your first take might be wonderful—you hit all the key words, get just the right inflection, and nail the attitude. Yet, the producer may have you do another 10 takes, looking for something better, all the while drifting off target. When all is said and done, that first good take may be the one that's used.

WHO ARE THOSE PEOPLE?

Some studio sessions may be crowded with many people deeply involved with the project, or you may have several people on a conference call if working from home. Of course, there will be an engineer, and there will usually be someone who is the obvious producer/director. But the client may also be there, as well as his wife, their best friend, the agency rep from their ad agency, the person who wrote the copy, maybe even an account executive from a radio or TV station and possibly a dog. Everyone there, except the dog, has an opinion about what you are doing, and may want to offer suggestions about what you can do to improve your performance. It's a nice thought, but too many directors will make you crazy.

One obvious problem with so many people is conflicting direction. As a performer, you must choose one person in the control room to whom you will listen for direction. Most of the time this should be the producer handling the session. However, if it is obvious that the producer cannot control the session, you might choose someone else, if you feel the person is a better director. Most studios that record voiceover have engineers who are very experienced in directing voice actors. It is not uncommon for an engineer to "take over" the session if he recognizes that the client or producer is not getting an effective performance or the desired results.

Once you have made your choice, you must stick with that person for the duration of the session. Changing directors in mid-session will only make your performance more difficult. Simply focus your attention on the person you picked and direct your questions to only that person, mentioning him or her by name when necessary. There's a way of doing this that won't offend anyone.

When someone else presses the talkback button and gives you some direction, you need to bring control back to the person you chose. Allow the interruption to happen, and then refer to your chosen director for confirmation or further comment. After this happens a few times, the would-be director will usually get the hint and let the person in charge handle the session. Future comments will then be routed to you via your chosen producer or director—as they should be.

Types of Sessions, Setups and Script Formats

There are many different types of voiceover projects, and recording sessions come in all shapes and sizes, with a variety of format styles.

DEMOS

A *demo session* is for a project that has not yet been sold to the client. It will be a demonstration of what the ad agency is recommending. The client may or may not like it. The ad agency may or may not get the account. A demo is a commercial on spec (speculation).

Mel Blanc, one of the great animation character voices of the 1950s and 1960s, once gave the following definition of working on spec:

> *Working on spec is doing something now for free, on the promise you will be paid more than you are worth later on. Spec is also a small piece of dirt!* (Mel Blanc, from *Visual Radio*, 1972, Southern California Broadcasters Association)

Ad agencies, television stations, and radio stations often do projects on spec when they are attempting to get an advertiser's business—sort of an audition for the ad agency. The potential profit from a successful ad campaign far outweighs the cost of producing a spec commercial—provided the agency lands the account.

Demos will not air (unless they are upgraded by the client), and are paid at a lower scale than regular commercials. They may have several different voiceover performers booked to do the demo session. Since completed spots will be produced, demo sessions are often intended to give the advertiser a choice of performers for the final commercial. If the demo is simply upgraded, your agent will be contacted and you will be paid an additional fee. If a separate session is booked, you will be contacted, scheduled, and paid an additional fee.

SCRATCH TRACKS

A *scratch track* is similar to a demo in the sense that it is the preliminary form of a commercial. The major difference is that a scratch track is used as a reference for a commercial that is already in the process of being produced. Scratch tracks are most often used for TV commercials and other video productions, and serve as a reference track for the video editor before the final voice track is recorded. A scratch track will often be voiced by the producer, director, or sometimes the editor or audio engineer, and the music, sound effects, and other elements of the spot may or may not be in their final placement.

As a voiceover performer, you may be providing the original voice for a scratch track, or you may be providing the final voice that replaces an earlier recorded voice used as a scratch track. Either way, your job will be to match the edited timing as much as possible. Your job is not to mimic the style of the person who recorded the scratch track. If the client wanted that style, they would have hired the person who did the scratch track (and it has happened).

Just as for a demo session, your performance for a scratch track may be good enough for use in the final spot. You or your agent will know if the scratch track session is for a demo or a final commercial, and you will be paid accordingly.

REGULAR SESSION

This is a session for production of a final commercial. Many engineers refer to *regular sessions,* to differentiate them from demos, tags, scratch tracks and so on. The only difference between this type of session and all the others is that it is for a complete production.

SESSION SETUPS

There are two basic session setups: *single session* and *group session*. At a *single session*, you are the only person in the studio, but this does not mean you are the only voice that will appear in the final project. Other performers, to be recorded at another time, may be scheduled for different sections of the project, or for the tag.

There will be only one microphone, a music stand, a stool, and a pair of headsets. Many recording studios also have monitor speakers in the studio, so you can choose to wear the headset or not. Let the engineer make all adjustments to the mic. You can adjust the stool and music stand to your comfort.

Multiple-voice, or *group sessions*, are often the most fun of all types of sessions simply because of the ensemble. Each performer normally has his or her own mic, music stand, and headset. Depending on the studio, two performers may be set up facing each other, working off the same mic, or on separate mics in different areas of the studio. A group session is like a small play, only without sets. Looping is almost always done as a group session with from a few to a few dozen voice actors in the studio.

SCRIPT FORMATS

There are a variety of script formats used in the business of voiceover. Radio, television, film, multimedia, video game, and corporate scripts all have slight differences. Regardless of the format, all scripts include the words you will be delivering and important clues you can use to uncover the building blocks of any effective performance.

The Session: Step-by-Step

Working from your home studio is pretty straight-forward. However, when you visit a recording studio, things change.

Let's walk through a typical session from the moment you enter the studio, until you walk out the door. Much of this is review from other parts of this book; however, this will give you a complete picture of a studio session. After reading this section, you will know what to expect and should be able to act as if you have done it all before. But keep in mind that there are many variables that can affect this scenario. Just "go with the flow" and you will be fine.

Once you enter the studio lobby, your first contact will be the receptionist. Introduce yourself, and tell her which session you are attending. If the studio is in an office building and you paid to park in the building's parking structure, don't forget to ask if the studio validates.

The receptionist will let the producer know you are there. If you don't already have the script, you might be given your copy at this time, or you might have to wait until the producer comes out of the control room. Depending on how the previous session is going, you may have to wait awhile.

The producer, engineer or an assistant will come out to get you when they are ready, or the receptionist will let you know that you can go back to the control room. Or, someone might come out to let you know that the session is running late. There are many things that can put a session behind schedule. Remember, this is a hurry-up-and-wait kind of business.

When you enter the control room, introduce yourself to the producer, the engineer, and anyone else you have not yet met. You can be certain that anyone in the control room is important, so be friendly and polite.

If you do not already have your copy, it will be given to you here. This is your last, and often only, opportunity to do a quick "wood shedding," or script analysis, set your character and ask any questions you might have about the copy. Get as much information as you need now, because once you are in the booth, you will be expected to perform. Get a good idea of the target audience and correct pronunciation of the product's and client's names. Make notes as to attitude, mood, and key words. Mark your script so that you will know what you are doing when recording begins. The producer or engineer may want you to read through the copy while in the control room for timing or to go over key points. When the engineer is ready, you will be escorted to the studio.

In the studio, you will usually find a music stand, a stool, headphones, and the microphone. Practice good studio etiquette and let the engineer handle any adjustments to the mic. Feel free to adjust the music stand to your comfort. If a stool is there, it is for your convenience, and you may choose not to use it if you feel more comfortable standing. Some studios will give you the option of performing without having to wear headphones, but for most you will need to wear them to hear the director. Find out where the volume control is before you put on your headphones.

Make sure your cell phone is turned off, or better yet, leave it in the control room either turned off or silenced.

The microphone may have a *pop stopper* in front of it, or it may be covered with a foam *wind screen*. The purpose of both of these devices is two-fold: first, to minimize popping sounds caused by your breath hitting the microphone and second, to minimize condensation of breath moisture on the microphone's diaphragm. Popping can be a problem with words containing plosives such as "P," "B," "K," "Q," and "T." If an adjustment is needed, let the engineer know. If the mic is properly positioned, the pop screen may not be needed.

When the engineer is ready to record, you will be asked for a *level* or to *read for levels*. He needs to set his audio controls for your voice. Consider this a rehearsal, so perform your lines exactly the way you intend to once recording begins. You may do several reads for levels, none of which will likely be recorded. However, the producer or engineer may give you some direction to get you on the right track once recording begins. Some engineers will record your rehearsals, which occasionally are the best takes.

The engineer will *slate* each take as you go. You will hear all direction and slates in your headphones. This is not the same as slating your name for an audition. The engineer may use an audio slate or identify the project or section you are working on, followed by "take 1," "take 2," and so on. Or he may simply use flag markers inserted into the digital project. Before or after an audio slate, you may receive some additional direction.

Do not begin reading until the engineer has finished his slate and all direction is finished. You will know when you can start by listening for the sound of the control room mic being turned off. If you speak too soon, your first few words might be unusable. Wait a second or two after the slate, get a good supporting breath of air, begin moving, then begin speaking.

As you are reading your lines, the engineer will be watching your levels and listening to the sound of your voice. He will also be keeping a log sheet and will time each take with a stopwatch. He may also be discussing your delivery or possible copy changes with the producer or client.

Common Direction Terms

Expect to receive direction from the producer after each take. Do not change your attitude or character, unless requested by the producer. Do not comment about things you feel you are doing wrong, or ask how you are doing. Let the producer guide you into the read he or she is after.

Marc Cashman (**cashmancommercials.com**) has compiled a list of common direction terms from numerous voiceover resources, including prior editions of this book. Here's his list:[1]

Accent it: Emphasize or stress a syllable, word or phrase.

Add life to it: Your reading is flat. One expert advises: *"Give it C.P.R.: Concentration, Punch, Revive it!"*

Add some smile: Simply put, smile when you're reading. It makes you sound friendly and adds more energy to your read.

Be authoritative: Make it sound like you know what you're talking about. Be informative.

Be real: Add sincerity to your read. Similar to *"make it conversational."* Be genuine and true-to-life in your delivery.

Billboard it: Emphasize a word or phrase, most always done with the name of the product or service.

Bring it up/down: Increase or decrease the intensity or volume of your read. This may refer to a specific section or the overall script.

Button it: Put an ad-lib at the end of a spot.

Color it: Give a script various shades of meaning. Look at a script as a black and white outline of a picture that you have to color, with shading and texture.

Don't sell me: Throw out the "announcer" voice, relax; the read is sounding too hard-sell.

Fade in/fade out: Turning your head toward or away from the microphone as you are speaking, or actually turning your entire body and walking away. This is done to simulate the "approach" or "exit" of the character in the spot.

False start: You begin and make a mistake. You stop, the engineer refers to this as a *false start* and either goes over the first slate or begins a new slate.

Fix it in the mix: What is done in postproduction, usually after the talent leaves. This involves fixing levels, editing mouth noises, etc.

Good read: You're getting closer to what they want, but it's not there yet.

Hit the copy points: Emphasize the product/service benefits more.

In the can: All recorded takes. The engineer and producer refer to this as having accomplished all the takes they need to put the spot together.

In the clear: Delivering your line without *stepping* on other actors' lines.

In the pocket: You've given the producer exactly what they want.

Intimate read: Close in on the mic more, speak with more breath, and make believe you're talking into someone's ear.

Keep it fresh: Giving the energy of your first take, even though you may be on your twentieth.

Let's lay one down: Let's start recording.

Less sell/More sell: De-emphasizing/stressing the client name/benefits.

Let's do a take: The recording of a piece of copy. Each take starts with #1 and ascends until the director has the one(s) they like. Also heard: *Let's lay it/one down.*

Let's get a level: The director or engineer is asking you to speak at the volume you're going to use for the session. Take advantage of this time to rehearse the copy. Any shouts or yelling will require you to turn your head 45–90 degrees away from the mic. If the mic needs adjusting, the engineer will come into the booth. Do not move the mic unless instructed to do so.

Make it conversational: Just like it sounds, make your read more natural. Throw out the "announcer" in your read, and take the "read" out of your delivery. If it sounds like you're reading, you won't be believable. Pretend you're telling a story, talking to one person. Believe in what you're saying.

Make it flow: Also heard as: **Smooth it out.** Avoid choppy, staccato reads, unless the character calls for it.

More/less energy: Add more or less excitement to your read. Use your body to either pump yourself up or calm yourself down. Check with the engineer (i.e., do a level) to make sure you are not too loud or soft.

Mouth noise: The pops and clicks made by your mouth, tongue, teeth, saliva and more. Most mouth noises can be digitally excised, but make sure that you don't have excess mouth noise, because too much is an editing nightmare and will affect your work. Water with lemon or pieces of green apple can help reduce or eliminate most mouth noise.

One more time for protection: The director wants you to do exactly what you just did on the previous take. This is similar to "that was perfect, do it again." This gives the director a few more options to play with, should they be needed in post-production.

Over the top: Pushing the character into caricature.

Pick it up: Start at a specific place in the copy where you made a mistake, as in: *Pick it up from the top of paragraph two,* or *Let's do a pick-up at the top of the second block.*

Pick up your cue: Come in faster on a particular line.

Pick up the pace: Pace is the speed at which you read the copy. Read faster, but keep the same character and attitude.

Play with it: Have fun with the copy, change your pace and delivery a bit, try different inflections.

Popping: Noise resulting from hard consonants spoken into the mic. Plosives, which sound like short bursts from a gun, are most evident in consonants like B, K, P, Q and T.

Punch-in: The process of recording your copy at an edit point in real time. In a punch-in, as opposed to a "pick-up," the engineer will play back part of the copy you recorded and expect you to continue reading your copy at a certain point. The director will give you explicit directions as to where in the script you will be "punched in," and you will read along with your prerecorded track until your punch-in point. From there, you'll continue recording at the same level and tone you originally laid down.

Read against the text: Reading a line with an emotion opposite of what it would normally be read.

Romance it: Also "Warm up the copy." Make it more intimate.

Run it down: Read the entire script for level, time, and one more rehearsal before you start recording.

Shave it by ...: Take a specific amount of time off your read. Also heard as "shave a hair." If your read times out at :61, the director might ask you to "shave it by 1.5 seconds."

Skoche more/less: A little bit, just a touch more or less. This can refer to volume, emphasis, inflection, timing, attitude, etc.

Split the difference: Do a take that's "between" the last two you just did. For example, if your first take comes out at :58, and your second take comes out at :60, and the director asks you to "split the difference," adjust your pacing so the third take should be in at :59. Or, if your first take is monotone-ish and your second one is very "smiley," and the director asks you to "split the difference," adjust your read so that the third take will be somewhat in-between the first two.

Stay in character: Your performance is inconsistent. Whatever character and voice you commit to, you have to maintain from beginning to end, take after take after take. Focus. Be consistent with your character and voice.

Stepping on lines: Starting your line before another actor finishes theirs. Sometimes the director wants actors to "overlap" their lines, or interrupt. Others want each line "in the clear," where there is no overlapping or stepping.

Stretch it/Tighten it: Make it longer/shorter.

Take a beat: Pause for about a second. You may be asked to do this during a specific part of the script, like in-between paragraphs, or inside of a sentence or in a music bed. A good sense of comic timing is particularly helpful.

Take it from the top: Recording from the beginning of a script.

That's a buy/keeper: The take that everyone loves—at least the director loves. If the client loves it, then it's accepted.

That was perfect—do it again: An inside joke, but a compliment. Usually the producer wants you to reprise your take "for safety" (i.e., to have another great alternate take).

This is a :15/:30/:60: Refers to the exact length of the spot in seconds, also known as a read or take.

Three in a row: Reading the same word, phrase, sentence or tag three times, with variations. Each read should have a slightly different approach, but all should be read in the same amount of time. The engineer will slate three in a row "a, b, and c."

Throw it away: Don't put any emphasis or stress on a certain phrase, or possibly the whole script.

Too much air: Noise resulting from soft consonants spoken into the mic. Most evident in consonants like F, G, H, and W, and word beginnings and endings like CH, PH, SH, and WH.

Under/over: Less or more than the time amount needed. If you were *"under or over"* you need to either shorten or lengthen your delivery and *"bring it in"* to the exact time.

Warm it up a little: Make your delivery more friendly and personal. Whatever makes you feel warm and fuzzy is the feeling you should inject into your delivery.

Wood shed: To practice or rehearse a script, reading out loud. From the old days of theater where actors would rehearse in a woodshed before going on stage.

Wrap: The end—as in "that's a wrap!"

You will hear many other directions. Do your best to perform as requested. There is a reason why he or she is asking you to make adjustments, although that reason will often not be clear to you.

One of my favorite directing stories is one that Harlan Hogan tells about a session he once voiced. He had just completed a delivery that the producer said was extremely good, but wasn't quite where he wanted it. In the producer's words, "... that last take was a bit burgundy, I'm looking for something a little more mauve." With direction like that, what could Harlan do? So he delivered the script exactly the way he had just done, and the producer's response was "... now that's what I'm looking for!" Go figure.

Producers usually have an idea of what they want, and may or may not be receptive to your suggestions. Find out what the producer is looking for when you first read the script. Once in the booth, you should be pretty much on track for the entire session. If you get a great idea, or if it appears that the producer is having a hard time making a copy change, by all means speak up. You are part of a team, and part of your job is to help build an effective product. If your idea is not welcome, the producer will tell you.

Recording studio equipment sometimes has a mind of its own. There are times when the engineer may stop you in the middle of a take because of a technical problem, and you may have to wait awhile until it is corrected. Once corrected, you need to be ready to pick up where you left off, with the same character and delivery.

If you left your water in the control room, let the engineer know and it will be brought in for you. If you need to visit the restroom, let them know. If you need a pencil, let them know. If you need *anything*, let them know. Once your position is set in front of the microphone (on-mic), the engineer will prefer that you not leave the booth, or change your position. If your mic position changes, you can sound very different on different takes, which can be a performance continuity problem for the engineer if he needs to assemble several takes to build the final commercial. If you must move off-mic, try to keep your original mic position in mind when you return to the mic.

Be consistent throughout your session. Changes in dynamics may be useful for certain dramatic effects, but, generally, you will want to keep your voice at a constant volume or in a range consistent with your character. If your performance does call for sudden changes in volume, try to make sure they occur at the same place for each take. If your levels are erratic, the changes in volume may become noticeable in the final edit.

You know what the producer wants. You stay in character. Your timing and pacing are perfect. Your enunciation and inflection are on track. Your performance is wonderful. The producer is happy. The engineer is happy. And, most important, the client is happy. That's it! You're done, right?

Not quite.

Wrap it Up

Before leaving the studio, make sure you read and sign the contract for your services. If you were booked for one commercial (spot announcement), and the producer had you do three spots plus tags, make sure the changes are made on the contract. Also make sure to let your agent know about the changes. If you are unsure of anything on the contract, call your agent *before* signing the contract.

For union work, send your SAG-AFTRA form to the union within 48 hours of the session to avoid any penalties. The union form is the only way AFTRA has of tracking your work, and making sure you are paid in a timely manner. If you are working freelance, make sure you are paid before you leave the studio, or that you have a signed invoice or deal memo—and make certain you have the contact address and phone number of your client. If you have a merchant account, you can take a credit card number to be processed, or to hold as a guarantee until your check arrives. You've completed your part of the agreement, and you are entitled to be paid. It's up to you if you agree to have your payment sent to you, but keep in mind that you take a risk of delays or not being paid if you do this.

It's good form to thank the producer, engineer, client, and anyone else involved in the session before you leave. If you think your performance was especially good, you can ask the producer for a copy of the spot when it is finished. If the project is a TV commercial, there may be a charge for you to receive a copy. In this digital age, finished commercials are increasingly being distributed to stations via ISDN networks directly from the studio's computer, emailed as digital files, uploaded to a website, or sometimes mailed as a one-off CD. One way to ensure that you get a copy is to include a clause to that effect in your agreement. However, even with that, it may never arrive or you may find yourself waiting several weeks, or even months, before you get it.

Once your session is over and the paperwork is done, you are free to leave. Your job is done, so don't stick around unless invited. After you are gone, the process of assembling all the pieces of the puzzle begins. It may take from several hours to several days before the final audio track is complete.

If your session is for a TV commercial, the completed audio will often be sent to a video postproduction house where the video will be edited to your track to create a final TV spot. In some cases, just the opposite occurs—the video may have been edited to a scratch track, and the purpose of your session would have been to place your voiceover against the preproduced video. Once mastered, copies are made and distributed to tradio and TV stations.

Follow up your session with a thank-you note to the producer. Thank him or her for good directing or mention something you talked about at the session. Be honest and sincere, but don't overdo it. A simple note or postcard is often all that's necessary to keep you in the mind of the producer or director and get you hired again. If you haven't already, be sure to add their names to your mailing list for future promotions you send out.

Of course, if you are working from your home studio, much of the above will still pertain. Many of the intricacies of working from a home studio are covered in Chapter 22, "Your Home Studio."

---

1 Adapted and compiled by Marc Cashman from the following sources:
    Alburger, J. R. (2006). *The Art of Voice-Acting* (3rd ed.). Focal Press.
    Blu, S. & Mullin, M. A. (1996). *Word of Mouth.* (revised edition). Pomegranate Press.
    Apple, T. (1999). *Making Money in Voice-Overs.* Lone Eagle Publishing Company.
    Whitfield, A. (1992). *Take It From the Top.* Ring-U-Turkey Press.
    Thomas, S. (1999). *So You Want to Be a Voice-over Star.* Clubhouse Publishing.
    Berland, T. & Ouellette, D. (1997). *Breaking into Commercials.* Plume Publishing.
    Douthitt, C. & Wiecks, T. (1996). *Putting Your Mouth Where the Money Is.* Grey Heron Books.
    Jones, C. (1996). *Making Your Voice Heard.* Back Stage Books.
    Clark, E. A. (2000). *There's Money Where Your Mouth Is.* Back Stage Books.

In this Chapter

28

Stop It!

What Are You Doing to Sabotage Yourself?

There's a simple fact of life that is true for all of us from time to time. I'm referring to those things we do, often unconsciously, that prevent us from moving forward in life and business. These could be behaviors or attitudes based in fear or things that have simply become habit. Whatever they may be, they can have the very deleterious effect of stopping us dead in our tracks.

So, what's the solution? It's quite simple, really. Just stop doing whatever it is that you are doing that holds you back. OK, it's often not quite that simple, but you cannot change a behavior, habit or fear until you are aware that it exists. Only then can you can begin work on reversing or stopping it.

Popular comedian Bob Newhart was known for the way he looked at common situations from an off-beat perspective. His routine titled simply, "Stop it!" was the inspiration for this chapter. Scan this response code to watch the Youtube video, or search "Bob Newhart Stop It" at **Youtube.com**. When you stop laughing, come back to this chapter and find out how many of these common behaviors might be holding you back. Then get to work and just stop it!

STOP ACTING

All acting is about creating a believable reality of the moment. If are "pretending," if your presentation is artificial in any way, or if you are trying to be real, you are acting. The best acting is not acting. To be real in the moment of any script ... Stop Acting!

STOP ANNOUNCING

On rare occasions, the character you create for your voiceover performance may be an "announcer." An announcer has a specific, detached, and slightly over-the-top delivery with an energy that is not conversational and may have the tone of a circus ring master.

The majority of voiceover work today requires a believable, relaxed and conversational delivery that connects with the listener on an emotional level. An announcer style might be excited and energetic, but it is generally not the type of sound that most people easily connect with.

To be conversational, your energy must be consistent with your telling of the story, you must be speaking to someone (not at them), and your tone of voice cannot be over-the-top. To be conversational, you must Stop Announcing!

STOP APOLOGIZING

Why do you say "I'm sorry" when you flub a line or stumble over a word in your script? You didn't do anything wrong. You just didn't get the words out correctly. That's no reason to apologize!

An apologetic attitude is generally nothing more than a bad habit. But it's a habit that can keep you from reaching your goals. Every time you say "I'm sorry," the perception of you as an expert and a professional is slightly reduced. Experts know what they are doing and have no reason to apologize—no matter what happens.

To be perceived as a professional, Stop Apologizing!

STOP ASSUMING

How many times have you recorded a script and delivered to your client, only to discover that you didn't fully understand the story, or the meaning and pronunciation of some words. Or perhaps your interpretation turned out to be completely wrong? Or you negotiate a fee for your work only to learn that you won't be paid for six months, if at all, or your work is being used inappropriately, all because your client says they misunderstood something you said, or because you didn't have a clear agreement in writing. It happens to all of us at one time or another!

The reason these things happen is because we tend to assume that we know how to correctly pronounce a word, or that our interpretation is what the client has in mind, or that our agreement is understood. It doesn't matter if our assumptions are correct most of the time or not. What does matter is that if we allow ourselves to make assumptions, eventually we will suffer the consequences.

This is an easy predicament to solve. All you need to do is have a policy of asking a lot of questions. Ask about pronunciation, interpretation, character, attitude, payment terms, conditions for use, and so on. If there is even the slightest hint of something you do not understand or about which you need more information, ask questions to get clarification. The best way to get your questions answered is in person or by phone. But in today's electronic marketplace, that is often not practical, which leaves email or texting. Whatever works! Just ask lots of questions.

To be perceived as a professional, Stop Assuming!

STOP CARING

Of course you care about your work and doing the best job you can with your auditions and paid projects. That goes without saying! That's not what I'm talking about.

When you care about whether or not your client will like you, or you care about whether or not your booth sounds OK, or if your performance choices are right, or if your client is ethical, or if you are going to be paid, you are setting yourself up for failure.

Amateurs and hobbyists care about how they and their work are perceived by others. Professionals don't care!

A professional actor is confident with their skills and expertise. A professional knows they are more than just "good" at what they do— they are an expert. A professional doesn't care about what people think of them. A professional knows that when they do an amazing job for their clients, they will get repeat business and referrals.

If you truly want to be perceived as a professional voice actor, you need to learn how to Stop Caring!

STOP GUESSING

Do you guess at the pronunciation of a word or do you look it up? Do you guess that your interpretation is going to be OK, or do you seek the advice of your coach or client? Do you guess at how your work will be used, or do you ask specific questions to get accurate information?

When you are guessing, you are making assumptions. Go back and re-read Stop Assuming and apply those concepts to your work and Stop Guessing!

STOP JUDGING YOURSELF

When you flub a line or make a mistake, do you kick yourself by loudly proclaiming to the world how much you suck? When you can't get the edits to sound right, do you begin to think that you might be better off working in a flower shop?

Self-judgment can be debilitating. And if you self-judge in front of your clients, it can result in loss of future work. Your clients expect you to behave as a professional. The occasional frustration with a word, a line of copy or with the client's direction is to be expected, but a continuing pattern of destructive self-judgment is considered unprofessional.

You need to know that you are OK and that what you do in the booth is on track to meeting your client's needs. This is not life and death ... this is voiceover.

Keep your cool in the booth. Stop Judging Yourself!

STOP NEGATIVE THINKING

Self-judgment is just one form of negative thinking. In fact, most of your bad habits have their roots in negative thinking. You're not good enough, you don't have the right equipment, you're not a good negotiator, you don't know how to use your software, you hate balancing your books. These are just a few of our typical negative thoughts. If not dealt with, they can take on a life of their own.

Negative thinking will stop you in your tracks, preventing you from making those necessary cold calls, negotiating the talent fees that you deserve, and even performing to the best of your abilities. A negative attitude is the ultimate outcome from negative thoughts. It will be picked up by those around you at an unconscious level, and can easily result in unhappy clients who would prefer to not work with you in the future.

If you truly want to work as a professional voice actor, learn how to maintain a positive attitude and turn your destructive, negative thoughts into constructive, positive thoughts. If you are going to take your voiceover work seriously, you must control, and ideally Stop Negative Thinking!

STOP PERFORMING

Remember the definition of a voice actor? A performer who creates compelling characters in interesting relationships.

In order to be compelling, an actor must be real and believable and the audience must experience an authentic representation of the moment in time being portrayed by the actor. If the actor is doing anything less than representing the honesty of the moment, he or she is performing.

Now, of course, we all know that when we stand in front of the microphone, we are "performing," but that doesn't need to mean that we should sound like we are performing. To be an effective—and compelling—voice actor, the direct opposite is true. We must sound like the "real thing." We must be true, honest, authentic, and usually conversational in our delivery. To be anything less is to be standing in our way of creating the reality of the moment.

Learn how to create a compelling reality of the moment and Stop Performing!

STOP PROCRASTINATING

Do you put off making those cold calls? Do you wait until the very last minute to record your auditions? Do you tell yourself you'll take that voiceover workshop later ... when you can afford it?

Can you really afford to put off getting the training you need, recording those auditions, or making the contacts you need to bring in business?

Procrastination is another of those bad habits many of us have to deal with. A wise individual once said "Hard work pays off later, laziness pays off now. I've always been one for being in the moment." Must have been an actor!

Or, look at it this way: The best part of procrastination is that you'll never be bored because you have all kinds of things you should be doing.

If you are going to be successful at anything, you need to learn how to manage your time and do the things that need to be done, when they need to be done. And that usually means now ... not later today ... not tomorrow ... now!

Do you really want to be a successful voice actor? If your answer is "yes," then do what you need to do and Stop Procrastinating!

STOP READING

This one is pretty simple: When you are only reading the script, you will sound like you are reading the script. That's not being real. That's reading out loud. Unless you are reading to your child at bed time, this approach to voiceover won't get you very far. Learn how to create believable, relatable characters—even if they are merely an extension of yourself. Learn how to put inflection and variety in your delivery as you speak. And learn how to tell stories in an interesting and compelling manner. In short ... learn how to Stop Reading!

STOP SECOND GUESSING YOUR CLIENT

Second guessing your client is not a good thing! You are making the assumption that you know better than your client. Now, the truth may be that you <u>do</u> know more and better than your client, but they are paying the bills. Don't forget the basic axiom of business: "The customer is always right … even when they are wrong."

When your client asks you to deliver their copy in a certain way, it is your job to meet their needs as much as possible—even if means going against every instinct in your body.

If you expect to get repeat bookings, don't argue with your director and Stop Second Guessing Your Client.

STOP SECOND GUESSING YOURSELF

This is almost as bad as second guessing your client!

All acting is about making choices and sticking with those choices until they need to be changed. When you second guess yourself, you are not being consistent with your choices. Your interpretation will vary from one take to another, which will make editing very difficult. Your tone of voice, characterization, and attitude will shift all over the place. And your performance will be perceived as little more than amateur.

Professionals are consistent in their choices. To do your best work, make solid choices, be consistent, and Stop Second Guessing Yourself!

STOP THINKING

In all the years of working with voice actors, there is one common challenge I have identified that consistently gets in the way of great performances. The simple fact is that most voiceover talent over-think their work. They over-analyze and often over-act as a direct result of thinking too much about what they are doing.

Sure, it's important to wood shed your script so you know the story and can pronounce any tricky words or phrases. But once you've done that, about 90% of your work is done. Let it go and stop thinking about it! Just get out of your way and let the words and phrases guide you through your performance.

When you think about how you are going to inflect a line, where you are going to breathe, or how quickly you are going to speak, you will be standing directly in the way of bringing the words to life.

To achieve your best performance, learn how to get out of your way and Stop Thinking!

STOP TRYING TO BE PERFECT

Perfection is elusive. In fact, most of the time, it's not possible. Your delivery might be exactly what you or your client wants, but it will never be absolutely "perfect." Yes, you can get very, very close, but perfection is one of those things that just doesn't happen every day.

Just as a good director will know when to accept a performance that meets the needs of the project and when the performance needs to be adjusted, so must you develop self-direction skills so you will instinctively know when you've got what you need and when to move on. You should absolutely strive to do your best whether its for an audition or a paid project, but also know that when you strive for perfection, you may never finish.

Learn how to critically listen to yourself and self-direct with skill and expertise so you can Stop Trying to be Perfect!

STOP TRYING TOO HARD

Trying too hard is closely related to trying to be perfect and thinking too much about what you are doing. When you try too hard, you will make mistakes and get frustrated. The resulting stress will affect your work whether you are aware of it or not.

Master your performing and business skills so they are second nature. To be your best at all times, simply Stop Trying Too Hard!

STOP WASTING TIME

Every time you get distracted or put off doing something that will move your voiceover work forward, you are wasting time, energy and often money. Learn how to focus your energy to increase efficiency and productivity. When you Stop Wasting Time, you will be more successful with your business.

STOP WORRYING ABOUT THE WORDS

Focusing on how you are going to "read the words" is a common problem that will take you out of a conversational delivery faster than just about anything else. Learn how to quickly interpret a script on the first read-through. Discover any challenging words or phrases and make any needed adjustments. Once you've got it … let it go and know that your delivery will be on track.

Your voiceover work will be much more consistent and you will have considerably more success with your auditions and bookings when you learn how to Stop Worrying About the Words.

In this Chapter

29

Tips, Tricks
and Studio Stories

Maxine Dunn
(MaxineDunn.com)

Maxine Dunn is a full-time voiceover artist and award-winning motivational business writer. Her voice has been heard in hundreds of commercials, documentaries, corporate narrations, voice-mail systems and websites. Maxine is a British native and her ability to also deliver a flawless American accent (without a trace of Brit) gives her voiceover work a tremendously wide range. She maintains an extensive voiceover clientele, locally, nationally, and internationally. She is the author of the eBook, *The Voice Actor's Tool Box - Beginner's Edition.*

Are New Clients
Even Reading Your Cover Letter?

Your marketing, your client outreach, and your individual efforts to attract and make contact with prospective voiceover clients who need your services, can have a HUGE impact on your bottom line.

As a professional voice actor, one of your primary skills is professional communication. That is, how you speak on the phone and how you compose emails, letters, and other communication.

It's important!

And one of the best ways to convey to a potential client what it is that you do, is by sending them a great cover letter (with or without your demos, depending upon whether you've also spoken to them in person).

Let's begin by defining what a "cover letter" is.

A cover letter is an introduction.

It's the written version of you holding out your hand and saying, "Hi! I'm so-and-so and I'd love to work with you!"

And a cover letter has ONE purpose: To pique the recipient's interest to encourage them to want to know more about you.

If you've sent out letters or emails to potential voice-over clients and you're not getting a positive response, you may be guilty of writing lousy cover letters!

Cover letters can compel clients to work with you but, if poorly written, they can be ignored and even repel potential clients.

But don't worry! No matter what your cover-letter-writing strategies or abilities are right now, by the time you've finished reading this article they'll be much better! No more lousy cover letters - yours are about to shine!

In the following tips, I've offered some suggestions for the basic structure of your voiceover cover letter and some specific items that you'll definitely want to mention in your cover letter.

BASIC COVER LETTER STRUCTURE:

Tip #1: Make your subject line clear and descriptive.

For example, "British voice actress specializing in corporate narration." Or, if you've already spoken to the client on the phone and have permission to send your website link or MP3, you can write your name in the subject line. For example, "Maxine Dunn - British voice-over demos." Avoid ALL CAPS in the subject line.

Tip #2: Make it personal, right from the start.

Before you ever write a single word to a prospective client you absolutely MUST know WHO you're sending your email to. No "mass mailings" where your opening salutation is just "Hello" or "Greetings." Those are a dead giveaway that you don't know who you're talking to.

Best case scenario: Take the time to call the company you're interested in working with and find out the name of the person who handles the voice talent. Make sure you get the correct spelling of their name.

Using a client's name in the opening salutation will set you apart from all those other people who just say "Hey!" or "Hello."

Tip #3: Make it easy-to-read. Keep it short and sweet.

Use bullet points. Check carefully for typos or grammatical errors. Clients are busy so they appreciate a short, to-the-point letter. Doing this one thing alone will set you apart from all those other people who send looooong emails with lots of typos.

Tip #4: Research your prospective client's company, in-depth.

Learn everything you can about them and mention something about your client in your cover letter. Don't just make it all about you. Whether you compliment them on their website design, congratulate them on an award they won or mention how much you enjoyed their demo reel on their site, show that you care about THEM.

Letting them know that you've researched their business and are familiar with the work they do will show them that you've done your homework. And it doesn't need to be a long mention. You can simply say, "Congratulations on your amazing demo reel - what an incredible body of work!" Or, "I notice that you specialize in creating corporate films, and that happens to be my voice-over specialty as well!"

Mentioning something about their business in your cover letter will set you apart from all those other people who only talk about themselves.

YOUR VOICEOVER INFORMATION TO INCLUDE:

Tip #5: Make your intention for writing clear, right from the start.

Don't waste time. Get to the point. For example, "Dear Ken, I'm a British voice actor based in the US and I specialize in corporate narration. I see on your website that you produce corporate videos and I'd love to work with you! I've included a link to my website and invite you to listen to my demos. I have 16+ years experience and can offer you a lightning-fast turn-around on projects from my professionally equipped home studio..."

Tip #6: Offer information about your vocal qualities.

Include the age-range of voices you perform, and any other interesting things about your voice that would help them know your abilities and remember you. Bullet lists work great here: For example:

> Age range: 30-50
> Accents: Native British and flawless American
> Vocal description: Sincere, warm, educated, trustworthy
> Specialties: Corporate narration, commercials

Tip #7: Include a short list of client credits.

For example, "My clients include AT&T, McDonald's, JC Penny's, Proctor & Gamble and Home Depot.

Tip #8: Include your home studio information and project turn-around time.

For example, "I have a professionally equipped home recording studio and can deliver your audio files quickly in any format that you wish. My turn-around time is typically 24-48 hours."

Tip #9: Include all your contact information.

Name, website address, email address, and phone number/ mailing address if you choose. Ladies, it's advisable to obtain a post office box address so you are not giving out your home address.

Tip #10: Follow up, follow up, and follow up again!

Don't just send and forget. (Which is what a LOT of voice actors do.) Mention in your cover letter that you'll follow up in a couple of weeks to see if they've had a chance to listen, and thank them very much for their time! I always like to end with, "I look forward to the possibility of working with you!"

TAKE TIME WITH YOUR COVER LETTERS

Be personal and engaging, include only the important information your prospective client will need, and just watch your results improve!

Deb Munro
(Canada)
(Debsvoice.com)

Deb is a voiceover powerhouse! She's a busy, and very talented voice actor, a writer, and a coach... among other things. From the moment I first met Deb, I was impressed with her seemingly unbounded energy. But all the energy in the world won't give you any more time to do what needs to be done. Here are some of Deb's ideas on Time Management.

How Well Are You Managing Your Time?

If you are a realist and manage your time well, you know exactly how much time it takes to get your duties done - you even know how to account for your personal time in that equation, while others aren't as lucky.

Or, you might be thinking: "Time management? What time!? Sometimes I think that's the category I fit into. There never seems to be enough time in the day for me to get done all that I set out to do.

The difference, however, is that I am a realist as well, and I do try to account for just the right amount of time.

I am known to never be early and never be late - but I get everything done just in the nick of time! Breaking myself into three careers isn't easy. I am a full-time voice talent/business owner, full-time coach, and full-time mom/spouse/grandma - so I tend to spread myself pretty thin. Not to mention that I have some big goals yet to accomplish.

It's very important for you to see where you want to go and then plan exactly what is required in both time and money to accomplish it.

In my case, I got so busy that I wasn't able to keep up. So hiring an assistant was my only hope. I was blessed when what I needed presented itself to me, and now I'm able to manage my time much better.

How much is your time worth to you? How are you best spending your time?

It's frustrating to watch talent have goals but do nothing with their time to achieve them. We all have circumstances that change our time management and daily routines, but much like the dreaded workout at the gym, if you don't keep at it, you will never grow. This is one industry where complacency can be your enemy.

Set a realistic schedule for yourself and start recording the time you spent on your craft. If you are devoting full-time hours to this, you will start seeing full-time results. But if you're only putting in an hour here and an hour there, that isn't commitment. That's a hobby, and most of us don't make money at our hobbies.

It's easy to make up excuses, so I encourage you to approach this in a productive direction - then stick to the plan you set out to achieve.

I truly believe there is power in writing out your goals and your schedule. I work best under a written schedule. How much time is spent per day doing the following?

Vocal and physical exercise	Auditioning
Editing	Educating
Research	Invoicing
Following up	Effective marketing
Social networking (a time sucker)	Family and friend time
Me time	

As you can see, there isn't enough time in the day to do all these things, but when you run your own business, you don't have a choice.

Also consider things that can steal time from achieving goals. For instance, how much time is spent per day doing the following?

Watching TV	Listening to music
Drinking coffee	Smoking
Driving	Sleeping
Eating	Complaining
Procrastinating	Playing games
Cleaning	Taking care of family
Working	Social networking (not business related)

Some things on this list are unavoidable, but if you monitor your days and write out exactly how much time is spent in each area of your day, you may be able to find more time.

If all else fails, hire someone to help achieve your goals and needs. Of course, you might resist hiring help because:

- You don't have the money, or
- You want to take on everything yourself to prove a point but the only point you have to prove is to succeed, and to show that you are worth the time and investment it takes to succeed.

I couldn't afford the time or the money to make this career happen, but I knew it wasn't going to do it itself. So I set out a schedule and a goal plan, and I've been following it and adapting it ever since.

How much is your time worth to you? Avoid overloading yourself. Set realistic goals so that you don't burn out. While you may be gifted to be all things to all people, until you take care of you - you will only let others down. Take care of your needs first.

Set boundaries for yourself and your support team so that you can realistically devote the time and effort you need to creating the best you that you can create.

Julie Williams
(Voiceoverchocolate.com
VoiceoverInsider.com)

Julie Williams is a voiceover talent with decades of experience and thousands of voiceovers to her credit. An acclaimed talent, she is also highly regarded as a voice-over coach whose students have gone on to do national commercials and narrations for Discovery Channel, DIY, and other national networks. Delivering a performance that meets her clients' needs is one of Julie's specialties. Julie shares two of the ways she does this.

Keep the Spotlight on the Star!

"Pay no attention to the man behind the curtain," the Wizard told Dorothy and her friends. And for good reason. Once they saw the Wizard, the magic was gone.

In voice-over, YOU are the man behind the curtain! The star?? It's the cartoon character to which you give life, the story you're telling, the message you're portraying, the lesson you're teaching, the reassurance you're giving, the product you're selling, and so on. That's why the voice itself is not only relatively insignificant in voice-over, it can actually get in the way.

"I've always been told I've got a great voice and I should do voiceovers," Newbies often say. They were misled to believe that they'd be "discovered" once someone heard their "great voice!" And most likely, the person recommending a voice-over career actually knows nothing about the industry!

But whether you're a voice-over Wanna-Be, Newbie, or Worker-bee, the message is still the same. Keep the spotlight on the star! You can't let your voice mask the message . This is easier said than done, of course. But it is essential. If the listener is distracted by your great voice, or an insincere delivery, they look to the man behind the curtain. And they can't see the star if the spotlight is on the man behind the curtain. It's nice for VO folks to get a little attention now and then, sure, but the client is paying good money for you to use your voice to focus the spotlight on the star!

How can you keep the spotlight on the star? Three ways.

First of all, understand the story, message, and purpose of what you are voicing, and the audience to whom you're talking. That will help you set the mood and tone for the VO. Then just "tell" the script!

Secondly, use all the tools in your arsenal to make the script your own. It must sound sincere—as if you wrote the words you're saying! Nothing moves that spotlight off the message and on to the man behind the curtain faster than an insincere read. And using improper inflection, punching words rather than coloring them, sounding like an announcer, and not "feeling what you're saying" are the fast track to sounding insincere.

And finally, focus YOUR attention on the star—and not the man behind the curtain! Don't think about how you sound when you're talking! Think about what you're saying! Just let it come out naturally. One well known coach, while producing a demo for a VO talent who was obviously enjoying the sound of his own voice, said to a colleague, "He's having himself!" If you cannot focus on the star as you voice the job—how can the end listener?

Like with the Wizard, once focus is on the star and not the man behind the curtain, magic happens! Of course, the process is not an easy one. Most voice-over artists cannot, or do not do it. That's why those who do have the potential to make very good money! By focusing the spotlight on the star—they deliver a stellar performance!

The Girl in the Red Coat

In the movie Schindler's List, scenes were shot in black and white. And the audience got used to that. But do you remember the girl in the red coat? Amidst the dreary black and white—your eyes were immediately drawn to the girl in the red coat, right? BE the girl in the red coat.

When a prospect is listening to dozens of demos or auditions, they all begin to sound black and white. But if you add an additional dimension to your read—through your own unique style (the style that is YOU and not just a nice generic, "anybody coulda done it" read,)—the ear will gravitate toward you.

Even if there are a couple of other competitors who have savvy enough to be in color, your odds are one in three, perhaps, to land the job. Then it comes down to—not who is the best talent, but who is the "right" talent for the job. In this way, you have no competition. There may be many voices—but there is only one you.

Who is the right talent? It may be the one who sounds like the voice in the clients head when he approved the copy. Or the style that makes him think, "Wow, I never thought of it that way."

We can't presume to predict what is in the minds of those who cast VO jobs. We can only know that if we do the copy well (as so many will) the one who will stand out is the one in the red coat.

Tom Dheere
(Tomdheere.com)

Tom is one of the most creative voice actor's I've met. His nearly two decades of experience narrating thousands of voiceover projects have given him insights that can only come from working in a variety of media. Here, he shares one of those insights:

Tom's Tip: The Scratch Track

Every once in a while I get a "scratch track" from a client before I start recording a project. Scratch tracks are used as a placeholder to assist in the timing of a video so the producer knows how much time they have to display certain visuals. Sometimes it's recorded by the producer, sometimes it's someone in the office who is good with pronunciations, often it's the sound engineer or maybe an intern.

While this is an extremely useful tool in the production process, it does not, I repeat NOT, help the voice talent! Why?

The voice talent is listening to a non-voice talent say their lines and it gets in their head. Sometimes it's difficult not to use the infections and cadence used on the scratch track. While the length of the scratch track may be correct, the speed in which certain words & phrases are uttered don't necessarily convey the proper emotion or message.

It's difficult to listen to a scratch track, look at the script, and then try to deliver the proper read at the same time. It's like trying to read a script written in German and then say it aloud in French!

With that in mind; if you're producing a project and you hired a voice talent, sending a scratch track does not necessarily help. Trust your talent to tell your story in the time allotted and in an engaging way!

Bill Holmes
(Voiceoverdoctor.com)

Bill Holmes has been a voiceover actor and director for more than 30 years. He started referring to himself as "the Voiceover Doctor" because of the style of teaching that he has developed over the years. It's a unique self-improvement system for voice actors that teaches the actor how to fix their own problems, enabling them to direct themselves and work through their performance weaknesses. In this article, the doctor talks about voiceover for commercials.

Commercial Voiceover: Yeah ... It's That Easy!

"We want an announcer but for God's sake we don't want him/her to sound like an announcer!" How many times have you heard that direction?

What exactly does that mean?

Well, in this man's opinion (and that's all it is, my opinion) they just want you to be yourself. That is when voiceovers for commercials goes from being a technical skill to an art. When you can actually make it your own. Taking someone else's words and making them sound like you talk like that all the time.

I can't tell you how many times students or clients (including lots of celebrity types) have looked up at me from the microphone and said, "I would never talk like this. I would never say these words the way they've written them!" I agree. Most people would not say the words, *"It has easy out roller seats that you can't get on any other minivan."*

But if you can get me to believe that you would say that and if you can say it as if you were just casually having a conversation with a friend, well, then I'll give you scale plus 10%.

One of the big problems a lot of actors have with commercials is they treat them like commercials and not like a conversation. Once you step into the booth to read commercial copy you have to realize that you're stepping into the world of advertising. It behooves you to start learning about the advertising game as well as the acting game. Advertising is written rather awkwardly at times. There certainly are exceptions to the rule but for the most part there's a lot of bad advertising on TV and radio. It's the actor's job, once he/she steps into the booth, to make it work.

So here are a few tips you can try to see if it helps you to become, not the person reading a script and just hitting the words, but the person who gets the listener to believe that they are talking just to him/her as they sit in traffic on the 405 freeway hoping to someday get to the beach.

When you're reading the copy don't worry so much about the words. Those words can really get in your way at times. Focus more on the pictures in your head. (Based upon the choices you've made as to Who am I, Who am I talking to, Where am I having the conversation, etc.)

When you approach a script you're going to be making choices. Make very specific choices of things that make you comfortable. Don't talk to an audience. Talk to someone you know very well. If you can picture one person that you know very well and that person is reacting to you (verbally) inside your head and you're just reacting honestly back to them, then that person sitting in traffic on the 405 freeway is going to believe you're talking just to him/her. It will make them feel comfortable to listen to you. They will hang on to that comfortable feeling next time they hear the name of the product that you were talking about in the commercial. When they see/hear the name of that product that you were comfortably talking about in the conversation you were having with that friend in your head, then that comfortable feeling may come back to them again and they will grab that product and put it in their shopping cart cause the comfortable feeling associated with the product makes them want to have it. (That's just a theory of how advertising is supposed to work).

"We want an announcer but we don't want them to sound like an announcer." That's what they are talking about. More often than not, the copy is going to be written very announcer-y! We as actors need to make it work by staying relaxed and chatting about things that make us feel comfortable.

We need to be what? (Who am I?) *We just need to be ourselves.* My experience directing actors over the years tells me that most actors think they need to be doing something in order to "get the job." Don't go into the booth trying to get the job. Go into the booth to do what you love to do. As you become more comfortable with the audition process, the jobs will start to come to you. It all comes down to being comfortable. Comfortable with the choices you've made, comfortable with who you are and sometimes just being physically comfortable while you're standing there talking to a stick.

There's an age old saying that most acting teachers tell their students more than once.

"Less is more!"

This couldn't be more true and better advice for the voiceover actor in commercials, primarily when you're directed to be casual or conversational. If you want proof go watch television. Watch the commercials and listen to Jeff Bridges on the Hyundai spots, Kevin Spacey on the Honda spots, etc. Those guys are just being themselves. Yes they're celebrities and some guy from the ad agency wanted to tell his wife that he worked with Jeff Bridges or Kevin Spacey or Demi Moore that day. That sometimes plays into why celebrities get most of the big lucrative jobs. But if you really sit and listen to what they're doing in the spots, you realize why they're so successful as actors. They are just being themselves within the scripts that have been provided them. Whether it's theatre, movies, TV or commercials these actors find a piece of themselves that lets the characters just be who they are. Hopefully that's what you're doing when you approach a script too. Why are these actors so good at being who they are? Because they're comfortable in their own skin (or at least they get us to believe they are) they know who they are and they know what they do well.

As I said earlier, this is just one man's opinion. There are other ways to approach commercial copy. For some actors substituting people, putting pictures and conversations with friends in their heads is a difficult thing to do. I'm just saying it's something you may want to try. It's a technique that most of the teachers out there are teaching. They all have their own approach but it's all pretty much the same thing. You just have to connect with someone who explains it in a way that *you* can understand.

So next time you hop into a voiceover booth and they tell you to NOT be announcer-y or they tell you to be casual or conversational. Relax! Stop working so hard. Make the obvious choice. Be specific. Be comfortable. Don't DO anything. Be yourself. You are interesting just the way you are. That's why they sent you the script in the first place. You're already the person that they're interested in. They don't want an actor. They want you to just be the person they have in their heads. So again I say, just be yourself.

Yeah. It's that easy! If you let it be.

Judy Fossum
(Voiceovervinyard.com)

Coming from a background in science and meteorology, Judy is a natural for technical narration. Based in the Rocky Mountains of Wyoming, Judy is one of those talented voice actors working from the middle of nowhere (or close to it). Because of her remote location, she has found that social media networking can be a powerful way to network with other professionals and make the critical connections generating voiceover work.

Link up with LinkedIn

Social media is a must in the world of voice over. From Facebook to Twitter to Pinterest to LinkedIn and more. They allow you to connect with colleagues, hear about new audio equipment (and not to mention do some troubleshooting), learn about classes and techniques, ask questions, build relationships and to socialize.

I don't know about you, but I've found it pretty easy to get distracted from time to time with social media. I've had to learn to discipline myself to spend only a set amount of time on various platforms and within that time to make the most of it.

For me, when it comes to LinkedIn, this is really where I try to focus my attention and to make the best use of my time. Sure, I have a lot of voiceover friends and colleagues on LinkedIn, but I like to look at it more as a great way to "link up" with businesses or organizations who just might have a need for my voiceover services. I do this in a step by step approach.

STEP 1: Send an Invitation:

When Linkedin comes up with a list of people you might know, I look through it and, although I do invite other voiceover colleagues and people I know, I more specifically look for companies who may have a need for my voiceover services. This can be ad agencies, production companies and actually any company or organization (both private and government). The point is that even though you may not know the person directly, you never know what their needs are. I go ahead and send an invitation and wait for their connection.

STEP 2: Introduce Yourself:

Just because you secure a connection on LinkedIn does not mean that "magic" will somehow happen and companies will automatically start asking for your services. Nope, you've got to introduce yourself. I always start with saying thank you for the connection and then go on to give a very brief synopsis of what I do as a voice actor. I feel the key here is to be brief and to explain to them how you can help them and their company. Speaking of their company, I like to check out their LinkedIn profile and website (if listed) to see if I can find a more personal connection to help personalize your introduction (thank you Maxine Dunn for this wonderful idea). A great way to save time is to have a template you can copy and paste for each introduction. Then you just customize it to the particular person/company you are building a relationship with.

STEP 3: Continue to Build the Relationship:

I'll admit that my invitations are not always accepted and that my initial introductions do not always get a response. However, for those that do, continue to foster those relationships. Ask if you can send them your demos, ask about their business, be interested. There are a ton of interesting people and businesses out there.

Does this work? Well, it has been my experience that things take time. In some cases I have heard from folks right away and in other cases it takes a few weeks. As with many things in voiceover staying persistent and having perseverance is relevant when it comes to networking as well. Of course, you don't want to nag, but short messages, sharing articles that might be of interest to them and saying a sincere "congratulations" on a recent accomplishment I feel cannot hurt.

Groups are another great thing about LinkedIn. I am a member of several voiceover groups, but here again is where I reach out to other groups. Groups of interest, groups I can learn from and those who perhaps could use my help on a future project. Be creative and think outside of the box here, as once again, you never know who you will connect with. In my groups I try to comment from time to time. This is not just "liking" a discussion (which I do as well), but it is commenting on a discussion or starting a new one.

This brings me back to the "Does this work?" question. Case in point, in making a comment on a discussion, I received an invitation, which I accepted and then proceeded to build a relationship with her and told her what I did. In the following weeks we corresponded via email and phone and are working on a series of webinars in which I will be able to provide some voiceover. In another instance, in following a discussion of interest I sent an invitation to the man who started the discussion. Once again I briefly introduced myself and how I could perhaps help him and his upcoming project. He put me in contact with a marketing agency who ended up hiring me to voice a power point presentation for a project the man was working on.

So for me, "Linking Up With LinkedIn" has so far been a great experience and has helped to build my career. Sure it takes some time, but so do all great things (at least in my opinion). I see LinkedIn as a relationship building social media network. I don't admit to have figured it all out and I know that I have a lot to learn, but so far I've found some effective ways to use social media and I hope that some of my ideas will help you in your endeavors as well.

Bobbin Beam
(Bobbinbeam.com)

Thoughts on Auditioning

I recently read an agent's comment that if you can't audition well, you have no future. So the truth is, for all actors, the real work is in the audition, and once booked, doing the job is play time. In both instances, you must act, and act well.

As voiceover talent, we spend most of our time looking for work when we are not working. I often say when the mic is off, my marketing and business hat is on. The days when we have little or no work are great for learning, reading and studying, improving our voiceover business systems, and working out, mentally, intellectually, and physically.

You can take classes and learn how to audition and learn all the etiquette, read the specs and audition your heart out, and do the job perfectly, and still not book it!

You may not be right for the role, your voice sounds like the casting director's ex wife, you sound too young, too old, or sound like you have spinach stuck in your teeth, your slate was your whole bio, or perhaps you didn't get the concept and weren't telling the story convincingly.

Whatever the reason, you must prepare and prepare well, and feel your confidence. Confidence comes through when you've made your strong choice and committed fully, forgetting about everything else. Fear, need and desperation have no place inside your head or in your audition. Instead, expect nothing from the audition other than you have another opportunity to create and work at your craft that brings you joy in the artistry of it all.

After you click send, you have to let it go and do not obsess, and second-guess yourself. The audition is over, so get over it fast. Congratulate yourself on a job well done. Most often we don't hear any feedback, unless we book the job. Most times, getting booked is the only feedback. And if you do get someone nice enough to get back to you and thank you for your time and audition, the next few words are, "but we've gone with another voice". Fat consolation, right?

It's true, that most times, we never know who booked the job until we see or hear it on the air … and then be stunned that the specs were thrown out completely and the job went to someone of the opposite sex!

There is so much to love about what we do. Yes, it's hard ... but the experience of creating art and voice acting, getting the concept and telling the story from your mouth to the listener's ears when you finally book the gig—PRICELESS !

Bob Hurley
(BobHurleyvoiceovers.com)

A Tip About Your Demo

No matter how many different demos you have out in the world, commit each and every one of them to memory so when a room full of clients on the other end of your ISDN say, "We loved the voice on your so and so ad", you'd better be able to remember what the hell they're talking about or it will be a very tedious session.

Or ...

A wide range of vocal deliveries is something we all initially want to be known for but keep that range on a character demo. Ultimately, you want to be known for YOUR voice and delivery. Having a whole slew of deliveries just becomes damned confusing for everyone.

Laura Bednarski

Tips for Voiceover Newcomers

My advice for newcomers would be, it is challenging to get into this business but not impossible. Do not quit your day job unless of course you are independently wealthy. I would recommend training in acting, improv and voice technique, especially. All the books tell you this. What will really get you into this business and allow you to start booking is to be honest about your abilities and to get to know who you are as a performer. Practice a ton in your own booth and explore all the areas of VO.

Figure out what you are best at and concentrate there. Ask people who you respect for advice. Sometimes an outside ear can tell you things you never could hear.

I can usually tell what I am good at by how easy things flow. If I am reading something a hundred different ways and it still does not sound right that is not my thing. I did a character recently for a radio drama. The minute I read the words the character came alive and I was excited and alive too. Character work is what I do best. Not impersonations or impressions but the ability to develop a character from the script and make it believable. On the other hand this morning I was sent an audition for a University ad. The pay was great so I wanted to try it. I kept reading it and it never sounded right. I knew I would not book the job so I did not even send it in.

Some other tips I have learned is having an agent will not get you the work. You have to take charge of your career. I have friends who were in VO in days gone by and they would just wait for their agent to call. The agent called a lot too. It is not like that now. You need to find the jobs yourself through networking, connecting with people who need the voices that you do best. This is a part of the business that is crucial. I get sent many auditions from my agent and I audition for most of them. But these auditions are going to many other agents and voice actors so the competition is fierce.

One more thing is, you need to have a focus on your goals and do something everyday toward reaching them. Study hard, get real good at what you do, believe in yourself, have confidence in your abilities and your clients will too.

Elley-Ray
(ElleyRay.com)

Elley-Ray is a crazy lady ... and I mean that in the best way possible. She's brilliant with an understanding of how to create characters and theater of the mind that is rare. Based in Toronto, and with over 30 years experience in voice overs, TV, film and theater, Elley-Ray is a leading voice talent and coach, specializing in animation, commercial announcing and multi-voice. She's won multiple awards, having voiced thousands of TV and radio commercials and countless animation series and films.

What You Eat is How You Sound!

Believe it or not, what you eat or drink can affect your instrument and how you voice, so listen-up. You are what you eat, as they say.

Anything ingested can have an effect on the vocal cords. Yes, that's right, so be aware of what you put into your mouth and system.

Imagine me flying into LA to do a spiritual retreat many years ago and finding out mid-flight that I had to do a big recording at Woodholly Studios in the morning.

I arrived late and hungry at my hotel, had a hamburger, fries and glass of wine, followed by a lovely piece of cheesecake and espresso.

I then went up to my room where I saw my bed turned down and a delicious chocolate mint left waiting - yummy! I called for a wake up, read a bit and turned out the lights.

The next morning early I received my wake up call and as I answered the phone, guess what?

Croak, croak, my cords were swollen and I tried to clear the burning at the back of my throat only to realize I was hoarse.

Without thinking, I had dehydrated my cords and created an acidic system in my stomach, allowing acid reflux and aggravating my vocal cords on an already dried-out system due to flying and exhaustion.

Yes, I had to learn the hard way.

To maintain vocal health, you must minimize foods that create acid production in the stomach.

The greatest offender for upsetting the acid balance is **caffeine**. It is a voicer's worst enemy, increasing acid production and loosening the muscles that separate the stomach from the esophagus. Yikes!

Caffeine is a diuretic, which induces urination and dehydration. As an irritant to the vocal folds, it induces mucous production and stiffness.

Carbonated drinks can contain caffeine and cause burping due to the carbonation, so beware gulping too much pop before a record.

Another huge offender is found in just about all foods we love to gobble: **fat**. Food with high fat content increases acid in our stomachs because it takes longer to digest - producing more acid and worsening acid reflux symptoms.

Similar to caffeine, **alcohol** wreaks havoc with its acidity and restricts flow in the blood vessels.

Other irritants to watch out for are certain **medications**, such as ibuprofen and aspirin, which can increase the risk of hemorrhage on the vocal folds.

Acid reflux is a common symptom of an overactive acid production in the body and can literally burn your vocal cords, causing a voice actor's worst fear: voice loss.

The acid from the stomach, once off balance, seeps up the esophagus and swells the tissue of the vocal cords, which then become inflamed and weaken our ability to express.

Sleep with the head of your bed raised or several pillows to help detract from the acid production moving up your esophagus.

Try to eat smaller, controlled portions, which keeps your stomach from getting too full. A full stomach can also cause acid over-production and force the stomach to work harder.

Below is a list of what to steer clear of before you have a big audition or voice job:

- Any meat with high fat content, including ground beef, marbled steak (increases acid).
- Processed chicken products (increases acid).
- Fats, oils, sweets, including chocolate, potato/corn chips, high-fat baked goods, creamy/oily salad dressings (increases acid).
- Coffee (dries out the vocal folds).
- Alcohol (dehydrates the system).
- High-acidic fruits and vegetables and acidic juices, such as orange, grapefruit, cranberry, tomato, lemon, and lime juices (irritates and causes acid).
- Mashed potatoes, French fries, potato salad.
- Raw onion, garlic (irritates and increases acid).
- Grains like macaroni and cheese. Pasta with marinara or heavy cream sauce.
- Regular-fat content dairy products like sour cream, milkshakes, ice cream, cottage cheese, high-fat cheeses (causes excessive mucous).
- Bananas (causes mucous).
- Mint (acidic).
- Nuts (can cause excessive mucous and allergic reactions).
- Spicy foods, fried foods, acidic foods (increase acid).
- MSG (increases acid).
- Hormones (increases acid).
- Allergens and pollutants such as dust and mold.
- Fatigue - sleep is good for your cords.
- Antihistamines and diuretics (very drying).

The sound of your voice is made by small internal muscle movements. Muscles need the energy furnished by well-metabolized food in order to function.

They also need to be hydrated to achieve peak energy, flexibility and elasticity.

Drinking room-temperature water as your principal beverage is best for hydration. If a beverage is too cold or too hot, it will affect the muscles of your larynx and focal folds, which are behind and adjacent to the esophagus where you swallow.

Vocal cords are fragile. Vocal hygiene involves drinking lots of water daily.

The recommended eight glasses a day are not adequate for a vocalist. Water is swallowed into the stomach, not the larynx. Water must be carried through the bloodstream to the vocal cords, so drink tons of H2O.

Supporting a "tone" or "placement" can work against the esophageal sphincter, causing the stomach contents to be pushed upwards towards the diaphragm, which in turn, can affect your breath support.

So remember not to eat a big meal before a gig. Do not eat late at night, either, as this leads to acid reflux overnight and into the next morning.

What to eat, you ask?

Fish, plain chicken, yellow veggies, rice, apples, eggs, almonds, fruits and whole grains are good options. And lots of water.

Rules:

- Do not drink coffee or caffeinated beverages within two to three hours of voicing.
- Do drink lots of room temperature water.
- Do not drink iced beverages within two to three hours prior to voicing.
- Do not drink hot beverages prior to or during records.
- Do eat high-water-content fruits for hydration and energy.
- Do eat high water content vegetables for hydration and minerals.
- Do stay fed, but don't overeat or stuff yourself.

Maintain a fabulous working environment for your voice. And be aware of what and how much of anything that you put into your body.

Everything affects this amazing apparatus we use to voice, and if you want to damage it then eat high-fat, high-caffeine, high-alcohol, sugar or dairy foods late at night before a gig and get no rest and drink no water. A pure recipe for disaster.

It can be a hard pill to swallow, but you are what you eat, so if you are a professional voicer, get on the VO diet.

Penny Abshire
(PositiveThinkersUnite.com)

Penny Abshire has gained a reputation for her exceptional copy writing skills, her outstanding performance coaching and directing, and, most of all her upbeat perspective on the business of voiceover. It has become a tradition that she close each edition of this book with a positive and motivational message.

So … What Happens Now?

Now that you have finished Jim's wonderful book, you may be asking yourself, "So what happens now?"

Is voiceover your PASSION? Do you think, eat, breathe, and sleep it? Would you do it for free just to be in the booth and performing? If all of these questions are true, then you simply cannot allow yourself to give up for any reason!

That being said, when you first decide to go for your dreams, your like a kid with a brand new toy. You play with it all the time … maybe even sleep with it at night. This lasts for a few weeks and then the newness wears off. Pretty soon this wonderful gadget is tossed into the toy box with everything else you've ever been interested in and is soon forgotten. Your dreams can suffer a similar fate.

I've had several students who start out so excited about having a voiceover career that they immediately run out and buy all their equipment. They sound-proof their room, sign up for all the pay-to-play sites and then sit back and wait for the work to come in. They are ready to see their dreams fulfilled! They haven't considered the fact that there will be WORK in the future to make this dream into a career.

Here's what I often see happen. When you announce to the world that you are going to be a voice actor, you're going to receive, in return, skepticism, utter disbelief and some downright negative comments from friends and relatives. And you will be dumbfounded!

This is your DREAM! Why don't they understand? For some, this will fuel the flame. For the majority of others, they will believe the negativity they hear and start to doubt their dreams. And pretty soon their equipment is collecting dust and they've given up the dream of being a voiceover artist - because of what OTHER PEOPLE THINK.

I know this will happen because it happened to me when I decided to follow my dream. I was 47 years old when I began my journey. So, the comments I heard from others were things like, "You're a little old to start a new career, aren't you?" Or, "You're going to quit a great paying job as a paralegal to be an actor!!??" Or, my favorite, "There's way too much competition out there! You're nuts to think you can compete!" Yes, every single statement was spoken. Some came from others who truly thought they were trying to save me from myself, but the biggest culprit and worst critic was ME.

I said these hurtful, discouraging things to MYSELF!

So how does one deal with these naysayers (which will probably include your own "voices?").

This is my suggestion: Create a positive statement that you can comfortably say to yourself and others. Something like this:

"I know you don't understand why I choose to go into a field that is highly competitive, involves many long hours of marketing, will cost me lots of money to take classes and get the right equipment, and seems (to you) to be kind of a silly thing to do to make a living. But I want you to know this is my dream. And since I only get one chance at life, this is the path I have chosen to take. I don't ask you to understand. All I ask from you is that if you can't find a way to encourage me in my journey, that you please keep your comments to yourself."

Starting any new career is difficult. And voiceover is no different. You must be committed to your journey and you must adopt a positive attitude about the journey. Because when you hit a bump in your road (and you will ...) you'll need the courage and fortitude to get up, brush yourself off, and get going again. You'll need a positive outlook to know that even though you've done 800 auditions without getting a job, that it's a numbers game and the producer who is looking for you will eventually find and hire you. It's looking at all those auditions as very valuable learning experiences in performing, negotiating fees, and editing.

Abraham Lincoln said, "Commitment is what transforms a promise into reality. It is the words that speak boldly of your intentions. And the actions which speak louder than the words. It is making the time when there is none. It is coming through time after time after time, year after year after year. Commitment is the stuff character is made of; the power to change the face of things. It is the daily triumph of integrity over skepticism."

You CAN do this. Have faith in yourself, your dream and your future! If the fire of passion burns true in your heart, nothing and no one can stop you!

Index

Index